To my father, John, who worked on
London Underground for 28 years.

And to Nina Fishman
(1946–2009).

UNDERGROUND WRITING

The London Tube
from George Gissing
to Virginia Woolf

Kath, to an dear
comrade — gre
& after

Dave
x

UNDERGROUND WRITING

The London Tube
from George Gissing
to Virginia Woolf

DAVID WELSH

LIVERPOOL
UNIVERSITY PRESS

First published 2010 by
Liverpool University Press
4 Cambridge Street
Liverpool
L69 7ZU

British Library Cataloguing-in-Publication data
A British Library CIP record is available

ISBN 978-1-84631-223-6 cased

Typeset in Perpetua and Gill Sans by BBR (www.bbr-online.com)
Printed in Great Britain by the MPG Books Group, Bodmin and King's Lynn

Change Wanderlust to Weltschmerz in the Underground
W. H. Auden, 'Thomas Epilogizes'

CONTENTS

ACKNOWLEDGEMENTS

The idea for a book about cultural history and the underground goes back to a discussion with Edwin Webb at the University of Greenwich but it has been 'in the making' for many decades. I would like to thank my wife Ev for inspiring me to write this book and for her unfailing support and kindness during its research and writing, and my three children, Tom, Laura and Robin, who have all grown up with a publicly owned Tube. My thanks to three great historians: Jan Pollock, Maggie Millman and Sheila Rowbotham. And I must mention the many union activists on London Transport, as well as more recently in the Campaign Against Tube Privatisation, with whom I have been associated for 30 years. Thanks to Birkbeck College for providing the opportunity to study, particularly to Professor Michael Slater and Nicola Bown and to Richard Temple at Senate House Library, University of London, and Beth Kingl. Finally, thanks to all the people who have supplied oral testimony about Tube sheltering during the *Workers' War* and *Talk About a Liberty* projects.

INTRODUCTION

I should like to see him clapped down in a third-class carriage on the underground, and asked to give the trades of all his fellow-travellers.

Dr Watson on Sherlock Holmes, 'A Study in Scarlet'[1]

When the novelist George Gissing was lampooned by *Punch* in 1885 the journal did not know that it had in its sights the man who would become the fictional cartographer of the Metropolitan Railway, the world's first underground system. Two weeks after an article punningly entitled 'Gissing the Rod' in which the author was taken to task for his belief in the 'artistic conscience',[2] *Punch* offered a caustic 'ballade' called 'By Underground' and a cartoon lambasting the Metropolitan Railway, one of its perennial targets.[3] Just under ten years later, Gissing published his novel *In the Year of Jubilee*,[4] containing an equally scathing account of the underground in which he compared King's Cross underground station to the infernal underworld of Hades. Gissing's topography featured demonic steam engines that pulled untold numbers of 'lost' commuters; windswept platforms that seemed to confine his characters; a cacophony of voices, banging doors and screeching wheels; and a pandemonium of advertising posters, steam, smoke and soot that swirled around the station. It was a metaphor for the psychological inferno into which Gissing pitched characters that were condemned to travel in endless circles.

Gissing's observations on King's Cross were a watershed in the development of writing about the subterranean railway. They were one component in a set of

1   A. Conan Doyle, 'A Study in Scarlet' (1887), in *The Complete Short Stories of Sherlock Holmes* (Ware: Wordsworth Editions, 2007), pp. 13–93, p. 23.
2   'Gissing the Rod', *Punch*, 3 January 1885, vol. 88, p. 1.
3   'By Underground', *Punch*, 17 January 1885, vol. 88, p. 34.
4   G. Gissing, *In the Year of Jubilee* (1894; London: Hogarth Press, 1987).

fictional perspectives that provided the foundations for underground writing in the years after his death. Gissing wrote a series of novels during the two decades of his residence in the capital, novels consistently highlighting the underground as a combination of steam technology and subterranean power that seemed to erupt from beneath the streets into the lives of his characters.

However, Gissing's attitude towards the underground railway in fiction was ambivalent. In the 1880s, he seems to have regarded it as a mechanical force, an implacable technology that carved the urban landscape into class-segregated enclaves. He initially adopted the common imagery of the infernal locomotive in novels like *The Nether World* (1889), an image that was reminiscent of Charles Dickens in *Dombey and Son* (1848) where the railway destroys vast tracts of the city. The steam locomotive and the railway arch seemed to enforce a geographical separation and vertical porosity in the urban landscape that sharply differentiated communities and helped to create a social abyss at the heart of the city. In the decade before his death in 1902, Gissing shifted the focus to the condition and experience of underground travel for a largely lower-middle-class public. In the novel *New Grub Street* (1891),[5] the subterranean railway is transformed into a vast circulatory system within which his characters encounter a psychological rather than a social inferno. In charting the development of the underground, Gissing exposed the fault-lines of suburbanization, thereby throwing into relief the massive shifts in the urban population that had been accelerating since the 1860s.

Gissing was not the first on the scene of this new urban phenomenon as it was already over 20 years old when he began to record its existence. He was almost by default the chronicler of the great wave of suburbanization that was facilitated by the most recent phase of transport development into districts like Crouch End, Camberwell, Willesden and Tottenham. His preferred habitat was the more compact social geography of mid-nineteenth-century London, a city whose northern boundary was reinforced by the construction of the underground and metropolitan road improvements. Gissing was not living in the capital when the first three-and-a-half-mile phase of the Metropolitan Railway from Paddington to Farringdon Street was opened in 1863 but he was the heir to the wild speculation that had greeted its inception. It was a sensation from the first day of construction, triggering outraged opposition, mockery and disbelief at the notion of running a steam railway under the streets of the capital. It opened up a subsurface world that had hitherto been populated by sewers, water and gas pipes, the electric telegraph, plague pits and crypts, giving London an

5   G. Gissing, *New Grub Street* (1891; Harmondsworth: Penguin, 1968).

'underworld' whose only equivalent seemed to be the Parisian catacombs. *The Times* poured scorn on the scheme, calling it 'Utopian and one which, even if it could be accomplished, would certainly never pay'.[6] A clergyman claimed that it would intrude into the 'infernal regions' and disturb the devil.[7] *Punch* dubbed it 'The Sewer Railway', publishing a 'prophetic' sketch showing two underground trains about to collide.[8] It lampooned the new railway after the official opening in a cartoon showing three crinolined ladies looking askance at being invited to enter the system through a sewer with one saying: 'Well I'm sure no woman with the least sense of Decency would think of going down that way'.[9] To the former Chartist leader Ernest Jones, incarcerated in prison in 1848, an underground railway was the epitome of Mammon, rushing demonically beneath a city that worshipped materialism.

So the underground had a history of its own but, as a novelist, Gissing annexed a vast territory from the past to describe the most modern technological phenomenon of the past 30 years. The quotidian world of the underground with its cavernous stations, sulphurous atmosphere and raucous steam locomotives offered comparisons with infernal and Gothic landscapes. The classical Hades or underworld that Gissing drew on had been filtered through the later Christian tradition of hell with Dante's *Inferno* and Milton's satanic abode in *Paradise Lost* as a place of torment for the damned. And Gissing discovered Dante in the 1880s, a legacy that had been particularly powerful following a revival in the middle years of the century. The ways in which the most modern of Victorian enterprises became embedded in layers of classical myth may have offered a vocabulary that deflected the shattering impact of modernity. But it also offered a metaphor for the secular abyss or 'nether world' of poverty that had been rediscovered by the sociologist Charles Booth.

Nevertheless, the Metropolitan Railway attracted a constant stream of good publicity, much of it shaped by systematic puffery in the press. The grandly titled 'Metropolitan Underground Railway', adorned with oak leaves and acorns, was feted by the *Illustrated London News* whose pages were given over to detailed drawings of tunnels and stations.[10] Its progress at street level was

---

6   *The Times*, 30 November 1861.

7   Quoted in S. Halliday, *Underground to Everywhere* (Stroud: Sutton Publishing, 2001), p.1.

8   *Punch*, 1846, vol. 11, p. 133. Not that *Punch* was only dismissive of subterranean projects: in 1846 it presciently pictured an overhead 'New Aerial Omnibus' showing two buses precariously suspended above London (*Punch*, 1846, vol. 11, p. 104).

9   *Punch*, 28 May 1864, vol. 46, p. 227.

10 'The Metropolitan Underground Railway', *Illustrated London News*, 27 December 1862, p. 692.

recorded by photographers like Henry Flather[11] and it managed the feat of being highly praised by Henry Mayhew in what was probably the first ever passenger opinion survey conducted on Britain's railways.[12] It soon began to appear on the London stage, including Dion Boucicault's *After Dark; A Drama of London Life* (1868), a dramatic incarnation that continued for many decades. Unlike the new sewer system built by Joseph Bazalgette in just nine years, the underground railway went on growing every year as it looped in all directions across the capital, including under the Thames to Shadwell in the former Thames Tunnel. And unlike the new sewers, the underground was neither invisible to the public, nor hidden from public opinion. Not only could the public travel on it but they could also read about it whilst on their journeys, a development much enhanced by the advent of the cheap press in the 1880s exemplified by Alfred Harmsworth's *Answers to Correspondents* (1888), culminating in 1896 with the *Daily Mail*. The new media hunted out weird and fanciful 'news' stories, with Harmsworth's *Answers* famously running a sensational story about a severed human finger found on an underground track at night. Even before the turn of the century then, the underground was fertile copy for the capital's journalists, providing a steady diet of information, sensation, entertainment and opinion for the suburban clerks who avidly consumed the news.

So when Gissing began to draw upon the Metropolitan Railway for his novels it was a case of writing transforming an already well-known location. Many of his middle-class readers were accustomed to the underground and would have accepted unquestioningly that its purpose was to assist them to travel more comfortably and speedily across the capital. To those of his readers not familiar with it, Gissing's visionary world would have seemed shocking in its 'realistic' depiction of modern life. As early as 1843, the pioneer of underground travel, Charles Pearson, had advocated a railway in order to provide the link to a new town for artisans on the then outskirts of the city in his 'Address to the Electors of Lambeth'. He would certainly have found Gissing's version of the Metropolitan Railway a truly gross distortion of the ideals he had attached to the project. But the shafts of daylight that pierced the smoke-filled platforms bore the coldly realistic message of economic downturn, forcing a drastic modification of Pearson's original utopian plans.

By the 1880s, when Gissing was an established resident in the capital, the underground had reached a nadir, being seen by the ever-watchful *Punch* as a

---

11   H. Flather, 'London Metropolitan Railway 1862', London Transport Museum Collection.
12   See H. Mayhew, *The Shops and Companies of London and the Trades and Manufactories of Great Britain* (London: Strand, 1865).

playground for cynical power struggles. What had begun as a battle to ensure regular dividends for shareholders had turned into a farcical scramble for every last penny of profit, as the two main railway companies waged guerilla warfare over yards of underground track. Progress on building the Circle line, despite the investment of £800,000 of public money by the City Corporation and the Metropolitan Board of Works, was held up by intercompany battles and technical and financial difficulties. In 1884, when the line finally opened, the service was diabolical with trains running up to three hours late. On one occasion, according to the *Railway Times*, a group of passengers attempted to escape from their train in protest at delays.[13]

If the underground railway thrilled audiences at the Metropolitan Music Hall a few stops down the Metropolitan Railway at Edgware Road, it was as much a parody of the Victorian class system as that to be found on the stage. Whilst it carried over nine million passengers in the first year of operations, they were separated into first, second and third-class carriages reflecting the already secure conventions of railway culture. Mingling with other classes on the platforms, working-class passengers were sharply observed by railway police who noted clothing, 'look' and the tools they habitually carried. Most were only able to travel at certain restricted times of day when workmen's fares were in operation with many simply unable to afford even the third-class fare at other times. They were segregated in stations in order to enter the appropriate overcrowded and poorly furnished third-class carriages. Whilst some novelists like Margaret Harkness noted the plight of these passengers, Gissing ignored them in his later novels, describing the journeys of his lower-middle-class characters without any trace of the capital's working-class inhabitants.

An 1862 pamphlet said that travellers were overloaded with sensory stimuli, distressed by lateness, and fearful of collisions and the sense of isolation in carriages.[14] In tunnels there were the added dimensions of claustrophobia and the danger of violent attack. Lewis Carroll had originally intended *Alice's Adventures in Wonderland* (1865) to be called *Alice's Adventures Under Ground* but his publishers advised against this on the basis of the infernal reputation of steam travel beneath the streets.[15] It would seem that what Wolfgang Schivelbusch has described as the 'technological accident' was a palpable fact, conveying the idea that the technological apparatus, in other words the train, had destroyed itself

---

13 *Railway Times*, 18 October 1884.
14 See *The Influence of Railway Travelling on Public Health* (London: Lancet, 1862).
15 A. Martin, 'Going Underground', *Evening Standard Magazine*, 26 March 1999, pp. 12–15, p. 12.

by means of its own power.[16] Detective fiction highlighted the underground's murky reputation with a number of murder mysteries, although Sherlock Holmes' only underground case had to wait until 1908, two years before a man was actually shot in a train between Baker Street and Swiss Cottage. It is arguable that the first 'moral panic' to hit the underground occurred in the 1880s after a series of terrorist attacks, such events providing fresh material for a range of apocalyptic tales in the early years of the next century.

Nicholas Daly has suggested that 'the railway, rather than the city street or the factory floor, represented the site of confrontation of the body and the forces of modernization'.[17] It was certainly the case that journeys in tunnels with no external view, poor ventilation and an utterly noxious atmosphere would have taxed even the most determined commuter. Nonetheless, it seems that passengers adjusted to the stress fairly quickly, finding new vistas inside the underground carriage: advertisements placed above the 'cant rail' opposite offered one way of coping with the problem of face-to-face contact without verbal communication. This was the world of the commuter who was repeatedly described in fiction as reading a daily newspaper. Such interior space came to dominate underground writing in the twentieth century as, by 1895, 400 million passengers a year were using suburban and underground trains—over two-and-a-half times more than in 1875.[18]

These interiors also represented a turn towards new worlds; the underground had seemed to be about the past and the present in Gissing's fiction but now it was linked to the future. William Morris opened his utopian novel *News from Nowhere* (1890) with six people exchanging views 'on the future of a fully-developed new society' pointedly followed by a lugubrious journey back to the west London suburb of Hammersmith on the Metropolitan Railway.[19] When the Time Traveller in H. G. Wells' short story 'The Time Machine' (1895) sets out into the fourth dimension he observes a 'great and splendid architecture rising up above me, more massive than any buildings of our own time, and yet, as it seemed, built of glimmer and mist'.[20] This is a vision of the future

---

16   W. Schivelbusch, *The Railway Journey: The Industrialisation of Time and Space in the 19th Century* (1977; Leamington Spa: Berg, 1986).

17   N. Daly, 'Railway Novels: Sensation Fiction and the Modernization of the Senses', *ELH (English Literary History)*, vol. 66, no. 2, Summer 1999, pp. 461–87, p. 468.

18   T. Barker, *Moving Millions, A Pictorial History of London Transport* (London: London Transport Museum, 1990), p. 45.

19   W. Morris, *News from Nowhere* (1890), in *Three Works by William Morris* (London: Lawrence & Wishart, 1968), pp. 181–401, p. 181.

20   H. G. Wells, 'The Time Machine' (1895), in *Selected Short Stories* (Harmondsworth: Penguin, 1958), pp. 7–83, p. 22.

city: a world in which transportation plays a key role in the integration of the various social, economic and political functions of urban society. In novels and short stories like 'The Time Machine', Wells was able to bring together Gissing's visionary imagery and the new technological advances of the period such as the first tube lines, the City and South London and Central London Railway, which pioneered electric traction in the capital. Indeed, as Gissing himself rather wistfully commented, in a reference to Wells' short story: 'in some future age, when the human population diminishes, climates such as ours will be forsaken: men will refuse to live under such conditions'.[21] But the rush to promote modernity, with its driven phenomenon of 'Metropolitan Man' outlined by Georg Simmel,[22] brought with it an ambivalence detectable in Wells' early fiction.

Both steam and electric technologies, although widely perceived as agents of progress and modernity, were also forces destructive of human identity and community. This emerged starkly in Wells' short story 'The Lord of the Dynamos' (1894) with its fearful invocation of the untamed energy of the tube that was no longer embodied in the infernal steam locomotive. Nevertheless, Wells can be described as bringing a utopian vision to underground writing as he, amongst others, believed that the new electric tubes were a harbinger of a future planned metropolis. Wells' switch from science fantasy to factual investigation in *Anticipations* (1902) and to contemporary social fiction in *Ann Veronica* (1909) and *Tono-Bungay* (1909), kept the focus on the underground but talked up its utopian value to the urban world and its social value in integrating urban communities. For Wells and other Fabians like George Bernard Shaw, the tube was a foretaste of a new political community. The London County Council was the chosen instrument of their will: only the veto of Council control over the underground by a Conservative government and the defeat of the Progressives on the Council in 1907 frustrated this strategy of municipal takeover. Other pathways branched from this particular conjuncture, with the underground beginning to develop its own history in fiction, particularly in the work of Arnold Bennett and Dorothy Richardson. Modernity in the form of electric tubes and trams also seemed to bring a nostalgia for the days of the Metropolitan Railway, most notably in Ford Madox Ford's *The Soul of London* (1905),

21   G. Gissing, 29 November 1895, in *The Collected Letters of George Gissing*, eds. P. F. Mattheisen, A. C. Young & P. Coustillas, 9 vols. (Athens, OH: Ohio University Press, 1990–97), vol. 6, p. 63.

22   See G. Simmel, 'The Metropolis and Mental Life', in D. Frisby & M. Featherstone (eds.), *The Sociology of Georg Simmel* (London: Sage, 1997), pp. 174–85.

published in the same year that the electrification of the old steam-driven lines was completed.

Modernities unfolded quickly in underground writing. Dr Seward in Bram Stoker's novel *Dracula* (1897) travelled with Mina Harker on 'the Underground to Fenchurch Street' recording the journey on his 'phonograph diary', along with that other new invention the typewriter.[23] Only a few years after *Dracula*'s publication, a further 26.5 miles of tube track was being built together with the development of a succession of 'new-fangled' inventions such as hydraulic lifts, escalators, maps and new types of train and station architecture. It was believed that such glamorously modern transit would attract passengers but with considerable competition from street-level transport and the first generation of tube lines, the success of the tubes was blunted. The older steam lines like the Metropolitan were rapidly electrifying their train stock and, although this did not substantially revive their fortunes, it did bring about a visible revolution on the ground. And from around 1905 the underground expanded its imaginative parameters to include artistic representation in paintings, posters and, in the cheapest and most accessible medium of the time, the postcard.

Such multiple perspectives were creating a more complex vision of the underground system. It seems that the bigger the system, the more diverse its imaginative tendencies, despite the fact that before the First World War the underground was little more than a patchwork of self-contained lines. Like G. K. Chesterton's idea of London in *The Napoleon of Notting Hill* (1904), it was a fragmented and localized world in which small enclaves mattered but culturally the underground was ubiquitous at this time: in novels and short stories, in newspaper articles and futuristic books, on posters, postcards and billboards. For literary modernists, the underground could move from the realism of Gissing towards technology on the one hand (Futurism) and the environment of personal and subjective consciousness on the other. Wyndham Lewis, the high priest of modernism before the war, included Gissing in the first issue of *Blast* (1914) calling him a 'futurist', a reminder that the gritty realism of Gissing's novels was another weapon in the battle to destroy literary conservatism.[24]

This outpouring of underground writing led to what may be called Tubism, a reconfiguring of cultural iconography and a new focus for the role of transport in the city. Tubism was detonated by forces both internal and external to the underground, one such being the succession of artistic avant-garde movements

---

23   B. Stoker, *Dracula* (1897; London: Penguin, 1993), p. 282.
24   P. W. Lewis, 'The Review of the Great English Vortex 1' (1914), in P. Faulkner (ed.), *A Modernist Reader* (London: Batsford, 1986), pp. 42–46, p. 43.

such as Futurism and Vorticism that emerged prior to the First World War and the slow-burning aesthetic philosophy of 'Fitness for Purpose'. It owes much to the iconoclastic figure of Filippo Marinetti who was to be found orating in French before a London audience in 1912. Tubism was not simply the result of an aesthetic process. Social and economic forces also played a role in its development. Commuting by bus and tube had grown phenomenally in the years before the war and in 1911 the underground had been affected by the biggest single strike in its history reflecting, in part, a bigger and more combative workforce. The more interventionist and collectivist ideologies of the early twentieth century were bound up with the future of urban transport, influenced by the need to give public transport a new role in the metropolis. The increased power of the state, already emerging in the report of the Royal Commission on London Traffic in 1905, and further accelerated by the impact of the First World War, meant that the underground was potentially seen as a publicly owned undertaking.

The London Passenger Transport Board of 1933 rapidly became a model public corporation and an iconic, ideological force with its innovative designs, and clean, efficient and remorseless technology. But the Tube (with a capital T), as it rapidly became known in these decades, became the subject of modernist writers, most notably Virginia Woolf, as well as the more traditional realist novelists of the past. In her novel *The Waves* (1931), Woolf employed much of the original thematic content of the underground in order to explore ideas about alienation, personal space and debates around individual and collective identity. If Woolf was the successor to Gissing as cartographer of the Tube, charting the writing of the interwar years, others, like T. S. Eliot and Ezra Pound, produced a Dantean London of impotence and despair revolving in a Gissingesque wasteland. What had entered writing in the Victorian era was now part of the arsenal of images that would make art *modernist* and, although Virginia Woolf dismissed realism as outmoded, she did not banish the Tube train from her novels. If modernism had run its course by 1930, it had nevertheless transformed the Tube from a place to a state, in the sense that T. S. Eliot meant when he talked about Dante's hell. But there were many other tensions within Tubism derived from the swift elision of steam and electric technology. The cultural landscape of the underground became a battleground for widely differing interpretations of its role and meaning with such authors as George Orwell, J. B. Priestley and Graham Greene expressing the more overtly political elements that Wells had highlighted whilst locating them within a more radical tradition.

Nearly 80 years after the opening of the original Metropolitan Railway, the artist Henry Moore drew two dramatic pictures that show an apparently infernal region below the streets of bomb-damaged buildings.[25] Moore's drawings strip open the road to reveal an underworld where shelterers take refuge from the Blitz, mirroring the massive changes that the Second World War had brought to the Tube. During the war, writers like Elizabeth Bowen and Louis MacNeice banished many of the infernal associations in underground writing, however, giving it instead an imaginative identity that shaped the 'real' utopia that emerged from a need for safety and security. For the first time in the history of the Tube, the imaginative construction of the system was almost unambiguously positive as it seemed to describe a whole submetropolitan society in the making, a microsociety that was overwhelmingly working-class in character. The experience of sheltering broke down the distinction between public and private spheres giving the underground a near mythological modernity; it also attracted writers like Vera Brittain who documented the sheltering communities. It appeared in a significant number of short stories and novels as well as radio plays, poems and films as a kind of running commentary on the extremely unusual and threatening experiences of the Blitz.

Why a cultural history of the Tube? There are many layers to the history of the capital's transport system but the least explored is the creation of a cultural framework in the 82 years between the opening of the Metropolitan Railway in 1863 to the end of the Second World War in 1945. It's hard to imagine the capital without subterranean transit because it's difficult to make sense of London without the cultural version of the underground that is 'hidden' behind the fabric of the system. On the Circle line, the brickwork of a Victorian steam railway reflects a massive 25-year construction project but one that was vigorously transformed by fiction. The commuter trains that speed up the Metropolitan line today are a remnant of utopian plans for a trunk railway linking the north-west of England with Paris via a Channel tunnel and the romance of this 'Metro-Land' has entered the cultural vocabulary of England. Reminders of gilt-edged Edwardian greed can be seen in the grandly tiled facades of stations such as Russell Square and it is salutary to read the dystopian stories that were its fictional counterpart in these decades. Tube stations of the 1930s reflect an ethos of public ownership coupled with modernist design but it was a contested cultural terrain. We still use the same platforms that were home to thousands of shelterers during the Blitz, shelterers who found a place

---

25 H. Moore, 'Devastated Buildings and Underground Platform Scene' (1940–41), British Museum, and 'Wrecked Omnibus and Figures in Underground Shelter' (1940–41), British Museum.

in wartime fiction. And all of these epochs in the history of the underground are compressed into the one system that is arranged neatly in the modern Tube map.

Underground Writing is, then, about the fictional landscape that was constructed from George Gissing's original depiction to the several decades of Virginia Woolf's writing. It is the first study to identify and trace the process of the Tube's cultural 'construction' in a variety of forms, ranging from the fictions of literary modernism to the art of the picture postcard. As Steven Connor has remarked, cultural history reads 'the novel not just as passively marked with the imprint of history, but also as one of the ways in which history is made, and remade'.[26] In other words, novels (and I would add other cultural products) do not simply reflect the various historical stages of the underground, but have actually helped to shape its cultural foundations.

There is, then, running in parallel with the complex historical map of urban transportation, a topography of the imagination, a world of visions, myths and artifacts. Underground writing began to locate it on a much wider canvas, going deeper into infernal underworlds or utopian futuristic multilevel mega-cities. It went outwards to construct suburban life in various ways, entering mysterious portals to remake London in parallel universes, or connecting to a more human-centred society whether reformist or revolutionary. In the period of deepest crisis during the Second World War, it brought together the human need for shelter and solidarity with the actual realm of war-torn stations and shattered trains.

In order to construct a cultural framework this study has drawn extensively on the literary aspects of the Tube, adding to those sources from Mass Observation and oral history in the final chapter. The approach adopted here is broadly based on Raymond Williams' ground-breaking work in *The Country and the City* (1973), *Culture and Society* (1958) and *The Long Revolution* (1961).[27] It draws on the notion of cultural materialism in order to highlight the relationship between the material base of a given society and its political/cultural elements. An analysis of the Tube is bound to explore its links to the city and Williams married the emergence of modernism to the metropolitan experience. He pointed to the urban novel as revealing an awareness 'intense and fragmentary, subjective only, yet the very form of its subjectivity including others, who are now with the buildings, the noises, the sights and smells of the city parts of

---

26   S. Connor, *The English Novel in History 1950–1995* (London: Routledge, 1996), p. 1.

27   R. Williams, *The Country and the City* (1973; London: Hogarth Press, 1985); *Culture and Society 1780–1950* (1958; Harmondsworth: Penguin, 1963); *The Long Revolution* (1961; Harmondsworth: Penguin, 1965).

this single and racing consciousness'.[28] Following Williams, we can say that the underground helped to detonate modernism's shift to multiple perspectives, contingency, novelty and friction.

Railways offer other perspectives: Lynda Nead has referred to 'a world devoted to the production of constant motion [...] inhabited by a new ideal citizen'.[29] Those who flocked to the underground at the end of the nineteenth century were increasingly from the lower middle class, forming an invading suburban army popularly embraced in the figure of Mr Pooter.[30] The underground was one of the things that brought an alteration in the construction of society through 'space-time compression'[31] as transport innovations shrank both the geography of the city and the time taken to traverse it. And this 'compression' brought with it a catapulting of writers into mythical exiles such as that expressed in John Davidson's *A Random Itinerary* (1894). Here, Davidson charted the trip out of London made by thousands of commuters to this day 'on a train from Baker Street to Amersham, [a journey] in a circle of Hades unexplored by Dante, being unknown in his day, the leprous land appointed for the punishment of descriptive writers.'[32]

Modernity brought other consequences. The underground itself has been an unfolding succession of modernities, reflecting broader technological, architectural and cultural changes. Underground writing by women depended on the ability to navigate the streets of the city and its public transport. Leonora Davidoff has pointed to the fact that 'cafes, the growth of tea-rooms, the use of buses, even the provision of public lavatories for women were important in freeing middle-class women'.[33] Such women were undoubtedly using the underground system independently by the 1880s and continued to do so for both work and leisure on a growing scale in subsequent decades, as did their lower-middle-class counterparts who came up to town on chartered trains for the sales. The suffrage movement pioneered the use of the new Tube system as a planned and organized means of bringing demonstrations, rallies and lobbies

---

28 R. Williams, *The English Novel from Dickens to Lawrence* (London: Hogarth Press, 1984), p. 164.

29 L. Nead, *Victorian Babylon: People, Streets and Images in Nineteenth-Century London* (New Haven & London: Yale University Press, 2000), p. 54.

30 See G. & W. Grossmith, *Diary of a Nobody* (1892; Harmondsworth: Penguin, 1965).

31 See S. Kern, *The Culture of Time and Space, 1880–1918* (London: Weidenfeld & Nicolson, 1983).

32 J. Davidson, *A Random Itinerary* (1894; Whitefish, MT: Kessinger Publishing, 2008), p. 40.

33 L. Davidoff, *The Best Circles: Society, Etiquette and The Season* (London: Croom Helm, 1973), p. 67.

into central London. The evolution of women's use of the transport system is therefore central to any discussion involving modernity and the urban world.

A cultural study requires more than the stringing together of various cultural artifacts or texts and it cannot simply 'read off' the cultural aspects as 'determined' in some straightforward way by the technological hard-wiring of the system. The underground embodied the most modern technology of mid-Victorian society, and it was one of the elements of the nineteenth century that 'invented' the twentieth.[34] Steam and electric power were required to make the underground work even if both technologies required extensive modification for successful implementation in an underground environment. Operating steam engines in tunnels was not a new phenomenon in 1863 even if it was soon evident that the underground was more than just a long tunnel. But it is important to remember that technology and society are not discrete spaces—that technologies, as Bruno Latour has shown, are not outside cultural processes.[35] This study has therefore tried to explore the relationship between the technologies and the emerging cultural trajectory of the underground.

By definition, the perspectives offered by *Underground Writing* are centred on writing about the Tube rather than reading about it. Writing has attempted to represent people in an underground environment doing what passengers do, whether it is standing or sitting, reading, thinking, sleeping or talking, and it has also tried to represent these underground journeys as part of an urban process. Doreen Massey's point that 'most people still live in places like Harlesden or West Brom [...] much of life for most people, even at the heart of the first world, still consists of waiting in a bus-shelter with your shopping for a bus that never comes' is equally applicable to the Tube.[36] In other words writing has shown, albeit imperfectly, how important such journeys are in daily life and just how their absence can also be significant. This suggests that modern forms of writing involve the move from the objective (sociological) to the subjective (psychological) as was evident from the start in the 'realist' fiction of Gissing, continuing through to the 'modernist' fiction of Woolf. But it also involves the opposite movement in terms of representation, notably in science fiction and polemical material. In terms of the reading, there were (and are) multiple connections between Tube passengers and the audiences that read, watched or listened to the literature, pictures, films or radio programmes that are discussed

---

34 See introduction to S. Rowbotham, *Edward Carpenter: A Life of Liberty and Love* (London: Verso, 2008).

35 See B. Latour, *We Have Never Been Modern*, trans. C. Porter (Cambridge, MA: Harvard University Press, 1993).

36 D. Massey, *Space, Place and Gender* (Cambridge: Polity, 1994), p. 163.

in this book. It is unlikely that infernal images ever discouraged more than a handful of people from ever actually using the Tube, although utopian accounts have almost certainly encouraged underground use even if only at the most mundane level of advertising. There are, after all, more practical reasons why people shun Tube travel, cost being the most obvious. But there are many less explicit ways in which these small cultural fragments have influenced perceptions of the underground system especially in the twentieth century. Myths about the Tube abound but they are founded on cultural deposits laid down in the period discussed in this book, in other words what we might think about the Tube may be composed not only of personal experiences of it but also of these residues of cultural material. The audiences of this material clearly did not consume it passively but we have only an imprecise idea of how these ideas are received. Raymond Williams' concept of 'knowable communities'[37] is relevant here. His personal experience of the Tube was described in very similar terms to those used by his bête noire George Orwell—the violent headaches caused 'whenever I passed through London and saw underground advertisements'.[38] Nevertheless, underground writing (and reading) has made the Tube a 'knowable community' if only because every generation of Tube users is materially rooted in certain locations whether they be stations or lines and comes to identify with them in certain ways. The residues of writing and reading have become a link, however tenuous, in that sense of community. Transport workers also form part of that loop as we know that at various times such cultural residues have emerged in a political form. For example, in recent decades many Tube passengers have voted for or supported policies at various levels such as in the 1981 Greater London Council's 'Fares Fair' plan[39] and that more latterly they have fought for improvements or to defend public ownership through political parties or pressure groups. Equally, Tube and bus workers in the capital took unprecedented strike action in the 1980s to keep transport services under the control of the Greater London Council, something unheard of in the previous two decades. Cultural fragments certainly played a part in these years and cannot therefore be separated from the wider social and

---

37 See Williams, *The English Novel from Dickens to Lawrence*.

38 R. Williams, 'Culture is Ordinary' (1958), in *Resources of Hope: Culture, Democracy, Socialism*, ed. R. Gable (London: Verso, 1989), pp. 3–18, p. 9.

39 The Fares Fair plan was ultimately declared illegal by a Law Lords ruling. The GLC Popular Planning Unit produced a number of publications that reflected these changes, for example *Notes from the Underground* (London: GLC, 1986) and a video *One Man: 2000 Jobs* (London: GLC, 1986), which highlighted the dangers of abolishing Tube guards.

political analysis of the underground system.[40] It is the argument of this book that these cultural fragments were and continue to be an important part of the wider history and the future direction of the underground in the capital.

---

40 See M. Mackintosh & H. Wainwright (eds.), *A Taste of Power: The Politics of Local Economics* (London: Verso, 1987) and *Tubewatch*, no. 9, September–October 1989. The fictional importance of Tube workers is evident in Sebastian Faulks's novel *A Week in December* (London: Hutchinson, 2009) in which one of the seven characters is a Circle line driver named Jenni Fortune.

Chapter One

THE KINGDOM OF SHADOWS:
THE INFERNAL UNDERGROUND
OF GEORGE GISSING

As always, it is the platform of the Terminus which seems alone real, and all behind it a mere dream.

George Gissing, *Collected Letters*[1]

In 'The Decay of Lying' (1889), Oscar Wilde's character Vivian observes that 'at present, people see fogs, not because there are fogs, but because poets and painters have taught them the mysterious loveliness of such effects'.[2] When these words were written, London was about to pass from one transport era to another as steam power was replaced by electricity. The steam underground railways of the capital had been in existence for 25 years, spreading from their original inner-city Metropolitan Railway as far as Richmond and Wimbledon and across the River Thames to New Cross, to Willesden Green in the north-west and Whitechapel in the East End. The underground had received plentiful coverage in Victorian newspapers and journals but it was only in the 1880s that underground writing emerged. This appeared in the fiction of George Gissing who began to offer a number of perspectives on the emergent underground network. In doing so, he constructed a key thread in the new genre of underground writing: an underworld which, like Wilde's fog, had not existed before. He was the first novelist to engage with the underground

---

1   G. Gissing, 17 August 1884, in *The Collected Letters of George Gissing*, eds. P. F. Mattheisen, A. C. Young & P. Coustillas, 9 vols. (Athens, OH: Ohio University Press, 1990–97), vol. 2, p. 243.
2   O. Wilde, 'The Decay of Lying' (1889), in *De Profundis and Other Writings* (Harmondsworth: Penguin, 1973), pp. 55–87, p. 79.

railway in a sustained way and his fictional depiction drew on much contemporary literary and sociological commentary. Gissing effectively manufactured a new underground that was able to live on in cultural terms far beyond the last days of underground steam railways.

This chapter explores the ways in which Gissing constructed key cultural perspectives for the underground railway that begin as a infernal visionary underworld in his 1880s novels such as *Demos* (1886), *Thyrza* (1887), *Workers in the Dawn* (1880) and *The Nether World* (1889). This underworld stretches across London and encompasses a vast urban wasteland criss-crossed by railway lines, embankments, underground cuttings and canals all linked by the powerful mechanical forces of steam power and the steam locomotive. But Gissing's fiction of the 1890s such as *New Grub Street* (1891), *The Odd Women* (1893), *In the Year of Jubilee* (1894), *Eve's Ransom* (1895) and *The Whirlpool* (1897), marks a major break with this approach. They depict the real underground as a key part of a new urban circulatory system in which his middle-class characters are increasingly trapped in their own vortex of suburbs, steam transport and consumerism.

The chapter will explore other cultural tendencies including the formation of newspaper and advertising media that gave the underground a much higher profile and the political fractions that were linked by it to some of the major industrial and political struggles of these decades. The chapter outlines the changing relationship between women and urban transit, the central pivot of which was the opening up of its interiors to the lower-middle-class women who helped to formulate the new 'rules' and conventions of subway consciousness.

'THE FUMES OF BAKER STREET STATION MUST BE POISONOUS': THE IMPACT OF THE STEAM RAILWAYS

The novels of Gissing represent the first sustained depiction of a new metropolitan transport system. They document the ways in which fiction attempted to both describe the underground railways and to understand their impact on the city and urban consciousness. Gissing's approach to the underground was understandably that of an 'insider', that is, he was a member of the social class for which first- and second-class underground transit catered, but Gissing was also an 'outsider' in that he brought other cultural references to bear in this first account of the underground. Gissing's representation of the steam underground railway in two decades of fiction produced a template for underground writing which meant the depiction of the underground as a powerful physical and mechanical force embodied in the dominant steam technology of the period. This would continue to assert itself even after a new era of electric technology had triumphantly overturned the steam underground, leaving a deposit of 'steam archaeology' embedded in literary history. Gissing's fiction outlined the ways in which the underground contributed to the physical and geographical fragmentation of the capital whilst, at the same time, bringing a new sense of unity to metropolitan life. This was done through an account of the new lines and stations that 'stretched' London's built-up area as well as segregating working-class communities. Gissing's novels began to bring out the impact of the underground on urban living in the form of its invasion of older modes of social life and the development of new systems of communication in an enclosed world of tunnels and trains. Finally, Gissing described the ways in which a form of subway consciousness emerged in the first urban subway system, a consciousness that was itself partly formed by his own fictional depiction of the underground.

Gissing was not the first novelist to register the appearance of the new Metropolitan Railway in the capital after its first phase of building was completed in 1863 from Paddington via King's Cross to Farringdon. Anthony Trollope, for example, referred to the early phase of the underground obliquely in his novels. As Robert Altick indicates, Trollope's novels chronicled the process by which the railways became an acceptable mode of travel for the middle-class.[3] It was either a vehicle for the journey to work from new suburbs like Swiss Cottage, a speculative opportunity or a convenient means for leisurely pastimes such as visiting friends. In *The Claverings* (1886–87) the financial aspects of the underground are exposed when Theodore Burton, the head of an engineering and land surveying company, is 'very keen at the present moment about Metropolitan railways [...] ridiculing the folly of those who feared that the railway projectors were going too fast'.[4] Burton wants to build a line 'from Hyde Park Corner to the Tower of London'.[5] Frank Greystock, in *The Eustace Diamonds* (1873), thinks that he will 'take a small house somewhere, probably near Swiss Cottage, come up and down to his chambers by the underground railway, and in all probability, abandon Parliament altogether'.[6] Such journeys involved only a short trip from Baker Street once Swiss Cottage station was opened

3   R. D. Altick, *The Presence of the Present: Topics of the Day in the Victorian Novel* (Columbus: Ohio State University, 1991), pp. 442–44.

4   A. Trollope, *The Claverings* (1886–87; Oxford: Oxford University Press, 1986), p. 450.

5   Trollope, *The Claverings*, p. 332.

6   A. Trollope, *The Eustace Diamonds* (1873), ed. J. McCormack (Oxford: Oxford University Press, 1983), vol. 1, p. 166.

in 1868. Hetta Carbury in *The Way We Live Now* (1874–75) 'trusted herself to the mysteries of the Marylebone [Metropolitan] underground railway and emerged with accuracy at King's Cross' in order to travel (probably from Baker Street station) to the fashionable north London district of Islington.[7] Trollope, however, did not convey the physical transformations that were affecting the capital in the 1860s and the frequent journeys of his characters are uninterrupted by road, sewer or railway construction projects.

Thomas Hardy described his first journey in a letter to Mary Hardy during his sojourn in the new railway suburb of Westbourne Park: 'I tried the Underground Railway one day. Everything is excellently appointed'.[8] Arthur Munby, a thoughtful observer of London for several decades, fulfilled the role of *flâneur* as he walked the capital's streets. But he also made use of the underground, noting in March 1863 that he had 'walked down with [his future wife Hannah] to Farringdon Street, avoiding the crowd by byways; and sent her home by the underground railway'.[9] Munby was not alone. Another prolific diarist, William Allingham, recorded a journey on the Metropolitan Railway only one year later, in 1864. He noted how he had visited the poet Robert Browning at Warwick Crescent and later walked with him 'to the Underground Railway, Bishop's Road [Paddington]'.[10] Bishop's Road was Browning's local underground station and he was a regular user of the service. From the 1860s, these middle-class circles were offered an affordable and comfortable form of travel by the underground, linking them with friends and associates and delivering them to parks and other pleasant destinations. Underground stations were already stages on extensive walking journeys across the capital as we find in 1876 when Allingham was walking with Thomas Carlyle 'through S. K. [South Kensington] station and up through Brompton Churchyard to Hyde Park' in 1876.[11] But there is a crucial difference: Allingham, like Munby, was a representative of a new underground railway generation whilst Carlyle was a member of the 'omnibus' generation and it is hard to imagine him as a frequent underground commuter. Allingham, for example, frequently uses trains in London

7   A. Trollope, *The Way We Live Now* (1874–75; Indianapolis: Bobbs-Merrill, 1974), pp. 634–35.

8   T. Hardy, 5 October 1865, in *Thomas Hardy: Selected Letters*, ed. M. Millgate (Oxford: Clarendon, 1990), p. 5.

9   D. Hudson, *Munby Man of Two Worlds, The Life and Diaries of Arthur J. Munby 1828–1910* (Boston, MA: Gambit, 1972), p. 150.

10   W. Allingham, *William Allingham: A Diary, 1824–1889* (1907), eds. H. Allingham & D. Radford (Harmondsworth: Penguin, 1985), p. 102.

11   Allingham, *Diary*, p. 251.

but notes in a diary entry from 1873 that he had helped Carlyle 'into a Chelsea omnibus' in Knightsbridge.[12] But from that point, people grew up using the underground and knew it as their own. Compton Mackenzie, according to his biographical recollections, was a typically youthful recruit to underground travel in the 1880s and recalled waiting at the age of five 'on the platform of the smoke-filled Temple station for the train to West Kensington'.[13]

When *The Times* called this first Metropolitan Railway 'the greatest engineering triumph of the day [...] ingenious contrivances for obtaining light and ventilation were particularly commended',[14] this description echoed the impact made by the Great Exhibition. This was in stark contrast to *The Times*' abrasive dismissal of the whole plan in 1861 when it had found the notion of putting trains underground offensive to all standards of reasonable conduct[15] whilst the journal *Punch* had similarly mocked the idea, saying the sewers 'would, with a little enlargement, answer all the purposes of the projectors of this scheme'.[16] It added scathingly that 'those who are disposed to sink a little capital cannot do better than bury it under the manner proposed'. *The Times* was at least partially correct in its initial assessment of the project. Yet to many of the architects of urban railway schemes who saw them as vehicles for street improvement, the alleviation of the housing crisis or an intervention into the lives of the lower middle classes in the city, this was a utopian project. No less than 55 proposed London railway schemes were deposited in the Private Bill office of the House of Commons in 1863.[17] It was Charles Pearson's plan for 'Suburban Residences for London Mechanics' that turned out to be the blueprint for the Metropolitan Railway. Pearson's plan included a village five

---

12 Allingham, *Diary*, p. 224.
13 C. Mackenzie, *My Life and Times, Octave One 1883–1891* (London: Chatto & Windus, 1971), p. 173.
14 *The Times*, 10 January 1863.
15 *The Times*, 30 November 1861.
16 *Punch*, vol. 2, 1846, p. 133.
17 A number of schemes had emerged in the previous two decades, many of the more fanciful plans linking urban subway transit with large-scale shopping arcades such as William Moseley's Crystal Way that stretched from Cheapside to Oxford Circus with a branch line near Seven Dials to Piccadilly. This was a glass-enclosed shop-lined arcade 25 feet above street level. Twelve feet below ground a large tunnel would have housed a train service propelled by atmospheric pressure. Joseph Paxton's Great Victorian Way suggested a glass-covered shopping arcade around central London through which eight railway lines and a roadway would pass. The most realistic concept was embodied in George Remington's plan for a deep channel railway to run down the middle of a wide thoroughfare from Paddington via King's Cross to Farringdon Street and Waterloo with a number of major stations at key intersections.

to eight miles outside the city where 10,000 houses and gardens were to be built for artisans displaced by his new railway terminus. Encompassing its own private station at the centre from which straight roads radiated, this was a model garden city with its own churches, schools, shops and public gardens. Pearson may have believed that his project would represent an example of Benthamite social planning, with London being linked by suburban rail to a series of communities on its outskirts based on an initial site in Hornsey or Tottenham. From the start therefore, the ideological roots of the Metropolitan Railway were to be found in a reforming utopian impulse even if the depressed economic climate of the Crimean War was distinctly unfavourable to the raising of the large sums required for such a project.

Gissing's response to the underground railway was of a different order. In his early novels, Gissing did not regard the underground as distinct from the already established steam railways that had carved out new routes into London from the 1830s. The underground was still a very visible part of the urban landscape: iron bridges appeared across railway tracks that disappeared into distant tunnels; smoke and soot from locomotives was ejected onto the streets or rose up between tenements. Gissing lived at 7K Cornwall Residences off Baker Street for six years from 1884 in a flat that 'overlooked the roaring engines of the Metropolitan Railway'. This coincided with the writing of four of his novels, and he could clearly witness the porously close relationship between the street level of the metropolis and the new subsurface level occupied by the 'inferno of the Metropolitan Railway'.[18] In 1888 he complained of 'the incessant hissing of steam from the Baker St. Station; it seems to annoy me more than formerly'.[19] The underground was presented to *Illustrated London News* readers as a supremely well-designed system with elegant yet utilitarian stations shown at street and subsurface levels.[20] Illustrations were designed to imprint on public opinion the notion of an orderly, simple and efficient means of transport for the middle class. Subsequent pictorial accounts invariably confirmed this stress on the underground as a middle-class travelling environment even when workmen's fares began to facilitate respectable working-class travel after 1864.

---

18 M. Roberts, *The Private Life of Henry Maitland: A Portrait of George Gissing*, ed. M. Bishop (1912; London: The Richards Press, 1958), pp. 60 & 90. Gissing also remarked that 'the fumes of Baker Street Station must be poisonous' (Gissing, 14 March 1888, in *Collected Letters*, vol. 3, p. 189).

19 G. Gissing, 6 June 1888, in *The Letters of George Gissing to Members of his Family*, eds. A. & E. Gissing (London: Constable, 1927), p. 216.

20 'The Metropolitan Underground Railway', *Illustrated London News*, 27 December 1862, p. 692.

Gissing himself would have been prohibited from using the underground during his early years in the capital on the grounds of cost.

Gissing's *The Nether World* offered a very different account of the construction of the underground. He carefully researched the Clerkenwell area, the key location for the novel, saying in a letter that 'I have something in hand which I hope to turn to some vigorous purpose, a story that has grown up in recent ramblings about Clerkenwell, dark, but with evening sunlight to close'.[21] Clerkenwell had been transformed after 1860 by the creation of Farringdon Road and the building of the Metropolitan Railway that terminated at Farringdon Street. Both events had had a seismic effect on the area as described by John Hollingshead in his 1861 *Ragged London* and it seems that Gissing drew on Hollingshead in preparing *The Nether World*. Hollingshead commented on Clerkenwell, placing it on the fringe of the Great Northern Railway Terminus and thus characterizing it as a railway suburb: half of Clerkenwell was 'down in the [Fleet] valley', and Hollingshead found it a place of 'social degradation'.[22] He noted the 'black arches of the Eastern Counties Railway running through the midst' of Shoreditch[23] and concluded that 'Wherever you sink a shaft— whether in the centre or the outskirts [...] you will find endless veins of social degradation'.[24] Gissing seems to have adopted Hollingshead's view of Clerkenwell by making it into a metaphorical gulf into which the working population of the area had fallen, bounded by the Metropolitan Railway tracks. It is described by Clara Hewitt, one of the central characters in *The Nether World*, who points to the 'surly bulk of Newgate, [...] the markets of Smithfield, Bartholomew's Hospital, the tract of modern deformity, cleft by a gulf of railway, which spreads between Clerkenwell Road and Charterhouse Street'.[25] Here, Gissing contrasts the old, medieval Clerkenwell with the modern 'deformation' brought about by the building of the Metropolitan Railway as the area is split by the embankments of the new railway in a way that is highly visible after the physical completion of the line. For Gissing, the underground was therefore a symbol of a massive rupture in the urban topography, a break in historical continuity that even the earlier effects of railway building as chronicled by Charles Dickens had not achieved because they had not struck at the heart of the city.

In his description of the physical impact of the Metropolitan, Gissing was forging the first component of underground writing—the notion of

---

21   G. Gissing, 25 July 1887, in *Collected Letters*, vol. 3, p. 139.

22   J. Hollingshead, *Ragged London* (London: Smith Elder, 1861), p. 19.

23   Hollingshead, *Ragged London*, p. 69.

24   Hollingshead, *Ragged London*, p. 232.

25   G. Gissing, *The Nether World* (1889; London: Dent, 1973), p. 280.

a mechanical force that entered the urban space, permanently dividing it as communities were broken up and remade as a result of housing demolition. The underground imposed a new technology, that of the steam locomotive, on the urban landscape in a way that no surface form of transportation did. The street remained a place of horse-drawn vehicles and pedestrians which was regulated by custom and convention even after the Traffic Act of 1867.[26] But the underground enforced its own regime of tracks, depots, stations and signals in a manufactured environment which was apparently disconnected from nature. Sensory observation is replaced by mechanical systems which are optical, auditory and telegraphic; a fact noted paradoxically by Gissing when he recorded a Metropolitan Railway journey to the British Museum in December 1890 in his diary: 'From Gower Street by train. Signals invisible, trains, without order, crawling from station to station. Damnable weather'.[27] Like most seasoned commuters on the underground, Gissing found nothing odd in the notion of travelling in an artificial environment beneath the streets, only complaining bitterly when nature invaded this environment.

Hollingshead's *Ragged London* chronicled the poverty to be found in the Clerkenwell area, adopting a critical view of the underground as a speculative venture that removed and fragmented working-class communities in the name of progress. He reported that the underground had not been well received by the women of Fryingpan Alley in Clerkenwell who had denounced 'the new underground railway that is forming in the neighbourhood; they look upon New Farringdon Street as a Corporation job, and they have got a rude notion that all local improvements put money into the pockets of Government'.[28] Such cynicism about the Metropolitan Board of Works, which had been formed in 1855, is unsurprising, since it was responsible for much of the physical upheaval in London in subsequent decades. Parliament was responsible for the social impact of railway improvements as parliamentary approval was required for all railway schemes in the capital. Some 76,000 people were evicted during the period to make way for a variety of railway tracks in the capital.[29] Only

---

26   J. Winter, *London's Teeming Streets, 1830–1914* (London: Routledge, 1993), chapter 3, pp. 34–49.

27   G. Gissing, *London and the Life of Literature in Late Victorian England, The Diary of George Gissing, Novelist*, ed. P. Coustillas (Hassocks: Harvester, 1978), p. 233. There can be no doubt that adverse weather affected the Metropolitan, one notable example being the storm that flooded Farringdon Street station in May 1915.

28   Hollingshead, *Ragged London*, p. 30.

29   See J. Kellett, *Railways and Victorian Cities* (London: Routledge & Kegan Paul, 1969) and H. J. Dyos, 'Railways and Housing in Victorian London', in D. Cannadine & D. Reeder (eds.), *Exploring the Urban Past* (Cambridge: Cambridge University Press, 1982), pp. 101–18.

307 people were officially evicted by the Metropolitan Railway but one source suggested that in fact some 12,000 people were displaced in the Fleet Valley alone. The vicar of St Bartholomew's near Smithfield, William Denton, accused the railway builders of choosing a route through poorer areas. In a pamphlet entitled *Observations on the Displacement of the Poor by Metropolitan Railways and by other Public Improvements'*, he declared that:

> The special lure of the capitalist is that the line will pass only through inferior property, that is through a densely peopled district, and will destroy the abode of the powerless and the poor whilst it will avoid the properties of those whose opposition is to be dreaded, the great employers of labour.[30]

But public opinion had been shaped by *The Times* which had posed as the Metropolitan Railway's most ardent champion, castigating those, like the Lambeth MP Thomas Hughes, who opposed its building on the grounds that it displaced working-class people to make way for middle-class travel. Hughes had attacked the underground as a 'social tyranny [against] the humbler classes, who have been turned out of their holdings [...] that a man might be able to get from one side of the town to the other in five minutes less time'.[31] *The Times* replied with disdain: 'Accustomed though we are to the exuberant zeal of the working man's champions, we were hardly prepared for a series of propositions so contrary to sound economical doctrines and so obstructive to legitimate enterprise'.[32]

Gissing took up this theme in *The Nether World* suggesting that Clerkenwell is at the heart of a social abyss that runs across London through the Victorian 'manufacturing belt' created in these decades.[33] These working-class inner-city suburbs were considered to be enclaves or appendages which Gissing described as 'a limbo external to society', referring to the 'great law of traffic and the spirit of the time'[34] apparently to describe the combination of steam technology and laissez-faire ideology that characterized London's ever-growing periphery from 1880 to 1900. It seems unlikely that Gissing was opposed in principle to the destruction of slum properties that lay in the path of the underground. However, he was aware of the dislocations that had occurred

---

30   Quoted in R. Trench & E. Hillman, *London Under London: A Subterranean Guide* (1984; London: John Murray, 1993), p. 139.

31   Quoted in S. Halliday, *Underground to Everywhere* (Stroud: Sutton Publishing, 2001), p. 25.

32   Quoted in H. Douglas, *The Underground Story* (London: Robert Hale, 1963), p. 112.

33   See G. Stedman Jones, *Outcast London: A Study in the Relationship between Classes in Victorian Society* (Harmondsworth: Penguin, 1991).

34   G. Gissing, preface to the new edition (1895), *The Unclassed* (1884; Brighton: Harvester, 1976), p. vi.

in the urban landscape—commenting later that 'very few indeed of our old London landmarks are left. London has changed indescribably since the days when I starved and wandered about the streets in 1877'.[35] In *The Nether World*, Shooter's Gardens is 'a picturesque locality which demolition and rebuilding have of late transformed' and now forms part of the social abyss in which the working-class character Pennyloaf (Penelope) Candy lives, dragged down by the daily struggle with insecurity. Clara Hewitt, whose artistic talents are shackled by poverty, feels despair at the prospect of entering this 'nether' world when she exclaims: 'Can I go out into a world like that-alone?'[36] Michael Collie correctly describes Gissing's ability to create a fictional locality which is 'grim, forbidding and precisely drawn', a picture which serves to reinforce the notion of both social and class segregation at a time when London's social crisis was topping the national political agenda.[37]

Gissing unfolds a fictional account that pitched the immutable economic forces of railways, factories and urban blight against seemingly powerless individuals and families. Chapter two of *The Nether World* opens with the release of the working class from the hell of work—'the hour of the unyoking of men'—followed by a kind of infernal rush hour after which there is 'silence and darkness and the sweeping wind'.[38] St John's Arch, a relic of medieval London, has 'a sad, worn, grimy aspect' reflecting the huge volume of pollution emitted over London by the steam locomotive, the factory and the domestic chimney. The underground has excavated and exposed London's archeological past but now buries the few remains of the visible past in soot and dirt. In this description of Clerkenwell, Gissing identifies the ways in which the underground had gouged out the urban landscape but had subsequently buried itself *beneath* the streets. He was very conscious of the constantly changing fabric of the central city, noting that in the 1860s 'It was then still the London of Dickens; now [in the 1890s], Dickens would lose his way anywhere except in a few main thoroughfares'.[39] Gissing asserts that the underground steam locomotive continued to have a real physical impact on the surface of the city throughout these decades. Underground trains and tracks may have been largely invisible to those on the streets but they were nevertheless a palpable

---

35 Gissing, 21 March 1897, in *Collected Letters*, vol. 6, p. 256.

36 Gissing, *The Nether World*, p. 74.

37 M. Collie, *The Alien Art: A Critical Study of George Gissing's Novels* (Folkestone: Dawson, 1979), p. 94.

38 Gissing, *The Nether World*, p. 10.

39 Gissing, 21 March 1897, in *Collected Letters*, vol. 6, p. 256.

mechanical presence through smoke, noise and the traces left on the pattern of human occupation.

Such a world is no longer linked with a known or knowable past, the railway having severed a historical artery and pushed many of its poorer inhabitants into an enclave physically and morally cut off from respectable society. His working-class characters are to be found in circles of hell. He refers directly to Dante in many of his novels after 1880, for example, *Workers in the Dawn*, *The Unclassed*, *Thyrza*, *The Emancipated* (1890), *New Grub Street* and *By the Ionian Sea* (1901), and was influenced by the Romantic and post-Romantic revival of Dante identified by Rick Allen.[40] Dante was, according to Michael Wheeler, 'the presiding genius of nineteenth-century social commentary'.[41] Gissing was particularly struck by his first serious reading of Dante, noting in two letters of 12 and 13 August 1885 that 'Dante I am engaged with at present, and he is glorious' and 'I have just finished the first three cantos of the Inferno in the original. Ye Gods, what glorious matter!'[42] But in Gissing's novels, as Michael Wheeler notes, the circles of hell are 'freed of their former doctrinal significance [...] secularized'.[43] This is a contemporary urban hell as indicated by Mad Jack, a character in *The Nether World*, when he cries out: 'This life you are now living is that of the damned; this place to which you are confined is Hell'.[44]

The underground has left open scars on the city's centre and this is the newest chapter in the life of the city. Those scars will act as the boundary along which main line railway termini will continue to be built thus condemning new areas like those around King's Cross to urban blight. This is what Gissing means in his novel *Thyrza* when he describes the splitting and fragmentation of Islington and Camden. He invites the reader to 'journey on the top of a tram-car from King's Cross to Holloway [...] You pass above lines of railway, which cleave the region with black-breathing fissure [...] All this northward-bearing tract, between Camden Town on the one hand and Islington on the other, is the valley of the shadow of vilest servitude'.[45] John Goode notes that London is 'charted, literally mapped out' in Gissing's fiction with railway lines, road improvements, construction projects and canals frequently providing

---

40   See R. Allen (ed.), *The Moving Pageant: A Literary Sourcebook on London Street-Life, 1700–1914* (London: Routledge, 1998).

41   M. Wheeler, *Death and the Future Life in Victorian Literature and Theology* (Cambridge: Cambridge University Press, 1990), p. 202.

42   Gissing, 13 August 1885, in *Collected Letters*, vol. 2, p. 333.

43   Wheeler, *Death and the Future Life*, p. 203.

44   Gissing, *The Nether World*, p. 345.

45   G. Gissing, *Thyrza* (1887; Brighton: Harvester, 1974), p. 319.

the boundaries of Gissing's social maps.[46] This is in stark contrast to Dickens who understands the city as an agglomeration of forces, a place of obscurity and mystery. For Gissing, the underground and other railway lines of the city have helped to change its nature, making it more factual, determined and predictable; closing down options of mobility to one social class whilst opening them up for another. The Metropolitan Railway is the southern boundary of *The Unclassed* as it runs along the North Road (Marylebone/Euston Road). The location of *Thyrza* is Lambeth, with a northern border made by the Thames and now reinforced by the District Railway housed inside the newly built Thames Embankment. Gissing's notion of a physical boundary was found in yet another major engineering project, the Regent's Canal. In *Demos* this is the 'maladetta e sventurata fossa' separating Hoxton and Islington, 'stagnating in utter foulness between coal-wharves and builders' yards' and dividing the area into 'two neighbourhoods of different aspects'.[47] The River Thames is an object to cross rather than travel along in *Thyrza* and Bloomsbury separates Clerkenwell from the West End in *The Nether World*.

As the underground disturbed ideas about existing boundaries and routes in the city, it helped to create a sense of vertical porosity in the environment. The first series of underground lines enveloped large swathes of central London in a maelstrom of railway construction. On the Thames Embankment the changes were dramatic, transforming an almost mythical district of the capital: the Adelphi Terrace. Built in 1768 as a massive luxury tier based on a network of arched catacombs leading down to the Thames, its riverside arches had achieved notoriety by the 1860s as a disreputable site of criminality and attempted suicide. The steam underground severed the past from the present in demolishing an older London, creating a new well-defined border along the Thames and changing the nature of public space. Arthur Munby observed in 1869 that: 'The bright morning sun shone on the broad bright river, and on the white walls of the Embankment, which stretch away as a noble curve to Westminster, under the dark contrasting masses of the bridges'.[48]

Gissing was therefore exploring the imaginative boundaries of the underground in relation to the new urban topography of the 1880s. Such fictional borders suggest that Gissing was an acute observer of the physical changes that continued to dominate the London landscape in the decades after his first arrival in the city in 1877. By the time he settled down to live in central

---

46 J. Goode, *George Gissing: Ideology and Fiction* (London: Vision Press, 1978), p. 91.
47 G. Gissing, *Demos* (1886; Brighton: Harvester, 1972), p. 25.
48 Hudson, *Munby Man of Two Worlds*, p. 265.

London, some of the underground railway landscape was nearly 15 years old, although the building of the Inner Circle continued until 1884. The older parts of the underground were by now covered in a layer of soot, a feature confirmed by a letter in the family correspondence of Mrs Richard Moore which recalled travelling on the Metropolitan Railway: 'Everything was covered with soot. To open a carriage door blackened your hand. After a train left the station the platform opposite was hardly visible for smoke. The smoke had a peculiarly strong smell'.[49]

Similar observations are found in Angus Evan Abbott's short story 'The Spawn of Fortune' (1896) when a carriage door is flung open in a tunnel and 'Steam and smoke in a purple cloud, and sulphur smells belched in and filled the compartment'.[50] The soot and grime of the underground railway soon became a regular feature of travel in the capital and were notable in the more enclosed spaces of tunnels and stations. But for Gissing the pollutants found on the underground were merely a reflection of the fog that characterized London's streets, as experienced by Gissing's character Edwin Reardon in *New Grub Street* when he exclaims: 'Ugh! That first mouthful of fog'.[51] An estimated 200 tons of fine soot escaped every day into the London atmosphere, causing the regular 'smoke fogs' in the capital which were particularly severe in the 1880s. Even Bram Stoker's vampire fighter, Van Helsing, remarked on the 'smuts' that had affected London when he had studied there as a young man.[52] Embankments and cuttings were 'softened' by the return of trees, shrubs and flowers on some of the less central parts of the system but the soot from under-ground locomotives quickly obscured tunnels.[53] A visitor to London, Hippolyte Taine, remarked on the streets of the city which were 'dirty and impregnated with the smell of soot. A thick yellow fog fills the air, sinks, crawls on the very ground; at thirty paces a house or a steam-ship look like ink-stains on blotting paper'.[54] The fog also appeared in a prose poem by another French visitor to the capital, Arthur Rimbaud. His poem 'Métropolitain' (1872) recorded the 'sheets of fog spread out in ghastly layers in the sky [...] formed by the most

49   Mrs Richard Moore, item from family correspondence, cited in G. Winter, *A Cockney Camera* (Harmondsworth: Penguin, 1979), p. 112.

50   A. E. Abbott, 'The Spawn of Fortune' (1896), in A. K. Russell (ed.), *The Rivals of Sherlock Holmes 2* (Secaucus, NJ: Castle Books, 1980), pp. 3–9, p. 4.

51   G. Gissing, *New Grub Street* (1891; Harmondsworth: Penguin, 1968), p. 26.

52   B. Stoker, *Dracula* (1897; London: Penguin, 1993), p. 149.

53   See A. Wohl, *Endangered Lives: Public Health in Victorian Britain* (London: Methuen, 1983), chapter 8.

54   H. Taine, *Notes on England 1860–1870*, trans. E. Hyams (London: Thames & Hudson, 1957), pp. 8–9.

treacherous black smoke that the Ocean in mourning can produce' as seen from the window of a Metropolitan Railway train as it steamed down to Wapping.[55] Compton Mackenzie remembered that in the 1880s Baker Street station was 'much fuller of fumes than the Temple [on the District], though not so full of them as Portland Road [Great Portland Street] or worst of all Gower Street'.[56]

London's soot and fog was as much an atmospheric envelope to the city as the other mechanical forces that imprisoned the working class and the so-called 'submerged tenth' or residuum. The railway was an important component of this envelope, a generic element in this social drama which unfolded at both surface and subterranean levels in the city. As Lynda Nead observes in *Victorian Babylon* (2000), from the 1860s London was in a process of transformation by demolition and construction projects behind which lay a complex bundle of ideas about social and sanitary improvement.[57] Gissing's fiction was part of a broad social message of the many liberal and radical arguments that were merging to form a loose radical, Christian or socialist critique of capitalism. Shortly after the publication of *Workers in the Dawn*, Gissing said that he would continue to combine fiction and social protest: 'I mean to bring home to people the ghastly condition (material, mental, and moral) of our poor classes'.[58]

He was describing in fiction a world that had already been included in the work of a number of popular writers like G. W. M. Reynolds in the 1840s and by the illustrator Gustave Doré just over two decades later. Gissing reworked a number of literary features in his first decade of novel writing, including, in a significant passage from *The Nether World*, the almost exact reproduction of a description of a railway journey from Reynolds' penny serial *The Mysteries of London* (1845). Reynolds' stories responded to the demand for lurid accounts of the criminal underground using Dantean imagery, eroticism and Gothic urban scenes. Despite his status as the most popular sensationalist author of the period, he was also a leading figure in the Chartist movement even in its attenuated 'late' phase. Reynolds described the way in which the Eastern Counties Railway intersected Spitalfields and Bethnal Green: 'The traveller upon this line may catch, from the windows of the carriage in which he journeys, a hasty but alas! too comprehensive glance of the wretchedness and squalor of that portion of

55 A. Rimbaud, 'Métropolitain' (1872), in *Rimbaud: Complete Works, Selected Letters*, trans. W. Fowlie (Chicago: University of Chicago Press, 1966), pp. 242–44, p. 243.

56 Mackenzie, *My Life and Times*, p. 178.

57 See L. Nead, *Victorian Babylon: People, Streets and Images in Nineteenth-Century London* (New Haven & London: Yale University Press, 2000), pp. 13–80.

58 Gissing, 3 November 1880, in *Collected Letters*, vol. 1, p. 307.

London [...] abodes of sorrow, vice and destitution'.[59] This passage seems to have given Gissing a literary context for contemporary social comment and allowed him to develop the panoramic urban perspective. Where Reynolds revealed the 'mysteries' of London from a railway carriage leaving Fenchurch Street station, Gissing steers a highly visible steam locomotive across an abyss of poverty, a world that is as desolate as Clerkenwell:

> Over the pest-stricken regions of East London, sweltering in sunshine which served only to reveal the intimacies of abomination; across miles of a city of the damned, such as thought never conceived before this age of ours; above streets swarming with a nameless populace, cruelly exposed by the unwonted light of heaven.[60]

Speeding across the infernal region of the East End from Liverpool Street station towards Chelmsford, the railway locomotive and its carriages are the privileged points of observation for the social observer but also, for Gissing, the embodiment of an unstoppable economic power that had helped to condemn the damned to their unsought fate. The steam locomotive had begun to dominate the capital, joining it together via the underground lines that were being vastly extended in the 21 years after 1863.

Gissing also drew on more recent visual documentation of London's railways. Gustave Doré's impressions of the city in *London: A Pilgrimage* (1872) include the often-reproduced illustration of a steam train as it crosses an urban wasteland of houses with the 'damned' in this case framed by the railway arch, a variation on the common use of the arches of bridges over the Thames, such as Waterloo, as a Victorian setting for suicide attempts due to the imaginative association of the arch with damnation. The arch belonged, Maidment suggests, to 'visual genres of social investigation', and had become 'menacing and oppressive'.[61] The riverside archway (like the Adelphi arches at Hungerford) framed Augustus Egg's 1858 painting *Past and Present, No. 3, Despair* with a moonlit backdrop and torn theatrical posters to the left of the picture,[62] whilst George Cruikshank's Plate VIII from *The Drunkard's Children* (1848) showed a woman falling from the parapet of a bridge on a misty but moonlit night,[63] an image invoked in a more romantic fashion by Gustave Doré in his portrayal of Waterloo bridge as *The*

---

59 See G. W. M. Reynolds, *The Mysteries of London* (1845; Keele: Keele University Press, 1996), ch. 42, 'The Dark House', selected chapters from vols. 1–2 of 4, vol. 1, p. 67.

60 Gissing, *The Nether World*, p. 164.

61 B. E. Maidment, *Reading Popular Prints, 1790–1870* (Manchester: Manchester University Press, 1996), p. 161.

62 Augustus Egg, *Past and Present, No. 3, Despair* (1858), Tate Britain, London.

63 G. Cruikshank, *The Drunkard's Children* (1848), Victoria & Albert Museum.

Bridge of Sighs (1850).[64] As Olive Anderson has pointed out, there was a rise in railway suicides after 1868,[65] and these earlier pictures were crudely reworked in the 1870s in publications like *Illustrated Police News*, adding sensationalist imagery to reports like 'The Suicide of Alice Blanche Oswald' (1872)[66] and the graphic print entitled 'Suicide on a Railway, A Young Woman Decapitated' (1877).[67] In this way, the use of bridge parapets, railway viaducts and the entrances to railway tunnels joined riverside arches in the imagination in these decades, and such suicide attempts were often portrayed on the London stage. The cover illustration for Charles Selby's play *London by Night* (1886) showed the overworked image of a woman jumping from a London bridge, and Dion Boucicault's *After Dark; A Drama of London Life* (1868) combined the steam engine *and* the attempted suicide of the heroine Eliza Medhurst who descends from a parapet into the Thames with a moonlit St Paul's Cathedral framed by the arch of the bridge.[68] Gissing would undoubtedly have sympathized with more contemporary social and secular responses to suicide if only because, as Ron Brown says, it was 'a concern that fell within the realms of the "condition of England" question'.[69] It seems that the looming presence of the railway arch figured as a 'portal of eternity' in his thinking, bringing together many of these visual elements in the creation of an imaginary underground in the 1880s. Gissing knew the Thames bridges well, contributing a short piece entitled 'On Battersea Bridge' to a London newspaper.[70]

The porous nature of these surface and subterranean worlds in Gissing's fiction may also be traceable to the ways in which the early Metropolitan Railway had been portrayed on the London stage in the 1860s. It soon made an appearance in *Punch* in an 1864 parody of its impact on the capital. In a short skit entitled 'Real Railway Advantages', *Punch* mockingly outlined the future

---

64   G. Doré, *The Bridge of Sighs* (1850), Victoria & Albert Museum.
65   O. Anderson, *Suicide in Victorian and Edwardian England* (Oxford: Clarendon, 1987) pp. 371–72.
66   'The Suicide of Alice Blanche Oswald', *Illustrated Police News*, 21 September 1872.
67   'Suicide on a Railway', *Illustrated Police News*, 23 December 1877.
68   'Eliza's attempted suicide', illustration for D. Boucicault, *After Dark; A Drama of London Life* (1868), in J. O. Bailey (ed.), *British Plays of the 19th Century* (New York: Odyssey, 1966), pp. 283–302.
69   R. Brown, *The Art of Suicide* (London: Reaktion Books, 2001), p. 153. See B. Gates, *Victorian Suicide: Mad Crimes and Sad Histories* (Princeton: Princeton University Press, 1988).
70   See G. Gissing, 'On Battersea Bridge', in *Selections Autobiographical and Imaginative from the Works of George Gissing. With Biographical and Critical Notes by his Son* (New York: Jonathan Cape & Harnon Smith, 1925).

development of the underground as an 'idea of great traffic and active Metropolitan Railway life'. It went on to describe that:

> Without the aid of a glass can be plainly read, on the Right Hand of the View, a large
> placard headed, BAYSWATER, BURLINGTON ARCADE, CHARING CROSS, AND BOROUGH LINE
> trains every five minutes! CHEAP FARES! and on the Left Hand a larger placard, adver-
> tising THE BROMPTON, PICCADILLY, CHARING CROSS, BOROUGH AND BLOOMSBURY LINE.
> TRAINS EVERY SEVEN MINUTES! CHEAPER FARES![71]

But the problem, in *Punch*'s short melodrama, is that the Metropolitan Railway
is causing an upheaval in the consulting rooms of 'MR MAGNEESHER, the
eminent M.D.'. In a preview of many later railway melodramas, Mr Magneesher
is constantly interrupted in his work by the sounds of railway bells, the shrieks
of engines, 'whistle screams like a war-whoop [...] the squeaking of ungreased
carriage-wheels and shouting of porters'. These terrors finally drive Mr
Magneesher to despair as he 'shakes his fists wildly at the Railway Stations'.
The mechanical world of the railway has finally invaded the central area of the
metropolis, adding a new dimension of noise to the fabric of city life. Although
this world is subterranean it erupts onto the surface and underlines the porosity
of the landscape.

David Pike has commented on the melodramatic treatment of the underground in Boucicault's *After Dark* and J. B. Buckstone's pantomime *Little Miss
Muffet and Little Boy Blue or, Harlequin and Old Daddy Long-Legs* (1861) in the
context of London's subterranean spaces. In *After Dark*, which ran for nearly a
year initially, the Metropolitan Railway is only separated by a brick wall from
the wine cellar of a gambling den named the Elysium Music Hall.[72] In the
'sensation scene', the hero Captain Gordon Chumley is drugged by the villains
and placed on the Metropolitan Railway track with tunnels converging in
perspective to the stage. Old Tom rescues him by breaking through the wall
from the gambling den to the underground as trains run up and down the
lines with all the atmospheric effects of locomotive power. Stage directions
make clear the power of the locomotive: 'Whistle, sound of train approaching
[...] Noise of train passing [...] Light shows at left [...] Light moves away'. Old
Tom jumps onto the track and finds Gordon but then 'Bell rings faintly, then
loudly; whistle sounds. The sound of train approaching begins and is continued
till end'. He grabs Gordon and 'The Train runs on, as a quick curtain falls'.[73]

---

71   *Punch*, vol. 46, January–June 1864, p. 67.
72   Boucicault took the plot from the French melodrama *Les Bohemians de Paris* and the climax
     from the melodrama *Under the Gaslight* (1867) by the American writer Augustin Daly.
73   Boucicault, *After Dark*, p. 300

The power of the oncoming locomotive in this scene is vividly shown in the cover illustration for H. L. Williams' adaptation of *After Dark*, in which a railway arch is a prominent part of the background, semaphore levers point ominously downwards, lamps revolve in the gloom, the train's light glares at Old Tom and the signalman is powerless to stop the train.[74] To Old Tom the railway line 'looks like a long, dark street, with green and red lights in the distance'[75] as though this subterranean world threatens to invade the rest of London. As Nicholas Daly suggests, *After Dark* envisions 'scenarios in which a human agent can beat a mechanical agent; the human for a moment comes to enter and master the temporal world of the machine'.[76] However, in Gissing's hands, the mechanical world is too powerful. The steam locomotive is figuratively and literally a force that threatens to overwhelm the capital through its ability to move through the porous urban landscape. The melodramas of the 1860s broke down the barriers between the subterranean and the surface worlds of London in a way that did not threaten Victorian middle-class audiences. But the conventions of the melodrama would take on a far more sinister character as Gissing's imagination transformed the underground into a formidable force capable of impacting on the metropolitan population in a variety of psychological ways.

By the 1880s, the mysterious and sensational elements of the railway had become part of theatrical stock-in-trade, especially with special effects that heralded the arrival of a locomotive on stage. These performances staged the railway as a reflection of the new subterranean experience, especially as the urban middle class was relatively unaccustomed to travelling underground. As David Pike suggests, the underground was 'rapidly assimilated to the middle-class world of which it played such an important role in the daily passage between suburb and city' in these West End productions.[77] Imaginary underground spaces had been frequently formulated for West End audiences in the 1860s and often based on a descent into hell using the classical mythology of Hades. Many other dramatic pieces had used underground spaces to stage comic turns about the building of the Thames Tunnel (1823–43), the projects of the Metropolitan Board of Works or the Metropolitan Railway. Dickensian images of locomotive power that intruded into human space were used, for

---

74   Cover illustration for H. L. Williams' adaptation of *After Dark* (1880?), British Library.

75   Boucicault, *After Dark*, p. 300.

76   N. Daly, *Literature, Technology and Modernity, 1860–2000* (Cambridge: Cambridge University Press, 2004), pp. 23.

77   D. L. Pike, 'Underground Theater: Subterranean Spaces on the London Stage', *Nineteenth Century Studies*, vol. 13, 1999, pp. 102–38, p. 129.

example in Trollope's novel *The Prime Minister* (1876), when his character Lopez travels by the underground to Euston and thence to Tenby Junction (apparently Willesden Junction) in order to commit suicide beneath an infernal 'flying engine' which smashes him 'into bloody atoms'.[78]

The London stage continued to use railway imagery throughout Gissing's period of residence in the capital with, for example, the murder mystery *The Great World of London* (1899), by George Lander and Walter Melville, featuring many scenes in railway stations. Gissing's early fiction echoes these stage dramatizations of the underground by placing much of the stress on the physical power and impact of steam locomotives rather than the experiences of those who travelled on the trains or waited on the platforms. Such melodrama was hugely popular in the period 1866–1900 with the revival of the West End theatre. There were, by the end of this period, 63 theatres in London and 40 music halls offering, according to Michael Booth, a huge range of sensational scenes and stage events including avalanches, horse races and train wrecks.[79] Turnham's Music Hall was renamed the Metropolitan in 1864 to cash in on the success of the nearby underground line at Edgware Road which had opened only a year before. Public space was much in vogue on the stage with bank interiors (*Ticket-of-Leave Man*, 1863); hansom cabs crossing Westminster Bridge (*The Great City*, 1867); real fire engines on stage in *The Streets of London* (1864) and Victoria Station and the Metropolitan Railway (*After Dark*). In addition, the hoardings temporarily erected during railway or road construction were plastered with posters, many of which advertised stage productions. An 1862 photograph[80] of the construction of King's Cross underground station shows a number of theatre and circus posters, including one for Boucicault's play *The Colleen Bawn* (1860) at the Theatre Royal, Drury Lane. The fact that these theatrical adverts increasingly featured violent images of death and destruction was a minor *cause célèbre* in the 1880s. *Punch*, for example, decried the moral dangers of new commercialism in a full-page cartoon entitled 'How We Advertise Now' in 1887.[81] This included a large number of lurid images, with the by now typical sight of a railway locomotive steaming at full throttle towards a hero tied to the tracks as though to advertise a play at an imaginary Newgate Theatre. The train as theatrical prop even entered the novel, appearing in Ella Hepworth Dixon's *The Story of a Modern Woman* (1894) in which the heroine, Mary Erle suggests

---

78   A. Trollope, *The Prime Minister* (1876), ed. J. Uglow (Oxford: Oxford University Press, 1983), p. 520.

79   See M. Booth, *Theatre in the Victorian Age* (Cambridge: Cambridge University Press, 1991).

80   *King's Cross Underground Station, July 1862*, Guildhall Library, London.

81   'How We Advertise Now', *Punch*, 3 December 1887, vols. 92–93, p. 262.

going to see 'that piece still at Drury Lane with the real railway-engine in it'.[82] This refers to the play *Pluck* (1882), which featured a double railway accident. The locomotive was also present in *The Whip* at Drury Lane Theatre in 1909. On stage, an overturned railway engine was framed by the ominous tunnel arch to the left of the stage and a Doré-like railway viaduct to the right.

Gissing lived in a city in which the steam locomotive was not only a real physical force but also a pervasive signifier for this technological power. His underground writing in the 1880s was related to the images of the railway that filled the streets and appeared on the London stage. This may help to explain why Gissing did not seek in this period to use the underground as a location for his characters (most of them would not have used it for reasons of cost) charting, instead, its technological impact on the urban landscape. The full-frontal railway locomotive that loomed out of a poster concealed behind its hoarding the real machine. Gissing's novels concealed both the real and imagined locomotive 'behind' the abyss in the sense that it represented an outside intervention in the lives of his characters. This confirms Rosalind Williams' seminal account of cultural perspectives on technology in *Notes on the Underground* (1990). Williams suggests that anxieties about industrialization and steam technology were increasingly being expressed primarily in the cultural rather than the political sphere during the Victorian period. These anxieties, she adds, 'were repeatedly shaped into subterranean images that were simulta-neously used as emblems of progress'.[83] The image of the locomotive was deeply ambiguous in mid-Victorian culture as it was repeatedly linked with a subter-ranean passage through landscapes. This subterrain, even if only marginally below the surface as it was in the first underground lines (unlike the later tube tunnels), presented writers and illustrators with elements of a cultural critique of capitalism. Steam locomotives were metaphorically demonic, being pictured as driving, infernal forces by George Cruikshank in his c.1845 illustration 'The Railway Dragon' and in John Leech's 1845 'The Railway Juggernaut'. Cruikshank portrayed the locomotive as a guillotine-like demon whilst Leech depicted it as an infernal 'speculator' gleefully driven by a devil.

By the 1880s, the technology of steam could clearly no longer be considered as an automatically benign social force, because, as Herbert Sussman points out, technological power and poverty were 'an intransigent condition of modern

---

82   E. Hepworth Dixon, *The Story of a Modern Woman* (1894; London: Merlin, 1990), p. 125.

83   R. Williams, *Notes on the Underground: An Essay on Technology, Society and the Imagination* (Cambridge, MA: MIT Press, 1990), p. 66.

life'.[84] Gissing was the heir to conservative critiques of industrial society as represented from Carlyle to Ruskin and Arnold. This ambiguous package of ideas informed Gissing's outlook and if, as Jacob Korg has suggested, Gissing had rejected the claims of both science and religion, steam technology would continue to be associated for him with the 'hell' of poverty and social degradation.[85] Gissing depicted the railway as literally destroying families as when, in *New Grub Street*, a railway accident in Crewe is cited as the cause of the descent from respectability of a walk-on character named Victor Duke. The story is recounted at a coffee stall beside Camden Town (Camden Road) station. Gissing returned to the destructive physical force of railway technology in one of his last short stories, 'Humplebee' (1906). Here, he actually depicts a train crash in which his hero Humplebee is directly involved: 'an accident—a collision! [...] in front of the engine lay a goods truck smashed to pieces; people were rushing about with cries and gesticulations'.[86]

Gissing's view of the railways may be compared with that of his fictional mentor, Charles Dickens. As the embodiment of modernity, the railways offered the benefits of progress that Dickens warmly welcomed. Dickens was keen to see fog, mud and other effluvia cleared out from the city in order to remove the 'blockages' to urban circulatory processes. This was clearly illustrated in Doré's print showing a steam train speeding across the viaduct at Ludgate Hill, in stark contrast to the massive traffic jam in Ludgate Circus below. In *Dombey and Son* (1848), Dickens portrayed the devastation caused by the arrival of the London and Birmingham Railway in the north London suburb of Stagg's Gardens (Camden Town): 'The first shock of a great earthquake had, just at that period, rent the whole neighbourhood to its centre. Traces of its course were visible on every side. Houses were knocked down; streets broken through and stopped; deep pits and trenches dug in the ground'.[87]

But the eventual result of this railway construction is, for Dickens, the growth of order, efficiency and the betterment of social conditions: 'from the very core of all this dire disaster [the Railway] trailed smoothly away, upon its mighty course of civilisation and improvement'.[88] Dickens was more concerned about incompetence and greed and, as Michael Slater points out, was severely

---

84   H. L. Sussman, *Victorians and the Machine: The Literary Response to Technology* (Cambridge, MA: Harvard University Press, 1968), p. 91.

85   See J. Korg, *George Gissing: A Critical Biography* (1963; Brighton: Harvester, 1980), p. 176.

86   G. Gissing, 'Humplebee', in *The House of Cobwebs* (1906; Edinburgh: Constable, 1926), pp. 68–87, pp. 79–80.

87   C. Dickens, *Dombey and Son* (1848; Harmondsworth: Penguin, 1970), p. 120.

88   Dickens, *Dombey and Son*, p. 121.

critical of the development of the railways 'from the irresponsibility of Boards of Directors playing fast and loose with the safety of the public to the surliness of refreshment room staff'.[89] Dickens exerted a major influence on Gissing's fiction and they shared a deep interest in the concept of progress and how it continually transformed the urban landscape. Dickens witnessed and testified to the massive fracturing of cities by industrialization, technology and the steam railway, processes that accelerated during his lifetime. But Dickens, as Efraim Sicher notes, 'reads the map of the city by walking its streets' whilst Gissing reads it by travelling on the underground railway.[90]

'THE UNDERGROUND IS A CONTRARY LINE': TURMOIL ON THE STEAM RAILWAY

T*he Nether World* is pivotal in the shift in Gissing's fiction away from an infernal underworld towards an engagement with writing the *actual* underground. In this novel Gissing has, as Rosalind Williams argues, reached the end-point of the 'subterranean social journey' in the sense that he simply cannot find more graphic terms in which to describe the social conditions of the abyss.[91] But *The Nether World* represents a new twist in Gissing's approach to subterranean London in that it points towards a greater interest in underground journeys. *The Nether World* contains an account of a Bank Holiday trip from Holborn Viaduct to Crystal Palace that is consciously staged as a reversal of normal social life as workers celebrate by escaping from Clerkenwell for the day. But they have to return to Gissing's 'city of the damned' in a circulatory motion that eventually denies them a suburban or pastoral future. Chapter 12, 'Io Saturnalia!', opens with trains disgorging from Holborn Viaduct: 'As soon as a train was full, off it went, and another long string of empty carriages drew up in its place.' There is 'No distinction between "classes" to-day; get in where you like, where you can.'[92] The working class is literally shipped off to a suburban paradise.

Gissing wants to remind his readers of this social message when he interjects with a rather staged and mocking lecture on the need to 'Destroy, sweep away,'

89   M. Slater, *An Intelligent Person's Guide to Dickens* (London: Duckworth, 1999), p. 71.
90   E. Sicher, *Rereading the City/Rereading Dickens: Representation, the Novel and Urban Realism* (New York: AMS Press, 2003), p. 41.
91   Williams, *Notes on the Underground*, p. 163.
92   Gissing, *The Nether World*, p. 105.

in order that the 'City of Man' may be built.[93] He appears to believe that such radical change is actually an illusion. The journey back to London from the Crystal Palace is a Bacchanalian scene in a *third-class* coach that underlines the crude realities of working-class life as Gissing sees them: Gissing's character, Pennyloaf Candy, has to return to Clerkenwell where she will have to suffer the indignity of pawning her wedding ring. The choice of the Crystal Palace for this chapter was significant because it represented for Gissing all the forces of contemporary capitalism, in other words, his characters were not sent there on a Bank Holiday excursion by accident. Gissing himself spent a Bank Holiday at the Crystal Palace in order to write this chapter, coming away with an extremely jaundiced view of the proceedings. The Palace itself stood out impressively from the surrounding streets like a colossal glass fairyland—a building six times larger than St Paul's Cathedral. It had been dismantled in 1852 and rebuilt by 1854 in Sydenham in south-east London and was joined to the city by the London, Brighton and South Coast Railway. In the 1860s, Hippolyte Taine had described it as a 'monstrous great pile devoid of style and bearing witness not to their taste, but to their power'.[94] It was perceived as a lower-class Arcadia of arts and sciences attracting over two million visitors in its first 30 years. The Palace's relocation in Sydenham was not, however, the only connection with railways. The glass arcade of manufactured goods and global commerce provided the young William Whiteley with the idea for a department store (opened in 1863)[95] and the symbiotic relationship between consumption and subterranean railways was being forged even before the building of the Metropolitan Railway had begun. As with the new underground, the original Great Exhibition had been charged with the duty to instil the virtues of hard work, diligence and duty into the lower classes. These were the same qualities that would be espoused by Jerrold in his description of workmen's trains on the Metropolitan Railway two decades later.[96]

The Great Exhibition was further linked to the underground through its contribution to the concept of utility in design, in this case through the application of art and science to industry. One of the organizers of the Exhibition, Henry Cole, had attempted to combine production and design, and the

---

93   Gissing, *The Nether World*, p. 109.
94   Taine, *Notes on England*, p. 188.
95   See L. Stratmann, *Whiteley's Folly: the Life and Death of a Salesman* (Stroud: Sutton Publishing, 2004).
96   G. Doré & B. Jerrold, *London: A Pilgrimage* (1872; New York: Dover, 1970), p. 113.

ideological roots of 'Fitness for Purpose'[97] lie in the style of Joseph Paxton's design for the Crystal Palace. Paxton was both an engineer and railway investor who had, as we have seen, produced a design for the Great Victorian Way in 1855, a subway that was to be part of a heated glass arcade and shopping emporium. However, the Crystal Palace that eventually appeared in Gissing's novel had passed through the critical condenser of Dickens and John Ruskin, both of whom expressed doubts about its contents and overall design. Dickens approved of it as a symbol of progress and a clear statement of liberal aims like Free Trade. But he also complained about the 'boredom and lassitude' of the public that might be brought on by the seemingly endless array of artifacts— causing a 'bewilderment of the public'.[98]

The Crystal Palace chapter points backwards to Gissing's concept of the railway as an elemental force. Holborn Viaduct station was on the only railway line to 'invade' the central business district, driving a permanent railway bridge across Ludgate Hill just above the major road junction at Ludgate Circus. It was an indelible mark on the landscape of the Fleet Valley, connecting directly with the Metropolitan Railway at Farringdon. Holborn Viaduct station offered the middle-class commuter a direct southern route out of the city but for Gissing's working class the railway is a formidable barrier. In *The Nether World* the station finally returns the working class to the abyss thus repeating Gissing's original conception of the demonic locomotive that divides and fragments the city. But this passage also points towards Gissing's new interest in the social content of the journey as the train's pathway is registered in terms of what is happening inside the carriages as people sing, smoke and savour the luxury of first-class cushions. For Gissing, the interior of the railway carriage is now a subject for fiction. On this occasion, Gissing suspends the 'normal' conventions of first, second and third-class travel in order to accommodate the fact that railways were generally a middle-class mode of transport. In reality, these conventions were a very visible part of the steam underground as station platforms displayed signs indicating where to wait for each type of accommodation as shown, for example, in contemporary prints of King's Cross, Gloucester Road and Baker Street underground stations.

After the publication of *The Nether World* in 1889, Gissing's underground writing undergoes a significant shift. In his novels of the 1890s, *New Grub Street*, *The Odd Women*, *In the Year of Jubilee*, *The Whirlpool* and *Eve's Ransom*, Gissing

---

97   'Fitness for Purpose' became the design philosophy for public transport in the capital during the first half of the twentieth century.

98   C. Dickens, 25 July 1851, in *The Letters of Charles Dickens*, eds. G. Storey, K. Tilliotson & N. Burgis, 12 vols. (Oxford: Clarendon, 1965–2002), vol. 6, p. 449.

develops a new set of perspectives that centre on the real underground rather than a visionary, infernal underworld. Characters in these novels are no longer drawn from the working class but are, instead, a middle-class group which is engaged in a struggle for survival in the vast circulatory system of the late Victorian city. Hell is still present though, as when his character Hugh Carnaby mutters 'The Whirlpool! [...] It's got hold of *me*, and I'm going down, old man—and it looks black as hell'.[99] As Jacob Korg notes, Gissing had continued to take an interest in radical politics and the working class throughout the previous decade, publishing three articles on socialism, for example, in the *Pall Mall Gazette* in 1880.[100] In 1885, he noted a visit to a socialist meeting in west London: 'And now I am obliged to go about attending Socialist meetings. To-night I go to one at the house of the poet Morris in Hammersmith'.[101] In a diary entry for June 1888, he recorded a journey on the Metropolitan Railway back to Baker Street, after a lecture on Christian Socialism. In July of the same year, Gissing attended a strike meeting of the Bryant and May Match Workers at Mile End Waste.[102] Annie Besant, a key strike leader and an important figure in the socialist revival of the 1880s, drew on the same Dantean imagery that appealed to Gissing in her newspaper *The Link*. She used it to describe the need for 'a people's Dante, to make a special circle in the Inferno for those who live on this misery, and suck wealth out of the starvation of helpless girls'.[103] A poem appeared in the *Star* entitled 'Lucifer in the East' which included the lines:

> Ay! go where the brimstone has shed its blight,
> Go, see, and consider it well
> How the daughters of women are perishing there,
> In your Lucifer's Brimstone Hell.[104]

Gissing was an avid purchaser of socialist publications like *The Link* noting, after the Mile End Waste visit, that it was 'remarkable, the extent to which revolutionary periodicals are multiplying [...] there must have been two dozen of them for sale'.[105] He would undoubtedly have responded to the regular use

---

99   G. Gissing, *The Whirlpool* (1897; London: Hogarth Press, 1984), p. 320.

100   See Korg, *Critical Biography*, p. 45.

101   Gissing, 22 November 1885, in *Letters to Members of his Family*, p. 174.

102   Gissing, *London and the Life of Literature*, pp. 32–33 & 35.

103   *The Link*, 7 July 1888, in E. Royston Pike, *Human Documents of the Age of the Forsytes* (London: George Allen & Unwin, 1969), p. 274.

104   'Lucifer in the East', *Star*, 27 January 1892.

105   Gissing, 15 July 1888, in *Collected Letters*, vol. 3, p. 224.

of such infernal metaphors. A Socialist League pamphlet by Edward Aveling and Eleanor Marx entitled *The Factory Hell* (1885) would also have been on sale at such gatherings. As Michael Wheeler notes, Gustave Doré's illustrations for *London: A Pilgrimage*, which depicted figures in the postures of the damned, offered more images of the Dantean Inferno, as did Charles Kingsley's novel *Alton Locke* (1849) and William Booth's *In Darkest England and the Way Out* (1890) with its focus on urban slums.[106] Beatrice Webb recorded the view of casual workers by a School Board Visitor: 'they are like the circle of the suicides in Dante's Inferno; they go round and round within a certain area'.[107] These infernal manifestations were a part of Gissing's cultural milieu.

By 1890 Gissing's interest in working-class politics and social questions was being replaced by a desire to describe the social and cultural consciousness of the urban middle-class groups. As early as 1887, Gissing reports that he was repelled by a meeting on Clerkenwell Green that he attended, describing it in a letter in the following terms: 'A more disheartening scene it is difficult to imagine,—the vulgar, blatant scoundrels!'[108] Gissing rationalized this move a decade later when he argued that the working class was for him no longer a living fictional subject and others were doing it better. After 1888 his diary never again records working-class industrial or political activity. A decade later he said in a letter to Gabrielle Fleury that 'it is […] so long since I took an active interest in socialism'.[109]

Gissing may be described as having a form of 'negative identification' with the working class after the publication of *Demos* in 1886. This term is used by Raymond Williams to describe the modification of Gissing's original radical commitment to social reform, possibly due to newly fashionable theories of pathological degeneracy amongst the poor.[110] Gissing seems to have lost faith in more ameliorative short-term solutions to the Victorian housing crisis such as the philanthropic or Metropolitan Board of Works's housing projects, describing the new Farringdon Buildings as 'barracks' in *The Nether World*.[111] The decision to shift the focus of his fiction to the middle class meant a new

---

106 See Wheeler, *Death and the Future Life*, chapter 4.

107 B. Webb, *My Apprenticeship*, 2 vols. (Harmondsworth: Penguin, 1938), vol. 2, p. 346.

108 Gissing, 27 August 1887, in *Collected Letters*, vol. 3, p. 145.

109 G. Gissing, 12 March 1899, in *The Letters of George Gissing to Gabrielle Fleury*, ed. P. Coustillas (New York: New York Public Library, 1964), p. 117.

110 See R. Williams, *The Country and the City* (1973; London: Hogarth Press, 1985), chapter 19, and F. Jameson, *The Political Unconscious: Narrative as a Socially Symbolic Act* (1981; London: Routledge, 1996), chapter 4.

111 Gissing, *The Nether World*, p. 274.

perspective on the underground and it assumed a much more significant role in his later novels, transporting his characters across the capital in a complex mix of work, business and leisure. The horizons of his characters were therefore considerably enlarged as the underground offered increased opportunities for travel that did not involve the vagaries of street-level traffic jams or the social mixing of the horse tramway system.

During Gissing's period of residence in London, the underground therefore represented a relatively fast circulatory system just below the surface of the city, literally only two dozen steps down from street to platform level. This passenger experience of the underground journey gave rise to what Lynne Kirby has called 'subway consciousness'[112] and Gissing was the first novelist to create underground writing that would encapsulate such an experience for his audience. This was an important new development in Gissing's approach to the system, a signpost for his interest in a middle-class segment of the urban population. However, the scope of this 'subway consciousness' was not confined to Gissing's fictional contribution as other contemporary writers were introducing a more radical dimension to this concept by focusing on the socially exclusionary role of the underground in a similar way to Gissing's earlier fiction. Margaret Harkness, in her novel *A City Girl* (1887), regarded the underground railway as a symbol of the impenetrable social barriers to advancement faced by working-class women. Her heroine, the East End seamstress Nell Ambrose, travels third class across the city but cannot traverse the class barrier between the East and West Ends of the capital. Taking a train: 'At the Mansion House station [she] seated herself in a third class carriage just as the guard gave the signal for the train to start' but loses her return ticket from West Kensington station and is forced to seek a cheaper means of travel back to the East End.[113] Like Reardon in Gissing's *New Grub Street*, Nell is suddenly excluded from the underground because of her lack of money but unlike him she has not descended from lower-middle-class genteel poverty. She is also the victim of a class betrayal when she is seduced by a West End radical—a vivid illustration of the callous behaviour of the politically committed bourgeois towards working-class women.

The response of radicals like Harkness to this inequality of access is also to be found in pieces by William Morris. In *Commonweal*, he berated the Metropolitan and District directors for forcing Londoners onto 'the beastly sewers

---

112   See L. Kirby, *Parallel Tracks: The Railroad and Silent Cinema* (Exeter: University of Exeter Press, 1997), chapter 3.

113   M. Harkness (writing as John Law), *A City Girl* (1887; London: Garland, 1984), pp. 95–96.

through which run stink-traps under the name of carriages' as part of his polemic against monopoly ownership in the capital.[114] *Punch* lampooned the District Railway whose speculative property developments threatened the Thames Embankment. In a cartoon entitled 'The Rough and the Rail; or The Embankment in Danger' (1883),[115] Mr Punch glares at the arrogant railway director and the 'London Rough', both of whom threaten the city. This was as much the case after the introduction of 'cheap trains' on the Metropolitan Railway in 1865 that enabled some 2,000 workers to travel third class at specific times of the day (out of a total of around 100,000 passengers). One of Harkness's other novels, *Out of Work* (1888), gives what is probably the best fictional account of workmen's trains. It includes a journey at 6.30 am from Fenchurch Street station to Tidal Basin: 'the carriage held about forty men, all untidy, unshaven, hungry people [...] full of stale tobacco. All the windows were up'.[116] *Out of Work* was set against a background of the Hyde Park unemployed riots whilst her next novel *George Eastmont, Wanderer* (1905) was placed against the 1889 Dock Strike.

A burlesque on the London stage by Edward Rose and Captain Coe, *Orpheus and Eurydice* (1891), mocked the Metropolitan Railway declaiming in the song 'Pluto comes by the Underground' that:

> At the top of the stairs
> Of the Underground deep
> Is the Office for fares
> Which we cannot call cheap.[117]

Baroness Orczy's short story 'The Mysterious Death on the Underground Railway' (1901) pinpointed the class nature of the Metropolitan Railway with a devious and successful plan by a 'poor shipper's clerk' Edward Hazeldene to murder his wife by poisoning her on the train. The plot turns on the regulated and orderly nature of travel in first-class compartments with middle-class commuters who are 'buried in the Stock Exchange quotations of [the] evening

---

114 W. Morris, *Commonweal*, vol. 2, no. 17, 8 May 1886, p. 45, in *William Morris, Journalism: Contributions to Commonweal, 1885–1890*, ed. N. Salmon (Bristol: Thoemmes Press, 1996), p. 71.

115 'The Rough and the Rail; Or, The Embankment in Danger', *Punch*, 17 March 1883, vol. 84, pp. 126–27.

116 M. Harkness (writing as John Law), *Out of Work* (1888; London: Merlin Press, 1990), pp. 127–28.

117 Quoted in Pike, 'Underground Theater', p. 112.

paper'.[118] The link between the underground and crime was reinforced by John Oxenham's short story 'A Mystery of the Underground' (1897) and Conan Doyle's 'The Adventure of the Bruce-Partington Plans' (1908). Sherlock Holmes and Dr Watson rarely use the underground although they do use it to travel to Aldersgate in 'The Red-Headed League' (1892) and High Street (Kensington) station is mentioned in 'The Six Napoleons' (1900). In 'The Adventure of the Bruce-Partington Plans', however, the only Holmes story that features the extensive use of the underground, the body of a senior civil servant, Arthur Cadogan West, is lodged on the roof of a train when it is stationary at a signal in the west London residential area of Gloucester Road. Cadogan West's body is carried around on the Inner Circle train until it falls off just outside Aldgate station on the edge of the East End where it may be assumed that he has been the victim of a casual robbery. The underground therefore briefly becomes a necropolis railway in this story, carrying the dead body of a man through the smoke-blackened underworld that runs beneath the whole city. A documentary aspect of the murder is pointed up by the fact that the window-sill from which the body is lowered is 'thickly covered with soot from the passing engines but the black surface was blurred and rubbed in places', an important clue in Holmes' investigation. Holmes and Watson wait at the window and 'the very next train roared from the tunnel as before, but slowed in the open, and then, with a creaking of brakes, pulled up immediately beneath us. It was not four feet from the window-ledge to the roof of the carriages'.[119] Some liberties are taken with the railway geography of Gloucester Road station. Inner Circle trains were hauled by Beyer-Peacock tank engines rather than the London and North Western engines that operated on the Outer Circle. Such engines had a pronounced 'fore and aft' surging motion that could be felt throughout the train, as one historian had remembered: 'on one occasion when leaving Victoria [Underground] a carriage full of passengers were swinging backwards and forwards after the manner of a University "eight".[120] On one of these trains, the body of the murdered Cadogan West would not have got much beyond Victoria let alone the points at Aldgate. But Holmes' attention to railway detail was in evidence in his account of a railway journey between Norwood Junction and London Bridge in 'The Adventure of the Norwood Builder' (1903). In this story Holmes concludes that a will was 'written in a train [...] drawn up on

---

118   E. Orczy, 'The Mysterious Death on the Underground Railway' (1901), in H. Greene (ed.), *The Rivals of Sherlock Holmes* (London: Bodley Head, 1970), pp. 217–37, p. 231.

119   A. Conan Doyle, 'The Adventure of the Bruce-Partington Plans' (1908), in *Sherlock Holmes: The Complete Illustrated Short Stories* (London: Chancellor Press, 1985), pp. 708–29, p. 723.

120   O. S. Nock, *The Railways of Britain* (London: Batsford, 1949), p. 105.

a suburban line, since nowhere save in the immediate vicinity of a great city could there be so quick a succession of points'.[121]

Conan Doyle's reluctance to use the steam underground in his detective stories seems odd, if only in the sense that other thriller writers adopted it with alacrity. Holmes and Watson use most of London's main-line stations but this is determined by their destinations which are, according to Franco Moretti's research, frequently outside London but easily reachable from the capital's termini.[122] Conan Doyle may have been influenced by 'sensation' crime novels like Wilkie Collins' *The Woman in White* (1860) where there are many railway journeys between London and Hampshire. Similarly, M. E. Braddon's *Lady Audley's Secret* (1863) features a detective who travels out of the capital to other cities. The streets of the West End seem to have offered Holmes a more congenial space and tunnels here are built by villains ('The Red-Headed League', 1891). It may be that Doyle's single story of the underground, which was written in 1908, provided him with the mythical smoke-filled Victorian world that he believed would satisfy his readers or perhaps he had noticed the successful use of the underground in other crime stories. Angus Evan Abbott staged a curious thriller called the 'The Spawn of Fortune' on the District Railway in which his character Arthur Brackenbridge enters a first-class carriage at Charing Cross in order to commit suicide. He is persuaded out of his decision by the 'Grays Inn murderer' who promptly commits suicide using Brackenbridge's revolver after Brackenbridge leaves the train at Earl's Court.[123] In 'The Tragedy of a Third Smoker' (1898), C. J. Cutcliffe Hyne concocted a similarly convoluted murder mystery on the Hammersmith and City. A drain contractor named Guide is alleged to have killed his foreman Andrew Walker on a Metropolitan Railway train after boarding it at Addison Road (Kensington) station. The train goes on a rather geographically fanciful journey to Shaftesbury Road (?) during which the two men have 'a fierce quarrel over money matters'[124] and Walker is killed. Resolution of the mystery turns on a basket of tools (a carpenter's straw bass) carried by Guide and he is found not guilty of murder. Some doubt is expressed as to whether an axe (the alleged murder weapon) could have been wielded effectively in a third-class compartment and it can only be assumed that the basket of tools did not exceed the 28 lbs in weight that was the regulation

121 A. Conan Doyle, 'The Adventure of the Norwood Builder' (1903), in *Holmes: Complete Short Stories*, pp. 456–75, p. 462.

122 See F. Moretti, *Atlas of the European Novel, 1800–1900* (London: Verso, 1999).

123 Abbott, 'Spawn of Fortune', pp. 3–9.

124 C. J. Cutcliffe Hyne, 'The Tragedy of a Third Smoker' (1898), in Russell, *Rivals of Sherlock Holmes*, pp. 317–23, p. 318.

on workmen's trains. As with all such thrillers the compartment is empty, as Abbott's character Brackenbridge observes ruefully in 'The Spawn of Fortune': 'at every station he prayed that some one would enter the compartment, but the Underground is a contrary line. No one disturbed them'.[125] Whilst the fictional steam underground seems to have become an ideal site for murder, it was obligatory for the purposes of detective stories that compartments remained empty!

By the 1880s the steam underground had begun to attract less favourable press comment with *The Times*, no longer a cheerleader for the system, describing the 'journey from King's Cross to Baker Street as a mild form of torture which no person would undergo if he could help it'.[126] A passenger interviewed for a Board of Trade inquiry in 1898 amplified this comment: 'I was nearly suffocated today on an Inner Circle steam train between Sloane Square and the Temple. The carriage was filled with sulphurous smoke, and my fellow-passengers in the packed compartment coughed incessantly'.[127]

As early as 1881 *Punch* magazine had begun to highlight contemporary middle-class fears about public transport when it featured a cartoon entitled 'Dangers of the Metropolis'[128] with a top-hatted gentleman harassed by bus conductors (cads) on the street and beaten up by 'roughs' on the underground. Another *Punch* cartoon of 1885 showed a rowdy party of 'Penny Hawkers' who lurk in a passageway under the watchful eye of a policeman.[129] In 1886 it portrayed a first-class carriage being 'invaded' by working-class passengers in a 'First Class Underground Study'. The caption commented that 'life at night on the Underground between South Kensington and Addison Road must be unpleasantly lively!'[130] The underground became the target for Fenian attacks in the 1880s with the detonation of two nitroglycerine bombs at Praed Street (Paddington) and between Westminster Bridge and Charing Cross in October 1883. Seventy passengers were injured in the former attack, prompting Queen Victoria to write to the Home Secretary William Harcourt that the perpetrators 'exhibit a diabolical spirit, and an utter disregard for human life dreadful

125 Abbott, 'Spawn of Fortune', p. 7.

126 *The Times*, 7 October 1884.

127 Board of Trade Report (1898), cited in T. C. Barker & M. Robbins, *A History of London Transport*, 2 vols. (London: Allen & Unwin, 1963–74), vol. 2, p. 370.

128 *Punch*, 30 April 1881, vol. 80, p. 204.

129 *Punch*, 17 January 1885, vol. 88, p. 34.

130 *Punch*, 25 September 1886, vol. 91, p. 148.

to contemplate'.[131] A third was exploded in the cloakroom at Victoria station in February 1884, followed by a fourth incident between Gower Street and King's Cross in January 1885. A final bomb blast hit an Inner Circle train near Aldersgate station in April 1897 killing one man and injuring ten other people although this was probably the work of a disgruntled former employee. Vivid illustrations of the attacks highlighted the vulnerability of the underground railway—in one a railway worker reels back in shock as an explosion occurs on board the last carriage of a train in a tunnel.[132] *Punch* offered a poem called 'By Underground' in which:

> the air was rent
> By dynamite; the Irish clan
> Had wrecked the Metropolitan!"[133]

As Bernard Porter points out,[134] a whole raft of popular fiction reflected these insecurities, with Big Ben being destroyed in E. Douglas Fawcett's *Hartmann the Anarchist, or the Doom of a Great City* (1893) and socialists using chemical weapons to dissolve London into dust in J. S. Fletcher's *The Three Day's Terror* (1901). Other stories by Donald Mackay, Fergus Hume and W. L. Alden featured a Fenian 'super-gun', bombs on the underground and anthrax in the water supply of Britain's cities.

This was the first media-generated 'moral panic' about underground travel. It combined a number of frustrations about the slow progress of the system and the constant in-fighting between railway companies as well as the perennial problems of steam pollution and sulphur poisoning. Middle-class opinion regarded conditions on the steam underground with increasing distaste, believing that it deserved better value for its money. The failure to develop an aesthetically pleasing feel to the underground became a recurring theme reflected, for example, in the comments of the architect and designer W. R. Lethaby from the late 1890s.[135] Platforms and trains were uniformly grimy and soot-encrusted and the physical dangers of underground travel were heightened following the crash that occurred on the District Railway near Earl's Court station in 1885. That passengers appeared to be especially vulnerable in this

---

131 Quoted in B. Porter, *The Origins of the Vigilant State: The London Metropolitan Police Special Branch before the First World War* (London: Weidenfeld & Nicolson, 1987), p. 28.
132 *Illustrated Police News*, 10 November 1883.
133 'By Underground', *Punch*, 17 January 1885, vol. 88, p. 34.
134 See Porter, *The Origins of the Vigilant State*, pp. 98–113.
135 W. R. Lethaby was closely associated with William Morris and Philip Webb in the Arts and Crafts Movement. He was co-founder of the Art Workers Guild in 1884.

subterranean environment brought an added sense of insecurity and urgency to the swing in public opinion. John Oxenham's short story 'A Mystery of the Underground' played upon these fears. Published as a serial in the weekly magazine *To-Day* in 1897, it featured apparently real newspaper extracts in a story about a mysterious assassin who is committing murders on the underground every Tuesday night. The murderer is as ingenious as the new technology of underground travel and we learn that he is a mechanical engineer named Hood who has a grudge against the District Railway Company. Asking whether the 'Underground Fiend [is] sated with blood', the press turn him into a Dracula-like figure.[136] This was a typical metaphor of these decades as exemplified in the press coverage of the Ripper murders in the late 1880s. Oxenham's story was so realistic that it provoked a complaint from the underground authorities to the editor of *To-Day*, Jerome K. Jerome.

The underground appeared to hold together very uneasily the many contradictory elements of transit highlighted in the press and popular fiction. It was more difficult to manage these contradictions within the changed political climate of working-class agitation in the capital when this class was emerging as a more coherent political and cultural force. By 1875 three-quarters of the passengers travelled on the Metropolitan Railway third class, suggesting that they were manual workers and low-paid clerks. Yet most contemporary illustrations and photographs show an almost uniformly middle-class patronage. One of the rare attempts to portray such third-class travel on the Metropolitan Railway appeared in Gustave Doré's and Blanchard Jerrold's *London: A Pilgrimage* showing workers boarding a train in an illustration entitled 'Work-a-Day London'. Jerrold's commentary indicates a specific purpose behind this picture as it suggests that underground travel facilitated a moral improvement in working-class character by instilling the virtues of discipline and respectability: 'He who falls from honest, methodical, skilled labour, and the regular travel by the workman's train, must earn his shilling or eight pence a day as boardman or dock labourer'.[137] However, whatever vestigial attachment the Victorian middle class still retained in terms of respectability and good habit, appears to have diminished in subsequent decades. Gissing both read and wrote for the *Illustrated London News* and its middle-class readership was not usually presented with images of working-class travellers, as found in Doré's 'productivist' vision, for it might have given the wrong impression to the middle-class commuters

---

136 J. Oxenham, 'A Mystery of the Underground' (1897), in P. Haining (ed.), *Murder on the Railways* (London: Orion, 1996), pp. 340–68, p. 364.

137 Doré & Jerrold, *London: A Pilgrimage*, facing p. 120.

who were first-class passengers.[138] The working class was more visible on the political landscape by 1885 but Gissing himself had moved on: whether the working class did or did not use the underground was by now of little interest to him. It is one of fiction's lost opportunities that Gissing might have explored the cultural world of the working class within the context of urban travel, but instead he explained that he had 'selected from the great mass of lower-middle-class life a group of people who represent certain grossnesses, weaknesses, etc., peculiar to our day'.[139] The underground experience of the working class was screened out and press coverage that was becoming more critical of the steam underground was not directly reflected in his later fiction. Gissing might have turned his attention to these questions but he was not interested in mounting a political crusade on behalf of a better transport system. This was despite the fact that working-class politicians were campaigning for cheaper, more efficient and better planned services. He commented in 1885 that his novel *Demos* was 'a savage satire on working-class aims and capacities'.[140] Like the other social realists Arthur Morrison and George Moore, he depicted the working class almost entirely as without a political outlook and, *Demos* excepted, there is no mention of class rebellion despite the intensity of the events unfolding in the capital. *Demos*, John Goode has argued,[141] comes closest to reflecting political struggles. Mutimer, the doomed hero the of the novel, is a mechanical engineer like John Burns and Tom Mann and, like them, he is sacked for his socialist activities. He is also an outstanding orator like Burns. But even if *Demos* does seriously engage with the problems of English socialism as Goode suggests, it fails to develop a critique of capitalism through the incorporation of contemporary struggles. Gissing was concerned to condemn socialism and to show that proletarian leaders were morally scarred by their social origins. He evidently sympathized with William Morris whom he thought had taken up social agitation in order to resist the destruction of all artistic impulses under the weight of commercialism. But Gissing felt that political activism on behalf of the working class was dangerous, arguing that being 'in the company of ruffians' would coarsen the artist.[142]

---

138 See Williams, *Notes on the Underground*, p. 107 for a distinction between producer-based and consumer-based viewpoints in her discussion of utopian writing.

139 J. Korg, 'Division of Purpose in George Gissing', in P. Coustillas (ed.), *Collected Articles on George Gissing* (London: Frank Cass, 1968), pp. 64–79, p. 74.

140 Gissing, 31 October 1885, in *Letters to Members of his Family*, p. 172.

141 See J. Goode, 'Gissing, Morris and English Socialism' (1968), in *Collected Essays of John Goode*, ed. C. Swann (Keele: Keele University Press, 1995), pp. 247–71.

142 Gissing, 22 September 1885, in *Letters to Members of his Family*, p. 169.

Gissing stood at a crossroads in underground writing. The system was in a parlous state with company rivalries, falling profits, service difficulties and competition from horse omnibuses. It was crying out for a novelist to capture the social essence of the system. The completion of the Circle was such an egregious example of company rivalries that it was described as 'almost disastrous' in 1886.[143] In this period there were industrial conflicts on the Metropolitan over the issue of Sunday working, a legacy continued into the next century with nearly a third of its workforce going on strike during the 1911 national rail dispute. Such events would have given Gissing ample ammunition for a fictional attack on the state of travel in the capital. Frederick Engels made much the same criticism of Margaret Harkness's novel *A City Girl*, praising its 'realistic truth' but saying it was 'not quite realistic enough [...] the rebellious reaction of the working class against the oppressive medium which surrounds them [...] must therefore lay claim to a place in the domain of realism'.[144] If Harkness didn't deserve this criticism, Gissing certainly did. In fact, as Jacob Korg argues, Gissing had opted to portray middle-class life partly from disillusion with social reform, an attitude influenced by an 'Arnoldian' view of culture as a fragile inward condition of mind and spirit that needed to be preserved in the face of a mechanical civilization. Gissing, Korg maintains, was now 'on the side of the middle-class in the social struggle, for only in a leisured environment could the potentialities of mind and spirit be fulfilled'.[145]

Gissing's new fiction offered a belated solution to the call by the *Illustrated London News* for a 'map' of the underground which would overcome the passenger experience of disorientation and establish a perfect sense of order. Whilst the location of this railway was unique, its mode of travel was not. The trains that ran on the Metropolitan in these illustrations were broadly the same as those that were used on the main-line tracks into the city. The Metropolitan was connected to the Great Western Railway at Paddington and was therefore built to accommodate the broad gauge trains operated by that company with wider tunnels and the tracks further apart than on other parts of the underground. The Metropolitan locomotives were supplied by Beyer-Peacock and the first 18 were named after classical deities such as Pluto, god of

---

143 Quoted in Barker & Robbins, *History of London Transport*, vol. 1, p. 237. *Punch* was sceptical of the arch railway developer Sir Edward Watkin's plans for a Channel Tunnel linked to the underground. In a cartoon 'Rule Britannia', Watkin is told to stop digging (*Punch*, 15 July 1882, vol. 83, p. 15).

144 Y. Kapp, *Eleanor Marx*, vol. 2, *The Crowded Years, 1884–98* (1976; London: Virago, 1979), p. 221.

145 Korg, *Critical Biography*, p. 94.

the underworld. This gave a comic dimension to the character of Pluto in the West End burlesque *Orpheus in the Haymarket* (1865), who sings:

> For Tartarus I happen to be bound
> And was just starting by the Underground.[146]

These trains ran below the great arteries of the city—the Marylebone, Euston and Farringdon Roads—for some 40 years, throughout the time of Gissing's residence in London.[147]

But we look in vain in Gissing's fiction for any social commentary on the steam underground of the kind advocated by Engels. He did set out to 'map' the underground system but in a way quite out of keeping with the *Illustrated London News'* quest for order: instead, his fiction traversed the social mores of the Victorian travelling public with an unerring ability to construct middle-class 'subway consciousness'. His writing showed for the first time what it was like to travel regularly on the capital's underground system, to use it for both work and leisure and to experience other (similar) people in the process. It was the equivalent of mid-Victorian diarist Arthur Munby's journal entries: the result of many journeys on the underground reinvented in fictional terms. Gissing did not attempt to register the alarming events that had dominated the building of new parts of the underground in these years and in this sense his fictional treatment of the system is flawed. But he did create an underground laced with social conflict, human longing and desire, a class and status-obsessed body of passengers, an account of travel that is not principally about specific journeys (although their destinations are carefully recorded). It was about the thoughts, innermost feelings and communication of his characters as they travel. John Goode points out that in *The Nether World* 'the city is no longer the meeting-place of classes, on the contrary, it is the structured space of separation'.[148] The underground became one of the principal sites of this separation as the working class was fictionally excluded from Gissing's new

---

146 Quoted in Pike, 'Underground Theater', p. 106.
147 The line offered 650 services per day and carried, on average, only 50 people on board each train for the full journey. The four carriages on each train were 40 feet long with first class containing six separate compartments whilst second and third class had eight compartments. Passengers paid three, four and sixpence for a single journey and five, six and ninepence return depending on the 'class' of travel. The carriages were lighted with gas and the gas was stored in India rubber bags located in wooden boxes on top of the carriages from which it was piped to the lights. Gas-making plants had to be built like the one constructed at Neasden depot, the smell at these sites being particularly overpowering.
148 Goode, *Gissing: Ideology and Fiction*, p. 107.

'map' of the capital. But even Gissing could not altogether ignore the poor as shown by Hugh Carnaby in *The Whirlpool*, who cries out from the suburban heights: 'It's bad to see the poor little squalling brats in the filth and smoke down yonder, and worse still in this damned London. Great God!'[149] However, in *The Nether World*, the working class is literally imprisoned in hell and there is no escape except by individual self-help (even the flight of Sidney and Clara Kirkwood to the suburb of Crouch End proves to be a dead-end). Whilst he shares many of William Morris's ideas—alienation is widespread, work is dominated by relentless inhumanity and human needs are not met—Gissing reifies the experience of the working class. By contrast Morris argued that 'this earthly hell is not the ordinance of nature but the manufacture of men [...] and it is your business to destroy it'.[150]

The prosperous middle class is able to look down on an urban world from a suburban eyrie to which it escapes by using the underground system. It was not always an easy escape route even in fiction. It was relatively simple for figures like Orpheus and Eurydice, in the 1891 burlesque, to escape from the 'Hades' of London into suburban mundanity but far harder for Ella Hepworth Dixon's heroine Mary Erle to understand the tortured relationship between the metropolis and its suburbs. In the former, Orpheus and his wife now occupy an outer London suburb and they travel by underground into the city (Hades):

> For its still to be found
> On the dark Underground—
> That City that's dark all day.[151]

But this regulated and mundane commuting lifestyle is full of tensions when, at the end of *The Story of a Modern Woman*, Mary Erle stands alone 'on the heights' and makes 'a feint as if to grasp the city spread out before her' but her attempt to comprehend this urban phenomenon ends 'in a vain gesture'.[152] It is hardly surprising that it was difficult for writers to come to terms with the massive changes that were happening in these decades due in part to the extension of transport services. In the period 1863–1900, the underground had encircled the central business district of London through the Metropolitan, District and Circle lines; it was extended from Swiss Cottage to West End Lane (Hampstead) in 1879; to Willesden and Harr ow in 1880 and Pinner (1885), Rickmansworth

---

149 Gissing, *The Whirlpool*, p. 184.
150 W. Morris, 'Misery and the Way Out' (1884), quoted in Goode, 'Gissing, Morris and English Socialism', p. 268.
151 Quoted in Pike, 'Underground Theater', p. 112.
152 Hepworth Dixon, *Story of a Modern Woman*, p. 271.

(1887), Chesham (1889) and Aylesbury (1892), and had begun to penetrate eastwards towards Bow (1902). This first phase of the underground, dominated by steam technology, was certainly the most concentrated public transport change ever witnessed in the capital, creating over one hundred new stations, laying down some 50 miles of track and transforming the landscape around London into suburban building land. Gissing's later novels read like a fictional gazetteer of the construction of the underground as he meticulously plotted the various stages by which the steam railway penetrated beyond what he called, in *In The Year of Jubilee*, the 'great smoke-area'.[153] He was not sanguine about the prospect of suburban development, describing in that novel:

> London, devourer of rural limits, of a sudden made hideous encroachment upon the old estate, now held by a speculative builder [...] the very earth had lost its wholesome odour; trampled into mire, fouled with builders' refuse and the noisome drift from adjacent streets, it sent forth, under the sooty rain, a smell of corruption, of all the town's uncleanliness.[154]

Gissing was not alone in his recording of the physical growth of the underground. The diarist Arthur Munby was a regular underground passenger, noting many journeys on the District Railway between 1859 and 1898. Similar to the younger Gissing, he was a liberal who sympathized with the lower classes, observing and taking photographs of working women. Munby married a domestic servant named Hannah Cullwick after having conducted an affair with her for 19 years and was associated with Pre-Raphaelite and Christian Socialist circles. Living in Fig Tree Court near the Temple, Munby was therefore well placed to record the vast changes that occurred on this stretch of the River Thames during this period. In 1864 he noted that 'Today I finally lost my view of the Temple gardens and the Thames [...] For the Embankment is coming'[155] and five years later was impressed by the redevelopment of this area: 'the course of the broad new street which is run from Blackfriars northeastward, is marked by heaps of ruin'.[156] He watched the building of the Embankment with a view similar to that of Charles Dickens, who had praised it as 'A really fine work, and likewise really getting on' but then characteristically attacked the 'muddle of railways in all directions possible and impossible, with no general public scheme, no general public supervision, enormous waste of money, no

---

153 G. Gissing, *In the Year of Jubilee* (1894; London: Hogarth Press, 1987), p. 402.
154 Gissing, *In the Year of Jubilee*, p. 218.
155 Hudson, *Munby Man of Two Worlds*, p. 193.
156 Hudson, *Munby Man of Two Worlds*, p. 265.

fixed accountability'.[157] The District Railway was creeping round from South Kensington to Westminster and opened to Blackfriars in 1870, passing through Charing Cross and Temple. The newly completed Victoria Embankment had to be ripped up to accommodate the District Railway because of the interminable delays to progress despite government financial intervention. Castigating the District for this ridiculous situation, *The Times* commented: 'it does seem too bad that we must now wait for the slow completion of this stupendous work [the Embankment] only to see it pulled down to pieces again'.[158] Munby observed the building of the District in 1869: 'Every day now, and for weeks past, the river along by the embankment wall is crowded at several points with strange craft, bringing sand and bricks for the underground railway they are making'.[159] Less than a year later he 'walked to the Blackfriars Station: for the railway beneath the Embankment is opened today, from Westminster to Black- friars. So by rail to Onslow Square'.[160]

Munby did not record his feelings about the subsequent lack of progress on the line eastwards from Mansion House, which remained the terminus for the next 20 years due to the intense rivalry between the two railway companies. But he did continue to use the District in a westward direction, often travelling to South Kensington, including a trip to the Albert Hall with Hannah to hear a performance of Haydn's *Creation* in 1873. Munby's diary is evidence of the key role being played by new underground services in the 1870s. It provided a fast and efficient circular service from the Embankment to Kensington, Paddington and Baker Street before tube lines offered a more direct route. It allowed a middle-class *flâneur* like Munby easy access to his friends and favourite walks in the city, and it transformed the north bank of the river into an imperial showcase as shown in John O'Connor's oil painting *The Embankment* (1874). It also provided a convenient route to the Drury Lane theatres from the west London suburbs with a young Compton Mackenzie being taken by his nurse on the District Railway in the late 1880s: 'The Temple station. Always the gloomiest on the District Railway [it] was gloomier than ever that afternoon'.[161] Mackenzie's childhood was romantically portrayed in *London Town* (1883) with the first illustration of children using the underground: it is a more pleasant scene in which a train gently puffs away whilst middle-class children wait on

157 Dickens, 30 November 1865, in *The Letters of Charles Dickens*, vol. 11, p. 116.
158 Quoted in Trench & Hillman, *London Under London*, p. 142.
159 Hudson, *Munby Man of Two Worlds*, p. 276.
160 Hudson, *Munby Man of Two Worlds*, p. 284.
161 Mackenzie, *My Life and Times*, p. 176.

both sides. Children can be glimpsed waving from the street above and the sign reassuringly says 'Wait Here for First Class'.[162]

The contrast between the more recent sordid past and the new efficient underground is pointed up by one of Munby's journeys on the South Eastern Railway between Charing Cross and Cannon Street. For a few years after 1866 these services had been used as a vehicle for prostitution during the brief seven-minute run. A combination of the new District Railway between Westminster and Blackfriars that diverted city men onto a quicker service and the new intermediate station at Waterloo ruined this trade and therefore brought a new respectability. In fact, the Embankment embodied the vision of Frederick William Trench who had proposed a Thames Quay in 1825, developed further by John Martin's 'Plan for Improving the Air and Water in the Metropolis' (1832) to include a three-level quay and Grand Sewer. Martin went on to paint a number of Gothic pictures of cataclysmic scenes, including the Biblical fantasy *Pandemonium* (1841)[163] that appears to incorporate his unrealized ideas for the Embankment. A new myth was in the making throughout these decades: that of an ultra-utilitarian underground that removed congestion from the streets above just as Bazalgette's sewer system had removed the effluent from the river and 'decontaminated' the city. The underground railway that occupied the new Embankment almost fulfilled this myth. But the apocalyptic message would not go away and re-emerged during Gissing's lifetime, with Martin's series of *Last Judgement* pictures being exhibited on a provincial tour in 1872, published as small mezzotints in 1870 and appearing at Earl's Court in 1897.

Gissing's diary and letters likewise record his own personal journeys to places now newly linked by the underground, including Westbourne Park and Gunnesbury. He moved from Islington to 55 Wornington Place in Westbourne Park in 1881 and dismissed north London as a place to live because transport links were 'very deficient'.[164] Westbourne Park was his nearest underground station being only about ten minutes walk from his new home. For him, this part of London was much better as there were 'numerous very cheap localities, and the communication with town is perfect'.[165] The newer parts of the Metro-politan Railway run like a thread on which his lower-middle-class characters are arranged. Continuously redefining places and locations in the Victorian period,

---

162 T. Crane & E. Houghton, 'The Underground Railway', illustration for *London Town* (1883), p. 29, Toronto Public Library.

163 J. Martin, *Pandemonium* (1841), Tate, London. The architecture in this painting resembles Carlton House Terrace and the scene is similar to his designs for the Embankment.

164 Gissing, 10 July 1881, in *Collected Letters*, vol. 2, p. 50.

165 Gissing, 10 July 1881, in *Collected Letters*, vol. 2, p. 50.

the underground created a dizzying development of districts or the movement of districts up and down the social scale. Set in the early 1880s, Gissing's novel *New Grub Street* (1892) is largely centred on the ways in which work, money and insecurity interact in the lives of the lower-middle-class inhabitants of the city. As Robert Selig comments, 'in a society that values only money, neither love nor art can flourish without sufficient cash',[166] and Gissing's main character, Edwin Reardon, finds that he cannot compete in the modern world of writing. However, another character, Jasper Milvain, is prepared to write what the market demands and is therefore able to reap the rewards of literary success. Reardon's wife, Amy, is a woman whose literary tastes are merely a cover for social competitiveness. Expecting Reardon to become a famous writer, she is mortified when he fails to succeed in the profession.

Reardon lives in Regent's Park but often travels to Westbourne Park. In *New Grub Street*, Westbourne Park is identified as a newly formed lower-middle-class underground suburb but 'characterless' like Royal Oak, the next station on the Metropolitan Railway. In chapter three, Gissing places Jasper Milvain and Marian Yule in what was once a pastoral setting now occupied by the growing station suburb of Westbourne Park. Jasper and Marian turn into a 'short lane which crossed the Great Western Railway, and thence by a stile into certain meadows forming a compact little valley'. The railway line runs 'along a deep cutting, from either side of which grew hazel bushes and a few larger trees [...] the leafy branches that grew out over the line swayed violently backwards and forwards in the perturbed air'.[167]

A perturbation caused by the passage of an express train. Here, then, Gissing registers the impact of both main-line and Hammersmith and City Railway routes on a formerly pastoral environment. The latter ran from Green Lane (Westbourne Park) into the fields of Porto Bello and Notting Barn farms, through Latimer Road and Shepherd's Bush to Hammersmith Broadway. In 1865 it had only reached as far as Shepherd's Bush as witnessed by a young boy named Frank Bullen who worked in an 'oil shop'. He described Westbourne Park as 'a funny little primitive station'[168] and found himself charged with an onerous trip on the underground to Moorgate Street in the City to collect an iron drum of treacle. Ladbroke Grove station in 1865 was like a Wild West site with empty building plots and open fields running northwards towards the Harrow Road. When *New Grub Street* was published, however, this was

---

166 R. Selig, *George Gissing* (Boston: Twayne, 1983), p. 34.
167 Gissing, *New Grub Street*, p. 63.
168 F. T. Bullen, *Confessions of a Tradesman* (London: Hodder & Stoughton, 1908), p. 3.

not a new railway landscape but one that was softened by bushes and trees that had gradually established a foothold alongside the embankment after the railway line to Hammersmith had been fully completed in the late 1860s. The physical impact of the railway tracks that passed through this district had been immense, cutting a wide and deep trench from Paddington station for about a mile until the separation of the two tracks just after Westbourne Park station. This topographical separation helped to facilitate new speculative development along the Hammersmith and City Railway on what had formerly been fields but it also opened up older residential areas like Westbourne Park and Ladbroke Grove to the middle classes like Gissing himself. In 1864 Arthur Munby recorded a very early trip made soon after the line had opened 'by underground railway to Westbournia to a party at Mrs Cunliffe's in Saint Stephen's Square'.[169] However, the area of Notting Dale in North Kensington was not salubrious, as William Law noted when he was appointed to run the Harrow Road Mission School: 'Nothing could have been more forlorn or desolate than the condition of this district at starting. The station of the Metropolitan Railway which bears the name Latimer Road was familiarly known as "Piggery Junction" from the miserable and unwholesome establishment for the feeding of [...] animals'.[170] Gissing did not find Westbourne Park an amenable place to live. He noted in a letter that 'I long for the neighbourhood of life and bustle and noise. Here in this wretched workman's suburb it grows intolerable' and he soon moved to Euston Square.[171]

In *New Grub Street* the express train has rushed 'with dread force and speed' along the 'gleaming rails which are visible to the west for more than a mile'.[172] The bridge over the Great Western on which Jasper and Marian converse crosses the Hammersmith and City Railway as it snakes towards Hammersmith but Gissing is able to use the bridge over this yawning chasm to connect the distant countryside with the city. In Gissing's novel, the underground suburb is the nodal point of a city that is gradually expanding into the surrounding countryside. The suburb offers Jasper Milvain future prosperity but it has begun to erase its pastoral history in much the same way as the Metropolitan Railway had almost destroyed the medieval past of Clerkenwell. Jasper can escape from the 'tumultuous' world that is denounced by one of Gissing's characters in

169 Hudson, *Munby Man of Two Worlds*, p. 198.
170 Quoted in S. Whetlor, *The Story of Notting Dale* (London: Kensington & Chelsea Community History Group, 1998), p. 33.
171 Gissing, 29 July 1881, in *Collected Letters*, vol. 2, p. 54.
172 Gissing, *New Grub Street*, p. 63.

his *Born In Exile* (1892), an escape from the 'triumphal procession that roars perpetually through the City highways'.[173]

Whilst the underground allows characters like Milvain a certain freedom, it also places vast unseen distances between others. Piers Ottway in Gissing's *The Crown of Life* (1899) is 'oppressed by the huge welter of common London' and laments that 'all London was between them, and their hands would never touch'.[174] Paradoxically, the underground is an instrument of joining and separation in these novels: it geographically and physically connects the distant pastoral world with the city but also 'stretches' the metropolis to a kind of physical breaking point. The effect of this is a further physical separation and segregation of social classes but there is a newer phenomenon: a psychological tension brought about by underground transit affecting Gissing's middle-class characters. In Gissing's fiction, the underground becomes a subterranean framework linking London, an imaginative construction that reflected its ubiquitous technological colonization of city space. In *New Grub Street* people and places are linked together by the physical presence of underground stations at street level, for example, when Amy Reardon walks to 'New Oxford Street from the nearest Metropolitan station' (Gower Street/Euston Road).[175] For Amy Reardon and Jasper Milvain, the underground is a part of the street furniture and a place of geographical separation when they walk 'the length of Gower Street' and reach 'the railway station' (Gower Street) where they part with an 'exchange of smiles which were something like a challenge'.[176] Whilst a new component in Gissing's cultural perspectives is the psychologically uncharted territory of underground travel, it is the fictional use of the underground to chart movement at *surface* level that is a feature of this writing, in a continuity with his previous approach to the railways.

Westbourne Park station appears in *New Grub Street* as the location of a meeting between Jasper Milvain and Edwin Reardon. The latter is failing in his ambition to be an independent writer and has already separated from his wife Amy, moving from Regent's Park to the cheaper district of Islington. Reardon has just visited his estranged wife in the respectable suburb of Westbourne Park and unexpectedly meets Milvain. The underground is instrumental in opening up a psychological gulf between the two men as Reardon stands outside the station below after Jasper remarks, casually: 'You are living a long

---

173   G. Gissing, *Born in Exile* (1892; London: Hogarth Press, 1985), p. 265.
174   G. Gissing, *The Crown of Life* (1899; Hassocks: Harvester, 1978), p. 55.
175   Gissing, *New Grub Street*, p. 398.
176   Gissing, *New Grub Street*, p. 401.

way from here [...] Are you going by train?'[177] Reardon walks back to Islington as he has ceased to play a part in the battle for survival. The underground appears to offer social integration and security but merely conceals the deeper dangers of metropolitan life for those who cannot successfully compete in the capitalist market. Reardon's separation from his wife Amy also points up the notion of social death on the underground as it carries him away from Regent's Park to his new lodgings in Islington. He is 'carrying a bag which contained a few things kept in his own care, he went by train to King's Cross, and thence walked up Pentonville Hill to Upper Street'. Reardon thus expects to return to the 'Obscure world whence he had risen [...] for two years and a half he had been a pretender. It was not natural for him to live in the manner of people who enjoy an assured income; he belonged to the class of casual wage-earners. Back to obscurity!'[178] And so he begins the slide into the status outlined by Doré and Jerrold in 1872. He is able to travel on the underground like the skilled artisans in *London: A Pilgrimage*, but is in danger of dropping out of respectable society into the social abyss. Later in the novel, Reardon walks the 'good six miles' from Islington to Westbourne Park instead of taking the underground. He walks 'Down Pentonville Hill, up Euston Road, all along Marylebone Road, then north-westwards towards the point of his destination' in a journey that points up both the physical distance *and* the topographical features of the urban landscape.[179]

This paradox of separation and integration is most evident in Gissing's *The Whirlpool*. In this novel, the Metropolitan Railway is at the hub of the city's circulatory system as a pathway to the distant suburbs with Baker Street as the pivotal central station. The Frothingham family is able to move from an obscure south London suburb to a one-class residential district called Fitzjohn Avenue (West Hampstead) and the childless Carnabys live in St John's Wood. Its central character Harvey Rolfe moves to Pinner because the Metropolitan Railway has opened up new prospects for relocation. Rolfe is at first living in a 'large house, within a few minutes walk of Royal Oak station' until he and his wife Alma move to the 'outer edge of the whirlpool' in Pinner, which is 'only about half-an-hour from Baker Street'.[180] Rolfe 'had never been beyond Swiss Cottage on this extension of the Metropolitan Railway; he looked with interest at the new districts springing up towards Harrow'. He later explores these areas 'to a greater distance on the same line, making a survey of the country

177 Gissing, *New Grub Street*, p. 301.
178 Gissing, *New Grub Street*, p. 290.
179 Gissing, *New Grub Street*, p. 381.
180 Gissing, *The Whirlpool*, p. 186.

from Harrow to Aylesbury'.[181] Baker Street station is placed at the centre of this urban whirlpool, a circulating mechanism through which 'Thousands of men, who sleep on the circumference of London, and go each day to business, are practically strangers to the district nominally their home'.[182] Arthur Munby travelled as far as Swiss Cottage in 1870 shortly after the underground had reached it, worrying that Hampstead Heath was going to be swallowed by urban sprawl. He 'went by rail to the Swiss Cottage, and thence walked across the fields (which begin close by) to Hampstead church and back [...] But all these fields are doomed: roads, houses, are closing in around'.[183]

The concept of London as a respiratory mechanism that inhales and exhales each day was not an unfamiliar image. Gissing's fiction underlined this by locating the underground as the technological means for this metaphorical process of urban circulation. Gissing added another element to underground writing, one that would come to dominate the thinking of the London Passenger Transport Board in the 1930s: that technology would be the 'fix' for urban development. In Gissing's perspective, London draws in and expels its commuters each day from the outer suburbs. William Greenslade suggests that Gissing's whirlpool image is about being trapped on the edge of a perpetual vortex, an entirely negative image of urban development.[184] Harvey Rolfe cries out, 'I feel as if we were all being swept into a ghastly whirlpool which roars over a bottomless pit',[185] in a clear reference to an urban psychological hell whose key mechanism is the underground system—a hell that will eventually contribute to his wife Alma's suicide. It is no longer the steam locomotive of Gissing's earlier fiction but the underground *as a whole*; a subterranean system which has honeycombed the metropolis. Gissing does not use this metaphor as a prelude to destruction or Armageddon but as a description of capitalism triumphant. The system will not implode from its own internal contradictions or be overturned by the proletariat as in Marx's analysis, but will be fuelled endlessly by population growth and London's imperial dominance.

---

181 Gissing, *The Whirlpool*, p. 183.
182 Gissing, *The Whirlpool*, p. 381.
183 Hudson, *Munby Man of Two Worlds*, p. 293.
184 W. Greenslade, *Degeneration, Culture and the Novel, 1880–1940* (Cambridge: Cambridge University Press, 1994), p. 136.
185 Gissing, *The Whirlpool*, p. 14.

THE STORY OF THE SEVERED FINGER:
THE UNDERGROUND IN THE 1890s

A wave of commercial development transformed the steam underground of the 1890s. New stations were architecturally undistinguished and further disfigured by hundreds of advertisements at both street and platform levels. The classical, spartan features of the early underground stations had been rapidly overlaid with commercial and corporate advertising giving the underground overall a very different character. *Punch*'s cartoon 'How We Advertise Now' (1887) suggested a 'sense of claustrophobia' in its depiction of the middle class as being penned in by the forces of advertising culture: a hansom cab is confronted by the grotesque figure of a man dressed in an elephant costume whilst a sandwich-board man cavorts in the foreground; the cartoon is framed on the right by a Charing Cross omnibus covered in adverts.[186] *Punch* then pictured 'Horrible London; Or, The Pandemonium of Posters' (1888) in which a demon slaps posters depicting violence and disorder on a wall.[187]

Gissing registers this sense of enclosure in his description of King's Cross underground station in Part Five of *In the Year of Jubilee*. Written as a means of exposing the crude, shoddy and false nature of late Victorian society, the novel centres on the celebrations for the fiftieth year of Queen Victoria's reign in 1887. The Jubilee certainly offered many commercial opportunities such as the sale of 'Jubilee Perfume', a 'Jubilee Drink' and a 'Jubilee Fashion Club'. In a letter to his sister Ellen in 1885, Gissing called the Jubilee the 'most gigantic organized exhibition of fatuity, vulgarity and blatant blackguardism on record'.[188] The Metropolitan Railway platform here embodies a kind of warfare as two of his characters, Jessica Morgan and Samuel Barmby, are assailed by advertising culture whilst waiting for a train to take them to Pentonville:

High and low, on every available yard of wall, advertisements clamored to the eye: theatres, journals, soaps, medicines, concerts, furniture, wines, prayer-meetings— all the produce and refuse of civilisation announced in staring letters, in daubed

---

186 J. Hewitt, 'Poster Nasties: Censorship and the Victorian Theatre Poster', in S. Popple & V. Toulmin (eds.), *Visual Delights: Essays on the Popular and Projected Image in the 19th Century* (Trowbridge: Flicks, 2000), pp. 154–69, p. 156.

187 'Horrible London; Or, The Pandemonium of Posters', *Punch*, 13 October 1888, vol. 95, pp. 170–71.

188 Gissing, 21 June 1887, in *Collected Letters*, vol. 3, p. 125.

effigies, base, paltry, grotesque. A battle-ground of advertisements, fitly chosen amid subterranean din and reek.[189]

In this infernal catalogue, Gissing pinpoints another essential element in underground writing: the ways in which public transport enables advertisers to bombard consumers with a seemingly endless stream of messages. It can be assumed that all of Gissing's characters in this fiction would have used the underground and were therefore exposed to this constant process.

William Morris, whom Gissing admired, also thought of the underground as one of the most assertive and pervasive vehicles of commercialism. Morris described the demise of commercial capitalism after the future revolution in *News from Nowhere* (1890): 'Nor could [commercialism] have been destroyed otherwise; except, perhaps by the whole of society gradually falling into lower depths, till it at last reached a condition of barbarism'.[190] And we can assume that, in Morris's utopian society, all advertising would have been removed from the underground.

No contemporary illustrations or photographs of King's Cross show the underground station in the state so graphically described by Gissing but some idea can be gained by an 1894 photograph in which a steam-hauled Inner Circle train is entering Charing Cross (Embankment) station. Nearly every available space on the platform walls is filled with advertisements for both services and goods, including property, theatrical performances, 'Marigold Flake', typewriters and Turkish Baths.[191] Advertising hoardings even appeared on open sections of the track as is apparent in a photograph taken just outside Edgware Road station around 1905 where adverts for 'Lipton's Tea' and 'Reid's Stout' can be seen.[192] Gissing's characters were therefore assailed by the most intense array of advertising forces to be found in Victorian capitalism.

The station bookstall was a growing trend in this period, provoking Gissing's ire in *New Grub Street* when he described the young people who were 'incapable of sustained attention' and needed 'something to occupy them in trains' and on

189 Gissing, *In the Year of Jubilee*, p. 309.
190 W. Morris, *News from Nowhere* (1890), in *Three Works by William Morris* (London: Lawrence & Wishart, 1968), pp. 181–401, pp. 136–37.
191 London Transport Museum Collection.
192 The proliferation of platform advertisements was deplored by W. R. Lethaby and other prominent critics who were active in the Society for Checking Abuses of Public Advertising. Meanwhile, the underground itself began to develop its own brand of 'corporate' advertising with the use of huge vertical illuminated signboards saying 'UNDERGROUND' on top of station buildings. These became standard after 1910 and can be seen in the second incarnation of King's Cross underground station entrance on King's Cross Bridge.

'buses and trams [...] the lightest and frothiest for chit-chatty information'.[193] Whelpdale's journal in the novel is called 'Chit-Chat', an allusion to the new media. Launched in 1888, a year after the Jubilee, Alfred Harmsworth's *Answers to Correspondents* was one such publication that featured 'true stories' about public transport in the capital alongside features on 'What the Queen eats', 'An Electrical Flying Machine' and 'How Dickens Read'. One notable example from *Answers* was the story of the underground railway worker who, walking along the line before the trains started in the morning, had found a human finger: 'The finger had been torn off roughly, and in a manner which must have caused the owner pain of the most terrible kind'.[194] Such stories undoubtedly moved Gissing to observe 'the flood of blackguardism which nowadays is pouring forth over society [...] Impossible to take up a newspaper without being impressed with this fact of extending and deepening vulgarity'.[195]

Advertising was plastered all over public transport in the city, including on a tram that Gissing uses in the novel to highlight how susceptible his characters are to the blandishments of the advertisers. When Barmby, Jessica and Nancy Lord travel by tram from Camberwell to Westminster Bridge, Gissing highlights Nancy's lack of cultural discrimination as she reads the adverts on the tram's lower deck: 'Somebody's "Blue;" somebody's "Soap;" Somebody's "High Class Jams;" and behold, inserted between the Soap and the Jam—"God so loved the world"'.[196] Both passages, on the platform at King's Cross and in the Westminster tramcar, testify to Gissing's moral and didactic purpose in this novel. His characters, particularly the female ones, are castigated for their cultural and moral impoverishment and their willingness to be sucked into the fabricated world of advertising represented by the Jubilee. Both journeys are the lower-middle-class equivalent of the fateful 'Io Saturnalia' train journey in *The Nether World* as both suggest that they are 'trapped' by the circulatory system of public transport. Gissing underlines the point, noting that the group had allowed themselves to become entangled with the working class by choosing to travel by tram instead of private cab.

This awareness of advertising culture as manifested on public transport is linked to the development of a 'subway consciousness' as used by Lynne Kirby in her discussion of the early years of silent cinema in North America.

---

193 Gissing, *New Grub Street*, p. 419.
194 P. Ferris, *The House of Northcliffe, The Harmsworths of Fleet Street* (London: Weidenfeld & Nicolson, 1971), p. 37.
195 Korg, 'Division of Purpose in George Gissing', p. 74.
196 Gissing, *In the Year of Jubilee*, p. 60. Selig makes the mistake of believing that the tram car in this scene is on the underground railway, see his *George Gissing*, p. 81.

The underground station and the interior of the underground carriage are intelligible: as Kirby notes, a 'condensed version of the commercial chaos of city streets and marketplaces'.[197] Using the interior of the railway carriage was a common conceit in the pages of *Punch* for both articles and cartoons. One notable example of October 1871 highlighted the very early impact of commercial advertising culture. In this short account, a correspondent is travelling on the Metropolitan Railway to Mansion House and has a dream induced by the 'advertisements at the Stations and in the carriages'. It consists of a series of surreal images including: 'Essence of Beef, washed down with several descriptions of Cocoa, India pale ale, German wines, Chloralum and Cognac' until awakened by '"Notting-Hill Gate! Notting-Hill Gate!" That familiar cry aroused me from what I was rather glad to find only a dream'.[198] *Punch* was one of the starting points for the new convention of the carriage in which figures are arranged in conversation such as its cartoon depicting two respectable middle-class women 'In the Metropolitan Railway' (1878). The two ladies are strangers but one ventures to the other: 'I beg your pardon, but I think I had the pleasure of meeting you in Rome last year!' The other replies, 'No I've never been nearer to Rome than St Albans.' 'St Albans? Where is that?' asks the first lady. 'Holborn!' comes the reply, referring to the church in that part of the city.[199] Such exchanges also appeared in Conan Doyle's 'The Adventure of the Naval Treaty' (1893) where an illustration shows Holmes and Watson discussing the south London landscape near Clapham Junction station,[200] and in 'The Adventure of Silver Blaze' (1892) where they converse in a compartment on the Great Western.[201] It is also memorably present in Lewis Carroll's *Through the Looking Glass* (1872) in which Alice is perused through a pair of opera glasses by the guard as she sits in a railway carriage opposite the Goat, the gentleman in white paper and the Beetle.[202] The carriage interior was also used with an advertising message as, for example, in an 1896 cartoon entitled 'The Underground Railway—As It Should Be', which shows a railway guard offering a 'Géraudel's Pastille' to a female passenger who is choking

---

197 Kirby, *Parallel Tracks*, p. 135.
198 *Punch*, 28 October 1871, vol. 61, p. 174.
199 'In the Metropolitan Railway', *Punch*, 12 January 1878, vol. 78, p. 6.
200 A. Conan Doyle, 'The Adventure of the Naval Treaty' (1893), in *Holmes: Complete Short Stories*, pp. 394–420, p. 406.
201 A. Conan Doyle, 'The Adventure of Silver Blaze' (1892), in *Holmes: Complete Short Stories*, pp. 235–56, p. 237.
202 J. Tenniel, 'Looking-Glass Insects', illustration in L. Carroll, *Through the Looking Glass* (1872; London: Penguin, 1994), p. 48.

from the effects of smoke in the tunnel.[203] So ubiquitous was advertising in the confined spaces of underground stations and the interior spaces of carriages that it is hardly surprising that Gissing was driven to comment on it.

Gissing is almost obsessive in the placing of his characters in the public space of underground trains and stations in these novels. During the chapter entitled 'Compassed Round' in *In the Year of Jubilee*, Gissing returns momentarily to the Dantean world. Jessica and Samuel make a descent to the platform at King's Cross underground station: 'he strode to the booking-office. They descended and stood together upon the platform'.[204] The descent is one of the conventions of epic poems such as Homer's *Odyssey* or Virgil's *Aeneid* and Dante, in the *Inferno*, descends into Hades in order to recognize the frailty of earthly things. It seems that Gissing wanted to make an ironic comment about the life of his two characters as they descend into the underworld of modernity where they immediately see the infernal locomotives that carry the 'shades' around the city: 'This way and that sped the demon engines, whirling lighted wagons full of people [...] an engine with glaring lights upon its breast' rushes towards them from the black mouth of the tunnel.[205] And the scene in King's Cross evokes Gissing's earlier novel *A Life's Morning* (1888) in which he had likened Hood's clerkships to 'an existence possibly preferable to that of the fourth circle of Inferno'.[206] King's Cross underground station is indeed the domain of Pluto, god of the underworld in Dante's *Inferno*: 'Hurrying crowds, in black fumes that poisoned the palate with sulphur [...] Shrill whistles, the hiss and roar of steam, the bang, clap, bang of carriage-doors, the clatter of feet on wood and stone—all echoed and reverberated from the huge cloudy vault above them'.[207]

This description has left an indelible mark on subsequent underground writing, making King's Cross an infernal world. In Angus Evan Abbott's 'The Spawn of Fortune' (1896), Charing Cross underground station appears particularly ethereal: 'A few waiting passengers sauntered up and down the platform. Smoke hung about in fantastic blue whiffs, writhing and twisting and swirling lazily towards the roof, and the gas burned yellow in the glass globes that hung from above the footway'.[208] A train then appears from the tunnel with full demonic power: 'two yellow eyes trembled and blinked in the darkness, and

---

203 O. Eckhardt, 'The Underground Railway—As It Should Be' (1896), in J. Coulter (ed.), *London of One Hundred Years Ago* (Stroud: Sutton, 1999), p. 98.

204 Gissing, *In the Year of Jubilee*, p. 309.

205 Gissing, *In the Year of Jubilee*, p. 309.

206 G. Gissing, *A Life's Morning* (1888; Brighton: Harvester, 1984), p. 64.

207 Gissing, *In the Year of Jubilee*, p. 309.

208 Abbott, 'Spawn of Fortune', pp. 3–4.

the next instant a Richmond train came wheezing, rocking, screeching, and grinding out of the blackness, and stopped with a jerk at the platform'.[209] In Gissing's novels, the underground engenders a lexicon of subterranean behaviour by his characters who beneath the streets play out the social struggle for middle-class existence in late Victorian urban society, a struggle that takes the form of a 'relentless warfare which ceases not, night and day, in the world above'.[210] Jessica and Samuel spend ten minutes on the platform at King's Cross waiting for a southward train to take them to Pentonville, 'a remote district'. They are on their way to a lecture ironically entitled 'National Greatness; its Obligations and its Dangers'; they walk towards 'the black mouth of the tunnel' to find a quiet space for conversation after Jessica warns Samuel that 'We may not be alone in the train'. A 'keen wind' sweeps the platform, drawing Jessica closer to Samuel.[211] This passage is charged with tension, particularly in the gender relations between the two characters, an aspect that has received much critical comment.[212]

The broader tensions of this scene in King's Cross show how underground writing embodies a sense of an 'uncontrollable', unknown landscape. This was evident in a letter of 1884 in which Gissing noted, rather mysteriously, that 'as always, it is the platform of the terminus which seems alone real, and all behind it a mere dream'.[213] He brings to bear all the forces of this city within the subterranean environment, drawing on his earlier fiction to underline the turmoil in the lives of his modern characters. Set in a noisy, crowded, smoke-filled station with the symbolic tunnel arch heralding a mysterious world beyond, the location of this scene is an interesting example of his ability to build other, more psychological, components of the imaginative underground. King's Cross station was at the centre of the first underground line, a pivotal point in London's transport geography. After Gissing moved to Gower Place he pointed out with some pride that 'From the three great railway Stations—King's Cross, St Pancras, Euston Square—I am about ten minutes' walk'.[214] King's Cross was an example of the traditional elevated glass and iron train-shed designed to help dissipate smoke and sulphur fumes and Gissing's characters have 'descended'

---

209 Abbott, 'Spawn of Fortune', p. 4.

210 Gissing, *In the Year of Jubilee*, p. 309.

211 Gissing, *In the Year of Jubilee*, p. 309.

212 See C. L. Bernstein, *The Celebration of Scandal: Toward the Sublime in Victorian Urban Fiction* (University Park, PA: Penn State University Press, 1991), B. L. Harman, *The Feminine Political Novel in Victorian England* (Charlottesville: University Press of Virginia, 1998) and M. Walters, 'Introduction', in G. Gissing, *The Odd Women* (1893; London: Virago, 1980).

213 Gissing, 17 August 1884, in *Collected Letters*, vol. 2, p. 243.

214 Gissing, 3 August 1881, in *Collected Letters*, vol. 2, p. 55.

to a 'subterranean' world, an imaginative 'inferno' located in a 'huge cloudy vault'. All the things that the underground 'imposes' on Gissing's characters are particularly modern and in some ways quite a mundane repertoire of activities: they try to avoid the crowds to talk privately within the confines of a narrow platform and are aware of the regularity of trains; they shout above the din of arriving and departing trains in order to communicate; they taste the sulphur in their mouths and throats in a more condensed way than in the streets above and move closer together as a cold draught emerges from the tunnel as though heralding the end of this platform episode.

The modernity lies in this episodic quality: we can observe the characters as if from a moving train or from the platform when they join the train, a fictional experience described by Sarah Grand in her short story 'When the Door Opened' (1898). It is set in a railway carriage but points to another part of the emerging subway consciousness of these decades when the narrator talks about 'the beginnings of episodes—tragic, heroic, amorous, abject; or the conclusions, which make the turning point the crisis of a life'. Such episodes can be observed from 'the top of an omnibus, from the platform of an underground station in a train that stops for a minute'.[215] They are one of the psychologically mysterious intervals in modern urban life because the viewer (or reader) cannot be sure what happens next. In Grand's story, the door having opened, it is closed as the train moves off again leaving the narrator 'tormented with conjectures as to what happened when that door opened'.[216] In *The Whirlpool*, Gissing amplifies this episodic quality by using the underground as a backdrop to the daily lives of his characters. Harvey Rolfe travels from Kensington High Street on a 'City train', Alma Rolfe travels to Queen's Road and both of them wander about on the platform at Notting Hill Gate station. Harvey Rolfe and Alma Frothingham travel 'by rail to Edgware Road, exchanging scarce a word on the way'.[217] In *In the Year of Jubilee* Nancy Lord changes at Baker Street station 'to go westward by another train',[218] reaching her destination with the 'help of train and omnibus'.[219] Gissing's characters spend an enormous amount of time on the underground, not to mention the odd journey on tram, bus and surface railway, but these are the first novels to engage deeply with underground travel, suggesting that it has become the transport method of choice

---

215   S. Grand, 'When the Door Opened' (1898), in A. Richardson (ed.), *Women Who Did: Stories by Men and Women, 1890–1914* (London: Penguin, 2002), pp. 217–24, p. 217.

216   Grand, 'When the Door Opened', p. 224.

217   Gissing, *The Whirlpool*, pp. 103, 144, 445 & 438.

218   Gissing, *In the Year of Jubilee*, p. 415.

219   Gissing, *In the Year of Jubilee*, p. 417.

in the metropolis. The journeys made by these characters occupy the same geographical co-ordinates as those made in *New Grub Street*, and highlight the ways in which the Circle line has linked the inner suburban shopping area of Kensington/Bayswater/Westbourne Grove with the outer suburban Metropolitan line to the north-west of London, the forerunner of twentieth-century 'Metro-Land'. In *The Whirlpool*, Alma is spotted by Harvey Rolfe, her future husband, as he watches 'in idleness, [...] the people who alighted from carriages' at Kensington High Street station—a sure sign of subway *flâneurie!*[220] Alma is able to travel 'frequently to Kingsbury-Neasden, and ran up to town at least as often as they (Dora and Gerda) did',[221] illuminating the new idea of underground shopping and leisure. Alma, however, finds herself harassed by Dymes as he pursues her onto the platform at Baker Street station. She has to listen for a quarter of an hour to 'remonstrances, flatteries, amorous blandishments, accompanied by the hiss of steam and the roar of trains'.[222] Harvey Rolfe and Alma move from Pinner to Gunnesbury: 'You know that we're going west to Gunnersbury', he explains during a visit to see Hugh Carnaby.[223]

What do all these episodes signify, particularly for women? Women's access to the metropolis had expanded, both in terms of leisure and employment and, as Deborah Parsons points out, although this new freedom was limited, 'its importance for emancipation should not be overlooked'.[224] Rachel Bowlby has described women's presence in the consumerist spaces of London[225] and Judith Walkowitz has highlighted the women who undertook social and charity work in the East End.[226] Women were represented as occupying the streets as shoppers, working girls and spinsters and would soon assert an even greater presence through the suffrage movement. But what about on the underground? Whilst this was a public space on a par with the streets, the nature of the environment imposed a different regime on women: the station platform was not like the street because it suggested the specific task of catching a train. There were no bus stops at this time so women and men did not queue at street level for the purpose of catching a bus. Trains were less crowded than

---

220 Gissing, *The Whirlpool*, p. 103.
221 Gissing, *The Whirlpool*, p. 188.
222 Gissing, *The Whirlpool*, p. 263.
223 Gissing, *The Whirlpool*, p. 320.
224 D. L. Parsons, *Streetwalking the Metropolis: Women, the City and Modernity* (Oxford: Oxford University Press, 2000), p. 43.
225 See R. Bowlby, *Just Looking: Consumer Culture in Dreiser, Gissing and Zola* (New York: Methuen, 1985).
226 See J. R. Walkowitz, *City of Dreadful Delight: Narratives of Sexual Danger in Late-Victorian London* (London: Virago, 1992).

buses because they were class segregated on the old steam lines and more spacious than horse-drawn vehicles. Women are represented as travelling in large numbers on the underground in this period, suggesting that it was not on the whole a hostile environment. Nevertheless, the platform and carriage were confined and potentially claustrophobic spaces where women might face harassment or violence. In Gissing's novels, women are subjected to greater pressures in public spaces. Edmund Widdowson, in *The Odd Women*, tries to restrict Monica's movement around the city by marrying her and removing her to Herne Hill; he argues that 'this cursed London [...] has come between us',[227] evidently blaming the underground and other transport services that have stretched the city making it into a place of separation. Edmund views her journeys as immoral as he suspects her of adultery. Two other shop-girls, Amy Drake and Miss Eade, use public transport locations for just such immoral activities; Amy Drake seduces Everard Barfoot in a railway carriage and Miss Eade becomes a prostitute at Victoria station. Here Gissing appears to believe that the freedom of such women is flawed by the attractions of independence and mobility. Like Mary Erle in Ella Hepworth Dixon's *The Story of a Modern Woman,* the female characters in Gissing's *The Odd Women* have a 'ready knowledge of London transit'.[228] Mary Erle, the writer and New Woman, uses the underground to prepare herself for an important meeting, telling herself 'as the train rattled on its way to Kensington that she could not afford to break down now'.[229] Monica Widdowson is employed as a draper's assistant in the Walworth Road and, as Sally Ledger observes, she enjoys a 'spatial liberation' brought about by frequent journeys on both underground and surface rail, travelling confidently, for example, from York Road station on the Piccadilly line to Walworth Road.[230] She too is able to use underground journeys to think as the railway carriage offers an interlude between events: during the journey from York Road, she looks 'like one whose mind is occupied with grave trouble. Fatigue had suddenly overcome her; she leaned back and closed her eyes'.[231] In chapter 17 of *The Odd Women*, Everard Barfoot spots Monica just outside Sloane Square station and they travel together on the Circle line westward in a first-class carriage. In a long conversation both characters spar over marriage and

---

227 G. Gissing, *The Odd Women*, p. 225.
228 G. Gissing, *The Odd Women*, p. 46.
229 Hepworth Dixon, *Story of a Modern Woman*, p. 155.
230 S. Ledger, *The New Woman: Fiction and Feminism at the Fin de Siècle* (Manchester: Manchester University Press, 1997), p. 164.
231 Gissing, *The Odd Women*, p. 46.

relationships in an 'intimate tone'[232] until 'Their eyes met, Barfoot sat forward from his place opposite Monica'.[233] The conversation terminates at Bayswater where Barfoot alights, leaving Monica alone with her thoughts until her stop at Portland Road. But it was men who 'loitered' on station platforms and commanded this subterranean space.

These instances point to the powerful influence of underground travel in the fiction of the 1890s. 'Subway consciousness' is being explored in these encounters as they take place in a now familiar environment that offers the possibility of easy access, endless opportunities to meet at stations or on platforms and a space in which to negotiate gender relations. We probably know more about these underground spaces in fiction than those encountered on omnibuses simply because station platforms offer more time and space for conversation. But it is also a subterranean, enclosed space in which characters may feel defeated by the seemingly endless pressure of the whirlpool or, in Mary Erle's case, 'Niagara [...] like London [...] the great power for ever driving forward'.[234] The underground, like Niagara, whirls Gissing's characters around London in the endless pursuit of 'worthless' jobs in service industries. Luckworth Crewe in *In the Year of Jubilee* is an advertising agent based at Farringdon Street whose clothes bear 'the traces of perpetual hurry and multifarious impact'.[235] Samuel Barmby in the same novel is in life insurance; Beatrice Peachey is the brains behind the South London Dress Supply Association; Cecil Morphew in *The Whirlpool* runs a photography shop; Rhoda Nunn teaches 'superfluous' women in *The Odd Women* and, in *Eve's Ransom*, Eve Madeley's friend Patty Ringrose works in a music shop in Camden Town. All these characters undoubtedly reflected the realities of lower-middle-class life in the capital.

Gissing returned to many of these themes in *Eve's Ransom*. Eve, the book-keeping heroine of the novel, has grown up in urban squalor and now lives in London. Gissing had originally planned to call the novel *The Gods of Iron*, a term he used in a letter to Algernon Gissing in 1893.[236] He described his intentions in writing the novel to Eduard Bertz in 1892:

> I shall use it as a picturesque background [he is describing the suburb of Birmingham
> in which the original story was to be set] to a story of middle-class life, insisting on

---

232 Gissing, *The Odd Women*, p. 192.
233 Gissing, *The Odd Women*, p. 193.
234 Hepworth Dixon, *Story of a Modern Woman*, p. 130.
235 Gissing, *In the Year of Jubilee*, p. 101.
236 Gissing, 28 February 1893, in *Letters to Members of his Family*, p. 332.

the degree to which people have become *machines* in harmony with the machinery amid which they spend their lives.[237]

And the most visible machines in Gissing's novel are trains. It opens on a railway station in the Midlands with a description of a train arriving with 'roaring, grinding, creaking and a final yell of brake-tortured wheels'.[238] In *Eve's Ransom*, Gissing counterposes the character of Hilliard to that of Eve Madeley, introducing Hilliard on a train journey from Dudley Port to Birmingham. As a draughtsman, Hilliard regards himself as being condemned to be a 'damned grinding mechanism'[239] and he is an expression of Gissing's deep ambivalence about technology. Hilliard wants to escape from the world of machinery, declaring that the human race will 'be driven mad and killed off by machinery'.[240]

Hilliard comes to London in order to escape from his old life and, once installed in the capital, he notices a young woman in a photograph album who is identified as Eve Madeley. Eve had also moved to London and Hilliard seeks out the house near Euston station where Eve is lodging even though he has only ever seen her in the photograph. He begins to 'stalk' her as she leaves the house to go to the Metropolitan Railway at Gower Street (Euston Square). Eve buys a ticket to visit the 'Healtheries; third return'[241] referring to the popular International Health Exhibition held at South Kensington in 1884 which drew over four million visitors.[242] Hilliard follows Eve on this underground journey and is soon sitting 'face to face with her in the railway carriage'.[243] Eve is 'at her ease, casting glances this way and that. When her eyes fell upon him he winced, yet she paid no more heed to him than to the other passengers'.[244] Eve, like Alma

---

237 G. Gissing, 2 December 1892, in *The Letters of George Gissing to Eduard Bertz, 1887–1903*, ed. A. C. Young (London: Constable, 1961), p. 163.

238 G. Gissing, *Eve's Ransom* (1895; London: Sidgwick & Jackson, 1911), pp. 3–4.

239 Gissing, *Eve's Ransom*, p. 34.

240 Gissing, *Eve's Ransom*, p. 37.

241 Gissing, *Eve's Ransom*, p. 81.

242 One of the visitors was George Bernard Shaw, himself a prolific user of the Metropolitan Railway, who recorded in a letter that he had waited in vain for his friend Alice Lockett to arrive at Liverpool Street station after her visit to the exhibition. Like the fictional Hilliard, Shaw did not actually make contact with Alice and fumed in the waiting room for over an hour until he gave up on her and 'came back by underground to Portland Road'. Shaw complained that Alice had left him 'to absorb a whole stationfull of rheumatism' at Liverpool Street (D. H. Laurence (ed.), *Bernard Shaw Collected Letters 1874–1897* (London: Max Reinhardt, 1965), pp. 98–100).

243 Gissing, *Eve's Ransom*, p. 81.

244 Gissing, *Eve's Ransom*, p. 82.

Rolfe in *The Whirlpool*, appears to symbolize the psychological dangers involved in the pursuit of an independent lifestyle in the capital—the public space of the underground carriage or platform allowing her to be covertly observed by men. Women and men shared this particular public space but, as Winter observes, they 'inhabited those spaces on different terms'.[245] It is interesting that Gissing sets one of the most dramatic scenes in the novel in an underground carriage, loading it with the suspense surrounding the first meeting of his two main characters in the midst of the busy Circle line. Later, when Hilliard is properly introduced to her, Eve vaguely recalls 'that I have seen you somewhere' and he jogs her memory with 'Perhaps in the train this evening?'[246] Eve is surprised that he was able to recognize her from the photograph but, of course, the twin technologies of underground transit and photography have combined in Gissing's hands to allow Hilliard the time to sit and study her face in the carriage. He even has time to doubt whether this is the woman in the photograph, asking himself if 'this could be the real Eve Madeley whose history he had heard'.[247] Rachel Bowlby comments on Gissing's *Eve's Ransom* to show how his middle-class characters have to inhabit a world of public transport as part of 'the demands of a competitive, monetary economy'.[248] But the use of the photograph also points to the forensic clarity that Gissing brought to his writing: having visited the Health Exhibition he would have noted Francis Galton's booth which asked visitors to volunteer their personal data such as fingerprints. Galton had focused on the importance of photographic records in the observation of criminal 'types'.

Eve was a fictional version of the many single middle-class women who struggled to make a living in the capital at this time. Women like Amy Levy, whose poem 'Ballade of an Omnibus' (1889) celebrated the 'new opportunities for mobility and expression' opened up by urban life.[249] Levy's two characters Phyllis and Gertrude, in her novel *The Romance of a Shop* (1888), are to be found confidently using both the underground and buses, with 'Phyllis disappearing to the underground railway', and 'Gertrude mounting boldly to the top of an Atlas omnibus'.[250] The basic plot is an account of the modern women who enter

---

245 Winter, *London's Teeming Streets*, p. 178.

246 Gissing, *Eve's Ransom*, p. 89.

247 Gissing, *Eve's Ransom*, p. 83.

248 Bowlby, *Just Looking*, p. 151.

249 L. Hunt Beckman, *Amy Levy: Her Life and Letters* (Athens: Ohio University Press, 2000), p. 139.

250 A. Levy, *The Romance of a Shop* (1888), ed. S. D. Bernstein (Peterborough, Ontario: Broadview Press, 2006), p. 86.

the public world of the city and, in particular, the four Lorimer sisters who set up a photography business. Phyllis and Gertrude are the two most independently minded sisters and the latter is fascinated by London's 'pageant'. Baker Street is at the centre of this experience and Gertrude is gladdened by the 'fate which had transported her from the comparative tameness of Campden Hill to regions where the pulses of the great city could be felt distinctly as they beat and throbbed'.[251] The pulse of the city may be detected by the regularity of trains on the Metropolitan Railway that travels virtually beneath their shop at Baker Street, an image of modernity. Levy was friends with the 'Gower Street' group—Olive Schreiner, Eleanor Marx and Vernon Lee—and was involved, like the novelist Margaret Harkness, in the new arts and politics of the 1880s. As Deborah L. Parsons has pointed out, Levy published 'Women and Club Life' (1888) in *Woman's World*, an article which defended the upper-middle-class women's clubs that had sprung up south of Baker Street.[252] The clubs mentioned—Somerville (1887), Albermarle (1881), Alexandra (1884) and University (1887)—were 'havens of refuge' for women but Levy used the image of the centre versus the periphery again: 'from the high and dry region of the residential neighbourhood the women came pouring down to those pleasant shores where their great stream of human life is dashing and flowing'.[253] This is a powerful evocation of journeys inwards rather than the outward escape routes of Gissing's characters. Beatrice Webb's diaries record her frequent travels on the Metropolitan Railway in the following decade with one entry in particular noting her 'steaming off to Baker Street' after a visit to the anarchist thinker Peter Kropotkin in the East End.[254] Webb, who lived for a time with her cousin Margaret Harkness, made regular journeys in the early 1880s between St Katherine Buildings at St Katherine Dock and Cheyne Walk in Chelsea. She sometimes travelled on the Thames steam ferry from Chelsea to Tower Pier although this service had been in decline since 1878 after the Princess Alice disaster when the overcrowded ferry capsized, drowning over 600 people. Webb was a regular user of the Metropolitan and District lines following her marriage to Sidney Webb when she moved from Hampstead to Millbank, an address near the Houses of Parliament and the Metropolitan

---

251 Levy, *Romance of a Shop*, p. 87.

252 See Parsons, *Streetwalking the Metropolis*, chapter 3.

253 A. Levy, 'Women and Club Life', *Woman's World* I (1888), pp. 364–67, reprinted in *The Complete Novels and Selected Writings of Amy Levy 1861–1889*, ed. M. New (Gainesville: University Press of Florida, 1993), pp. 532–38, p. 532.

254 B. Webb, 16 February 1890, *The Diaries of Beatrice Webb*, eds. N. & J. MacKenzie, 4 vols. (London: Virago, 1982), vol. 1, p. 327.

Board of Works council chamber at Spring Gardens. She contributed to early discussions on the relationship between the local economy and the growth of the new suburbs, arguing in 'A Lady's View of the Unemployed' (1886) that unemployment in the capital was being increased by new machinery, changes in the structure of industries like the docks, and cheap fares to the suburbs.[255] Karl Marx's daughter, Jenny, was a seasoned underground traveller, recalling her journeys on 'the dark underground, to Farringdon Street, where when I was not stifling with asthma, I could at least indulge in my morning daily'.[256] One of his other daughters, Eleanor, was also a regular user of the Metropolitan and District in the 1880s, particularly during the Dock Strike and the four-month strike at Silver's factory in Silvertown. Her journey to the factory would have taken her from Farringdon Street to Aldgate and thence to Silvertown station on the Great Eastern and Blackwall Railway. The Metropolitan Railway was literally the northern geographical boundary of the 'ardent young men and women' who traversed a 'fictional grid of one square mile, south of Euston Square'.[257]

London's economy was being driven by the development of the West End as it extended westwards to take in areas like Bayswater and Westbourne Grove, a growth fuelled by the massive expansion of the London docks to the east of the city. This was the consumer equivalent of the manufacturing belt which ran across north London, a mainly residential area first connected to the rest of central London by horse omnibus services. The Bayswater/Westbourne Grove area chronicled by Ana Parejo Vadillo was at the important western edge of the Metropolitan Railway.[258] It was the western boundary of Gissing's *New Grub Street*, a world that had been semi-pastoral in previous decades and clearly retained something of that character when Gissing became more familiar with it in the mid-1880s. In *Shopping for Pleasure* (2000), Erika Rappaport has shown how much was done in print to develop the links between public transport and the shopping districts of the West End. Women were furnished with 'consumer-oriented knowledge gained by reading magazines' with, for

---

255 B. Webb (writing as Beatrice Potter), 'A Lady's View of the Unemployed', *Pall Mall Gazette*, 18 February 1886.

256 J. Marx, letter to Laura Marx, March 1882, in O. Meier (ed.), *The Daughters of Karl Marx, Family Correspondence, 1866–1898* (Harmondsworth: Penguin, 1984), p. 152.

257 C. Steedman, 'Fictions of Engagement; Eleanor Marx, Biographical Space', in J. Stokes (ed.), *Eleanor Marx (1855–1898), Life, Work, Contacts* (Aldershot: Ashgate, 2000), pp. 2–39, p. 29.

258 See A. Parejo Vadillo, *Women Poets and Urban Aestheticism: Passengers of Modernity* (Basingstoke: Palgrave Macmillan, 2005).

example, *The Lady* publishing a series called 'London Locomotion' (1891) which described the history of the public transport system.[259] The link between shopping and transit was also highlighted in *Orpheus and Eurydice*. It has the mythical couple living in the suburbs and commuting into the city for business and pleasure. They travel

> On the dark underground—
> That City that's dark all day!
> The place where gold buys everything
> All's marked with the price somehow
> From an MP's seat to a wedding ring.[260]

Here, the underground has been linked with a West End of consumption in a way that is consistently repeated in the social lives of the characters in Gissing's fiction. In *Orpheus and Eurydice*, the underground is no longer mysterious or particularly threatening as the metaphorical gateway to Hades. It has been stripped of the former infernal associations of steam power and is therefore merely a convenient route into the city and West End for the middle class.

The underground was also closely connected with the growth of the South Kensington complex. The Department of Science and Art had moved to the area in 1856 and was housed in the corrugated iron structure known as the 'Brompton Boilers' until the opening of the Victoria & Albert Museum in 1899. Nearly six million people attended the International Exhibition in 1862, six years before the Metropolitan Railway reached it and nine years before the District. As we have seen, the International Health Exhibition of 1884 was immensely popular and led to the Colonial and Indian Exhibition (1886) that featured Indian tea manufacture. In the 1870s each annual International Exhibition attracted nearly one million visitors with two-and-a-half million going to the Greater Britain Exhibition at nearby Earl's Court in 1899, exhibitions having been transferred there after 1886 following the start of construction of Imperial College. The District Railway opened a pedestrian subway under Exhibition Road in 1885, charging people one penny and offering a return fare of one shilling for artisans travelling to South Kensington. The Diamond Jubilee in 1897 was celebrated by a Victorian Era Exhibition at Earl's Court, a site owned by the District Railway, and was just one of the

259 See E. D. Rappaport, *Shopping for Pleasure, Women in the Making of London's West End* (Princeton: Princeton University Press, 2000), p. 125.

260 Quoted in Pike, 'Underground Theater', p. 112. Pike says that the new 'tube' lines were readily accepted by the travelling public. In terms of the writing, the tube was more problematic as its image was already being shaped by Gissing's perspectives.

many held there between 1887 and 1913. Another major attraction was the Ferris wheel that towered over the railway tracks for over ten years whilst the nearby Olympia, originally opened as the National Agricultural Hall in 1884, was directly linked to Earl's Court Station. The Hungarian-born entrepreneur Imre Kiralfy was the organizing force behind the Earl's Court exhibitions in the 1890s. The first of his projects was the Empire of India Exhibition held in 1895, followed by the Greater London Exhibition, his most ambitious project after forming London Exhibition Limited. In 1907 Kiralfy erected his own exhibition hall at Wood Lane—the Great White City and Stadium covering 140 acres at which he launched the Imperial International Exhibition in 1909 featuring exhibits like the 'Alpine and Submarine Railways'. The site replaced Earl's Court as London's biggest exhibition centre and large shows were held there until 1914. The Central London Railway used the opportunity to extend its services and the opening of the new extension in 1908 coincided with Kiralfy's first exhibition on Franco-British relations. Many of these exhibitions stressed the Empire as an integral part of Britain's economic success and the various underground companies tapped into this notion of imperial power with, for example, the District Railway publishing special Jubilee maps that featured images of the Empire.

The late Victorian fashion press evaluated the different modes of transport available to educated middle-class women, arguing that they could avoid the dangers of assault, harassment or embarrassment. Images of assault were common in Victorian melodrama, poster advertising and magazine illustration, and were often associated with the railways. A *Strand Magazine* illustration accompanying the Conan Doyle story 'Wisteria Lodge' has a female character fighting to escape from a male assailant in a railway carriage.[261] But as early as the 1870s, J. J. Tissot's painting *Waiting at the Station, Willesden Junction* (c.1874), showed how female servants could travel unmolested.[262] Disturbing images were now being firmly countered in the more up-market parts of the media and it was essential to highlight the ease of access to department stores that came with the new tube lines, for example at the new Selfridge's store in Oxford Street. A stream of favourable information and opinion began to dominate discussion of the 'new' West End, paving the way for the very positive views of tube expansion that were to appear in the mainstream media in the later years. As Erika Rappaport points out, 'the fashion press proposed

261 A. Conan Doyle, 'Wisteria Lodge' (1908), in *Holmes: Complete Short Stories*, pp. 683–707, p. 703
262 J. J. Tissot, *Waiting at the Station, Willesden Junction* (c.1874), Dunedin Art Gallery.

that middle-class travellers could avoid becoming the endangered heroines of Victorian melodrama. Armed with a consumer-oriented urban knowledge gained by reading magazines, one could evade the dangers and the discomforts associated with urban existence'.[263]

Gissing contributed indirectly to this process of integration through his repeated depictions of the steam underground. When Biffen in *New Grub Street* says that 'we form our ideas of London from old literature',[264] he provides an apt statement of Gissing's own role in delineating late-Victorian London. Gissing constructed the foundations for underground writing and his novels completed a fictional process whereby the steam underground was firmly established as an integral part of everyday urban life for the middle class. This was an important statement about the social and psychological impact of technology within the city, particularly as it imaginatively situated the underground as the key subterranean thread, surpassing the sewers. Gissing's earlier perspectives on the underground focused on an infernal battleground with the steam locomotive as the central symbol of capitalist power; this came to shape his more mature exposition of lower-middle-class urban consciousness in the following decade. Gissing's fiction therefore transformed the series of images and concepts that informed the conventional portrayal of railways into a powerful set of imaginative perspectives. The underground writing that Gissing fashioned did integrate it into the wider urban context but also dislocated it psychologically, physically and emotionally in the imaginative sphere. The paradox was that Gissing's creation of these perspectives actually identified and put in place a number of themes that would inform the much wider debate about the metropolis in the coming century.

Gissing did not introduce the electric or tubular railway into his later work despite the fact that the first deep-level, electrically powered tubes, the City and South London Railway and Central London Railway were opened in the final decade of his life. Gissing was living in France for some years until his death and the new tubes were a novelty and perhaps better suited to journalistic treatment than fiction. Nevertheless, the steam underground made a final appearance in the novel *Will Warburton* (1905), published two years after his death. Warburton's life is filled with journeys from Whitechapel to Chelsea, to Putney, Walham Green and Clapham Junction. Many of these trips would clearly have been on Gissing's familiar underground lines, as when Warburton

---

263 Rappaport, *Shopping for Pleasure*, p. 124.
264 Gissing, *New Grub Street*, p. 474.

alights 'from a train at Notting Hill Gate'[265] station to visit Norbert Franks the artist. This station was, by then, intersected by the newly completed Central London Railway, but the electric tube does not intrude into the pages of this novel. Gissing's legacy is one in which the middle class is trapped in a whirlpool of urban modernity. Their prison is the *steam* underground carriage of the Metropolitan, District and Circle lines, in which they are figuratively locked to endure endless journeys around the system.

---

265 G. Gissing, *Will Warburton* (1905; London: Hogarth Press, 1985), p. 183.

Chapter Two

THE UTOPIAN UNDERGROUND
OF H. G. WELLS

Bank-clerks [...] were heard to declare, as they sped home
from the City, that the Underground Railway was beautiful
from London Bridge to Westminster, but not from Sloane
Square to Notting Hill Gate.

Max Beerbohm, '1880'[1]

I n his 1902 book *Anticipations of the Reaction of Mechanical and Scientific Progress upon Human Life and Thought*, H. G. Wells declared that the 'People of today take the railways for granted as they take the sea and sky; they were born into a railway world, and they expect to die in one.'[2] For Wells, the underground was the epitome of this railway world as it brought together all the components of his reforming vision. George Gissing's visionary underground was anchored in a securely realistic setting, developing a number of literary perspectives for an entirely new mode of travel in the capital. Wells, on the other hand, adopted many of Gissing's conventions but redefined them first through science fantasy and then, especially after 1900, in reforming journalism and social fiction. In Wells' scientific romances of the 1890s, the underground is projected into the future as the mechanized, enclosed city of a far-distant period. Contemporary developments in electrically powered technology and underground tunnelling are presented as part of a deterministic process of human evolution. A more utopian vision is revealed in Wells' campaigning journalism with non-fictional polemics such as *Anticipations* and *A Modern Utopia* (1905)

---

1   M. Beerbohm, '1880' (1894), in *The Works of Max Beerbohm* (London: Heinemann, 1922), pp. 35–47, p. 40.

2   H. G. Wells, *Anticipations of the Reaction of Mechanical and Scientific Progress upon Human Life and Thought* (London: Chapman & Hall, 1902), p. 12.

in which the underground appears as the key underpinning of the planned metropolis. In the Fabian phase of his career between 1903 and 1908, Wells drags the underground back from the future in order to give shape and order to his projected contemporary city. Wells' post-1900 fiction offered the transit system as a means of mapping the increasingly complex, seemingly incoherent and often puzzling urban environment of the capital city for his characters in a way that picks up and tries to answer the more pessimistic account of urban life in Gissing's novels. Wells' perspectives represented an extraordinary leap in underground writing as it placed the technology of the emerging electric tube system squarely in the context of a construction of the present and the future.

This chapter will explore the development of a new paradigm that enabled the underground to be inserted into a public discourse combining science, technology, sociology and urban reform, particularly in relation to the suffrage movement and the ideology of National Efficiency. Wells' linking of London's underground with science fiction is discussed as well as his contribution to a new political landscape for urban public transport debates. The work of a number of other writers including E. M. Forster, Arnold Bennett and Dorothy Richardson is also explored as they rewrite the fictional boundaries of the underground in relation to its vast suburban extensions.

THE DISCOVERY OF THE UNDERGROUND: H. G. WELLS AND A VISION OF THE FUTURE

Wells had considerable personal experience of the underground in London whilst studying at the Normal School of Science in South Kensington from 1884 to 1887. He lived in the Euston Road and recalled in *An Experiment in Autobiography* (1934) the steam-driven Metropolitan and Circle lines, travelling regularly 'by train from Gower Street station (Euston Square they call it now) to Praed Street at a cost of three half-pence'.[3] He coupled the old London of steam and gas lighting with the very new political ideas of the Fabian generation that dominated radical thinking at the turn of the century when he further recorded his journeys 'through the gas-lit winter streets of London and by the sulphurous Underground Railway, to hear and criticise and cheer and believe in William Morris, the Webbs, Bernard Shaw,

---

3   H. G. Wells, *An Experiment in Autobiography*, 2 vols. (London: Gollancz, 1934 & 1966), vol. 1, p. 280.

Hubert Bland, Graham Wallas and all the rest of them, who were to lead us to that millennial world'.[4]

At this point Wells was at the confluence of steam technology, new political ideas of rational progress and the speedy arrival of the future in the present. In his early stories, however, the underworld generalized is a key thread but it is no longer a social abyss or a location through which people travel. It is, instead, an entirely new subterranean city-state constructed to house populations that have retreated below the surface of their world at some stage in history and have successfully adapted to a subterranean environment. Notably, there is a descent into the earth at some distant future point in 'The Time Machine' (1895); the discovery of a lunar underworld in *The First Men in the Moon* (1901) and the construction of a rather indeterminate multilevelled city enclosed in a vast dome in his novel *When the Sleeper Wakes* (1899). All of these subterranean locations suggested that underground railways could be perhaps the first stage in a process of migration beneath the city.

Wells was certainly not the first writer to describe such underworlds in the last quarter of the nineteenth century. As Rosalind Williams points out, there was a fast developing genre of novels and stories that explored common themes such as the environmental effects of changes to the earth's atmosphere, the possible evolutionary direction of the human species and the potential of engineering technology to allow human habitation of deep-level zones within the earth. For example, William Delisle Hay's social-Darwinist novel *Three Hundred Years Hence* (1881) describes a new world 50 feet below the surface reached by a subway of 'terra-cars' and Bulwer-Lytton's *The Coming Race* (1871) shows a future human group called the 'vril-ya' occupying vast chambers within the earth. In Gabriel Tarde's *Underground Man* (1896), the human race flees from a catastrophic 'cliff composed of rocks and overturned engines, of the wreckage of bridges, stations, hotels and public offices'[5] and seals itself off in subterranean galleries. Elsewhere, Camille Flammarion's *La fin du monde* (1893) and William Hope Hodgson's *The Night Land* (1912) highlighted the effects of global cooling. This fiction also frequently contains speculation about the future social organization of society alongside theories of 'racial' degeneration and social-Darwinist ideas of the survival of the fittest. Common to all, though, is the important role played by motive power, as represented in *The Coming Race* by a mysterious force called 'vril', and in *Three Hundred Years Hence*

---

4   Wells, *Experiment in Autobiography*, vol. 1, pp. 265–66.
5   G. Tarde, quoted in R. Williams, *Notes on the Underground: An Essay on Technology, Society and the Imagination* (Cambridge, MA: MIT Press, 1990), p. 102.

by an energy source named 'basilico-magnetism'. If, as fiction suggested, the life of the future was likely to be subterranean then such fantasy writers simply took their cue from the cities they actually lived in. London, Paris and New York either already had or were being furnished with underground railways that offered an existing model for travel but could also be seen as the harbinger of a whole life beneath the ground. The future subterranean city-state would require a highly developed transit system as locomotion would clearly be a crucial element in the lives of the inhabitants enabling them to reach all levels of the city efficiently. This model of an underground society crossed national boundaries to inspire, for example, a new genre of utopian/dystopian literature in Russia, a trend accelerated by a flood of translated science fiction including the works of Wells and Jules Verne.[6]

For Wells, the London underground system offered this range of possibilities in the form of an imagined future city. In 'The Time Machine', his Time Traveller journeys into the far-distant future of the year 802,701 where he discovers a world composed of two degenerate species: the Eloi who live above ground and the Morlocks who inhabit a subterranean world. The Time Traveller's experiences in this world are reminiscent of Wells' own youthful journeys in the Metropolitan Railway's sulphurous environment when he was transcribing the new electric tubular railways through the perspectives of the steam underground writing of Gissing. When he discovers that there are entrances to a subterranean world, the Time Traveller realizes that 'the earth must have been tunnelled enormously and these tunnellings were the habitat of a New Race'. This 'new race' is called the Morlocks but the Time Traveller calls them 'Undergrounders'.[7]

In order to explain this strange world, Wells again resorts to the real underground. The Time Traveller points out that the 'existing circumstances' of his own time, the 1890s, already suggest a division between social classes, 'the Capitalist and the Labourer', adding that 'There is a tendency to utilise underground space for the less ornamental purposes of civilisation, there is the Metropolitan Railway in London, for instance, there are the electric railways, there are subways'.[8] The Time Traveller decides that the Morlocks

---

6   Novels like N. N. Shelonski's *In the World of the Future* (1892), V. N. Chikolev's *Electric Tale* (1902), Valery Bryusov's *Earth* (1904) described underworlds. A. Rodnykh's *St Petersburg–Moscow Self-Propelled Underground Railway* (1902) showed how science fiction was a powerfully imaginative vehicle for the technological development of tube railways.

7   H. G. Wells, 'The Time Machine' (1895), in *Selected Short Stories* (Harmondsworth: Penguin, 1958), pp. 7–83, pp. 46–48.

8   Wells, 'The Time Machine', p. 47.

live in an 'artificial Under-world' and later climbs down a shaft towards their domain whilst 'the thudding sound of a machine below grew louder and more oppressive'.[9] Whilst this fictional underworld is a constructed, manufactured city, Wells' London was already a place in which the noise and reverberation of subterranean railways affected the surface. This was particularly notable as the old underground was far from silent and the new electric tubes introduced a whole range of extra sounds to the aural vocabulary of their passengers. In a travel essay on London, the Swedish journalist Sigurd Frosterus wrote that passengers are 'sucked in unawares through the mechanically opening double iron doors into the bogie-carriages of the accordion-like train'. The end of the journey is marked by 'a sudden jolt, a metallic clicking, the doors burst open'.[10] Such sensations of sound and movement are a prominent part of what Wells' Time Traveller poignantly calls 'the stir that makes the background of our lives' when he beholds the uninhabited earth towards the end of the story.[11]

In *The First Men in the Moon* (1901), this concept of a subterranean world is further highlighted when Wells' travellers hear a sound 'from beneath our feet, a sound in the ground [...] Its dull resonance was muffled by distance, thick with the quality of intervening substance', a sound which Wells links with 'sleepless nights in crowded cities'.[12] Wells is sign-posting the sounds of the deep tube at around 60 feet below the surface, giving a new sense of daily vibration to the urban world. Here, the sound seems to be prophetic in some way as vibration may be viewed as undermining the urban environment as seen in Arthur Machen's short story 'Opening the Door' (1931). Set in the year 1907, a 'teacup and saucer on a side-table trembled slightly' setting off an apoca-lyptic sequence in which the main character, a clergyman named Jones (the 'Canonbury clergyman'), foresees the end of London: 'Jones heard the tea-cup rattle and laid the universe of London in ruins'. He imagines the city collapsing in a tangle of water-mains, drainage, gas and electric wires whilst being undermined by 'great processions of huge omnibuses carrying fifty, seventy, a hundred people' and 'the earth would be rent with explosions, and the myriad streets of London would go up in a great flame of fire'.[13] The investigation of

---

9   Wells, 'The Time Machine', p. 50.
10 S. Frosterus, 'London Rhapsody' (1903), quoted in R. Allen (ed.), *The Moving Pageant: A Literary Sourcebook on London Street-Life, 1700–1914* (London: Routledge, 1998), pp. 209–11, p. 210.
11 Wells, 'The Time Machine', p. 78.
12 H. G. Wells, *The First Men in the Moon* (1901; New York: Airmont, 1965), p. 57.
13 A. Machen, 'Opening the Door', in *Holy Terrors* (Harmondsworth: Penguin, 1946), pp. 54–65, p. 56.

the subterranean world brought about by increased tunnelling fired the imaginations of those who reflected on the metaphorical process of undermining the urban environment. In fact, the real vibrations produced by the new deep level lines *did* cause complaints about subsidence with the original locomotives on the Central London Railway (1900) accused of causing high levels of vibration that were damaging property along the surface of the line. Two contemporary *Punch* cartoons picked up the immediate impact on the capital's surface life, the first entitled 'Vibration of the Tube' showing a series of London statues collapsing in ruins whilst the second furnishes London's domestic servants with a new explanation for that broken vase: 'They must 'a been shook by that there 'orrid Tube that they talk about!'[14] A Board of Trade enquiry into vibration was set up with three scientific experts including Sir John Wolfe-Barry, the designer of Tower Bridge. The 43-ton locomotives were blamed for the vibration and some were adapted but the problem was not solved until the introduction of lighter multiple-unit trains. In the fictional world the underground remained unsettling and the physical impact of the tube on the streets of the capital was swiftly mediated by narratives of urban destruction.

In 'The Time Machine' Wells' Time Traveller spends much time exploring the subterranean world of the Morlocks by descending and ascending shafts. At one point he thinks of 'trying to go up the shaft again, and leave the Underground'.[15] He later enters a gallery in the 'Palace of Green Porcelain' which is just like an underground station platform: 'Singularly ill-lit, the floor of it running down at a slight angle from the end at which I entered. At intervals white globes hung from the ceiling—many of them cracked and smashed, which suggested that originally the place had been artificially lit'.[16] Here, Wells has combined the elements of an underground station and the museums at South Kensington with which he was closely acquainted, South Kensington underground station being by now linked to these museums by a subway. It seems that the Time Traveller's entrance to the Morlock world can only be via a more familiar, historical level identified with steam traction. For Wells, the steam underground is a portal to even deeper and more threatening lower levels in a way similar to the idea of a portal discussed in chapter one. The Green Porcelain gallery is set below ground level 'like the area of a London house' and it runs down 'into a thick darkness',[17] sloping away from

---

14   'Vibration of the Tube', *Punch*, 6 February 1901, vol. 120, p. 122 and 27 February 1901, vol. 120, p. 173.
15   Wells, 'The Time Machine', p. 51.
16   Wells, 'The Time Machine', p. 62.
17   Wells, 'The Time Machine', p. 62.

the known world of the platform towards a dangerous deep tunnel inhabited by the Morlocks. The gallery contains derelict machinery dating from the Traveller's own time but the only useful implements are a box of matches and a steel bar or lever. The Traveller grabs and breaks off this 'lever not unlike those in a signal-box'[18] from one of the machines in order to defend himself and his Eloi companion Weena from attack by the Morlocks. Both images illustrate an inchoate and indistinct world but the lever is enough to reassure the Traveller of an old and faithful friend, the Victorian signal-box. This familiar image of order is one that fortifies the urban traveller in confronting the deep tubes, the Time Traveller having already admitted that he is 'more in his element' amongst this old machinery.[19]

The 'area' or basement entrance of a London house is linked with coal (often leading to the entrance to a coal cellar) and, after he discovers a block of sulphur, the Time Traveller soon becomes fixated with it. This sulphur, he says, 'hung in my mind, and set up a train of thinking'.[20] Wells brings the image of sulphur into play here because the Time Traveller is thinking of a means of self-defence, but it may be linked with the sulphur matches that prove to be one of his last defences against the Morlocks and therefore another safe reminder of the stable Victorian past to shore up as protection against the unknown future. It seems possible that Wells naturally associated this environment with the smell of sulphur and flickering lights. He had already used the poignant image of the lighted match in an article 'The Rediscovery of the Unique' (1891) published in the *Fortnightly Review*, saying that 'science is a match that man has just got alight [and] now that the preliminary sputter is over and the flame burns up clear [...] around him, in place of all that human comfort and beauty he anticipated— darkness still'.[21] If Wells imaginatively linked underground places and tunnels with underground railways, his fictional reflex would be to include such images because they powerfully evoked in his audience the infernal qualities of steam underground journeys. Even in *The First Men in the Moon* he cited the 'use of steam' as the most advanced technological achievement on the earth.

Most of Wells' readers would have had considerable experience of the smell and taste of sulphur from coal-burning fires and steam engines. The

---

18   Wells, 'The Time Machine', pp. 62–63.
19   Wells, 'The Time Machine', p. 62.
20   Wells, 'The Time Machine', p. 61
21   H. G. Wells, 'The Rediscovery of the Unique' (1891), in R. M. Philmus & D. Y. Hughes (eds.), *H. G. Wells: Early Writings in Science and Science Fiction* (Berkeley: University of California Press, 1975), pp. 22–31, pp. 30–31.

underground was a notable example of its effects as recorded in 1887 in the diary of the American-born journalist R. D. Blumenfeld:

> I had my first experience of Hades today, and if the real thing is to be like that I shall never do anything wrong. I got into the Underground railway at Baker Street [...] The atmosphere was a mixture of sulphur, coal dust and foul fumes from the oil lamp above; so that by the time we reached Moorgate Street I was near dead from asphyxiation and heat'.[22]

Blumenfeld was still complaining 13 years later in 1900 after a journey on a steam train between Sloane Square and Temple stations on the Inner Circle, declaring that 'the carriage was filled with sulphorous smoke and my fellow-passengers in the packed compartment coughed incessantly'. Like *Punch* he looked forward to electric traction noting that 'Some day the electrification plans of this stuffy line may be completed but in the meantime the smoke nuisance is trying'.[23] Not for nothing did *Punch* dub steam traction the 'Demon King Sulphur'.[24] In fact, despite the introduction of electric traction, sulphur remained at alarmingly high levels in the underground until filtered and ozonized air was pumped into the tunnels from 1911.

Even as late as 1900, sulphur and coal were key mediating forces in the construction of an infernal underground but for Wells, who was on the technological fault-line between steam and electric power, sulphur appears to be a saviour not a killer, and the Time Traveller can protect himself against the Morlocks with one of the ubiquitous substances of 'carboniferous capitalism'.[25] Wells was exploring the concept of descent through the visionary steam underground bequeathed by Gissing but was using familiar images of stability as a context for an abstract, unknown and possibly problematic future. For Wells, the tubular railway in London was the next step into the future but a future that might produce the Morlocks. The steam underground was a portal to the future as one form of technology gave way to another, but it might bring about an irrevocable breakdown in human values and the emergence of a cannibalistic master race which preyed on surface-dwelling Eloi. As Roger Luckhurst has observed, this 'ambivalence towards technologies is often the presiding

---

22   R. D. Blumenfeld, *R. D. B.'s Diary, 1887–1914* (London: Heinemann, 1930), p. 7.

23   Blumenfeld, *Diary*, p. 114.

24   'The Good Fairy Electra of the Continuous Current banishes the Demon King Sulphur', *Punch*, 18 December 1901, vol. 121, p. 449.

25   See A. Briggs, *Victorian Things* (1988; Harmondsworth: Penguin, 1990), chapter 8. A popular brand of match was called 'Locomotive'.

spirit of engagement'[26] and Wells was using his fiction to bridge the cultural dissonances thrown up by his own personal experiences of steam travel and the as yet uncharted territory of electric technology.

By the time Wells published *The First Men in the Moon* there was less ambivalence in his attitude to the future underworld. In the novel, two Englishmen, the businessman Bedford and a scientist Cavor, travel to the moon in a sphere coated with the antigravity substance Cavorite. Captured by the moon's inhabitants, the Selenites, Cavor is taken beneath the surface through a great shaft which is 'one of an enormous system of artificial shafts that run, each from what is called a lunar "crater" downwards for very nearly a hundred miles towards the central portion of our satellite'.[27] The Selenites' ruthless adaptation of the individual to efficiently carry out their assigned function is deplored in the story but Cavor's interview with their leader, the Grand Lunar, reveals a different agenda. Cavor's hapless description of the earth's achievements brings about his eventual demise but the message does point towards the positive sides of science and technology. For instance, Cavor has to tell the incredulous Grand Lunar three times 'that of all the 4,000 miles of substance between the earth and its centre men knew only to the depth of a mile' but that people on earth 'were now taking their railways and many establishments beneath the surface'[28] with the implication that human beings are making progress along the lines of the moon's advanced Selenite community. Wells reinforces the message by saying that 'there are new elements, new appliances, new traditions, an overwhelming avalanche of new ideas'.[29] As John Huntington suggests, *The First Men in the Moon* points towards a new direction in Wells' thinking with some resolution of his doubts about whether such subterranean cities could represent an admirable social order.[30]

Wells now believed that if technology could be properly controlled and guided, the city would be transformed into a viable future city-state. In this transition, Wells now began to reconsider Gissing's portrayal of a social abyss because it seemed to offer no solution to contemporary urban problems. As a close friend of Gissing, Wells acknowledged his views in *Anticipations* during a discussion of the modern city. According to Wells, Gissing had named: 'nineteenth-century London in one of his great novels *The "Whirlpool"*, the

---

26   R. Luckhurst, *Science Fiction* (Cambridge: Polity, 2005), p. 5.

27   Wells, *First Men in the Moon*, p. 133.

28   Wells, *First Men in the Moon*, p. 153.

29   Wells, *First Men in the Moon*, p. 147.

30   See J. Huntington, *The Logic of Fantasy: H. G. Wells & Science Fiction* (New York: Columbia University Press, 1982), pp. 87–97.

very figure for the nineteenth-century Great City, attractive, tumultuous, and spinning down to death'.[31] If Gissing's London continued to develop along these existing Victorian lines it seemed clear to Wells that class divisions would harden inexorably into the biologically divided society of 'The Time Machine'. Gissing's working class had been incarcerated in geographical enclaves by the railways, canals and roads of late Victorian London but Wells' proletariat is trapped in an evolutionary dead-end which condemns them to a biological future as cave-dwellers. Wells' pinpointing of the whirlpool or vortex as a metaphor suggests that he was acutely aware of this possibility. In 'The Time Machine' the Traveller asks, rhetorically, 'Even now, does not the Eastend worker live in such artificial conditions as practically to be cut off from the natural surface of the earth?'[32] Wells feared not so much that these divisions would occur biologically but that they would, in fact, place the working class (Morlocks) in a position of dominance over the educated middle and upper classes (Eloi) as the Morlocks have power—both technological and political. As Rosalind Williams correctly notes, Wells, like many intellectuals of this period, was using biological language to express political convictions, a 'general concern about human nature [...] was in fact a specific fear of particular groups—a race, a nation, a gender, a class'.[33]

Wells wanted to save the city. To achieve this he turned to the idea of a social and political elite of guardians who would use authoritarian control, if required, to enforce a new city-state and harness new technology in a rational and planned way. *The War of the Worlds* was designed to show how such a new society might emerge in Britain as a result of a catastrophic external threat. London would grow from the ruins of the Martian invasion as a new city, one unknown to 'those who have only seen London veiled in her sombre robes of smoke' but now with a 'naked clearness and beauty of the silent wilderness of houses'.[34] In this novel, the Martian invaders create enormous colonial bases on Earth in which they can prepare their campaign of terror against London's unsuspecting population. They converge on London, bringing alarm 'to the clients of the underground railway [...] the Sunday excursionists'.[35] Showing how crucial the railway system was to him, Wells highlights its role in the collapse of the social order as a result of the Martian attack: 'by mid-day even

---

31   Wells, *Anticipations*, p. 44.

32   Wells, 'The Time Machine', p. 47.

33   Williams, *Notes on the Underground*, p. 126.

34   H. G. Wells, *The War of the Worlds* (1898; New York: Tor Books, 1988), p. 188.

35   Wells, *War of the Worlds*, p. 83.

the railway organizations were losing coherency, losing shape and efficiency, that swift liquefaction of the social body'.[36]

London's commuters quickly panic in a 'roaring wave of fear that swept through the greatest city in the world'.[37] At Chalk Farm station in north London the 'engines of the trains that had loaded in the goods yard there ploughed through shrieking people'[38] whilst the authorities are militarily weak in relation to the Martians' heat rays, a much superior use of advanced technology. But for Wells the collapse of the social order presages the stirrings of a new and better world created by an elite. This must be started by finding concealment beneath the ground, as the authoritarian artilleryman who is hiding from the Martians outlines: 'You see, how I mean to live is underground. I've been thinking about the drains. Then there's cellars, vaults, stores [...] And the railway tunnels and subways'.[39] The artilleryman describes a complete strategy for survival until the Martians can be overthrown, a strategy with no place in it for 'lackadaisical ladies'[40] or the commuters who 'skedaddle off to work [...] running wild and shining to catch their little season ticket train'.[41] In this instance, Wells seems interested in diverting the biological destiny of 'The Time Machine' towards an underground city-state, converting the 'miles and miles—hundreds of miles'[42] of drains beneath London into a temporary refuge. Wells' narrator appears to reject this strategy largely on the grounds of impracticability since the scale of the task seems beyond the capacity of scattered individuals.

Wells' fictional destruction of London's population is precipitated by an external invasion and colonization from Mars. Other contemporary writers used miasmic imagery to describe the destruction of London. William Delisle Hay's *Doom of a Great City* (1880) concerns the effects of a poisonous fog that has come from the impoverished classes of the East End, and Richard Jefferies' novel of ecological Armageddon, *After London* (1885), surveys the 'utterly extinct city of London'[43] after flood waters have overwhelmed the capital. Unlike Wells, Jefferies wanted the complete destruction of London and it appears that the city has brought about its own demise through a moral decline. He connects

---

36   Wells, *War of the Worlds*, p. 100.
37   Wells, *War of the Worlds*, p. 100.
38   Wells, *War of the Worlds*, p. 100.
39   Wells, *War of the Worlds*, p. 174.
40   Wells, *War of the Worlds*, p. 173.
41   Wells, *War of the Worlds*, p. 172.
42   Wells, *War of the Worlds*, p. 174.
43   R. Jefferies, *After London or Wild England* (1885; Oxford: Oxford University Press, 1980), p. 206.

this process of urban moral degeneracy with that of tunnelling beneath the surface. The flood waters that overwhelm the city 'began to overflow up into the deserted streets, and especially to fill the underground passages and drains' and 'the ancient city had been undermined with vast conduits, sewers and tunnels'.[44] Contemporary London has undermined itself leaving only mythical tales of its former grandeur in the period in history of the novel's hero, Felix Aquila. He hears that there were 'places where the earth was on fire and belched forth sulphurous fumes, supposed to be the combination of the enormous stores of strange and unknown chemicals collected by the wonderful people of those times'.[45] London has been destroyed by the forces of nature which overwhelm the artificial, chemically constructed life of the city; the steam and electrical Victorian technology of the city is counterposed to the pastoral world. As the underground railway tunnels cannot be sealed off from flooding, they therefore contribute to the rapid inundation of the city. Jefferies also drew attention to the wilderness that seemed to lie beyond the power of modern technology when London is overwhelmed by snow in the short stories 'Snowed Up' and 'The Great Snow'.[46] His concept of the capital is hardly more hopeful than Gissing's desolate urban merry-go-round, particularly in his comments on the underground railway itself: 'What a sermon on this is to be found in the carriages of the Metropolitan and District Railway which run deep under houses. At the stations people are shot about—and quick in the current—are lost. They rush on—with no attention'.[47]

All individuality has been lost in this underworld, leaving commuters at the mercy of the rush-hour tide as it floods through the system. Again, in the short story 'A Wet Night in London' (1885) Jefferies likened human beings to 'mere hurrying machines [...] to the condition of the wooden cabs [...] pulled along by the irresistible horse Circumstance'.[48] His response to London was influenced by his identification with a class of small working farmers, manual workers who feared the power of the city and industrial capitalism. He welcomed the downfall of civilization in order to bring an end to a 'machinery

---

44 Jefferies, *After London*, pp. 36 & 214.

45 Jefferies, *After London*, p. 206.

46 Jefferies drew particular attention to the *Princess Alice* steamboat disaster on the Thames in 1878. See R. Jefferies, *The Story of My Heart* (1883; London: Macmillan, 1968), p. 103.

47 R. Jefferies, quoted in J. Maynard, 'A Marxist Reading of "Snowed Up"', in J. Wolfreys & W. Baker (eds.), *Literary Theories: A Case Study in Critical Performance* (London: Macmillan, 1996), pp. 129–56, p. 149.

48 R. Jefferies, 'A Wet Night in London' (1885), in C. H. Warren (ed.), *The Open Air* (London: Eyre and Spottiswoode, 1948), p. 196.

for extortion' and Felix Aquila in *After London* stands alone against the world of bourgeois society, a sentiment to be found in a letter of William Morris in which he declared 'I *know* now [civilization] is doomed to destruction, and probably before very long; what a joy it is to think of!'[49]

Alexandra Warwick has commented on the Gothic tradition which drew extensively on the historical relevance of the decline of Rome to imperial London and Wells, she argues, foregrounded notions of infection and invasion of the civic body in *The War of the Worlds*. The capital is 'a living body from which the life is sucked' by the Martians,[50] it is a city that seems to be dead even after the defeat of the invaders. The threat to Wells' London comes from outside through the imperialist attack on earth by the Martians, organic creatures who build mechanical carapaces in their factories and use heat rays to defeat human beings. The lesson seems to be that humans as similarly organic creatures need to 'arm' themselves with better technology, town planning and leadership if 'civilization' is to survive. By contrast, Jefferies appears to believe that this civilization will inevitably generate its own nemesis from within and that 'wilderness' is the necessary step towards redemption. This tradition can be traced back to John Ruskin who in 1865 had lamented the way in which 'every creature is only one atom in a drift of human dust, and current of inter-changing particles circulating, here by tunnels underground, and there by tubes in the air'.[51]

Other contemporary short stories illustrate this trend such as 'London's Danger' (1898) by C. J. Cutcliffe Hyne, where the capital is engulfed by a blizzard followed by a massive fire. There is no safe haven, even at King's Cross station where 'the place seemed deserted. Half the roof was off'[52] and from the 'great shelter of Charing Cross Station there came a stream of shrieks which made us shudder'.[53] Paralysed by riot, starvation, death and disorder, the empire collapses leaving 'a nation with a glorious history but no future'.[54] Three

---

49   W. Morris, 13 May 1885, in *The Collected Letters of William Morris*, ed. N. Kelvin, 4 vols. (Princeton: Princeton University Press, 1987), vol. 2, part B, p. 436.

50   A. Warwick, 'Lost Cities: London's Apocalypse', in G. Byron & D. Punter (eds.), *Spectral Readings: Towards a Gothic Geography* (Basingstoke: Palgrave Macmillan, 1999), pp. 73–87, p. 78.

51   J. Ruskin, 'The Study of Architecture in Our Schools' (1865), in *The Works of John Ruskin*, eds. E. T. Cook & A. Wedderburn, 39 vols., vol. 19 (London: George Allen, 1905), pp. 19–46, p. 24.

52   C. J. Cutcliffe Hyne, 'London's Danger' (1898), in A. K. Russell (ed.), *Science Fiction by the Rivals of H. G. Wells* (Secaucus, NJ: Castle Books, 1979), pp. 341–48, p. 342.

53   Cutcliffe Hyne, 'London's Danger', p. 347.

54   Cutcliffe Hyne, 'London's Danger', p. 348.

stories by Fred M. White pictured the destruction of London by dramatic climate change or technological failure. In 'The Four White Days' (1903) London is in the 'Grip of an Arctic Winter'[55] when a snowstorm destroys all services including main-line trains, rendering 'Deep cuttings and tunnels [...] impassable by drifted snow'.[56] There is 'practically no motive power beyond that of the underground railways'[57] and no fuel for the population. The main-line stations where coal is stored become the targets for looters and martial law is about to be declared when the story ends with a miraculous thaw. In White's story 'The Four Days' Night' (1903) London succumbs to a vast oil-based fire which generates a huge black 'grotesque mushroom' cloud that settles over the capital. It becomes 'A city of the blind! Six millions of people suddenly deprived of sight!'[58] The fog is eventually dispersed by an explosive charge dropped from an airship. And in 'The Invisible Force' (1903) White turned to the new tubes as the source of disaster—an earthquake appears to hit the capital caused by 'an accident in the tubes; and they have been blown all to pieces'. It is revealed that 'the steel core [...] lay bare with rugged holes ripped in it'[59] and the tube has been ejected from the ground like a giant earthworm. Entering the system at 'Park Road Station', search teams discover some survivors of what is the first tube disaster in fiction. The horror of the accident is conveyed by an eyewitness: 'We got on just as usual for the first ten minutes or so, the train running smoothly and plenty of light. Then all at once we came to a sudden stop that sent us flying across the carriage [...] You could hear the wind go roaring past the carriages, and then it stopped as soon as it had begun'.[60] He reports that 'many were killed [...] but the others are sitting in the carriages waiting for the end to come'.[61] White's purpose seems to have been, like Wells, to warn readers of the dangers of unregulated technology. The tube is destroyed by an 'invisible force' and the most sanguine comment comes after the disaster: 'in the long run we shall benefit by the calamity, great communities do [...] Come,

55   F. M. White, 'The Four White Days' (1903), in Russell, *Science Fiction by the Rivals of H. G. Wells*, pp. 457–68, p. 457.

56   White, 'Four White Days' , p. 458.

57   White, 'Four White Days', p. 459.

58   F. M. White, 'The Four Days' Night' (1903), in Russell, *Science Fiction by the Rivals of H. G. Wells*, pp. 441–53, pp. 442–44.

59   F. M. White, 'The Invisible Force' (1903), in Russell, *Science Fiction by the Rivals of H. G. Wells*, pp. 483–94, pp. 487–88.

60   White, 'Invisible Force', p. 494.

61   White, 'Invisible Force', p. 493. White confusingly refers to the dead bodies of an 'engine-driver' and a 'stoker' as though referring to a steam train followed by a reference to the more authentic electric cables.

let us get to work and try to forget'.[62] Such stories illustrate how powerfully the notion of London's vulnerability had taken root in these years.

Wells did try to find a solution to this question of moral and social imbalance in the metropolis. When creating a world of perfect harmony in the short story 'The Door in the Wall' (1905), he used the Gissingesque image of porosity between surface and subterranean levels. As Martin Tropp notes, doors had been used by R. L. Stevenson in *The Strange Case of Dr Jekyll and Mr Hyde* (1886) to 'connect two dissimilar but proximate realms', and Wells had already used the device of entering another world in his short story 'Mr Skelmersdale in Fairyland' (1903) suggesting that an improvement in well-being and happiness could ensue from a change of environments.[63] In the 'Door in the Wall', Lionel Wallace, an immensely rich and successful MP, decides to make a final break with his career by going through 'a real door, leading through a real wall to immortal realities'.[64] In other words, Wallace believes there is a perfect world that can be entered through a door in a Kensington street. He first encounters the door as a child: 'the white wall and the green door stood quite distinctly'[65] and he enters an enchanted Edenic garden. At the climax of the story, Wallace actually attempts to pass through this portal to enter 'an altogether more beautiful world'[66] but instead falls to his death in a 'deep excavation near east Kensington station [...] one of the two shafts that have been made in connection with an extension of the railway southward'.[67] The narrator speculates on the perceptual causes of his mistake: 'did the pale electric lights near the station cheat the rough planking into a semblance of white? Did that fatal unfastened door awaken some memory?'[68] A number of threads from Wells' early fiction come together here. The use of a shaft to an underground line echoes the shaft down which the Time Traveller journeys towards the Morlock underworld but in this case it is a real underground line in the real city of London. Wells uses the door as the portal between two worlds similar to how Gissing uses the railway arch in his fiction. He retains the mystery of this doorway by leaving the reader guessing whether the underground is actually a magic realm when his narrator reflects in the closing lines: 'We see our world fair and common, the

---

62 White, 'Invisible Force', p. 494.

63 M. Tropp, *Images of Fear: How Horror Stories Helped Shape Modern Culture, 1818–1918* (Jefferson, NC: McFarland & Co., 1990), p. 107.

64 H. G. Wells, 'The Door in the Wall' (1906), in *Selected Short Stories*, pp. 106–22, p. 108.

65 Wells, 'Door in the Wall', p. 108.

66 Wells, 'Door in the Wall', p. 122.

67 Wells, 'Door in the Wall', p. 121.

68 Wells, 'Door in the Wall', p. 121.

hoarding and the pit. By our daylight standards he walked out of security into darkness, danger and death. But did he see it like that?'[69] Wells may have been thinking of the false frontages that were built in Leinster Gardens in Bayswater to disguise the passage of the underground beneath houses in the 1860s.

Wells' Gothic tendencies were reinforced by the popularity of the Gothic horror genre in late Victorian England with such tales offering an even more literal version of Wells' engagement with the underworld. In *The Three Impostors* (1885), for example, Arthur Machen describes an infernal world just below the streets of London that threatens to engulf urban life: 'a street of grey houses and blank walls […] a veil seems drawn aside, and the very fume of the pit steams up through the flagstones, the ground glows, red-hot, beneath his feet, and he seems to hear the hiss of the infernal cauldron'.[70] This image of the London street erupting in a sea of infernal lava must have sent a thrill rather than a chill down the spine of every Victorian reader. The infernal demon which in Gissing's fiction had typically been a snorting steam locomotive, was now an image in transition to the deeper underground. In fact, victory over the infernal steam locomotive remained an important priority despite the coming of the electric tube. For *Punch*, this heralded a new era in underground travel and it pounded the demonic steam train in a series of cartoons featuring monstrous and malevolent steam trains. In one cartoon the figure of Electra serves 'Notice to Quit' on the Steam Locomotive Underground Demon soon after the opening of the London Electric Railway (Central line) in 1900 with the words: 'Now they've seen *me*, I fancy your days are numbered'.[71] Machen's visitor in *The Three Impostors* is carried by steam railways from the west country into Paddington station through an urban landscape tainted by the 'sickly fume of brickfields about Acton' and 'neglected backyards […] near Paddington'.[72] Machen found London an irredeemably artificial and alien place that was undermining itself in an inexorable process of decay. Even Wells subscribed to this view at times, for instance in *The New Machiavelli* (1911) when he describes the 'crust' on the surface of society, a crust of custom overlaying the ferment at the heart of human activity like the 'hot new lava' at Vesuvius.[73]

The fiction of Machen and his contemporaries suggested that the underground railway was one of the forces that could be held responsible for undermining the Victorian city in moral as well as physical terms. Fears voiced

---

69   Wells, 'Door in the Wall', p. 122.
70   A. Machen, *The Three Impostors* (1895; London: Everyman, 1995), p. 13.
71   'Notice to Quit', *Punch*, 4 July 1900, vol. 118, p. 5.
72   Machen, *The Three Impostors*, p. 19.
73   H. G. Wells, *The New Machiavelli* (1911; London: Penguin, 2005), p. 412.

in the 1850s about the construction of an underground railway were therefore revived in the context of a debate pioneered by Max Nordau in his seminal work *Degeneration* (1895). The city was a place of frenetic activity that separated its population from the natural world, a separation between urban and pastoral exacerbated by suburban railway growth. Railways were identified as a cultural threat to society in a manner reminiscent of Ruskin's polemics in which he had denounced 'the mere trampling pressure and electric friction of town life' in the 1880s.[74] Nordau connected railways with both individual and national decline, declaring in *Degeneration* that the late-twentieth-century generation might adapt to 'live half their time in railway carriages or in a flying machine' or 'allow railways to disappear' altogether. He also remarked on the terms 'railway-spine and 'railway-brain' caused by railway accidents and the 'constant vibrations undergone in railway travelling'.[75] A decade earlier, James Cantlie in his essay 'Degeneration Amongst Londoners' (1885) suggested that the 'degeneration' of urban dwellers was due to 'urbo-morbus' or city disease. He asked rhetorically: 'Are we not at the end of the generation who lived before steam, manufactories, large cities, and all the modern developments which have made our air impure'?[76] Cantlie voiced the contemporary condemnation of urban social divisions that would find its way into Wells' vision of a determinist future in 'The Time Machine' when he noted how 'we have two classes living exactly opposite lives, one condemned to labour incessantly indoors, the other called upon to do no manual labour'.[77] Many contemporary stories dramatized these degenerationist fears describing either the dangers of human regression to savagery or fears of progress—the evolutionary outcome of 'over-civilization' driven by urban modernity. Patrick Brantlinger describes the stories of Machen, Jefferies and Bram Stoker as 'imperial Gothic' and it is clear that the genre fed into Victorian science fiction through Wells' *The War of the Worlds*.[78]

Never slow to exploit the opportunity offered by frenetic urban lifestyles, the media played on the disorders apparently induced by urban transit. A contemporary advert for a medicine called Purgen was illustrated with images

74   J. Ruskin, 'Fiction, Fair and Foul' (1880), in *The Genius of John Ruskin: Selections from His Writings*, ed. J. D. Rosenberg (London: Routledge, 1963), pp. 435–44, p. 438.

75   M. Nordau, *Degeneration* (1895; London: University of Nebraska Press, 1968), pp. 541–42 & p. 41.

76   J. Cantlie, 'Degeneration Amongst Londoners' (1885), in L. Hollen Lees & A. Lees (eds.), *The Rise of Urban Britain* (New York: Garland, 1985), pp. 7–61, p. 30.

77   Cantlie, 'Degeneration', p. 40.

78   See P. Brantlinger, *Rule of Darkness: British Literature and Imperialism, 1830–1914* (London: Cornell University Press, 1988), pp. 227–53.

of a crowded tube train and a bus to depict the stresses and strains of modern urban life. It declared that 'Business Men on the way to the City often feel out of sorts, owing to hasty meals and lack of outdoor exercise'.[79] Pierre de Coulevain, in his travel book *The Unknown Isle* (1906), was struck by 'the expression of utter weariness on [City men's] faces. Some of them looked as though they could scarcely turn the pages of their newspapers'.[80] He also noted the ever-present advertisement posters that he claimed had left 'a brutal impression on the brain'.[81] Ford Madox Ford, in his comments in *The Soul of London* (1905), made similar assumptions about the railways, comparing them with the natural and ancient highway of the River Thames. Ford argued that London's railways were unnatural, 'a kind of underworld' and invoked an image of degeneration, saying that the metropolis was built on 'sliding sands' and was threatened by 'those black and sulphurous clouds, Neurasthenia, Decay, and the waters of the Earth'.[82] Ford jumped backwards and forwards from organic to mechanical images to describe the city, concluding that the back streets of London were 'like the cells in an electric battery'.[83]

Like these writers, Wells tried to overcome the contradictions between the vision of an ideal organic society and the rapid technological developments of the period. However, his 1899 novel *When the Sleeper Wakes* (revised as *The Sleeper Awakes* in 1910) represents a significant step towards a fully utopian fictional vision. It introduces a multilevel world reached by 'underways' which are strongly reminiscent of the tunnels in 'The Time Machine' but this narrative, by contrast, opens up a comprehensive vision of a city-state. This is not a bipartite world but a multi-tier London with an endless series of gradations between the glass dome that encloses it and the underground factories of the community's Labour Company. Graham, the hero of the novel, finds himself in a place of 'overwhelming architecture [...] Titanic buildings, curving spaciously in either direction'.[84] Every form of locomotion is available in this city—from

---

79 Author's collection.

80 P. de Coulevain, *The Unknown Isle* (French edition 1906, trans. 1911), in J. Coulter (ed.), *London of One Hundred Years Ago* (Stroud: Sutton, 1999), pp. 97–98.

81 Coulevain, *The Unknown Isle*, p. 98.

82 F. M. Ford, *The Soul of London* (1905; London: Everyman, 1995), pp. 40–41.

83 Ford, *The Soul of London*, p. 42. Wells had prefigured such a world in 'A Story of the Days to Come' (1899) in which London of the twenty-second century is composed of many storeys with the prosperous inhabitants living in the upper tiers and the industrial workers in lower tiers or 'underways'. Workers travel on 'moving platforms' at 50 miles per hour and its male hero Denton descends through the various social strata of London to work in the Labour Company 'Tile Trust'.

84 H. G. Wells, *The Sleeper Awakes* (1899; London: Sphere, 1976), p. 36.

microlights to high-speed tube trains linked by a series of 'moving ways' or suspended travelators. He refers to 'endless platforms of narrow transverse overlapping slats with little interspaces'[85] that permitted the trains to follow the contours of the streets. In this 'quasi-subterranean labyrinth', Graham notes the 'strange traffic of narrow, rubber-shod vehicles, great single wheels, two and four wheeled vehicles, sweeping along at velocities of from one to six miles a minute'.[86] Amidst this riot of public transportation, Graham emerges onto 'the roof of the vast city structure which had replaced the miscellaneous houses, streets and open spaces of Victorian London'[87] and later notes that 'man had entered upon a new stage of his development'.[88] Wells inserts Graham's observation of 'a few embankments remained as rust-crowned trenches here and there', the remains of the obsolete Victorian railway system.[89] This was a world that he would reproduce in non-fiction only three years later in *Anticipations*.

When *The Sleeper Wakes* achieved the first fictional portrayal of the utopian city in which public transportation was given a central role in structuring the environment. The underground railway is no longer literally under the ground as the concept of the subterranean has ceased to have its normal meaning. For Wells, the utopian city exists in a state of independence from terra firma with a mass transit system providing the axes around which the life of the city orbits. This is truly *transit* architecture that could only be sketched in the new architectural movements of the twentieth century, such as Tony Garnier's plans for an Industrial City (1904) which featured a linear urban environment with a cantilevered railway station, later partially realized in the film *Metropolis* (1927).[90] However, the rather more grim reality of the social abyss does intrude into the utopian world of London as Graham is thrown into the power politics of the city and finds that it has not kept pace with technological progress. He descends by lift into 'great and dusty galleries' populated by the workers of the Labour Company and the imagery of 'The Time Machine' recurs with 'shrouded isles

85 Wells, *The Sleeper Awakes*, p. 37.
86 Wells, *The Sleeper Awakes*, p. 112.
87 Wells, *The Sleeper Awakes*, p. 61.
88 Wells, *The Sleeper Awakes*, p. 113.
89 Wells, *The Sleeper Awakes*, p. 112.
90 Wells panned the film *Metropolis* (1926) in a review he wrote for the *New York Times Magazine* (17 April 1927). He said that its conception of the future was outdated even though it owed much of its futurology to *When the Sleeper Awakes*. Wells now adopted a more positive view of technology, arguing that it brought liberation rather than enslavement. See 'Mr. Wells Reviews a Current Film', in M. Minden & H. Bachmann (eds.), *Fritz Lang's Metropolis: Cinematic Visions of Technology and Fear* (Rochester, NY: Camden House, 2000), pp. 94–100.

of giant machines [...] ill-lit subterranean aisles of sleeping places, illimitable vistas of pin-point lights'.[91]

Such images suggest that Wells was not portraying any kind of socialist utopia in this novel. At one point, Graham reflects on the work of the American author Edward Bellamy, whose book *Looking Backward* (1888) had provoked strong opinions a decade earlier: 'Bellamy, the hero of whose Socialistic Utopia had so oddly anticipated the actual experience but there was no utopia, no socialistic state'.[92] Wells is saying that his utopia is more technocratic than socialist, particularly in the light of his subsequent remarks in the 1921 edition when he described *When the Sleeper Wakes* as no more than a grim picture of 'capitalism triumphant'.[93] Nevertheless, E. M. Forster judged *When the Sleeper Wakes* to be part of Wells' utopian output, claiming that his own dystopian short story 'The Machine Stops' (1909) was written as 'a reaction to one of the earlier heavens of H. G. Wells'.[94] In Forster's story, a nebulous 'Machine' controls all aspects of a perfect future society which is located 'deep beneath the surface of the earth'. Kuno, the main character, is a social misfit who is driven to explore the surface beyond the control of the Machine because travel, originally facilitated by railways, has been largely eliminated as science has made the earth the same all over. One day, Kuno ascends towards the surface until he reaches the 'railway tunnels of the topmost storey'.[95] The tunnels and platforms of this tube railway are illuminated, and have 'live' rails just like the London tubes; here 'everything is light, artificial light'.[96] As Kuno explores these tunnels he is suddenly confronted with a swiftly passing train and he pulls himself back towards a 'black gap in the tiles' as 'a train passed. It brushed by me; but I thrust my head and arms into the hole. I had done enough for one day, so I crawled back to the platform, went down in the lift, and summoned my bed'.[97]

The experience with the tube train cleverly brings together the contemporary London tube lines of Forster's time with the parody of Wells' utopian city. In 'The Machine Stops', the tube train passes Kuno in an image reminiscent of the express train that thunders beneath Gissing's characters Jasper Milvain and Amy Reardon in *New Grub Street*. In Forster's story, however, the train is

---

91 Wells, *The Sleeper Awakes*, p. 173.

92 Wells, *The Sleeper Awakes*, p. 51.

93 Wells, *The Sleeper Awakes*, p. 8.

94 E. M. Forster, 'Introduction', in *Collected Short Stories* (Harmondsworth: Penguin, 1954), pp. 5–7, p. 6.

95 E. M. Forster, 'The Machine Stops', in *Collected Short Stories*, pp. 109–46, p. 126.

96 Forster, 'The Machine Stops', pp. 126.

97 Forster, 'The Machine Stops', pp. 125–26.

not a harbinger of progress. The controlling mind of the Machine directs the tubes according to their mechanized timetable, suggesting contemporary fears of machine-based societies that also appeared in Forster's novel *Howard's End* (1910). Forster's story also contrasts the artificial world of the Machine with the organic or natural world that survives above ground, a pastoral vision of a place that remains inhabited. At the end of the story, 'scraps of the untainted sky' are glimpsed by Kuno and the other doomed inhabitants as the city is broken 'like a honeycomb' when the Machine fails.[98] For Forster, the electric tube has become the real symbol of an invasion of the pastoral world—the decisive moment in history (located geologically) when humans have ceded agency to the machines allowing the city-state to develop in an unfettered way through suburbanization. A detached form of human agency has been able to emerge. As they shared the generic sense of the tube system as the classic stage of urban development, both Wells and Forster therefore helped to turn fictional perspectives in this direction, albeit in different ways. Writers in the 1920s and 1930s went on to react either for or against technological solutions along lines broadly laid out by them before the First World War.

Around 1902, Wells was making a final transition to a utopian underground writing and beginning to flesh out his plans for a decisive break with the Victorian past. In the opening chapter of *Anticipations*, Wells announced himself as the key protagonist in a popular campaign to overturn the old ways and bring about a modern form of urban life. He rejected fiction as the means of achieving this goal because it was 'necessarily concrete and definite; it permits of no open alternatives'.[99] Wells has been described as the 'magus of a mechanistic age' by I. F. Clarke as he was broadly in tune with a more optimistic attitude to social change around 1900.[100] 'Despite the misgivings', Roslynn Haynes writes, 'the beginning of the 20th century was characterized by a wave of optimism [...] a renewed belief in progress that mushroomed with the material triumphs of technology'.[101] This triumphant technology of the future was reflected in Wells' writings. It was built on electricity, the new motive force for the tubular railways in London and Paris, and the overhead railways, trams and subways in the United States. This revolution in transit hit the United States and Europe in the pre-war decades, the key reason for which was probably that 'it proved

98   Forster, 'The Machine Stops', p. 146.
99   Wells, *Anticipations*, p. 2.
100 I. F. Clarke, *The Pattern of Expectation, 1644–2001* (London: Jonathan Cape, 1979), p. 213.
101 R. Haynes, *From Faust to Strangelove: Representations of the Scientist in Western Literature* (Baltimore: Johns Hopkins University Press, 1994), p. 162.

extremely profitable for the operators'.[102] Electric power was invested with a dynamic, unlimited and mythical power at this time, convincing a number of thinkers that an era of 'neo-technics' had dawned which would speedily replace the old steam and labour-driven 'paleo-technic' world. Electric power was popular—it appeared in a rash of books like *The Romance of Modern Electricity* (1908) and was celebrated in Wells' novel *Tono-Bungay* (1912). Teddy Ponderevo, the hero of the story, says ''Lectricity' is the only feasible way to 'run the country [...] Make it a Scientific-Organised-Business-Enterprise. Put ideas into it. 'Lectrify it'.[103] In *The World Set Free* Wells asked 'could anything be more emphatic than the appeal of electricity for attention?'[104] Paul Meuriot's 1898 book *Des Agglomerations urbaines dans l'Europe contemporaine* offered electric power as one of the keys to future social and economic development. Meuriot stressed that the combination of better transit and electric power would make it:

> possible to reduce the excessive population of the towns [and] keep the industrial worker in his home and do away with those concentrations of men that the modern factory system makes necessary [...] In a word, one scientific revolution caused the extreme development of the urban economy, and in the same way another scientific revolution will produce the remedy for these evils of excessive growth.[105]

Other thinkers from a variety of political traditions such as the anarchist Peter Kropotkin and the socialist Graham Wallas argued that electrical technology could rescue civilization from industrialism (although Wallas later changed his mind).[106] The theme was picked up by Patrick Geddes writing on behalf of the Garden City Movement who stated that 'the smoke fiend is well within bounds in Garden City' where 'all machinery is driven by electric energy'.[107] Geddes was an important figure in this movement and, according to Carey and Quirk, 'the first to offer a full-scale utopia systematically within a theory of electrical technology'.[108] Urban transport was one of the key fields

---

102 R. Bessel, 'Transport', in C. Chant (ed.), *Science, Technology and Everyday Life, 1870–1950* (London: Routledge, 1989), pp. 162–99, p. 168. See also J. P. McKay, *Tramways and Trolleys: The Rise of Urban Mass Transport in Europe* (Princeton: Princeton University Press, 1976).

103 H. G. Wells, *Tono-Bungay* (1909; Harmondsworth: Penguin, 1946), pp. 88 & 252.

104 H. G. Wells, *The World Set Free* (1914; London: Hogarth Press, 1988), pp. 15–16.

105 P. Meuriot, *Des Agglomerations urbaines dans l'Europe contemporaine* (1898), quoted in Clarke, *Pattern of Expectation*, p. 173.

106 Kropotkin lived in Harrow, Ealing and Bromley after his exile from Russia in 1876. Wallas was a member of the Fabian Society from 1886 to 1904.

107 P. Geddes, quoted in J. W. Carey & J. J. Quirk, 'The Mythos of the Electronic Revolution', *The American Scholar*, 39, no. 2, Spring 1970, pp. 219–41, p. 230.

108 Carey & Quirk, 'Mythos of the Electronic Revolution, p. 232.

where electric power was already prominent by 1900. The advent of electrically powered trains on the new tubular railways in London represented an important breakthrough for the advocates of this utopian future, with electric companies in the capital supplying power to large installations for lighting as early as 1875. The advance of electric power in London was given a boost by the 1888 Electric Lighting Act and by 1890 there were ten electricity suppliers in the city. The Electric Generator and Light Company was installing electric lighting on Metropolitan stations such as Aldersgate (Barbican) in the 1880s followed by electric lifts in the next decade, and two new power stations were built at Chelsea and Neasden between 1906 and 1916 exclusively to supply the needs of the underground network.

The first tubular line to be built in London was the City and South London Railway in 1890. It pioneered electric traction with each train consisting of a small, squat electric locomotive hauling three cars of only 32 seats each and internal electric lighting. *The Times* was as much of a cheerleader as it had been after the opening of the original underground. It described the arrival of the tube as 'an epoch in the development of the internal communications of London which may, perhaps, hereafter prove to have been even more important than the opening of the Metropolitan Railway in 1863'.[109] *Punch* summed up the new mythos of electric power with a cartoon entitled 'The Young Spark and the Old Flame' and verse which poured scorn on the old steam world:

> His murky monopoly, Madam is ended.
> Come down, my dear love, to my subterrene hall! …
> Electrical traction with sheer stupefaction
> Strikes Steam, the old buffer, and spoils his small game
> You're off with the old love, so try the new bold love,
> And let the Young Spark supersede the Old Flame.[110]

The opening of the City and South London Railway was a watershed in the history of London's transit system and also of underground writing. The original stretch of line between King William Street in the City, south of the river to Stockwell was soon extended to Euston and southwards to Clapham Common. However, reports of its early days were far from positive: stations were described as dull and poorly lit, carriage lighting was inadequate and passengers found their journeys uncomfortable, noisy and rough, giving carriages the nickname 'padded cells'. The small oblong windows of frosted

---

109 *The Times*, 4 November 1890.
110 *Punch*, vol. 94, 15 November 1890, pp. 230–31.

glass prevented passengers from identifying stations and the names had to be called out by guards. A number of accidents occurred in the early years, leading one historian to conclude that 'regulations were frequently broken to keep an incredibly intense service operating, controlled by an inadequate mechanical signalling system'.[111]

Wells used the new tube as the key thread in his 1894 short story 'The Lord of the Dynamos', located in a shed at Camberwell housing the three dynamos that 'kept the electric railway going'. In the story, the 'Lord' of the title is the biggest of the three dynamos: 'How great it was! How serene and easy its working! [...] The great black coils spun, spun, spun, the rings ran round the bushes and the deep note of its coil steadied the whole'.[112] The dynamo is invested with the organic power of a massive snake coiling around the machinery. The real generator was actually located at Stockwell, and Wells had paid a visit to it with all the enthusiasm of a scientist interested in the potential of electricity to provide the motive power for underground transit in the capital. The Stockwell generating station certainly had an impressive interior with four massive engines that entirely filled the gigantic brick and steel shed.

Henry Adams, in his essay 'The Dynamo and the Virgin' (1900), had described the dynamo which he found at the Paris Great Exposition of 1900 as 'a symbol of infinity' despite its reliance on 'a dirty engine-house carefully kept out of sight' that housed the coal supply. Adams was deeply impressed by the 'huge wheel, revolving within arm's length at some vertiginous speed, and barely murmuring'.[113] Wells was equally fascinated by the potential embodied in the dynamo and in his story it is presented as a new god of technology. His chauvinistic and materialist manager, Holroyd, believes in capitalism's infinite power to command the earth and demand obedience: 'Kill a hundred men. Twelve per cent on the ordinary shares [...] and that's something like a Gord'.[114] The other main character is an irrational spiritualist, Azuma-zi, who represents an uncorrupted but misguided notion about technology. These two play the roles of imperialist and colonized in a way similar to the description of the Martian invaders and humans in *The War of the Worlds* but also represent Wells' attempt to show two polar views of technology from which he can

---

111 P. P. Holman, *The Amazing Electric Tube: a history of the City and South London Railway* (London: London Transport Museum, 1990), p. 51.

112 H. G. Wells, 'The Lord of the Dynamos' (1894), in *Selected Short Stories*, pp. 185–92, p. 186.

113 H. Adams, 'The Dynamo and the Virgin' (1900), in *The Education of Henry Adams* (1918), ed. I. B. Nadel (Oxford: Oxford University Press, 1999), pp. 317–26, p. 318.

114 Wells, 'Lord of the Dynamos', p. 186.

draw a practical conclusion. In 'The Lord of the Dynamos' the power of the dynamos in the suburban Camberwell shed is separated from the novitiate tube travellers on the City and South London Railway. Here, Wells identified an important change from the steam underground as the motive power of the tubes is no longer generated from the train itself. The dynamo controls the fate of tube passengers and, by implication, the life of the city as the circulation of people can be prevented merely by the flick of a switch. Even the tracks themselves are now more dangerous to both staff and passengers in that an electric current has been added to the 'normal' danger of vehicular traffic. Azuma-zi underlines this change when he says 'The people of London hid their gods'.[115] At the climax to the story, determined to sacrifice Holroyd to the dynamo 'god', Azuma-zi pushes him into it and Holroyd is 'swallowed'. However, after Holroyd's murder, a new scientifically qualified manager, who seems to be an early representative of Wells' benevolent technocratic elite, comes to run the dynamos. After a botched attempt to kill the new manager, Azuma-zi commits suicide by jumping into the main dynamo himself. The story concludes as the new manager 'went towards the switch in the shadow and turned the current into the railway circuit again'.[116] The moral of the story is that the old ways of understanding technology need to be replaced with a modern guided utilitarianism which will set aside the 'cash nexus' of laissez-faire capitalism. Wells made the point clearer in the following year when the Martians appear with a more formidable technology of destruction than that perfected by the human species, suggesting that scientific rationality is the only means of human survival.

'The Lord of the Dynamos' embodies many of the contradictions in Wells' attitude to technology. The electric tube represented the attractive technology of the future located in the present towards which Wells was drawn by his scientific training and desire for a rationally planned society. On the other hand, the tube suggested a state of helplessness on the part of the individual commuter, 'trapped' in a metal 'sardine-box' as *Punch* dubbed it.[117] The dramatic and frightening power of this technology was underlined in Sigurd Frosterus's

---

115 Wells, 'Lord of the Dynamos', p. 187.
116 Wells, 'Lord of the Dynamos', p. 192
117 *Punch*, quoted in S. Halliday, *Underground to Everywhere* (Stroud: Sutton Publishing, 2001), p. 46. *Punch* continued to use the 'sardine' image to describe any kind of crowded railway carriage, for example in 1902, showing a crowded third-class carriage in 'A Bank Holiday Sketch' from which someone shouts: 'Change 'ere, 'ave we? Then kindly oblige me with a sardine-opener!' (*Punch*, vol. 122, January–June 1902, 21 May, p. 377).

'London Rhapsody' (1903) in which he recounted the impact of a tube train arriving in the platform of the City and South London Railway:

> A slow rumbling, an indeterminate reddish gleam that adds colour to the dark rat-hole, which gapes blackly in the black wall of the station. And the next moment there stops at the platform a strange, coiled monster with staring insect's eyes, behind which, like a brain, the train driver hides.[118]

The snake-like coils of the dynamo, the monstrous insect-like 'face' of the engine and the strange notion of a brain which controls its human driver all point to Wells' dystopian vision of the future. This tube train is like one of the Martian invaders in *The War of the Worlds* transplanted beneath the earth's surface and mixed with Wells' Morlocks. Inadvertently, Wells had conjured up a new demonic power in the Camberwell dynamo shed!

It is no wonder that Wells turned to fiction to explore the anxieties about the possible impact of new technology on society when it could show a dynamo as a modern god which demanded sacrificial victims from those responsible for its efficient running. Like the Machine in Forster's short story, the dynamo was already exerting a fearful power over its guardians and was literally regulating the lives of millions of commuters on the underground. In Gissing's novels, the steam underground had been dimly perceived as a circulatory force in the capital; in Wells' fiction, the underground is becoming a circulatory mechanism, a metal machine which governs the city. Whilst the revolution in electric urban transport only really hit London in the 1900s, Wells was obviously writing in a decade of visible change throughout Europe and the USA. In his *Experiment in Autobiography* (1934), Wells argued that new forms of electric transport opened up possibilities for progress, thus reading off the relationship between technology and human consciousness as a direct one. He believed that services like gas, electricity and transport could only be operated efficiently on a larger scale and that faster transit services were 'delocalizing' people, that is, they increasingly lived in one place, worked in another and had children at school in a third area. The 'delocalized' type of mind, Wells believed, was to be found in an uprooted group severed from traditional class positions in society, a kind of Fabian intellectual elite. Electric transport, alongside other innovations, was increasingly making it possible for this group to govern, with Wells saying that he was trying to 'modernise a world in which the modernized types were deprived of any influence'.[119] The rapid growth of electric tube and tram

---

118   Frosterus, 'London Rhapsody', quoted in Allen, *The Moving Pageant*, p. 209.
119   Wells, *Experiment in Autobiography*, vol. 1, p. 259.

services in the capital suggested massive opportunities for urban development to Wells who perceived transport as the 'wiring' in his future city-state.

Wells wrapped his mechanical vision in an organic metaphor, like a blood transfusion, and he recalled coughing up blood in a 'dingy compartment' of the District Railway.[120] This vampiric relationship between the old and the new appears in Wells' science fiction such as *The Island of Dr Moreau* (1896), *The War of the Worlds* and 'The Time Machine'. Wells' new scientific class of managers has to battle with the weight of old prejudices and myths and, like many of his science fiction characters, they successfully overcome the forces of social and cultural inertia in order to build the new world but in a much more pragmatic fashion. Steam railways, Wells said, had been a 'great stimulus to still further expansion'[121] of London but the Victorians had failed to think out a better and more efficient means of transportation than the railway system. Remington, the hero of *The New Machiavelli*, proclaims that:

> the Victorian epoch was not the dawn of a new era; it was a hasty, trial experiment, a gigantic experiment of the most slovenly and wasteful kind [...] The nineteenth century was an age of demonstrations [...] but will anyone, a hundred years from now, consent to live in the houses the Victorians built, travel by their roads or railways [...]?[122]

For Wells and many of his contemporaries, the old steam underground epitomized the 'slovenly' approach of the Victorians with both *The Times* and *Punch* remarking on the general improvement that would result from electrification of the underground. *Punch* noted gleefully, in the strap-line accompanying a 1901 cartoon about the Metropolitan Railway, that the 'good fairy Electra of the continuous current banishes the Demon King Sulphur' as the defeated demon sinks into the ground beneath a station platform.[123]

Wells wanted to use the existing steam underground as part of his programme for social reform, transforming the old system into a modern, clean and efficient form of transit in the capital. Writing in a positive climate for reform after 1900, he advocated views that commanded respect across a wide layer of Britain's intellectual and political class. Wells was inserting himself into the tradition of using public transport to effect social change. This reforming impulse had been revived in the later nineteenth century as a coalition of political forces including the veteran socialist John Burns and social reformer

---

120 Wells, *Experiment in Autobiography*, vol. 1, p. 367.
121 Wells, *Experiment in Autobiography*, vol. 1, p. 274.
122 Wells, *The New Machiavelli*, p. 41.
123 *Punch*, vol. 121, 18 December 1901, p. 449.

Charles Booth began to articulate the need for a more vigorous transport policy. Booth in particular argued for 'a large and really complete scheme of railways underground and overhead, as well as a net-work of tram lines on the surface; providing adequately for short as well as long journeys'.[124] Consensus was emerging on the need for rational reform in the capital that would be best guided by experts. Wells entered the debate with his 1903 lecture for the Fabian Society entitled 'Locomotion and Administration', a talk in which he outlined revolutionary changes in transport technology. He had published *Anticipations* in 1902, and in that polemic had laid down a blueprint for his reform programme, declaring that the old 'railway begotten great cities' would become 'urban regions' with likely populations over 20 million.[125] London had inflated and grown 'as a puff-ball swells' but transport technology and immigration had shattered its containing walls and 'the modern Great City looks like something that has burst an intolerable envelope and splashed'.[126] London, he went on, was no longer a Gissingesque 'whirlpool'[127] in that new social forces were producing a centrifugal rather than centripetal effect. This brought about the 'star-shaped contour of the modern Great City, thrusting out arms along every available railway line, knotted arms of which every knot marks a station'.[128] The transport system was the means by which this more open city would successfully communicate and exchange people between centre and suburbs.

The underground was a vital part of this developing city but Wells' *Anticipations* saw it transformed by electric power into a utopian world in which urban travel would be an aesthetic pleasure for commuters. Wells asked the reader to 'imagine that black and sulphurous tunnel, swept and garnished, lit and sweet, with a train much faster than the existing underground trains perpetually ready to go with him and never crowded'.[129] And yet Wells was only pushing forward what was already technologically feasible by 1902: the recent Paris Exposition had highlighted a 'people-mover' or 'rolling platform'; a 'Stepped Platform Railway', capable of carrying 12,000 passengers an hour, had been described and illustrated in the publication *Scientific American* in 1890.[130] Wells,

---

124 C. Booth, *Improved Means of Locomotion as a first step towards the cure of the housing difficulties of London* (1901), pp. 15–16.

125 Wells, *Anticipations*, p. 39.

126 Wells, *Anticipations*, p. 45.

127 Wells, *Anticipations*, p. 44.

128 Wells, *Anticipations*, p. 45.

129 Wells, *Anticipations*, p. 29.

130 One illustration showed passengers descending to the underground at an interchange station for 'cars' to Strand and Chancery Lane, the 'cars' in fact being small two-person booths placed on a continuous belt. As the accompanying article stated, there would be

however, wanted the underground of the future to be more than just a utilitarian addition to the city when he asked the reader to 'further imagine on this train a platform set with comfortable seats and neat bookstalls and so forth, he will get an inkling in just one detail of what he perhaps misses by living now instead of thirty or forty years ahead'.[131] In this vision the underground of the future would be aesthetically pleasing, a place of leisured cultural exchange and relaxed social intercourse. In *A Modern Utopia* (1905), he went on to point out that 'embankments and railways and engineering devices are not obliged to be ugly' adding that the 'tramway, the railroad, the culverts and bridges [...] will all be beautiful things'. There would be no 'smoke-disgorging steam railway trains in Utopia, they are already doomed on earth'.[132] In his essay 'Socialism and the Family' (1906), Wells envisioned a socialist future where 'an unfettered hand [would] make beautiful and convenient homes, splendid cities, noiseless great highways, beautiful bridges, clean, swift and splendid *electric railways*' (my italics).[133]

This put Wells into the orbit of a major revival of the Arts and Crafts Movement which called for a new design philosophy for a scientific age. This set of ideas derived many of its underlying attitudes from William Morris but was coming to terms with machinery and machine-driven production, a shift very much reflected in contemporary design. Wells was also linked with the vigorous utopianism that Matthew Beaumont detects as arising from two changes in Victorian society in the 1870s: the first deriving from the impact of the Great Depression which had evoked alternatives to capitalist society and the second from the newly emergent conditions of modernity—the 'time-space compression' as described by Stephen Kern.[134] Morris was well qualified to enter this debate and he combined a number of its strands in the novel *News from Nowhere* (1890). The novel opens with the narrator sitting disconsolately 'in a vapour-bath of hurried and discontented humanity, a carriage of the underground railway'[135] on his way home to Hammersmith after a meeting of

---

'neither smoke nor dirt; no time-table, no late arrival; no waiting for trains' and, as an incentive to would-be investors, 'the number of employees can be very small' (L. De Vries, 'The Stepped Platform Railway', in *Victorian Inventions* (London: John Murray, 1971), p. 36).

131   Wells, *Anticipations*, p. 29.

132   H. G. Wells, *A Modern Utopia* (1905; London: Thomas Nelson, undated), pp. 113 & 53.

133   H. G. Wells, *Socialism and the Family* (London: Fifield, 1906), pp. 21–22.

134   See M. Beaumont, *Utopia Ltd., Ideologies of Social Dreaming in England 1870–1900* (Boston: Brill, 2005) and S. Kern, *The Culture of Time and Space, 1880–1918* (London: Weidenfeld & Nicolson, 1983).

135   W. Morris, *News from Nowhere* (1890), in *Three Works by William Morris* (London: Lawrence & Wishart, 1968), pp. 181–401, p. 181.

the Socialist League which had hotly debated the outcomes of a revolution.[136] Morris not only denounced the sewer-like underground but in his newspaper *Commonweal* also attacked the 'fat cat' companies that held a 'monopoly we may be sure the railways won't give up until they are *forced* to'.[137] Seven years before, in 1883, Morris had written to his wife Jenny that he was 'quite sick of the underground', adding that he had an intense dislike for 'the sweltering train-business'.[138] To reach Merton from Kelmscott House Morris had to endure a two-hour journey by both underground and main-line rail, so it is hardly surprising that these negative experiences, coupled with his dislike of the way transport was organized solely for profit, led him to join the protest against a Channel tunnel project in 1882.[139]

Wells paid tribute to Morris's utopian writing in 1896 saying, in a discussion of Morris's *The Well at the World's End* (1896), that his 'dreamland was no futurity but an illuminated past'.[140] He clearly recognized the debt he owed to Morris's approach, whilst rejecting or ignoring the latter's more Marxist analysis of power relations and the communist future found in *News from Nowhere*. However, both Morris and Wells accepted that technology would have to exist in a future society with Morris, for example, vaguely pointing to the use of hydroelectric power and 'force-vehicles' having replaced 'old steam-driven carrying'.[141]

In *News from Nowhere*, Morris also anticipated many of the wider themes taken up by Wells after 1900. The narrator, William Guest, exclaims in the opening sequence, 'But is this the Thames?', continuing: 'The soap-works with their smoke-vomiting chimneys were gone; the engineer's works gone; the lead-works gone; and no sound of riveting and hammering came down

---

136 It was published in the same year that Morris and his supporters in the Hammersmith branch had left the Socialist League.

137 W. Morris, *Commonweal*, vol. 2, no. 17, 8 May 1886, p. 45, in *William Morris, Journalism: Contributions to Commonweal, 1885–1890*, ed. N. Salmon (Bristol: Thoemmes Press, 1996), p. 71.

138 W. Morris, 19 May 1882 to Jenny Morris, in *Collected Letters*, vol. 2, part A, p. 192.

139 The Channel tunnel was a project that remained a serious possibility from the 1870s until effectively halted by a combination of company rivalry, shortage of funds and military warnings of invasion. The engineering opportunities were based on the technological advances embodied in the growth of the underground—the Inner Circle, for example, having reached 13 miles in length by 1884. The railway 'baron' Edward Watkin envisaged a Manchester–Paris Railway that would have been pivoted around the Metropolitan Railway which he owned.

140 H. G. Wells, quoted in P. Parrinder, *Shadows of the Future: H. G. Wells, Science Fiction and Prophesy* (Liverpool: Liverpool University Press, 1995), p. 43.

141 W. Morris, *News from Nowhere*, p. 350.

the west wind from Thorneycroft's',[142] and his description sounds curiously like London after the Martian invasion. The smoke, pollution and industrial noise of London have disappeared from Morris's utopia, a picture that would undoubtedly have appealed to Wells in a decade when the general pollution of the urban environment was probably worse than at any other time. The frustration for Wells and many others was that the solution seemed so simple and the means so close at hand. This explains perhaps why he was drawn to Edward Bellamy's rival utopia outlined in the novel *Looking Backward* (1888) in which the narrator Julian West wakes up in twenty-first-century Boston. Morris had denounced *Looking Backward* as embodying Bellamy's personal bourgeois attitudes: 'The only ideal of life which such a man can see is that of the industrious professional middle-class men of today purified from the crime of complicity with the monopolist class, and become independent of being, as they are now, parasitical'.[143]

In other words, the novel enjoins the reader to reject middle-class political leadership on the grounds that all around him, the wider professional middle class collaborated with the upper bourgeoisie in the exploitation of the working class under capitalism. Morris gave Wells a consciousness about the importance of culture in a future society but Wells was prone to grasp at Bellamy's techno-logical solutions as a short cut to utopia. Morris also refused to accept that the transition to utopia would be an automatic, inevitable or painless process devoid of serious class conflict and dismissed Bellamy's vision as nothing more than 'state communism'. Bellamy's *Looking Backward* set out a blueprint for the survival of capitalism offering, as Matthew Beaumont points out, a world of 'clean lines and gleaming white surfaces [...] a consumerist utopia'.[144] Bellamy's narrator observes a department store of the future:

> a vast hall full of light [in which] a magnificent fountain played [...] the walls and ceiling were frescoed in mellow tints, calculated to soften without absorbing the light which flooded the interior. Around the fountain was a space occupied with chairs and sofas [...] legends on the walls all about the hall indicated to what classes of commod-ities the counters below were devoted.[145]

This passage is in sharp contrast to Wells' dystopian science fantasy but very much in tune with his later writing. Morris's criticisms of Bellamy's vision

142 W. Morris, *News from Nowhere*, pp. 186–87.

143 W. Morris, *Commonweal*, vol. 5, no. 180, 22 June 1889, pp. 194–95, in *Contributions to Commonweal*, pp. 419–25, p. 421.

144 Beaumont, *Utopia Ltd.*, p. 75.

145 E. Bellamy, *Looking Backward 2000–1887* (1888; Harmondsworth: Penguin, 1982), p. 92.

could equally well have been levelled at Wells, whose utopia embodied 'an ideal, rational order—planned, centralized and secure from disruptive forces' including 'the most efficient mechanisms of social control'.[146] It was Bellamy rather than Morris who inspired Wells' futurological writings such as *Anticipations*, creating department stores that seemed to draw on the pavilions at contemporary world expositions and, as Susan Buck-Morss observes, 'the message of the world exhibitions as fairylands was the promise of social progress for the masses without revolution'.[147] Like Bellamy, Wells sidestepped the question of how the future society would be achieved by replacing Morris's agency of transition, the working class, with an intellectual elite. This left open the question of political consent and representation with Wells simply believing in a kind of benevolent despotism. He thought that a progressive and enlightened group of entrepreneurs and thinkers could influence and educate public opinion as well as providing efficient public transport and viable manufacturing industries. Wells was therefore in tune with broadly 'progressive' or new liberal opinion in the period 1900–14 that shared the belief that the capitalist system should be modernized, particularly at a national level. As part of a consensus within a section of the British political elite, he could reach wider layers of public opinion.

It is ironic that the idealism of the various liberal advocates of better public transport in the capital was based on the largely speculative strategies of the infamous 'traction baron' Charles Tyson Yerkes. This notorious character had developed the street railway system in Chicago, connecting it into a network via a downtown loop and controlling over 400 miles of street railway. Having realized that London's Circle line could be similarly developed if connected with tube and tram 'feeder' lines, Yerkes arrived in London as an American representative of the kind of unbridled and corrupt capitalism despised by Wells and other colleagues at the Fabian Society, such as George Bernard Shaw and Sidney and Beatrice Webb. According to Theodore Dreiser, who immortalized Yerkes as Frank Algernon Cowperwood in his last novel *The Stoic* (1947), there were 'snarls of rage' in Chicago when it was discovered that 'such a ruthless trickster, so recently ejected from that city, should proceed to London'.[148] Nevertheless, by 1901 Yerkes had acquired a large part of the London network and had created a new company, the Underground Electric Railways of London Limited, and had begun the construction of three tube lines. The 'London underground

---

146 C. Ferns, *Narrating Utopia* (Liverpool: Liverpool University Press, 1999), p. 97.

147 S. Buck-Morss, *The Dialectics of Seeing: Walter Benjamin and the Arcades Project* (London: MIT Press, 1989), p. 86.

148 T. Dreiser, *The Stoic* (1947; New York: Thomas Y. Crowell, 1974), p. 125.

situation' was always on the lips of Cowperwood/Yerkes in Dreiser's account, a gripping phrase from the first novel to be entirely concerned with London's underground. Yerkes may have modernized the old and increasingly unprofitable steam underground but it was Wells who most effectively modernized and popularized the debates around public transport by combining the imaginative with the non-fictional, moving skillfully from one medium to the other throughout his subsequent career. By actively intervening in a debate about the underground itself in order to shape its future, he was able to place himself in the vanguard of transport policy-making in this period, gradually unfurling a series of proposals that would bring him into the emerging transport elite in the capital.

Wells was always only slightly ahead of the latest developments but this meant that the imaginative construction of the underground was being pushed in a more technical direction. Having projected the underground into the far distant future, he now aligned it very closely with the rapid developments of his own time. Wells emerged as the champion of the new modernizing underground before the First World War, thereby making him an important figure in the emerging idea of Tubism in the post-1918 period. He championed corridor trains as an alternative to the old-fashioned compartments found on the Metropolitan and District railways and argued against the 'archaic' class structure of the Victorian era that the railways seemed to embody in their use of first, second and third-class sections. Writing in *A Modern Utopia*, Wells asserted that 'there will be no distinctions of class in such a train, because in a civilised world there would be no offence between one kind of man and another'.[149] He turned instead to the new electric tubes that had already introduced 'cars' and abolished these class distinctions on their services. The City and South London was operating a fare of two pence for all passengers provoking *The Times* to declare that 'All the complicated apparatus of booking clerks and tickets, first, second and third class, single and return and season, is swept away'.[150] Price was also reflected in the moniker 'Tuppeny Tube' adopted for the Central London Railway that was simply a nickname derived from that flat-fare system. The tube was certainly successful if measured by the 15,000 passengers who used it each day within a few weeks of its opening by the Prince of Wales.[151]

---

149 Wells, *A Modern Utopia*, p. 54.
150 *The Times*, 4 November 1890.
151 The introduction of women-only cars on the New York Hudson-Manhattan in these years would have appealed to Wells as an advocate of women's rights. They were mooted in London by *The Times* correspondent Janet Hogarth who called for 'ladies' coaches' on the Central but the idea was not adopted in London except on suburban trains.

The Fabian Society, which Wells joined in 1903, also provided a source of ideological support for many of his policy ideas. The Fabians, including Shaw and the Webbs, were passionate advocates of the concept of efficiency and played an important role in the National Efficiency Movement of the 1890s. They had campaigned for a properly organized electricity supply for London, with the Progressives on the London County Council fighting to advance that Council's role in supplying electricity at a municipal level. The Fabians also called for a Greater London Authority to organize both transport and electricity in the capital and were undoubtedly part of a so-called 'chorus of lament' around 1900 which argued that London was not keeping up with the new technology compared with cities like Chicago and Berlin.[152] In the Fabian Society Wells encountered George Bernard Shaw, a great advocate of efficiency at a personal as well as governmental level. Shaw was himself a prolific user of the underground, recording dozens of trips on the Metropolitan, Circle and District lines to destinations throughout London in the 1880s and 1890s.[153]

The National Efficiency Movement took a pessimistic view of British technological development, comparing it unfavourably with the United States. This had a particular relevance to the London tubes, as an editorial by Norman Lockyer in the journal *Nature* (1901) pointed out:

> how different is the role that Britain is playing at the beginning of the new century to that she filled at the beginning of the old one. We import instead of export. The chief London electric railway is American, American coal is producing gas to light the streets of the metropolis, American cars are found on our English trains, which on some lines are drawn by American locomotives.[154]

And in the same year, *Punch* laconically noted the American interest in a cartoon entitled 'Jonathan Shopping' in which the shop-keeping figure of John Bull asks an American millionaire 'Now, my little man, what can I do for you?' and gets the reply 'Wal, guess I'll buy the whole store!' and he is clutching a toy Metropolitan locomotive.[155] When the nickname 'Baker-loo, London's latest

---

152 Quoted in T. P. Hughes, *Networks of Power: Electrification in Western Society, 1880-1930* (Baltimore: Johns Hopkins University Press, 1983), p. 257.

153 G. B. Shaw, 17 February 1895, in *Bernard Shaw: The Diaries, 1885–1897*, ed. S. Weintraub, 2 vols. (London: Penn State University Press, 1986), vol. 2, p. 1066. Shaw recorded all these trips in his diaries, including details of his fares. This included a journey in 1895 to a lecture on 'Twentieth Century Politics' at the Reformers Club in Kennington using the 'Electric Railway' (City and South London Railway).

154 J. N. Lockyer, 'Editorial', in *Nature*, 3 January 1901, p. 2.

155 'Jonathan Shopping', *Punch*, 8 May 1901, vol. 3, p. 341.

Twopenny Tube' was coined by the *Evening News* in 1906, this 'gutter title' was blamed on the American owners. Significantly, the building of the first tubular railway, the City and South London Railway, had been hailed as a glowing example of 'English' innovation, with the *South London Press* featuring a speech in 1890 by the local MP in which the project was praised as a sign of national progress: 'by this electric railway you have shown our great competitors in electrical sciences that we in England are moving forward'.[156] The ideology of National Efficiency brought together a number of strands of thought which, as G. R. Searle has indicated,[157] were stimulated by the impact of the Boer War and the rapid emergence of Germany as a world power. As one of the many admirers of the German state's scientific and technical education system, Lockyer was able to join with Liberals like Richard Haldane and Fabians like George Bernard Shaw to lobby for Britain to emulate the German model. Sidney Webb claimed that supporters of the principle of National Efficiency brought a 'clear vision of how they intend to work this principle out'. He pointed to the Progressives on the London County Council who 'at the risk of calumny and misunderstanding at the West-end and in the City, did not shrink from painting the sky red with their projects'.[158] Lockyer founded the British Science Guild in 1905, with Haldane as its first president, as a means to obtain more public funding for science in universities whilst Richard Gregory, a close friend of Wells, succeeded Lockyer as editor of *Nature* in 1919. The National Efficiency Movement therefore represented an important fraction of the ruling elite in Britain, offering a major vehicle for debates on urban transport.

---

156   *South London Press*, 8 November 1890. The takeover of the City and South London Railway by US traction baron Charles Tyson Yerkes of the Underground Group of Companies spoiled this celebration. Yerkes was undoubtedly one of the 'millionaire company promoters' that C. F. G. Masterman complained about.

157   See G. R. Searle, *The Quest for National Efficiency: A Study in British Politics and Political Thought* (Oxford: Basil Blackwell, 1971).

158   S. Webb, 'Lord Rosebery's Escape from Houndsditch', in *The Nineteenth Century and After*, vol. 50, July–December 1901, pp. 366–86, p. 385.

OVERCOMING THE ENDLESS STREETS:
H. G. WELLS MAPS THE METROPOLIS

n 1901, Wells proclaimed in a letter to R. A. Gregory that he was 'going to write, talk and preach revolution for the next five years'.[159] By 1905, the year of the publication of *A Modern Utopia*, his revolutionary élan had cooled sufficiently for him to adopt the gradualist perspective that began to appear in his social fiction. The motif of efficiency loomed large in Wells' thinking as shown in *The New Machiavelli* (1911) when the main character in the novel, Remington, comments that 'the picture of the splendid Working Man cheated out of his innate glorious possibilities [...] began to give place to a limitless spectacle of inefficiency, to a conception of millions of people not organized as they should be'.[160] Wells put fictional flesh on some of his arguments and London's transport system offered a means of highlighting the social issues that affected the lower middle class in the metropolis. Like Gissing, Wells did not find that social conditions in the capital were propitious for the lower middle class and was dismayed by the vast panorama of the London streets. The characters in *Ann Veronica* (1909), *The New Machiavelli* and *Tono-Bungay* are confronted by a monstrous urban underworld with its 'endless streets of undistinguished houses, undistinguished industries, shabby families, second-rate shops [...] the unorganised, abundant substance of some tumorous growth-process'.[161] And Wells' characters, like Ann Veronica Stanley, are often inexperienced arrivals in the metropolis seeking to establish themselves in an alien urban milieu. They are faced with the two urgent problems of housing and employment but also need to make sense of London's atmosphere: 'London seemed to be so full of meanings—all mixed up together', exclaims Margaret in *The New Machiavelli*[162] and Ann Veronica finds that 'London is very dark and foggy and greasy and forbidding' as she searches for a job.[163] The social writing of the underground could now be tuned to the need to navigate this ever-moving city and it offered his characters a genuine 'lifeline' to survival in an urban environment.

If, as Wells' fiction suggested, there were considerable barriers facing lower-middle-class arrivals, then such barriers were undoubtedly both more numerous and less surmountable by women. Ann Veronica was involved, Wells tells us, in

159 H. G. Wells, letter to R. A. Gregory, quoted in R. Haynes, *H. G. Wells, Discoverer of the Future: The Influence of Science on his Thought* (London: Macmillan, 1980), p. 66.

160 Wells, *The New Machiavelli*, pp. 100–01.

161 Wells, *Tono-Bungay*, p. 95.

162 Wells, *The New Machiavelli*, p. 178.

163 H. G. Wells, *Ann Veronica* (1909; London: Dent, 1966), p. 105.

the suffrage movement and was therefore a fictional beacon in these struggles when she is 'in the very forefront' of a raid on the Houses of Parliament.[164] Wells commented disparagingly that the New Women of this time 'were good pure women rightly struggling for a Vote, and that was all they wanted'.[165] However, the suffrage movement was a significant influence, especially during the heightened campaigns of 1906–11 by the Women's Social and Political Union (WSPU) and National Union of Women's Suffrage Societies with their focus on national demonstrations and parades in central London. These organizations had an unprecedented effect on the visual environment in the capital, particularly on various routes from the Embankment and the Strand to the Albert Hall and Hyde Park, routes which were frequently adjacent to underground stations where women could fly-post both tube stations and advertising hoardings with visually powerful images. One huge advertising poster for a WSPU march in June 1908 featured a map of Hyde Park that resembled one of the newest underground maps (UERL, 1908). The suffrage campaigns, it has been argued by Lisa Tickner, were linked by 'the use of a new kind of political spectacle, and the production of an iconography of their own'.[166]

The suffrage movement also transformed the underground by using it on an unprecedented scale for access to events. This was not just because the Central, Bakerloo and Piccadilly lines had opened new corridors through the West End, north-east and north-west London, but because many of these demonstrations were national in character rather than being largely drawn just from the capital's populace. The massive Hyde Park rally of 1908, which brought an estimated quarter of a million people to London, was supplied by 64 trains and processions joined it from all over the city, with 700 floating banners and 40 bands. The scale of the rally depended on the underground network to bring people together in a way never before seen in the history of radical protest and the assembly points themselves were now chosen because of their proximity to underground stations.[167]

---

164 Wells, *Ann Veronica*, p. 193.

165 Wells, *Experiment in Autobiography*, vol. 2, p. 484.

166 L. Tickner, *The Spectacle of Women: Imagery of the Suffrage Campaign, 1907–14* (London: Chatto & Windus, 1987), p. 10.

167 After the completion of the new Embankment, demonstrators used it to follow routes from Tower Hill via Mansion House when marching into central London venues such as Trafalgar Square or Hyde Park. By comparison, the marches of the 1880s protesting against unemployment—for example in 1886 when demonstrators marched from Dodd Street and other points in London's East End to Trafalgar Square; 'Bloody Sunday' in 1887 with marches coming from Clerkenwell through St Martin's Lane and from many points in south London traversing Westminster Bridge; and the 1889 Dock strike marches from

This was graphically recorded in suffrage fiction when, in *Suffragette Sally* (1911) by Gertrude Colmore (based on the real events of 1908), a march assembles 'on the crowded Embankment':

> All the way from Westminster to Blackfriars Bridge stretched a line of waving banners; all the way, in file four deep, close pressed together, ranks of women, ranks of men, massed densely on either side, crowds of spectators; and beyond the Embankment wall, the river rising in its banks, swelled by the flow of the incoming tide driven upwards by the sea.[168]

Throughout these years, thousands of women used the underground to travel to and from meetings, rallies and protests. The most renowned Suffrage Society, the WSPU, was centrally located in Clement's Inn, Holborn and the International Franchise Club was close to Russell Square tube station. During the week of action in November 1910, 'women poured through the long tunnel from South Kensington [station] to the Albert Hall. The railway official on duty in that dim place took a fatherly interest in us all'.[169] Built by the District Railway in 1885 to coincide with the start of the Inventions Exhibition, this particular pedestrian subway under Exhibition Road had only been opened permanently two years before. The rally itself was the culmination of a 'long week entirely devoted to Suffrage. The average woman must have become a little tired of turning out night after night in the wet'.[170] The campaigner Violet Hunt, who lived in Kensington, recalled giving out suffrage leaflets at her local underground station, Kensington (High Street), surely the first recorded example of station leafleting.[171] Mary Stocks describes the funeral of Emily Davidson in 1911, when they 'took the tube to Holborn in the fond hope of seeing Miss Davidson's funeral; but when we got near the church we found the densest crowd I have ever seen—right along Holborn and all down those little streets that lead off to the British Museum'.[172] Such activities utilized the underground as an accepted mode of transport, a shift made possible by the

---

Commercial Road to Tower Hill—all largely reached their assembly points on foot. The International May Day demonstrations of 1890–92 also brought massive numbers of up to 300,000 to Hyde Park, reflecting the growing strength of unskilled trade unionism and the radicalism of the metropolis.

168 G. Colmore, *Suffragette Sally* (1911), reissued as *Suffragettes: A Story of Three Women* (London: Pandora, 1984), pp. 287–88.

169 *Common Cause*, 17 November 1910, quoted in J. Marlow (ed.), Marlow, *Votes for Women: The Virago Book of Suffragettes* (London: Virago, 2000), pp. 124–25, p. 124.

170 *Common Cause*, 17 November 1910, p. 124.

171 See V. Hunt, *My Flurried Years* (London: Hurst & Blackett, 1926).

172 M. Stocks, *My Commonplace Book*, quoted in Marlow, *Votes for Women*, pp. 198–99, p. 198.

more middle-class composition of the suffrage movement and the cheaper fares offered by the new tube lines. This is similarly reflected in fiction such as the 'militant suffragette' Una Blockley in W. L. Courtney's 'The Soul of a Suffragette' (1913), who smashes a shop window in Bond Street with a hammer. She is then whisked away by a (male) stranger in a hansom cab who asks 'but whither are we driving?' to which she promptly replies: 'Take me to any Tube station—Marble Arch will do. Or perhaps we might go up to Edgware Road station. That would be still more convenient'.[173] Sally Simmonds, the working-class representative amongst the three female protagonists in *Suffragette Sally*, is a housemaid who can afford to use the tubes because of the relatively low cost. This was a watershed in the political history of mass campaigning in the capital, one that highlights a dimension in the use of the underground that did not appear alongside the images of women that featured on official posters and publicity in this decade.

One propaganda device used to good effect by the suffrage movement was the picture postcard. It was also a means of communication for the various underground companies and the postcard formed an important part of contemporary visual media for transport advertising before the take-off of the poster. They were especially popular with the urban working class as they were a relatively inexpensive medium whilst trade cards with illustrations of underground themes were an ideal way to locate companies based in London. A 1915 trade card featuring an early tube map was issued to customers of Woolland Brothers of Knightsbridge and the original 'UNDERGROUND' sign was displayed on a trade card saying 'Shop in Comfort' with insets of women travelling on an underground train, shopping and dining.[174] Virtually nothing on the underground escaped the attentions of the postcard artists and designers. One very imaginative illustration from 1902 showed a Central line train entering a tunnel with a Central line route map placed above the tunnel entrance and a far-distant view of the train ahead entering the next station with the slogan 'This is the Best Way to Get About London: The Tube'. The period 1904–10 was the golden age of postcards so that by 1910, 866 million of them were sent

---

173 W. L. Courtney, 'The Soul of a Suffragette' (1913), in C. Christensen Nelson (ed.), *Literature of the Women's Suffrage Campaign in England* (Peterborough, Ontario: Broadview Press, 2004), pp. 313–25, pp. 313–18.

174 Other postcards showed Moorgate Street (1907) and Notting Hill Gate stations (1902); the interior of the great Northern, Piccadilly and Brompton Railway electric car shed at Lillie Bridge (1906); tube station platforms such as Piccadilly Circus, a Central line platform and spacious car interiors on the Central (1910); and even a Central line 'whitewashing' train which sprayed the track between stations for the benefit of drivers (1902).

by post each year, helping to bring images of and messages about the underground to audiences with little or no personal acquaintance with tube travel, thus doing to a lesser extent what the silent cinema was doing in the United States. The cards' widespread circulation and availability have shaped modern perceptions of the underground by providing reasonably reliable illustrations of train stock, station décor and the general 'atmosphere' of the system, for example in the artist's impression of 1915 which featured a spacious car interior with men in top hats and bowlers reading newspapers and women in flowing gowns.[175] This image appeared in contemporary observations such as the travel book *The Unknown Isle* (1906) when Pierre de Coulevain recorded that: 'On all the platforms of the underground, there are women and girls to be seen wearing very brightly-coloured dresses, frequently white ones, feather boas and picture hats'.[176] Such images entered the visual vocabulary of the underground, subtly mediating its cultural construction in a way similar to the posters of the interwar period—with brightly coloured illustrations. It is not surprising that the term 'TUBE' entered popular usage quickly as it was emblazoned on vertical signs saying 'TUBE Station', appeared on hundreds of postcards and in novelty giveaways like the folder designed as a pillar box with the slogan 'Quickest Way to Exhibition by Tube'. Even Christmas cards featured the 'Tuppeny Tube', such as the slightly risqué image of an Edwardian woman perched on a tube of 'First Quality Moist Colours—2d per tube—must be well squeezed', saying 'I've Just Come Up on The Tuppeny Tube'.[177]

The rapid expansion of public transport in London during this decade offered Wells the opportunity to 'map' the city for his often disoriented characters, allowing them to navigate the 'interminable procession of horse omnibuses [which] went lumbering past, bearing countless people we knew not whence, we knew not whither'.[178] Ann Veronica comes to the city for the first time from suburban Surbiton in order to escape from her overbearing family. She becomes a self-supporting university student, attends socialist and feminist meetings and has an affair with a married man. She is found travelling out of London to Morningside Park on a train from Waterloo station 'with both her feet on the seat in an attitude that would certainly have distressed her mother to see and horrified her grandmother beyond measure'[179] and leaves

---

175 On the reverse side of this particular card is the slogan 'Bakerloo & Piccadilly Tubes afford the maximum speed, safety, comfort and convenience in all weathers'.

176 Coulevain, *The Unknown Isle*, p. 98.

177 Christmas card, 1901, author's collection.

178 Wells, *The New Machiavelli*, p. 65.

179 Wells, *Ann Veronica*, p. 1.

the city at the end of the novel on a train from Charing Cross station with her lover Capes. Morningside Park is a new 'suburb that had not altogether, as people say, come off' but one that is accessible by means of public transport.[180] Ann Veronica followed in the footsteps of George Moore's heroine *Esther Waters* (1894), who had to travel frequently across London from Dulwich to West Kensington using both underground and main-line railways. Moore's novel opens on a railway station platform as his eponymous heroine stands watching a departing train. Esther's life in London is dominated by her job as a domestic servant as she travels fruitlessly 'on long journeys from Brixton to Notting Hill to visit poor people who could hardly afford a maid-of-all-work [...] a house in Bayswater, and thence she had to go to High Street Kensington, or Earl's Court; a third address might be in Chelsea'.[181] Later, she frequently visits east Dulwich to see her young son, travelling from Ludgate Hill station as she is 'living in' with Miss Rice in Avondale Road, West Kensington. The city has continued to expand uncontrollably with 'great new forces, blind forces of invasion, of growth', Wells said in *Tono-Bungay*.[182] This process had forced many people to travel vast distances involving tubes, buses, trams and railways; in other words, public transportation is an *organizing* force for the individual inhabitants of the capital.

Wells presents public transport as a thread that leads Ann Veronica either to safety or towards personal freedom whilst for Moore it allows Esther Waters to juggle the competing claims of domestic service and motherhood. Ann Veronica does a considerable amount of walking and Wells describes only two of her train journeys, but it is safe to assume that, like Wells himself, she would have been a regular tube user. Wells does tell us that 'It was rare that Ann Veronica used hansoms, and to be in one was itself eventful and exhilarating'.[183] On the streets, Ann Veronica's confidence evaporates when she is pestered by a man and is driven 'from street to street [...] in a stream of hurrying, homewards workers' until she reaches 'the Euston Road Corner of Tottenham Court Road, and there, by the name on a bus and the cries of the conductor, she made a guess of her way'. By now, 'all the glory of London has departed' but public transport has allowed her a safe passage and a protected journey away from the attentions of her male harasser.[184] The message in this scene is that even the sounds of public transport, with bus conductors and tube guards

---

180   Wells, *Ann Veronica*, p. 1.
181   G. Moore, *Esther Waters* (1894; London: Dent, 1962), p. 163.
182   Wells, *Tono-Bungay*, p. 95.
183   Wells, *Ann Veronica*, p. 126.
184   Wells, *Ann Veronica*, pp. 83–84.

calling out the names of places and stations to passengers, may be reassuring rather than part of the threatening thunder of the underworld so powerfully evoked by Gissing. Wells is saying that the machinery of public transport that he had described in his non-fiction has a *human* dimension. The human voice can actually transcend the tumult and human faculties could be complemented rather than drowned out by technology.

Arthur Kipps in Wells' 1905 novel *Kipps* travels up to Charing Cross station from Folkestone on a 'train [...] composed of corridor carriages' and forgets 'his troubles for a time in the wonders of this modern substitute for railway compartments'.[185] Later, Kipps discovers 'another means of locomotion in the Underground Railway', travelling with his friend Sid in a third-class car.[186] Kipps can feel that his journeys in the metropolis are manageable as it is easier to apprehend the city through the underground map rather than through other types of description. As Ford Madox Ford perceptively commented, the generic figure of Kipps will have 'acquired an alertness of eye that will save him from asking the way. On his "Underground" he will glance at a board rather than inquire of a porter'.[187] *Kipps* contains a social diagramming of place in the same way that Wells had described the simple class structure of the Potteries in *The New Machiavelli*, comprising the 'meanly-housed workers [...] a small middle-class quarter [...] the big house of the employer'.[188] London was 'limitless confusion'[189] by comparison and Wells' search for a simplified diagram of social structure was at least partly supplied by public transport. The underground did not eliminate the segregation by class that was so obviously visible in the metropolis but it could offer the rational underpinning to a social structure that seemed to defy all known models of the city. In one sense, the new tubular railway seemed to soften Edwardian class structure: Eric Banton in 'Underground Travelling London' (1903) said that the tubes enabled 'the

---

185 H. G. Wells, *Kipps* (1905; London: Fontana, 1961), pp. 210–11.

186 Wells, *Kipps*, p. 214.

187 Ford, *The Soul of London*, p. 10. The first complete underground maps were not actually issued until 1908, three years after *Kipps* and one year before the publication of *Ann Veronica*, offering practical guidance to passengers and complementing Wells' attempts to simplify and domesticate underground travel in fiction. Innovations in typography should also not be underestimated. Edward Johnston, the calligrapher who designed the new block lettering sans-serif type for the underground, said to his students that 'If you know where an omnibus is going you owe that to me because your fathers and mothers did not ever know where an omnibus was going: you could not read the letters on the old omnibus' (P. Johnston, *Edward Johnston* (1959; London: Barrie & Jenkins, 1976), p. 204).

188 Wells, *The New Machiavelli*, p. 134.

189 Wells, *The New Machiavelli*, p. 134.

office boy [to sit] himself down in great content beside the City magnate, and still the heavens do not fall'.[190] For the Prince of Wales, who had opened the City and South London line in 1890, the electric tube would benefit 'Business men who have great distances to come [and be] a material boon to the working man who is obliged to work all day in a not always pleasing atmosphere'.[191] The social class 'levelling' of the tubes would not radically disturb the wider class structure above ground but, for Wells and others, such change represented the gradual breaking down of social barriers.

For Wells, the underground is the way to organize London's subterranean levels. In other words, he has crystallized the role of the subterranean rather than merely describing the experience of travelling in it. His conception of the underground indicated that writing had rapidly 'caught up' with the new electric technology of the tubular railway and its deep level operation. This had occurred within a few years of the opening of the City and South London and continued in the next decade as additional lines such the Central London Railway from Shepherd's Bush to Bank were completed in 1900. Its 14 stations were uniformly white-tiled and over a hundred feet long, lit by electricity and furnished with stone slabs on its platforms after the serious fire on the Paris Métro in 1903 which had been fuelled by wooden flooring. Wells' writing was probably reflecting the high profile of the Central that was undoubtedly enhanced by the favourable press coverage of the new line. The *Daily Mail*, for example, opined that 'if this kind of thing goes on, London will come to be quite a nice place to travel in'[192] and it was the *Mail* that dubbed it the 'Twopenny Tube'. But Wells was also reflecting the optimism of Edwardian consumerism that was to be found in many media descriptions of the tube. Illustrations for the Central pinpoint the ease with which passengers could travel across the city and the line rapidly became a new link between the West End shopping district and exclusive suburbs like Bayswater, linking them beneath the surface as the buses had done previously at street level. On board the trains the company had introduced fitted straps for standing passengers, creating the new figure of the 'straphanger' who provided the dividends to shareholders according to the American 'traction baron' Charles Tyson Yerkes.[193]

Underground writing turned positively towards suburbia. The realism

190   E. Banton, 'Underground Travelling London' (1903), in G. R. Sims (ed.), *Edwardian London*,
      4 vols. (London: Village Press, 1990), vol. 4, pp. 60–63, p. 63.

191   *South London Press*, 8 November 1901, p. 2.

192   *Daily Mail*, 30 July 1900.

193   See J. Franch, *Robber Baron, The Life of Charles Tyson Yerkes* (Urbana & Chicago: University of
      Illinois Press, 2006).

of Arnold Bennett expresses the same sentiments as Wells in relation to the security role of the underground. Richard Larch, in Bennett's novel *A Man from the North* (1898) is one of a number of characters to arrive in London from the Potteries. He rents a place in Raphael Street in Fulham that is 'within the sound of the central hum and beat of the city'[194] and travels on the District line from Parson's Green station. For Bennett, the underground is a lifeline that carries his characters into a suburban oasis: 'The curving rails [at Parson's Green] stole away mysteriously into a general greyness, and the twilight, assuaging every crudity of the suburban landscape, gave an impression of vast spaces and perfect serenity'.[195] And the underground is central to his vision of a better life as it threads a course above the streets and roof-tops of the west London suburbs before descending beneath the central city. It offers a pathway through the vast metropolis: 'A signal suddenly shone out in the distance; it might have been a lighthouse seen across unnumbered miles of calm ocean'.[196] Some ten years later, Bennett returned to the underground in *Buried Alive* (1908). The novel actually opens at No. 91 Selwood Terrace which is described as 'one of ten thousand similar houses between South Kensington Station and North End Road'.[197] Bennett offers his readers a useful sociological account of underground stations, revealing that South Kensington has a cloakroom and workmen's trains run through East Putney in the early morning. For Bennett, the older lines like the Metropolitan and District represented the main thoroughfares of the city. The former had already had a major impact on London's north-western development as it extended out of London towards Harrow and Uxbridge, a line which was electrified as early as 1907 despite the fact that the capital's suburbs still only reached as far as Dollis Hill in 1914. Bennett grasped the key role of these railways during these years, making similar observations in his novel *Hilda Lessways* (1911), in which the heroine arrives at King's Cross station and journeys into the north London suburbs 'level with the top of vague, far-reaching acres of houses [...] And always it travelled on a platform of brick arches'.[198] Hilda alights at Hornsey station and an express train whizzes by 'like a flying shell'[199] in a manner reminiscent of the express train in Gissing's *New Grub Street*. Similarly, Marion, a character in Wells' *Tono-Bungay*, sets 'her mind

---

194 A. Bennett, *A Man from the North* (1898; London: Hamish Hamilton, 1973), p. 61.

195 Bennett, *A Man from the North*, p. 60.

196 Bennett, *A Man from the North*, p. 61.

197 A. Bennett, *Buried Alive* (1908; London: Methuen, 1913), p. 1.

198 A. Bennett, *Hilda Lessways* (1911; London: Eyre Methuen, 1976), p. 90.

199 Bennett, *Hilda Lessways*, p. 91.

quite resolutely upon Ealing',[200] the more prosperous railway suburb in west London notable for its District Railway links to the city. The characters of Bennett and Wells are sometimes nearly overwhelmed by the 'endless, endless arches'[201] of London's suburbs but both writers saw women in particular as benefiting from transport improvements, placing great value on the newly won power and freedom of 'salary-earning girls' in the capital.[202]

The railway network was the essential link between work and the more private world of the suburbs as famously memorialized in George and Weedon Grossmith's *Diary of a Nobody* (1892) in which the railway track lies at the end of the garden.[203] Bennett's character Richard Larch in *A Man from the North* is planning to write a book called the *Psychology of the Suburbs* because 'the suburbs *are* London!'[204] The suburb was the realization of the pastoral dream. No longer imprisoning the lower middle class in the old London, the underground liberated it at the end of the working day and at weekends. The salary-earning girls and boys could use the underground for leisure, an aspect of the system that would be much developed in the interwar years. These suburbanites also featured in Bennett's *The Sinews of War* (1906), where the 'Tube Railway threw up quantities of the same sort of people out of the earth'. They were 'the vanguard of the blackcoated workers'.[205] This was also the theme that C. F. G. Masterman developed in *From the Abyss* (1902), an attempt to fashion a new political alliance for liberalism. Masterman noted that 'the mass [...] have been hurried up in incredible number through tubes sunk in the bowels of the earth, emerging like rats from a drain'.[206] In *The Condition of England* (1909), he depicted the urban masses 'struggling from the outskirts of the city into tramcars and trains which are dragging it to its centres of labour'.[207] He wanted this process to be the basis for a new political alliance between the 'Suburbans' who represented 'unconquered human aspiration'[208] and the 'Multitude' or 'Crowd'. Masterman believed that peaceful progress could be achieved if 'aided by any loosening of the city texture by which, and through improved means

---

200 Wells, *Tono-Bungay*, p. 158.
201 Bennett, *Hilda Lessways*, p. 91.
202 A. Bennett, *Our Women: Chapters on the Sex-Discord* (London: Cassell, 1920), pp. 124–47.
203 See G. & W. Grossmith, *Diary of a Nobody* (1892; Harmondsworth: Penguin, 1965).
204 Bennett, *A Man from the North*, p. 71.
205 A. Bennett, *The Sinews of War* (1906), quoted in J. A. Morris, *Writers and Politics in Modern Britain (1880–1950)* (London: Hodder & Stoughton, 1977), p. 31.
206 C. F. G. Masterman, *From the Abyss: Of Its Inhabitants by One of Them* (1902; New York: Garland, 1980), p. 2.
207 C. F. G. Masterman, *The Condition of England* (London: Methuen, 1909), p. 119.
208 Masterman, *Condition of England*, p. 70.

of transit, something of the larger sanities of rural existence could be mingled with the quickness and agility of the town'.[209]

Transport was assigned the role of joining the city with the pastoral world of the suburb with the aim of bringing about social harmony without the need for the more radical reforms of the Garden City Movement. The author and journalist Mark Twain (Sam Clemens) focused on the romantic aspects of the pastoral dream. Twain, who attended the opening of the Central in 1900 alongside the Prince of Wales, enthusiastically wrote to his friend Joseph Twichell that:

> From the house you can see little but spacious stretches of hay fields and green turf [...] Yet the massed brick blocks of London are reachable in three minutes on a horse. By rail we can be in the heart of London, in Baker Street, in seventeen minutes—by a smart train in five.[210]

David Reeder has pointed out the importance of the new suburbs with their 'mingling of density and rurality [...] where the charm of rural seclusion seems to merge itself in that of proximity to the city market'.[211]

Not all observers agreed with this belief in a social idyll. T. W. H. Crosland, in *The Suburbans* (1905), mocked the Twopenny Tube as a 'ghastly burrow' of suburbanism.[212] Crosland argued that the 'bowels of the earth, no matter how so well lighted, how so well tiled and how so well ventilated, were never intended for the journeyings of mortal man'.[213] There was considerable debate about the struggles of the 'two-penny clerk' or 'thirty-bob-a-week' man who was typically identified with underground travel in these pre-war years. John Davidson's 1894 poem 'Thirty Bob a Week' immortalized the clerk who travelled 'like a mole [...] along the underground'.[214] E. M. Forster placed Leonard Bast, the unfortunate clerk in his novel *Howard's End* (1910) on 'the extreme verge of gentility [...] not in the abyss'.[215] Tormented and frustrated by the underground, Bast uses the District Railway to get to Wimbledon

---

209 Masterman, *Condition of England*, p. 95.

210 M. Twain, *The Selected Letters of Mark Twain*, ed. C. Neider (New York: Harper & Row, 1982), p. 261. A 'smart train' was a non-stop train that ran through Dollis Hill station on the Metropolitan line, a then almost rural district to which Twain had moved in the same year from a central London apartment in Knightsbridge.

211 D. Reeder, *Suburbanity and the Victorian City* (Leicester: University of Leicester, 1980), p. 3.

212 T. W. H. Crosland, *The Suburbans* (London: John Long, 1905), p. 31.

213 Crosland, *The Suburbans*, p. 33.

214 J. Davidson, 'Thirty Bob a Week' (1894), in J. Hayward (ed.), *The Oxford Book of Nineteenth Century English Verse* (Oxford: Oxford University Press, 1964), pp. 900–03, p. 901.

215 E. M. Forster, *Howard's End* (1910; Harmondsworth, Penguin, 1941), p. 58.

only to find 'gas lamps for hours'[216] instead of a pastoral utopia. He travels by rail out of King's Cross on suburban services, reaching 'the embankment at Finsbury Park' where he has 'his first sight of sun'.[217] Bast suffers torment over the price of a tram ride and instead walks under the South-Western railway tunnel at Waterloo where he is assailed by the roar of the train above. The situation of this stratum of London's working people in regard to their choice of transport remained deeply ambiguous both before and after the First World War, an ambiguity that would remain central to the experience of many suburbanites throughout the period. It reflected, moreover, the growing insecurity of clerical workers after the Great Depression and the narrowing of the gap in pay with manual workers in the last decades of the nineteenth century. An insurance clerk like Bast would have earned around £85 a year in 1909 and his youthfulness in Forster's novel was an accurate portrayal of the fact that 72 per cent of clerks were under 35 as against 54 per cent in all other occupations.[218] A tradesman like Frank Bullen endured nearly four hours travelling each day in order to 'live at a low rent and have a little house' in the suburbs.[219] Women were also entering the profession, making them part of a commuter workforce in the city, as can be seen in Olive P. Rayner's novel *The Type-Writer Girl* (1897). Rayner's story centres on a lower-middle-class heroine Juliet Appleton, who learns shorthand and typing in the East End and joins the struggle for the 'survival of the fittest' declaring that 'I could earn my own bread [...] the sole remaining question was could I adapt to my environment? If so, I had fulfilled the whole gospel of Darwinism'.[220]

If this suburban experience of transport inevitably played a big part in 'subway consciousness' then Wells tended to 'iron out' the ambiguities of this subterranean social interaction. In his writing, the unspoken rules and protocols of social intercourse on the underground are reduced to simple formulas for efficient travel in the city, and are largely drained of social tension or angst. Henry James broadly shared with Wells the more upbeat evaluation of underground travel but, like Gissing, drew on the notion of an 'interlude' in the underground. James had briefly included a short journey from Victoria to Temple station on 'the mysterious underground' in his short story 'A London Life' (1888) and he was very familiar with the steam underground, having lived

216 Forster, *Howard's End*, p. 126.
217 Forster, *Howard's End*, p. 314.
218 See G. Anderson, *Victorian Clerks* (Manchester: Manchester University Press, 1976).
219 F. T. Bullen, *Confessions of a Tradesman* (London: Hodder & Stoughton, 1908), p. 97.
220 Quoted in Anderson, *Victorian Clerks*, p. 27.

in Piccadilly and then Kensington in the 1880s.[221] He had said, in 1877, 'my interest in London is chiefly that of an observer in a place where there is most in the world to observe'.[222] In the novel *The Wings of the Dove* (1902), he used its transit system to stage a short interlude in the lives of Kate Croy and Edward Densher. A long way from the Venetian sunshine, the two characters look across 'the choked compartment' of a first-class carriage on a journey from Sloane Square to Queen's Road in a way that develops the concept of 'subway consciousness'.[223] In this crowded environment, both verbal and non-verbal communication are not only possible but deeply significant for the love affair of his two characters. They are part of the Lancaster Gate 'set' in which the role of wealth is paramount and Kate enters the train 'at Sloane Square to go to Queen's Road' (Bayswater) on the Circle line.[224] This is a chance meeting as Densher is already on the train when Kate boards but they 'exchange the greeting of movements, smiles, abstentions' across the car.[225] Indeed, the value of non-verbal interaction is actually enhanced as they play a game of tube 'musical chairs' in order to sit next to one another when at 'Notting Hill Gate Kate's right-hand neighbour descended, whereupon Densher popped straight into that seat'.[226] On reaching Queen's Road six stations later she alights and Densher 'instantly followed her out of the train'[227] and they walk together to Lancaster Gate. It is clear from this passage that the interior of the underground car is no longer a tense and suspenseful world of estrangement and separation but is a location of emotional fulfilment and engagement. Kate's 'consciousness had gone to him straight as if they had come together in some bright stretch of a desert',[228] a confirmation of mutual attraction which will finally be fulfilled when they sleep together in Venice. It is also really inventive in its playful comedy—the first novel to treat the system as a playground. It seems clear that these users of the underground are being shown as possessors of the kind of mental map of their journeys that had been first developed in Gissing's *The Odd Women*, but they can do much more than simply travel on the underground. It is also important to note that the privileges of class status are being represented in this passage—the train is

---

221 H. James, 'A London Life' (1888), in *A London Life; and, The Reverberator* (Oxford: Oxford University Press, 1989), pp. 3–146, p. 77.

222 H. James, 7 August 1877, in *The Letters of Henry James*, ed. P. Lubbock, 2 vols. (London: Macmillan, 1920), vol. 1, p. 55.

223 H. James, *The Wings of the Dove* (1902; Harmondsworth: Penguin, 1965), p. 90.

224 James, *Wings of the Dove*, p. 89.

225 James, *Wings of the Dove*, p. 90.

226 James, *Wings of the Dove*, p. 90.

227 James, *Wings of the Dove*, p. 55.

228 James, *Wings of the Dove*, p. 54.

busy, it is evening but the other passengers are solidly respectable, one being 'a youngish man with a single eye-glass which he kept constantly in position'.[229] James saw no need to disguise the simple class realities of underground travel experienced by his moneyed characters and his reflection of them in this novel is a reminder that class distinctions were stubbornly maintained—there can be no greater contrast than that between James' Kate Croy and George Moore's heroine Esther Waters who travels third class. Whilst it is undoubtedly true that railway stations mixed social classes in a 'carnivalesque' way, as Richards and MacKenzie argue,[230] the 'old' underground system was not compelled to adopt the 'levelling' approach of the new tube lines and the old first, second and third-class carriages persisted on main-line trains. It was not simply a question of railway apartheid but a measure of the deep social gulf that divided Kate Croy from Esther Waters, a gulf that widened in the Edwardian years.

This fictional understanding of social and mental mapping parallels what was appearing in motion pictures in the United States. There, as Lynne Kirby reveals, two short silent films—*A Rube in the Subway* (1905) and *2AM in the Subway* (1905)—showed the process of acquiring tube etiquette on the New York system. This represented a telescoping of the learning process that had been chronicled in relation to the underground in London. It was now possible to show the most modern transit systems like the New York subway to large cinema audiences in a way that had been technologically impossible for the London system in its first three decades of existence. Where fiction and the press had been the main means available to portray the underground, the cinema offered simpler and more immediate lessons on urban travel. Silent film could reflect and mould habits of subway travel whilst entertaining habitual passengers. In *A Rube in the Subway*, the 'Rube' is a gullible innocent who is visiting New York. The film features three characters, one man and two women who appear amidst the 'anarchy' of the subway platform. The 'Rube' steps off a train and is robbed but jumps onto the track in order to chase the departing train. After a puff of smoke a police officer and a subway official march the 'Rube' back to the platform. In a similar style, *2AM in the Subway* shows a sleepy policeman dozing on the platform. A train pulls in and deposits a drunken trio of 'city folk' and various comic incidents follow. Kirby argues that both films project an 'urbaneness [which] connotes a particular, middle-class position', a visual American version of the purely fictional portrayal of the underground in

---

229 James, *Wings of the Dove*, p. 55.
230 J. Richards & J. M. MacKenzie, *The Railway Station: A Social History* (Oxford: Oxford University Press, 1986), p. 137.

London.[231] They appealed to the rising class of white-collar and white-blouse workers in American cities who could laugh at the antics of unsophisticated visitors. Kirby points to the ways in which early cinema captured forms of urban mass transit visually as fiction had been doing in the descriptions of characters in underground writing. As she concludes, 'if the train station was a microcosm of the social sphere, the train car itself was simply a smaller, more condensed version of the station'.[232] In film, the railway carriage was sometimes a location for a more daring portrayal of human relationships: a picture postcard entitled *In the Tunnel* (c.1904) based on the British film *Kiss in the Tunnel* showed a couple embracing in a railway compartment.[233] Another postcard entitled *Boys Will be Boys* evoked the comedy in this situation by showing a mischievous boy lighting matches in a compartment to show two couples kissing in the tunnel.[234] By 1909, Wells' hero in *Tono-Bungay* explained how he was kissing Marion in a first-class carriage on the underground on their way back from the Birkbeck Institute until 'two other people got in with us and terminated my wooing'.[235]

John Galsworthy's *The Man of Property* (1906) demonstrates a similar sense of familiarity when it notes that 'everyone today went underground', by which was meant everybody who was anybody.[236] This was a retrospective narrative of social life in London in which class divisions on the older sections like the Metropolitan and Circle are identified by placing the two Forsyte brothers, Nicholas and Soames, in separate first and second-class compartments on the same train travelling from Praed Street (Paddington) to Notting Hill Gate and South Kensington stations. It is Nicholas Forsyte who declines to travel second class on the grounds that 'you never know what you may catch',[237] reflecting

---

231 L. Kirby, *Parallel Tracks: The Railroad and Silent Cinema* (Exeter: University of Exeter Press, 1997), p. 139. Whilst the US silent motion picture industry was quick to portray the New York subway following its initial fascination with the building of the trans-American railroad, in Britain filming on the underground was of a purely documentary nature—see the 14-minute short film by London Transport Museum (2002).

232 Kirby, *Parallel Tracks*, p. 83.

233 See J. Barnes, *The Beginnings of the Cinema in England, 1894–1901*, 5 vols. (Exeter: Exeter University Press, 1997), vol. 5, p. 266.

234 Mischievous boys have serious repercussions in another railway incident, when a small boy throws a stone at a train in Henry Green's novel *Blindness* (1926) and John Haye is blinded for life. See H. Green, *Blindness* (1926), in *Nothing/Doting/Blindness* (London: Picador, 1979), pp. 343–505, p. 365.

235 Wells, *Tono-Bungay*, p. 116.

236 J. Galsworthy, *The Man of Property* (Forsyte Saga, vol. 1) (1906; Harmondsworth: Penguin, 1951), p. 269.

237 Galsworthy, *Man of Property*, p. 28.

that this is an underground which once again highlights the class system. Later, Soames Forsyte travels from Sloane Square station in 'a first-class compartment filled with City men [opening] *The Times* with the rich crackle that drowns all lesser sounds and, barricaded behind it, set himself steadily to con the news'.[238] But it is an underground of concealment too. The previous evening saw him rape his wife Irene, asserting the rights of property ownership, and this episode is placed in the familiar first-class carriage in order to highlight the contrast between that awful event and the apparent normality of middle-class commuting. Here, the steam underground of the 1880s is imagined as a necessary part of the structure of wealthy upper-middle-class life in the capital. Galsworthy invokes the Dantean underground in this 'Voyage into the Inferno',[239] using the Circle line for an extraordinary series of encounters in a fog-bound Victorian London. Characters attempt to follow and observe one another in the underground as the mundane world of the Circle line flickers in and out of focus and the underground has become a conduit for the fog that swirls around Sloane Square station, even as far as Trafalgar Square where figures are like 'spectres'.[240] However, Galsworthy's underground is more a stage-set for the lives of his characters and in many ways this serves to underline the novel's historical sweep into the Victorian period. In Galsworthy we find the beginnings of a mythical Victorian underground akin to the process of myth-making around Victorian London itself with its fog-bound streets and clattering horse-drawn carriages that would come to dominate cinematic portrayals of the capital. A whole epoch later, in *Swan Song* (1928), Galsworthy reacted angrily to the tanks that occupied the Embankment during the 1926 General Strike: here the solid achievements of Victorian London with its underground railways was being mocked by a Baldwin government intent on behaving like the thugs that *Punch* had portrayed in its 1883 cartoon 'The Rough and the Rail'.[241]

---

238 Galsworthy, *Man of Property*, p. 265.
239 Galsworthy, *Man of Property*, pp. 264–74.
240 Galsworthy, *Man of Property*, p. 271.
241 J. Galsworthy, *Swan Song* (*Forsyte Saga: A Modern Comedy*, vol. 3) (1928; Harmondsworth: Penguin, 1968), pp. 37–38.

THE INVENTED HISTORY OF THE
UNDERGROUND: FICTION DIGS UP THE PAST

The historical element rapidly became another component in underground writing and inaugurated the creation of a distinct historical tradition at the moment of a major technological break. This was prompted at least in part by the transformation of the underground with the advent of electric power and the disappearance of steam in the central area over a relatively short time. This can be seen in Baroness Orczy's comments in her short story 'The Mysterious Death on the Underground Railway' (1901) when in the 'days of tubes and motor traction [...] the good old Metropolitan Railway carriages cannot at any time be said to be over-crowded'.[242] The underground now had its own 'history' in which separate periods could be identified and explored for their power to mark off or evoke Victorian London. In fictional terms this took the form of a nostalgic recreation of the steam underground and starts with G. K. Chesterton's portrayal of Victorian stability in *The Man Who Was Thursday* (1908). Chesterton connected a secure Victorian past with the insecurity of the Edwardian present, with his character Gabriel Syme describing the underground as the 'victory of Adam' and adding that 'every time a train comes in I feel that it has broken past batteries of besiegers, and that man has won a battle against chaos'.[243]

Arnold Bennett went back even further to the actual building of the Metropolitan Railway in his novel *Riceyman Steps* (1927). Bennett invoked the construction of the underground in its King's Cross/Clerkenwell context as a 'marvellous outstanding event'[244] and detailed 'the construction of the Underground Railway from Clerkenwell to Euston Square'. Bennett conveys the dramatic events involved in building the line by the 'cut and cover' method when the 'earth opened in the most unexpected and undesirable places. Streets had to be barred to horse traffic; pavements resembled switchbacks'. But 'the culminating catastrophe' was the collapse of the workings as the crown of arch of the mighty Fleet sewer' breaks, unleashing a torrent of 'dark and fetid liquid [...] into the mouth of the new tunnel'. But Bennett is quick to say that 'the Underground Railway was begun afresh and finished and grandly inaugurated,

---

242 E. Orczy, 'The Mysterious Death on the Underground Railway' (1901), in H. Greene (ed.), *The Rivals of Sherlock Holmes* (London: Bodley Head, 1970), pp. 217–37, p. 220.

243 G. K. Chesterton, *The Man Who Was Thursday* (1908; London: Penguin, 1986), p. 13.

244 A. Bennett, *Riceyman Steps* (1923; London: Pan, 1964), p. 31.

and at first the public fought for seats in its trains'.[245] In other words, he was convinced that the moral of this tale was the great step forward brought by the underground and he further reminded his readers of the 'hell of noise and dust and dirt' that existed in the streets of contemporary King's Cross.[246] Both Chesterton and Bennett clearly identified with the steam underground in a way very similar to Wells even if they rejected much of the wider Victorian legacy. Such writers constructed a fictional past for the steam underground that would 'store' it for future generations of readers unacquainted with the original reality. Even Edgar Wallace's thriller *The Four Just Men* (1905) places the underground in a romantic past even though the story features contemporary political themes. Towards the end of this thriller, an informer who threatens the gang's plot to kill a government minister is assassinated: he is lured into a first-class District Railway carriage at Charing Cross station but between Victoria and Sloane Square his killer appears in the adjoining car 'standing on the footboard of the swaying carriage, holding the half-opened door' and smashes a phial of prussic acid on the floor. When the train reaches Kensington station (South Kensington) 'a passenger leisurely selecting his compartment [...] opened a carriage door and staggered back coughing. A solicitous porter and an alarmed station official ran forward and pulled open the door, and the sickly odour of almonds pervaded the station'.[247] Both compartments are obligingly empty, the killer escapes undetected and no harm comes to any other passengers.

Radclyffe Hall and Dorothy Richardson created a fictional past for the underground that fixed it in a time of the original steam lines as though the speedy electrification of the system between 1898 and 1905 was the end of one historical era and the beginning of another. Radclyffe Hall's *The Unlit Lamp* (1924) portrays the visit of her heroines, Joan and Elizabeth, to London where they are engulfed in fog and struggle 'furiously for overcrowded buses, or filling their lungs with sulphur on the Underground'.[248] The steam underground also features prominently in Dorothy Richardson's novel sequence *Pilgrimage* (1938), where we meet Miriam Henderson, an unattached middle-class woman trying to establish herself in a largely male literary world. Miriam travels along an important urban boundary, one that had been carved out by the building of the Metropolitan Railway in the 1860s. Later, she walks along the Euston Road and visits some houses at the back of the Metropolitan Railway: 'one high long

---

245 Bennett, *Riceyman Steps*, pp. 11–12.
246 Bennett, *Riceyman Steps*, p. 2.
247 E. Wallace, *The Four Just Men* (1905; London: House of Stratus, 2001), p. 96.
248 Radclyffe Hall, *The Unlit Lamp* (1924; London: Jonathan Cape, 1933), p. 211.

lifeless smoke-grimed facade fronted by gardens colourless with grime'.[249] This sense of a railway polluted environment is strong in Richardson's novels, with smoke from the Metropolitan line pouring 'up over their faces as the smoke from the kitchen fire pours over the back of a range',[250] an interesting domestication of the steam locomotive. The houses evoke the underground in Miriam's mind: 'the sight of them brought nothing to her mind but the inside of the Metropolitan Railway; the feeling of one's skin prickling with grime, the sense of one's smoke-begrimed clothes'.[251]

Miriam is also to be found travelling on the Metropolitan Railway before electrification after having journeyed on a 'north London omnibus' to Portland Road Station. She later travels from Gower Street with 'its familiar sulphurous gloom, the platform lights shining murkily from the midst of slowly rolling clouds, grey smoke, the dark forms and phantom white faces of waiting passengers emerging suddenly as she threaded the darkness'.[252] These were Miriam's 'first London years'[253] and in a very combustible image, the city is 'her pillar of cloud and fire'.[254] Furthermore, the 'sense of a complex London life' comes to her on the platform at Gower Street station.[255] Richardson invests the steam underground with a profoundly symbolic power, the train rolling 'slowly in behind its beloved black dumpy high-shouldered engine with its large unshrieking mushroom bell-whistle'.[256] This is a journey from 'outside the radius into blackness'[257] to attend a lecture on Dante. After the lecture, Miriam travels back into London to Gower Street station 'in a dream',[258] and thinks that she must 'give up the sense of the train going along in the darkness'.[259] In *Pilgrimage*, Richardson is transforming the imagery of underground writing by consciously associating it with the past, successfully bringing together the surface and subterranean worlds so that they are almost a mirror image of one another. Whilst for her character Miriam the underground steam railway is more of a refuge than the streets above, Richardson makes the real, external underground into an internal, imaginative one in these journeys. She has also

---

249 D. Richardson, *Pilgrimage* (1938), 4 vols. (London: Virago, 1979 & 1992), vol. 2, p. 257.
250 Richardson, *Pilgrimage*, vol. 2, p. 257.
251 Richardson, *Pilgrimage*, vol. 2, p. 257.
252 Richardson, *Pilgrimage*, vol. 2, pp. 352–53.
253 Richardson, *Pilgrimage*, vol. 3, p. 107.
254 Richardson, *Pilgrimage*, vol. 3, p. 107.
255 Richardson, *Pilgrimage*, vol. 2, p. 358.
256 Richardson, *Pilgrimage*, vol. 2, pp. 352–53.
257 Richardson, *Pilgrimage*, vol. 2, p. 353.
258 Richardson, *Pilgrimage*, vol. 2, p. 355.
259 Richardson, *Pilgrimage*, vol. 2, p. 358.

placed a historical ring-fence around the steam underground, a world which had largely disappeared by the time she started writing *Pilgrimage*. The building of the tubes brought about the beginning of the end of the steam underground, heralding the close of what could be identified as the first historical era in the underground's relatively short history. It was in fiction like Richardson's that the old underground was mediated from outside its historical time-frame as a device to convey the life journey of an individual character—in this case Miriam. But her character's journey also anticipates many of the psychological themes of the postwar years. The carriage fills up at Praed Street station and Miriam is engaged for several pages in an intense interior monologue about these passengers, trying to find her way through this very Dantean underworld of 'the thick roots of evil in her to bring her through into the Paradiso'.[260]

Underground writing was influenced by other forces during these decades. One major development was the building of tube systems in other European cites against which the original London experience could be measured. The London underground exercised an almost mystical influence over those who wished to innovate in other cities, offering a practical example of the mechanics of the subterranean transport system. The fact that London had successfully completed both steam and electric lines by 1900 was an indication to urban planners and city governments that underground transit was a necessary part of the modern and modernizing city. At the same time, tube advocates were conscious of the need to avoid the apparent mistakes of the London system, particularly as tubes were only one of a number of possible transit options in other capital cities. The opening of the Paris Métro (1900) and the first New York subway line (1904) made possible a cross-cultural influence between the two. Both systems were from the start electrically powered and therefore images of sulphurous infernal underworlds were not valid, but there was nonetheless a transference of this generic imagery to the new systems, particularly as the London one had appeared in Huysmans' novel *A Rebours* (1884). Here his character Des Essientes describes in a hallucinatory way a London where 'trains raced by at full speed; and down in the underground sewers, others rumbled along, occasionally emitting ghastly screams or vomiting floods of smoke through the gaping mouths of airshafts'.[261] The Paris Métro had no smoke or sulphur but it quickly developed an infernal reputation, particularly after the 1903 fire which killed 84 people. The Paris Métropolitain was

---

260 Richardson, *Pilgrimage*, vol. 2, p. 356.
261 J. K. Huysmans, *A Rebours (Against Nature)* (1884), trans. R. Baldick (Harmondsworth: Penguin, 1959), p. 134; see also J. Campbell, 'To London, for love', *Guardian*, 20 November 2004.

dubbed the 'Nécropolitain' as a result of the disaster with a special edition of *L'Assiette au Beurre*, a leading left-wing illustrated magazine, depicting passengers buying tickets to the Métro from the skeletal figure of death in the booking office.[262] Inevitably, perhaps, *Punch* had prefigured this image for the London underground over 20 years before in a cartoon entitled 'THERE AND (NOT) BACK!' (1878) where seaside excursionists queue happily to buy tickets from a spectral ticket clerk.[263] These other metro systems were also threatened by the noxious vapours that seemed to pervade subterranean locations. As Benson Bobrick notes, the 'perennial question'[264] was the ventilation system of the tube and neither London nor Paris offered non-toxic air. Similar concerns led the London County Council to investigate pollution on the tubes, finding that levels of carbon dioxide were not dangerous but sulphur and nitrous oxide were, with exhaust fans being introduced at several stations as a result. In New York, considerable play was made of the effects of 'non-diluted' air by opponents of the subway, with the suggestion being made by them that such toxic air could produce epidemics of typhus, consumption and pneumonia. The Paris Métro was described as 'a badly ventilated cellar, recalling at times a sewer [...] a succession of unnamable odors, unbreatheable emanations, a mixture of sweat, coal-tar, carbonic acid, metallic dust, etc'.[265] It was also, as Christopher Prendergast has pointed out, a cause of bitter political debate centred on fears of modernization in the French capital as the tearing up of the Paris streets was controversial in a city still haunted by the 'Haussmannization' of the 1860s. Prendergast suggests that the Métro occupied an unstable position in public consciousness even though it stressed relatedness rather than separation.[266]

As in the first phase of underground development, journalism was better equipped to describe and comment on the new system and, at least in the initial years, to offer a positive account of the experience. Writing was slower to take shape with most authors only engaging seriously with the steam underground some 20 years after its inception. In the new phase of electric power, writing emerged almost contemporaneously in the 1880s and was quick to catch up with the reality of tube travel. Wells' approach encouraged a more multilayered description of the system: it tended on the whole to be positive and was in line with media accounts. The opening of the Central London

---

262 See B. Bobrick, *Labyrinths of Iron: A History of the World's Subways* (New York: Newsweek Books, 1982), chapter 5.

263 'There and (not) Back', *Punch*, 14 September 1878, vol. 75, pp. 114–15.

264 Bobrick, *Labyrinths of Iron*, p. 232.

265 Bobrick, *Labyrinths of Iron*, p. 157.

266 C. Prendergast, *Paris and the Nineteenth Century* (Oxford: Blackwell, 1992), p. 100.

Railway's first section between Bank and Shepherd's Bush in 1900 was described in glowing terms. One of its trains was said to have 'glided with an ease that was almost magical, out of the brilliantly lit Bank Station [and] slipped through brilliantly-lit white-tile stations, one after the other, until [...] it climbed smoothly up into the sunlight once more at Shepherd's Bush'.[267] And Frosterus, in his 'London Rhapsody' described the hansom cab as an heroic symbol of the past and the underground its modern future; whilst the electric railway was 'a parabola of energy [...] with its apex at the Bank of England [...] a work of art, monumental in its practical simplicity, splendid in its solid elegance'.[268] Frosterus was making the link between old and new technologies, with the bold utilitarianism of the tubes needing to make a strong impact on the surface. Journalism quickly focused on a number of important themes in this new tube travel, finding much more that was modern in the Central, Bakerloo and Piccadilly lines than in the 'sardine box' City and South London Railway with its so-called 'padded cells'. The newer tubular railways offered ease and speed of travel, clean white-tiled stations and access to platforms via fast and effective lifts. Tube trains permitted more comfortable conditions for a greater number of passengers, easier loading and unloading and more visual contact with the outside world. Many accounts pointed out to readers that the deep tubes returned to daylight at the surface as though to reassure them that the tubes were not cut off from the 'human' world and encased in a purely mechanical and artificial underworld. William Dean Howells, in his *London Films* (1905), describes a journey on the City and South London Railway from central London to Islington creating a curious picture of the experience: 'We dropped from the clouded surfaces of the earth to depths where the tube-trains carry their passengers from one brilliant-lit station to another [...] when we ascended to them [Highbury Fields] from our tubular station, the lawns were of an electric green in their vividness'.[269] There is a sense of relief in Howells' remarks, as though the ascent to the surface reminds the writer of a more stable world to which he has returned, a world grown more important after the experience of tube travel. This would not be inconsistent with Howells' views of the elevated railway in New York which he had attacked as a mechanization of morality in his novel *A Hazard of New Fortunes* in 1890.

However, journalism strengthened the dominant opinion that the new tubes would make a major contribution to improving the *entire* transport system in

267 Quoted in J. Day & J. Reed, *The Story of London's Underground* (Harrow Weald: Capital Transport Publishing, 2001), p. 56.

268 Frosterus, 'London Rhapsody', quoted in Allen, *The Moving Pageant*, p. 209.

269 W. D. Howells, *London Films* (London: Harper & Brothers, 1905), pp. 218–20.

the capital. Eric Banton in an article entitled 'Underground Travelling London' (1903) noted that 'few Londoners have a good word for the Underground' but hastened to add that the Central London Railway was a big step towards London having 'a perfect network of underground thoroughfares which will make the city one of the best equipped in the world'.[270] The illustrations accompanying Banton's article showed bowler-hatted gents waiting for lifts at Bank Station and well-dressed men, women and children strolling through the subways at the station. To give even more positive assurance to readers, police officers are frequently in evidence, in one case, giving directions to passengers. Such reassuring images were important for public perception of the new tube lines. By contrast, older lines were represented, for example, as subject to the female pickpocket who 'respectably attired [...] haunts the Metropolitan Railway and the suburban lines, or spends her days on omnibuses and tram-cars in quest of purses and other valuables'.[271] The underground was also responding to the need for a new London of imperial culture, to be reflected, some writers thought, in Edwardian architecture.[272] A new generation of stations designed by Leslie Green was being built all over the city and their solid design and powerful external presence on London's streets appeared to give a new dimension to the underground. In an era when the successful marketing of transport services in the capital was vital to private companies, these stations were designed to be important statements of railway architecture. The companies aimed to produce better services for the commuter under the direct influence of the late Arts and Crafts Movement and the growing design movement in the 1900s that included C. R. Ashbee and W. R. Lethaby. Such luminaries insisted that art should serve the people at all levels in society, making even public transport into an integrated aesthetic world as well as an efficient transit system.

There was broad agreement in the Design and Industries Association that the railways were part of a mechanized society, but were nonetheless aesthetic objects. It often shared with Wells a highly critical view of the city, with Lethaby, for example, voicing his dismay at the failure to improve architectural design in the early years of the new century. Lethaby argued, in a lecture entitled 'Architecture and Modern Life' (1917), that even 'the new Tube stations are draughty and untidy—gashes in the street's side—and now they are running down into

270 Banton, 'Underground Travelling London', pp. 60 & 63.

271 E. A. Carr, 'Criminal London' (1902), in Sims, *Edwardian London*, vol. 3, pp. 221–27, p. 225.

272 See J. Schneer, *London 1900: The Imperial Metropolis* (New Haven: Yale University Press, 1999).

accepted dirt and ineptitude'.[273] If the first generation of tube stations was to act as a suitably attractive portal to the subterranean system, they already required a major overhaul in terms of design or needed entirely rebuilding to reflect the modern city. Lethaby argued that a more scientific age had dawned after 1900, an age demanding a new philosophy of art and design more suited to a commercially based society. Lethaby's voice was heard throughout the interwar years and the underground seemed to be moving in the direction indicated by him. Noel Carrington found that the underground had managed to achieve a new pioneering design role after the war. In his article 'Need Our Cities be Ugly?' (1930), Carrington chose to illustrate this change with a series of photographs including a telling comparison between the old and the new St James's Park stations, pointing out that 'the Underground have led the way, not only in poster design, but in the efficiency and tidiness of their stations'.[274] The art critic Roger Fry described underground advertising in 1926 as a 'matter of hypnotism on a large scale [...] the poster has become the great weapon of the industrial companies, and the poster designer their great ally'.[275] But on the whole the more utopian advocates like Wells and Lethaby were able to signpost the future. Based on Lethaby's concept in a discussion on 'Art and Workmanship' (1913), the design philosophy 'Fitness for Purpose'[276] would emerge as the cardinal value of the Underground Group of Companies and its successor the London Passenger Transport Board. This was 'the well-doing of what needs doing',[277] indicating that everyday objects like tube stations should combine utility with beauty or good design. The tube station, Lethaby argued, should be integrated into the urban environment at a design as well as a functional level, an aspiration that was to be increasingly found in writing after the war. This stream of design ideas was effectively linked to writing through the work of Wells, giving it more wide-ranging imaginative perspectives of the kind that had been merely implicit in Gissing's fiction, for example, in the painterly perspective of the railway arch or portal. The new generation of tube stations was clearly a failure in Lethaby's view—they deserved to be the portals to and from the utopian city and it was the street level that mattered. In theory, at least, Gissing's infernal arches had been laid to rest by modernist

---

273 W. R. Lethaby, 'Architecture and Modern Life' (1917), in *Form in Civilization: Collected Papers on Art & Labour* (London: Oxford University Press, 1927), pp. 106–21, p. 110.

274 N. Carrington, 'Need Our Cities be Ugly?', *Listener*, 22 January 1930, pp. 149–51, p. 149.

275 R. Fry, quoted in O. Green, *Underground Art* (London: Studio Vista, 1990), p. 14.

276 'Fitness for Purpose' was the criterion for an effective underground poster developed by Frank Pick, who became Commercial Officer for UERL in 1912.

277 W. R. Lethaby, 'Art and Workmanship' (1913), in *Form in Civilization*, pp. 208–13, p. 209.

aesthetics and, like the magic door in Wells' 'The Door in the Wall', the future seemed like heaven. In other words, it was as though the deeper the tubes went, the more they needed to make an impact on the surface. It was here that a new aesthetic emerged, one that eschewed the functional entrances of the first decades of the steam underground. For Lethaby, the station entrance was primarily part of street architecture and needed to be designed as such. But for Wells the entrance represented a portal to an equally important underground world of travel—a potential underground city as prefigured in his science fantasy.

Where Gissing had identified a vertical porousness that was based on the physical proximity of the steam underground and the streets, the tubes were distinctly separate. But the psychological connection between the surface of the city and its subterranean levels could not be severed and became even more important with the building of deep tubes. The station lift and escalator were the new interface between street and sublevels, the kind of descent that would be increasingly remarked upon in writing in these decades. Electric lifts took on a special significance: often shown as part of a set of illustrations of the new tubes, they were frequently crowded but had a liftman reassuringly present at the lift gates. The ease with which the gulf between street and tube could be negotiated is also demonstrated in the corporate publicity that surrounded the new generation of department stores such as Bourne & Hollingsworth and Selfridges that colonized the West End after 1880. Advertising for Selfridges pictured the entire store from fourth floor to sub-basement, indicating the presence of the Central line running along Oxford Street and, of course, the store location is shown to be almost equidistant between Marble Arch and Bond Street stations.[278] As Alan Trachtenberg also notes in his study of American stores, 'these places created a unique fusion of economic and cultural values; they were staging grounds for the making and confirming of new relations between goods and people'.[279] Whilst the London department stores were greatly enhanced by the new tube lines, similarly all underground advertising was now strongly oriented to shopping with, for example, the new G. N. Piccadilly and Brompton highlighting its route through the theatre and shopping areas.[280] The pleasant shopping ambience was shown on many postcards and the official 'UNDERGROUND' poster entitled *Winter's Discontent*

278 *Selfridge's Department Store 1909*, reproduced in H. Clout (ed.), *The Times History of London* (1991; London: Times Books, 2000), p. 107.

279 A. Trachtenberg, *The Incorporation of America: Culture and Society in the Gilded Age* (New York: Hill & Wang, 1982), pp. 130–33.

280 See M. I. Bray, *Railway Picture Postcards* (Ashbourne: Moorland Publishing, 1986).

Made Glorious (1909) located illustrations of a theatre audience, a store interior and a restaurant inside an underground car.

A further link in the circuitry of tubes and shopping centres in the capital was the new generation of newspapers such as the *Daily Mail*. Alfred Harmsworth, the *Mail*'s proprietor, called his paper 'The Busy Man's Daily Journal', launching it in 1896 to compete with London's more staid titles which probably had a combined circulation of less than a million a day. Living in a newly built terrace near West Hampstead railway station, Harmsworth had a shrewd understanding of his commuter readership, particularly in his appreciation of their need to find the news quickly without wading through advertising supplements. 'The economy of the reader's time effected by the absence of the most puzzling maze of advertisements is [...] of the first importance' declared its first leader page.[281] The *Mail* was not a tabloid but it was concise and compact as well as cheap in comparison with the other London dailies, and it offered aspirant young clerks the chance to be seen reading a newspaper that did put them 'in the cheap-newspaper-reading class'.[282] Appearing without front page news was a badge of the *Mail*'s respectability. With both front and back pages of display and small advertisements offering 'charming semi-detached villas' in the suburbs and 'clothes in the latest West-end styles',[283] it was making the invisible connection between suburb and shopping, a reality that made the *Mail* increasingly dependent on advertising revenue for survival. It also provided the kind of news on basic issues that directly affected Londoners, with stories about the re-routing of horse omnibuses, the failings of London's trams and frequent comments on the new tube lines, not to mention the coining of phrases like 'Tuppeny Tube' and words like 'suffragette'. The *Mail* was pre-eminently the newspaper of London's transport system in these decades, both reflecting and shaping the perception of services to the ever-growing lower-middle-class commuter groups in the capital. It brought with this extensive coverage an apolitical campaigning approach which eschewed formal political affiliations (Liberal or Conservative) and therefore appealed to the tube or bus commuter who was angry about corruption in local government or the failure to provide decent services. It was an example of campaigning popular journalism, whether on larger patriotic, imperialist, anti-German themes or on local ratepayers' issues. The *Mail* had sales of a million and a half on 23 January 1901 when Queen Victoria died, settling to around 700,000 in the years before the First

---

281 P. Ferris, *The House of Northcliffe, The Harmsworths of Fleet Street* (London: Weidenfeld & Nicolson, 1971), p. 85.

282 Ferris, *House of Northcliffe*, p. 85.

283 Ferris, *House of Northcliffe*, pp. 85–86.

World War. It had a formidably large reach for its campaigning, another example of the ways in which London's underground system was integrated into wider cultural and political frameworks in these years.

Harmsworth had also launched *Forget-Me-Not* in 1891 which included a high proportion of fiction in a very portable A5 format and billed itself as 'The Pictorial Journal for Ladies' (1893). Here was the beginning of a modern mass readership fiction for women and men with, for example, the story 'The Man, the Girl and the Dog' (1915) focusing on an 'office slave' in the City.[284] This type of story, as Lynne Hapgood points out, was part of the transition in the lives of its commuter readership which was to be reflected in the fiction of the interwar period.[285]

These media changes shaped underground writing. Passengers had to adjust from one type of travel to another in a very short space of time and London was the only urban system to make such a transition. Writing adjusted to this process far more quickly than in Gissing's time, rapidly conflating the two stages. In this sense, the media representation of the tubes became synonymous with that of fiction, offering an increasingly unified blueprint of the underground system. The underground even had its own much condensed history in fiction to form a repository of images of the steam period even though the writing of the interwar years largely ignored the original sections of the system. It seems clear that the writing of H. G. Wells framed the literary responses to the London underground in the crucial period of its transition from steam to electric technology. Wellsian perspectives emerged through his work which largely drew on Gissing's original contribution but enlarged or rejected certain parts of Gissing's fictional mapping of the steam underground. Wells managed the technological transition in fiction in a utopian fashion, highlighting the positive contribution to the city of public transport that was embodied in the new tube lines. In Wells, public transport facilitated rather than impeded communication. Human faculties would not be drowned out by technology but instead would be complemented by it, in both the macro-sense of the whole city and the micro-sense of communication between people in the tube car or in the station. Wells could practise a formulaic account of underground travel because he was writing in the grain of the early 1900s, largely in tune with the press and opinion-formers of the period. In fact, Wells was a major opinion-former in his own right and transport organizations like the Underground

---

284   *Forget-Me-Not*, 23 January 1915, pp. 323–26.
285   L. Hapgood, *Margins of Desire: the Suburbs in Fiction and Culture, 1880–1925* (Manchester: Manchester University Press, 2005), pp. 127–28.

Group undoubtedly benefited from his practical endorsements of tube travel. Wells prepared the literary perspectives of the underground for the development of its powerful Tubist phase but his utopianism, however dominant, could not entirely rule out the more infernal perspectives inherited from Gissing, and Wells had himself reflected such perspectives in his science fantasy. That the London underground would be projected into the future or onto the Moon was hardly a predictable outcome but the more earthbound experiments in transportation, mediated however imperfectly by the earlier fiction of Gissing and others, offered the opportunity to pose a number of questions about the future. Ironically, Wells' swift elision of steam and electric systems into a single utopia simply concealed some elements that re-emerged in the aftermath of the First World War. Infernal images were given added cogency by the impact of the technology of modern warfare and in wartime, and 'a generation that had gone to school on horse-drawn tramcars now stood under the open sky in a landscape where nothing remained unchanged but the clouds and, beneath those clouds, in a force field of destructive torrents and explosions, the tiny, fragile human body'.[286] In similar fashion, the male generation that had travelled on the underground in London, reading the jingoistic Harmsworth press, breathing in the sulphur on steam trains or using the first escalators to the deep tubes, now found itself sheltering in a very different system of tunnels. Its female counterpart would find itself for the first time transformed from passengers into workers.

---

286 W. Benjamin, 'The Storyteller' (1936), in *Illuminations* (London: Fontana/Collins, 1973), pp. 83–109, p. 84.

Chapter Three

'THE ROAR OF THE UNDERGROUND RAILWAY': THE MAKING OF THE TUBE IN THE INTERWAR YEARS

At each station of the Outer Circle a train stopped every two minutes.

Graham Greene, *It's a Battlefield*[1]

When Virginia Woolf said that human character changed 'in or about December, 1910' she was probably not thinking of the London Tube.[2] Woolf appears to have taken the date from the year of the art exhibition 'Manet and Post-Impressionism' in her essay 'Mr Bennett and Mrs Brown' (1924) and it seems a far cry from the subterranean world of the London underground. In the 1930s, however, Woolf might have added that the Tube had as much of an effect on perception as Post-Impressionism but this would have been at least in part due to her own writing. Woolf's writing *changed* the way we think about the underground system and she was the literary inventor of the Tube after 1910, laying down a blueprint that would mark out new boundaries as a subject for writing. Her essay asserted a major shift in human relations that was based on her perception of changes in society, a view that could equally well have been applied to the writing of the new electric tubular railway. Woolf's essay suggested a move beyond fictional realism towards more expressive forms of art and the Tube offered many new possibilities. This was the literary creation of *the* Tube (with a capital T) even though, ironically, the

1   G. Greene, *It's a Battlefield* (1934; London: Heinemann, 1970), p. 19.
2   V. Woolf, 'Mr Bennett and Mrs Brown' (1924), in *Collected Essays*, ed. L. Woolf, 4 vols. (London: Hogarth Press, 1966), vol. 1, pp. 319–37, p. 320.

earliest appearance of this abbreviation in fiction was in Arnold Bennett's short story 'The Fire of London' (1904), the 'Mr Bennett' whom she had attacked in her essay. After 1910, an unprecedented amount of artistic and literary energy went into trying to find ways to construct the Tube in writing and this chapter will explore how and why modernism engaged with the underground until the beginning of the Second World War. Whilst still firmly located within the city, modernism moved the apprehension of the urban world from its political and economic structures to what Lynne Hapgood calls a 'geography of ideas'.[3] But the Tube was as much a fictional vehicle for a realist like George Orwell as it was for Arnold Bennett who wrote about it in the public spirit that Woolf referred to when she said that 'to complete [the novels of Bennett] it seems necessary to do something—to join a society, or, more desperately, to write a cheque'.[4] This chapter will explore these questions through an analysis of the components of what may be called Tubism, a formation of literary, artistic and cultural artifacts and practices that emerged in these decades.

A TOTALLY NEW IDEA OF MOTION: THE FORMATION OF TUBISM

How did the Tube come to occupy such a central place in writing in 1910? The simplest explanation is that it was taken up in the whirlwind of Futurism, the Italian cultural movement that swept Europe just before the outbreak of the First World War. The central aim of Futurism was to redefine the boundaries of culture, reviving the traditional arts but also creating an aesthetic of speed, mobility and technological power. Its leader, Filippo Tommaso Marinetti, employed every medium to disseminate Futurism's message in order to reach a mass audience. Virginia Woolf's description of the seismic change in human character might as easily have been ascribed to the impact of the Futurist exhibition held in London just over a year later, in early 1912. Marinetti had taken London by storm with his fervent acclamation in an interview with the *Evening News* that 'London itself is a Futurist City!'

---

3   See L. Hapgood, 'The Unwritten Suburb: Defining Spaces in John Galsworthy's *The Man of Property*', in L. Hapgood & N. Paxton (eds.), *Outside Modernism, In Pursuit of the English Novel 1900–30* (London: Macmillan, 2000), pp. 162–79, p. 164.
4   Woolf, 'Mr Bennett and Mrs Brown', p. 326.

and praised the capital's 'coloured electric lights that flash in the night'; its 'enormous glaring posters' and its 'brilliant hued motor buses'.[5]

Marinetti reserved his most extravagant praise for the underground, describing a tube journey as 'what I wanted—not enjoyment, but a totally new idea of motion, of speed'. It was, for him, the key to a new kind of city, a city of the future in which bodies were perpetually in motion so that human beings would become 'non-human and mechanical [...] constructed for an omnipresent velocity'.[6] Men, Marinetti said, would one day be 'endowed with surprising organs: organs adapted to the needs of a world of ceaseless shocks'.[7] The tube pointed to a future of man and machine, a world in which commuters would develop shock absorbers for the rigours of the rush hour and be visually, chemically and electronically plugged into their journey to and from work. Marinetti made the all-important breakthrough as the tube had not been described like this before: it was a new and compelling vision of urban transit that seemed to capture the essence of modernity. Marinetti was not the first writer to identify the tube as a transformative entity, but he was one of the first to associate it with forces that were reshaping consciousness, propelling human populations into a future in which electric technology would generate limitless possibilities. The hugely expanded tube network, tunnelling 26.5 miles under London in the years between 1903 and 1908, presented to Marinetti a powerful imaginative metaphor for the future. The stress on speed, deplored by cultural critics like John Ruskin and Max Nordau, was now to be celebrated by the Futurists. As Judy Davies argues, Marinetti wanted transit to be imperceptible 'in order that the earth-bound integument of the Futurist self may be forgotten'—in other words, the unity of man and machine.[8]

Marinetti's celebration of the tube was one of the formative elements in a redefinition of underground writing. These cultural perspectives may be labelled Tubism, an aesthetic cluster that brought together ideas, images, literary and visual genres and the technology of electric power in a shifting and often

---

5   *Evening News*, 2 March 1912, quoted in R. Cork, 'Art & the Underground', in E. Paolozzi, *Eduardo Paolozzi Underground*, ed. R. Cork (London: Weidenfeld & Nicolson, 1986), pp. 28–42, p. 28. This was Marinetti's second visit to London and on this occasion he had come with other Futurist artists to talk up the Futurist exhibition which had moved from Paris to the Sackville Gallery at 28 Sackville Street in March 1912. His visit included a lecture delivered at the Bechstein Hall in which he castigated English culture in French.

6   F. T. Marinetti, 'War, the World's Only Hygiene' (1911–15), in *Marinetti: Selected Writings*, ed. R. W. Flint (London: Secker & Warburg, 1972), p. 91.

7   Marinetti, 'War, the World's Only Hygiene', p. 91.

8   J. Davies, 'Mechanical millennium: Sant'Elia and the poetry of Futurism', in E. Timms & D. Kelley (eds.), *Unreal City: Urban Experience in Modern European Literature and Art* (Manchester: Manchester University Press, 1985), pp. 65–79, p. 72.

contradictory form. Tubism ranged from the celebrated poster art through the elegant design unity of trains, stations and maps to the potent imagery of the tube in the work of modernist writers like Virginia Woolf. Tubism signified that the underground was a machine for travelling in, a vast and unified public space through which travel, everyday communication, cultural exchange, business and pleasure could be routed. The Tube was incorporated into culture (as defined in 1910), admitted into an artistic movement (Futurism) and was therefore performing a new role in the vocabulary of the modern world. At no point in its cultural history had the underground explicitly entered the public realm as a world or an environment in the way that Futurism projected it into a much wider public arena. The underground could now be encountered as a place of altered consciousness. From this moment people could read and think about this experience and become more aware of themselves as travellers in this uniquely compact, crowded and artificial world. Now, Tube travellers were to be interrogated by modernism.

At another level Tubism was the expression, in more popular and consciously propagandistic forms, of the comparatively sudden unification of London's underground railways and tube lines. The system had taken on a more unified cultural form by 1912, in the early days of the new and dynamic leadership of Albert Stanley and Frank Pick. In these years, the newly formed Underground Group of Companies had begun the vigorous growth of the Bakerloo, Piccadilly and Northern lines; completed the electrification of the inner Metropolitan, Circle and District lines and had begun to introduce escalators, Otis lifts and innovations like illuminated platform indicators. The sheer scale of building and innovation during these years stamped the underground as an indelible example of modernity and the tube remapped the capital below ground, giving form to the notion of deep level underground systems as a subterranean reflection of the metropolis. During these years, the abbreviation of tubular railway to the 'tubes' or the 'Tube' came into vogue. The word 'tubes' seems to have appeared in popular fiction for the first time in a short story by Fred M. White called 'The Invisible Force' in 1903, and the following year as the 'Tube railway' in Arnold Bennett's 'The Fire of London'. In this sense, Tubism was the expression of what Ford Madox Ford called 'the modern spirit' in his essay *The Soul of London*, suggesting that it was to be found 'in terms not of men but of forces [...] great organisations run by men as impersonal as the atoms of our own frames, noiseless, and to all appearances infallible'.[9] The

---

9   F. M. Ford, *The Soul of London* (1905; London: Everyman, 1995), pp. 29–30. Leonard Woolf went as far as to suggest that human life was determined by transport systems: 'In London

Tube was a good example of this modern force, an organization seemingly run by impersonal and hidden systems through the 'invisible' technology of electric power. It symbolized the future, carving out a more democratic, accessible and leisure-based city that was in line with the utopian approach of H. G. Wells. It was an underground that had come to represent London as a city, as Ford had suggested in *The Soul of London*, where he noted that 'for the Londoner, there is a convenient station on the Underground'—a station which grafted an identity onto the seemingly anonymous streets of the capital.[10]

In other respects, Tubism reworks what Michael Saler has called 'medieval modernism'. Saler stresses the medieval roots of transport modernity because of its links with the nineteenth-century Arts and Crafts Movement and correctly identifies the extent to which the philosophy of 'Fitness for Purpose' guided the aesthetic development of the underground system.[11] Saler argues that it was 'the London Underground, rather than the continental futurists, surrealists, or constructivists that was the most successful embodiment of the early twentieth-century avant-garde's aim of integrating modern art with modern life'.[12] Whilst it is certainly true that the design policy of the underground was rooted in the attempt to conciliate between tradition and modernity, this analysis seriously undervalues the great diversity of visual ideas in the years around 1910 which placed the tubes in a new artistic context. For modernists like Virginia Woolf, it was not the fact that the look of the tube was informed by modernist principles of design, but how the tube was perceived, what it represented and how it could be fashioned in terms of an inner vision. As Samuel Hynes has noted, Woolf 'chose that occasion [the Post-Impressionist exhibition] as an appropriate symbol of the way European ideas forced themselves upon the insular English consciousness during the Edwardian years'.[13] The official design policy of the Underground Group was, in fact, a form of 'conservative modernity', an attempt to create a trademark ideology that would market the underground in an era of competitive urban transport. Whilst it has been persuasively argued by David Harvey that modernism was ultimately about the attempt to bring order out of chaos, this does not mean that the modernists could be relied upon to

---

we are made in the image of the Tube and Underground' (L. Woolf, 'Politics in Spain', in *Nation and Athenaeum*, 21 April 1923, vol. 33, no. 3, pp. 74–75, p. 75).

10   Ford, *The Soul of London*, p. 97.

11   See F. Pick, 'Art in Modern Life', in *The Nineteenth Century and After*, February 1922, pp. 256–64.

12   M. Saler, *The Avant-Garde in Interwar England: Medieval Modernism and the London Underground* (Oxford: Oxford University Press, 1999), p. 28.

13   S. Hynes, *The Edwardian Turn of Mind* (London: Oxford University Press, 1968), p. 326.

produce reassuringly positive images of the underground.[14] It is evident that many modernists believed that 'the rationalization of culture in the present form of the metropolis was [...] an unrealizable utopia'.[15]

In other words, some variants of modernism were either resolutely opposed or indifferent to attempts to make art serve the wider community, a project that involved incorporating the reforming impulses that Saler identifies in the policies of the Underground Group. T. S. Eliot, for example, attacked the nineteenth-century poets for meddling with social affairs[16] and, as Raymond Williams suggests in *Culture and Society*,[17] such modernists turned instead to a nostalgia for the pre-modern even whilst they were looking for new audiences *within* modern culture. All strands of modernism responded to the Tube, widening the aperture of underground writing. Furthermore, whilst Saler describes the historical tradition of the Arts and Crafts Movement in relation to the interwar underground system, he fails to comment on the fact that the underground also had a material and representational history stretching back to the original Metropolitan Railway. The literary perspectives generated in the fiction of Gissing, Wells and others point towards the more varied and non-linear nature of the cultural features of the system in the interwar years.

Marinetti's futurist advocacy sign-posted the emergence of this Tubist mentality: for him the tube was an aesthetic kaleidoscope that simply could no longer resemble the underground writing of late Victorian fiction. Marinetti's future was very much in the present, and it helped to drag the underground of the imagination back into the present, also ensuring a shift from the far-distant Wellsian utopias to more contemporary portrayals of the system. He gave everything a 'here and now' feeling—the underground should be experienced as a transport of delight, not as the grinding of a hideous underworld. Later, Marinetti would take the cult of energy and machine technology into the nascent fascist movement of Mussolini, finding continuity in its stress on Sorelian myth, militarism, violence and war and iconoclastic rhetoric.

Marinetti's utopian influence on the visual imagination of other writers was profound. He was important in the early work of the volatile artistic avant-garde

---

14 See D. Harvey, *The Condition of Postmodernity* (Oxford: Blackwell, 1990).

15 T. Miller, *Late Modernism: Politics, Fiction and the Arts Between the World Wars* (London: University of California Press, 1999), p. 40.

16 Eliot dismissed the middle nineteenth century as 'an age of progressive degradation'. T. S. Eliot, 'Baudelaire', in *Selected Essays* (1932; London: Faber & Faber, 1972), pp. 419–30, p. 427.

17 See R. Williams, *Culture and Society 1780–1950* (1958; Harmondsworth: Penguin, 1963), part 3, chapter 3.

of pre-war London and there were many affinities between Futurism and the Imagism/Vorticism movement of Ezra Pound and Percy Wyndham Lewis. Pound was the key figure in this artistic coterie, believing that London was, at this time, the creative capital of the arts in Europe. It has been suggested that Marinetti's barn-storming performances, including his keynote address on English culture at the Bechstein Hall, led Pound to overstate the differences between Futurism and Vorticism: in a letter to H. L Mencken, Pound said that 'Vorticism is not Futurism, most emphatically NOT'.[18] But there can be no doubt that Pound was strongly influenced by Futurism's bold attempt to proclaim a new aesthetic ideology and he was later quoted by an Italian critic as claiming that 'the movement which I began with Joyce, Eliot and others in London would not have existed without Futurism'.[19]

Imagism was the opening salvo in the battle to overturn the poetic conventions of the period. Led by T. E. Hulme and Pound, it insisted on accuracy of presentation, precision of language and the objectivity of the poem. It was Pound who, on a visit to Paris, produced a seminal Imagist poem entitled 'In a Station of the Metro' (1913) included in his collection *Lustra* (1916). He provided the spark that would ignite a new poetic account of the Tube that was to inspire the generation of modernist writers like Virginia Woolf. Gone was the lifelike context and apparatus of the steam underground with its realistically shaped characters and solid steam trains and in their place the fragmentary, the contingent, the ephemeral and momentary features of the electric tube:

> The apparition of those faces in the crowd;
> Petals on a wet, black bough.[20]

This was Pound's evocation of a Paris Métro platform, what he later called the 'sense of sudden liberation; that sense of freedom from time limits and space limits' in 'A Retrospect' (1918).[21] Pound describes the moments as Métro passengers cluster fleetingly like petals that momentarily adhere to a wet surface and are then blown away. No-one had written a poem about a scene on the underground like this, just as no-one had viewed the underground in this way

18   E. Pound, 17 March 1915, in *The Selected Letters of Ezra Pound, 1907–1941*, ed. D. D. Paige (London: Faber & Faber, 1982), p. 57.

19   M. Bradbury & J. McFarlane, *Modernism: A Guide to European Literature, 1890–1930* (Harmondsworth: Penguin, 1976), p. 254.

20   E. Pound, 'In a Station of the Metro' (1928), in *Selected Poems* (1928; London: Faber & Faber, 1968), p. 113.

21   E. Pound, 'A Retrospect', in *Literary Essays*, ed. T. S. Eliot (London: Faber & Faber, 1954), pp. 3–14, p. 4.

or employed such compressed imagery to capture the scene. On another more mythical level, the Métro can be related to the underworld visited by Odysseus and Orpheus, and the word 'apparition' suggests the shades or phantoms of Dante's *Inferno*. Whatever else Pound's haiku-like poem achieved, it immortalized the Paris Métro as the location for an iconic moment in the formation of the modern poetic.

Pound described how the poem had come out of his noticing faces on the platform at La Concorde station and identifying them as 'spots of colour'.[22] It was simpler, he thought, to paint such a scene. It is easy to see why: the Italian Futurists who exerted such a powerful influence over Pound were obsessed with painting trains, stations, trams and streets, notably Gino Severini's painting *Nord-Sud* (1912) and Umberto Boccioni's *States of Mind I: The Farewells* (1911).[23] It did not take much prompting from Futurists in the case of Ford Madox Ford, who, like so many other writers in this period, turned repeatedly in his writing to the London transport system. In 'The Prose Tradition in Verse' (1914), Pound singled out two poems by Ford Madox Ford, both of which focused on stations: 'Finchley Road' from which he quoted the opening lines:

> As we come up at Baker Street
> Where tubes and trains and 'buses meet
> There's a touch of fog and a touch of sleet;
> And we go on up Hampstead way
>
> Towards the closing in of day ...[24]

And then the refrain from the poem 'The Three-Ten':

> But see, but see! The clock marks three above the Kilburn Station,
> Those maids, thank God, are 'neath the sod and all their generation.[25]

Pound's comment on the 'The Three-Ten' is telling: 'there are very few song-writers in England, and it's a simple old-fashioned song with a note of *futurism*

---

22   H. Carpenter, *A Serious Character, The Life of Ezra Pound* (London: Faber & Faber, 1988), p. 190.

23   See U. Apollonio (ed.), *Futurist Manifestos* (London: Thames & Hudson, 1973), pp. 102 & 57.

24   F. M. Ford (writing as Ford Madox Hueffer), 'Finchley Road' (1910), in *Collected Poems* (London: Max Goschen, 1914), p. 73

25   F. M. Ford (writing as Ford Madox Hueffer), 'The Three-Ten' (1910), in *Collected Poems*, p. 74.

in its very lyric refrain' (my emphasis).[26] Both poems were first published in *Songs from London* (1910), a celebration of the capital, and public transport is woven into them to produce an almost pastoral idyll. Pound believed that Ford was important because of his 'insistence upon clarity and precision, upon the prose tradition; in brief upon efficient writing—even in verse'[27] despite many of Ford's poems being conventional in form and metre. For the avant-garde, mass transit in Europe's cities became part of a visual or poetic language that crossed national boundaries, helping to formulate a more universal vocabulary.

The significance of Pound's intervention in the development of the new perspectives of Tubism should not be underestimated. He was indifferent to the realities of underground travel, saying laconically, in a letter to the poet Iris Barry, that the District line was on 'a map with black lines on it, moving in that direction [to Wimbledon]' and preferring to walk or travel by bus in London.[28] But in the imaginative sphere, Pound toned down Marinetti's garish palette, offering a simple contrast between light and darkness.

A year after the publication of Pound's 'In a Station of the Metro', another Imagist, F. S. Flint, produced an acerbic attack on the bourgeois complacency of those who travelled on the underground in the poem 'Tube' (1914):

> You look in vain for a sign,
> for a light in their eyes. No!
> Stolid they sit, lulled
> by the roar of the train in the tube,
> Content with the electric light,
> assured, comfortable, warm.[29]

In these first six lines, no attempt has been made to tone down the antagonism and distance that seems to exist between the observer and the observed, the first sign of a radical breakdown in the Marinettian paradigm. Here is the 'roar' of the tube train that would reappear in many texts and the 'electric light' that will transfix commuters throughout the interwar years. This belief pervaded much of the modernist avant-garde both before and after the First World War. Of course, crowds had always been a feature of the underground but by now

---

26   E. Pound, 'The Prose Tradition in Verse' (1914), in *Literary Essays*, pp. 371–77, p. 377.

27   Pound, 'Prose Tradition in Verse', p. 377.

28   Pound, 13 July 1916, in *Selected Letters*, p. 85. Pound *was* aware of the sound and vibration of the underground—he remarked on sitting in 'a not over-heated studio with the railroad trains rushing overhead' when recalling visits to Gaudier-Brzeska's studio in Putney (E. Pound, *Gaudier-Brzeska, A Memoir* (1970; New York: New Directions, 2009), p. 48).

29   F. S. Flint, 'Tube', *The Egoist*, vol. 1, no. 1, January 1914, p. 14.

the full weight of 'elite' theory had transformed commuters into the masses. Here is Flint's modernist critique of mass conformity:

> this is the mass, inert;
> intent on being the mass,
> unalarmed, undisturbed;
> and we, the spirit that moves,
> we leaven the mass,
> and it changes;[30]

And here on the Tube is an interrogation of the collective unconscious. In his discussion of 'Savage Crowds', Robert Nye has explained the complex relationship between the avant-garde artist and the crowd or masses.[31] At least in writing, it seemed possible for the modernist to influence the world even if the masses appeared 'inert' and unresponsive. If Marinetti and the Italian Futurists wished to mobilize the crowds they aroused in their 'performances' in order to bring the masses into the cultural arena, Flint and the Imagists shared their ambition to propel the public into motion. The Tube symbolized the technology of modernization that would allow the poet to enter the collective unconscious.

If that collective unconscious could not be moved by the poet then at least the Tube and its occupants could be closely observed, a response that can be found in the work of the poet T. S. Eliot. He was to be a regular user of the Tube over some 40 years but his first recorded reference to the underground appeared in a review of Igor Stravinsky's ballet *The Rite of Spring* (1913). Here, Eliot argued that the ballet seemed to:

> transform the rhythm of the steppes into the scream of the motor horn, the rattle of machinery, the grind of wheels, the beating of iron and steel, the *roar of the underground railway*, and the other barbaric noises of modern life; and to transform these despairing noises in music [my italics].[32]

Eliot believed that *The Rite* contained a reordering of the past, translating it into a modern musical idiom, as he commented that 'The spirit of the music

---

30 Flint, 'Tube', p. 14.
31 See R. Nye, 'Savage Crowds, Modernism and Modern Politics', in E. Barkan & R. Bush (eds.), *Prehistories of the Future: The Primitive Project and the Culture of Modernism* (Stanford: Stanford University Press, 1995), pp. 42–55.
32 T. S. Eliot, 'London Letter', *The Dial*, vol. 71, no. 4, October 1921, pp. 452–55, p. 453. See also L. Gordon, *Eliot's Early Years* (Oxford: Oxford University Press, 1978), p. 108.

was modern, and the spirit of the ballet was primitive ceremony'.[33] The underground railway, the apogee of modernity, was the world into which the past flowed. Stravinsky had successfully brought the sounds of the tube into music—the first time that the sounds of modern city life had been heard in a ballet score, even if the Italian Futurists had already attempted to bring such noises into their performances. It seems that Eliot perceived the primitive as a source of renewal. By analogy, if Stravinsky had captured 'modern barbarism' in the music of *The Rite of Spring* and the music gave a 'sense of the present', Eliot might transform the Tube sufficiently in poetic terms to make its discordance intelligible at the level of artistic modernity.

The Tube could be made intelligible in other ways. In 1914, the same year as the publication of *Blast*, C. R. W. Nevinson produced a painting called *The Non-Stop*. The picture, now lost, was exhibited at the London Group show in March of that year and represented the interior of a Tube car. Its title suggests metaphorically that the train is out of control, carrying its passengers inexorably towards disaster. At a literal level, the title refers to the Non-Stop Services on the Hampstead Tube, portrayed in a 1910 publicity poster in which three passengers are left bewildered on the platform in the powerful slipstream of a departing Non-Stop service. The *Westminster Gazette* commented on the 'mixture of streams of light, the fragments of advertisements, and curves, and colour, with lines that suggest straphangers here and there' in the painting.[34] This suggests that Nevinson was attempting to grasp the dynamism of the Tube in a pictorial form similar to that of the Italian painters like Russolo and Boccioni who had signed up to the Manifesto of Futurism published in *Le Figaro* in 1909. The manifesto urged artists to 'sing of the multicoloured, polyphonic tides of revolution in the modern capitals; [...] greedy railway stations that devour smoke-plumed serpents'.[35] Other reviews of Nevinson's painting underlined its Italian Futurist roots by likening it to the work of Severini, whilst the *Evening Standard* observed that it was a 'rag time subject of many figures, cubistically treated, but with just enough reference to reality to

---

33 Eliot, 'London Letter', p. 453.

34 *Westminster Gazette*, quoted in R. Cork, *Vorticism and Abstract Art in the First Machine Age*, 2 vols. (London: Gordon Fraser, 1976), vol. 1, p. 218. Frank Rutter, in *Some Contemporary Artists* (1922), described Nevinson's painting as 'a circular picture of the interior of a compartment in a "Tube" in which the vibration of seated figures and strap-hangers was kaleidoscopically expressed in vivid bright colours' (cited in Cork, *Vorticism*, vol. 1, p. 218).

35 F. T. Marinetti, 'The Founding and Manifesto of Futurism' (1909), in Apollonio, *Futurist Manifestos*, pp. 19–24, p. 22.

make the picture intelligible'.[36] Nevinson was using Futurist techniques and subject matter to express, for the first time, a feature of everyday life—the journey to work inside a tube train.

Nevinson was not alone in his response to Futurism. Wyndham Lewis, in his play *Enemy of the Stars* (also published in the first issue of *Blast*), positioned his characters above the opening of a mine-shaft so as to be hit by 'A GUST SUCH AS IS MET IN THE CORRIDORS OF THE TUBE [...] THEIR CLOTHES SHIVER OR FLAP, AND BLARES UP THEIR VOICES'.[37] Wyndham Lewis rejected the 'automo-bilist' tendencies in Futurism, commenting acidly that British culture had long been acquainted with industrial artefacts.[38] As a proponent of Vorticism, he was attracted nonetheless to Futurist ideas, particularly in Boccioni's painting *States of Mind I: The Farewells* where the artist has created a vortex of swirling forms with human shapes, electricity pylons and a cityscape. On the London underground, the steam engine was largely banished, as *Punch* had gleefully proclaimed a decade earlier; for Vorticists like Wyndham Lewis, the energy of the steam engine had become concentrated, like a coiled spring, inside the Tube train as a whole. Pound was also attracted to the technological possibil-ities embodied in Marinetti's project, particularly in the 'Vorticist manifesto' published in the first issue of *Blast*, in which he likened pure language to efficient machine technology: 'The vortex is the point of maximum energy. It represents, in mechanics, the greatest efficiency [...] the most highly energised statement [...] which is most capable of expressing THE TURBINE'.[39]

The publicity poster was not far behind in its depiction of this new world of restless momentum and novelty. In 1912, Marc Laurence's poster *Always Warm and Bright* was published by the Underground Group as part of its publicity campaign to attract passengers. This poster combined the exaggerated colour scheme of the Fauvist movement with a serene and comfortable image of an underground car interior, its mix of social classes symbolized by the bowler hats, top hats and cloth caps worn by the men and the full Edwardian hats of the women.[40] Like many others produced by the Underground Group, this poster

36   M. J. K. Walsh, *C. R. W. Nevinson: This Cult of Violence* (London: Yale University Press, 2002), p. 83. The most striking development of Nevinson's approach is Cyril Power's work. Linocuts like *The Tube Train* (c.1934) and *The Escalator* (c.1929) convey anxiety and alienation whilst *The Tube Staircase* (1929) seems like a descent to a Wellsian underworld. See C. S. Ackley (ed.), *British Prints from the Machine Age: Rhythms of Modern Life 1914–1939* (London: Thames and Hudson, 2008).

37   P. W. Lewis, *Enemy of the Stars* (1914), quoted in Cork, *Vorticism*, p. 291.

38   *Blast*, no. 1, June 1914, p. 40.

39   *Blast*, no. 1, June 1914, quoted in Carpenter, *A Serious Character*, p. 246.

40   London Transport Museum Collection.

articulated a vision of the tubes that derived from the growing correspondence between journalism, commercial art and the needs (and resources) of modern transportation companies. Laurence was able to wrap the 'old' underground in the warm glow of artistic modernism, conveying the supremely comfortable, orderly and safe environment that Wells had tried to describe in *Anticipations*.

The various strands of Tubism emerged from an underground that was in a transitional phase. Such phases in the underground's history are not uncommon but this was a period of particularly spectacular change with many innovations. It was also a time when the old and new existed very much side-by-side and the poster, like fiction, had to portray both old and new. The traditional image, the idyllic world of suburban life as shown in the 1908 poster entitled *Golders Green. A Place of Delightful Prospects*[41] (in the north London suburb) was only gradually developing a more strongly technocratic emphasis. In the earlier period, the construction of the underground and its new role in the daily life of the metropolis had been carefully recorded on camera and had been represented in fiction. Now, the underground was increasingly recorded in the poster as well, adding a new dimension to underground writing. Tubism found expression in the poster, projecting itself more and more into the public view as an *official* cultural construction of the system. Tubism transformed the architecture of a new generation of stations that were built in the 1920s and 1930s, stations that became galleries for Tubist poster art and design. But, like T. S. Eliot's troubled description of the Tube as a barbaric mode in modern society, other modernist art did not lend itself to the comfortable depiction of this underground world.

In fact, Eliot's response was eclipsed by a poster art that offered more positive and comfortable images of Tube travel for nearly 40 years, a spectacular success for Tubism as public relations. Artistic representations that aimed to show the more sinister effects of a modernized system simply could not compete with the sheer volume of positive images emerging from first the Underground Group and then the London Passenger Transport Board. In this way, official accounts of the underground established a dominant hold on the representation of subterranean reality. Even the image of the vulnerable Edwardian woman was wiped away by underground posters like Alfred France's *The Way for All* (1911) which prominently depicted a confident young woman set against a green-tiled background and underground logo.[42] Here was the Ann Veronica of the tubes, the new woman with the independent status of underground guide, a female replacement for Dante's Virgil in his journey through hell. The new Tube lines

---

41   London Transport Museum Collection.
42   London Transport Museum Collection.

were not initially a financial success and needed to find appealing images that reached the middle class with money to spend on leisure. As Oliver Green points out, 'developments in transport technology were accompanied by new organisational structures [...] improving the Underground's poor public image was an essential part of the recovery process'.[43] The Underground Group was able to use its industrial weight to promote itself in a way never possible in the Victorian period. It was this emerging corporate power that was focused on transforming the image of the underground in order to attract desperately needed passenger revenue. The modernism of the poster was ultimately tied to the need for financial survival; the posters *had* to work in the short term in order to ensure that Tube lines were viable in the long term.

The power of Tubist imagery and the relationship between modernism and commercial publicity posters is evident in four contemporary paintings of the underground: Maxwell Armfield's *The Tunnel* (1905), Roger Fry's Omega mural (1916), Walter Sickert's *Queen's Road (Bayswater) Station* (c.1915–16) and Gladys Hynes' *Underground* (1920s).[44] Armfield's painting *The Tunnel* highlights a Tube train that bursts from the tunnel at Oxford Circus station. An Edwardian lady appears far from the train against the wall but the platform is otherwise an almost empty expanse of wooden flooring. Fry's mural suggests a strange, almost desert-like landscape in which an orchidaceous lady ascends the staircase beneath a huge 'UNDERGROUND' sign, an odd choice perhaps for a domestic interior. In a manner superficially reminiscent of Wyndham Lewis's paintings, the female figure seems to be weighed down by a kind of inertia— almost as though she is held down by a subterranean gravity. Various perspectives are juxtaposed: a sinister newsagent lurks inside his kiosk whilst a strange emptiness surrounds her, with only a dog and the glimpse of another passenger disappearing behind her. The 'UNDERGROUND' sign is a clear reflection of the ubiquity of Tube advertising in these years. In Hynes' *Underground*, the interior of a Tube car is filled mainly with bowler-hatted city gents. The car is a crowded mix of social classes including a number of seated women. One of the women holds a small child who appears to represent the next generation of commuters who will fill the ever-growing ranks of the rush-hour crowd.

All these paintings are an indication of a changed visual perception of the underground that heralded the Tubist period, where artists found the Tube environment symbolic of a new world. *The Tunnel* represents a threatening

---

43   O. Green, *Underground Art* (London: Studio Vista, 1990), p. 7.
44   Maxwell Armfield, *The Tunnel* (private collection); Roger Fry, Omega mural for Arthur Ruck's house, 4 Berkeley Street, London (later destroyed); Walter Sickert, *Queen's Road* (Courtauld Gallery); Gladys Hynes, *Underground* (private collection).

environment, practically denuded of human presence in a way that recreates the Gissingesque portal, suggested by the tunnel archway from which the train emerges. We find a subject from everyday life, an attempt to draw out a new visual meaning from the experience of Tube travel. Fry's mural seems to place the figure in a Dantean ascent as though the electric tube somehow needed to repeat visually the secular myths found in the late Victorian fiction of Gissing. *The Underground* is a more playful portrait, using to the full the conventions of a packed interior. There is a sense of a robot-like (almost steel-helmetted) conformity of the standing bowler-hatted men and seated men and women who are immersed in their daily newspaper. The painting is almost a parody of Laurence's poster *Always Warm and Bright* as the perspective is the same but the message is hardly comforting. Certain key elements stand out: there are harsh electric lights that illuminate the Tube car in Hynes' painting (with the clear shadows of the standing passengers); the prominent 'UNDERGROUND' sign in Fry's mural which frames the picture; the brightness of the platform walls compared to the darkened tunnel and the female figure in Armfield's painting; and the solitary figure in Sickert's painting that appears to be a soldier set amongst the everyday world of the platform. All four paintings are therefore realistic treatments of the underground which contain strikingly contrasting themes within themselves. These novel elements helped to frame the ambiguity in the perception of this Tube environment, and were part, as David Harvey suggests, of modernist approaches that were 'expressive of alienation, antag-onistic to all sense of hierarchy [...], and frequently critical of "bourgeois" consumerism and life-styles'.[45] The tubes could be seen as the embodiment of bourgeois values, in other words, the development of the electric tubes coincided with contemporary views that were at least embryonically antago-nistic towards the modernizing effects of Tube travel. In fact, all the paintings establish one key fact: that the Tube was exerting an imaginative grip on artists that started a mere 15 years after the opening of the first Tube line in 1890. Recording the Tube, as photographers and illustrators had done of the steam underground, was now extended to reordering it visually.

We have seen that the Tube was structured in writing under the auspices of Futurism and its associated avant-garde influences like Imagism. In this process, it came to have a wider purchase on the public imagination, giving the Tube a more existential feel in these years. Travelling on the Tube was to become the most normal of daily experiences exactly as the Underground Group intended. But this is an experience of the self in an alien environment

---

45 Harvey, *Condition of Postmodernity*, p. 29.

or an interrogation of the masses who sat or stood in the same Tube car or platform. Thus the foundations for Tubism were laid in the years immediately before the First World War but it was the experience of the war or the observation of war that would add a number of new meanings to underground writing in the interwar years.

EVERYONE IN THAT AGE MUST HAVE FELT CAUGHT IN A TUNNEL: THE IMPACT OF THE FIRST WORLD WAR

The First World War was a watershed for the underground. There was a dramatic increase in usage with 67 per cent more passengers in 1918 than in 1914—more than half the entire passenger traffic in the capital was now travelling by underground. This increase was due largely to the rise in London's population as a result of the wartime expansion of the civil service and of industries such as munitions. The underground must have seemed a confusing mixture of contrasts and similarities: the contrast between troops on leave mingling with the rush-hour commuter and West End shopper was as sharp as the contradiction between being voluntarily underground rather than corralled in the trenches of the Western Front. The difference between the 'normality' of everyday Tube travel and the surreal world of war was evident. There were similarities between the metallic and automated world of the underground and the armed automation of the front line with its machine guns, tanks and artillery. The occasional threat of aerial bombardment by German aircraft and Zeppelins brought home some of the reality of war and the sense of postponed domestic conflicts which might be resumed at any time (and indeed were with the outbreak of Tube strikes in 1918). The underground was also transformed by the changes in its workforce brought about by the call up and conscription of its staff after 1916. The most visible manifestation of this change was the presence of female staff on platforms, in lifts and on trains, roles from which they had hitherto been excluded.

The impact of the war on the underground was most vividly translated into writing in the short story 'The Fisher of Men' (1918) by the Russian engineer Evegenii Zamiatin, more famous for his novel *We* (1924). Zamiatin's story drew on the striking dissonances of Futurism in order to present the underground during a Zeppelin raid on the capital during the First World War. Zamiatin visited England in March 1916, during the airborne attacks, on a mission to build ice-breaking ships for Russia. He noted that 'Everything there was as new and strange as it had been in Alexandria and Jerusalem. Here at first was all iron, machines and blueprints'.[46] In an essay Zamiatin had said that 'the picture of the world and of people in the works of the neorealists often strikes you with its exaggerations, its grotesque and fantastic qualities'[47] and this notion was certainly expressed in this short story. The imagery of 'The Fisher of Men' is startling, a fictional restatement of Nevinson's *The Non-Stop*: 'Zeppelins over London! Extra! Extra!', the newsboys cry and 'The lifts did not have time to swallow them all. The ants poured down the emergency stairs. They clung to the footboards and then with a roar sped along the tubes'. London is 'in a frenzy' and will 'burst its banks [...] if there had not been an outlet down into the Underground and the subterranean lines of the "Tube"'.[48] The people 'take refuge in the catacombs' and crowd together in a futurist ideal of a 'delirious underground world with its concrete sky hanging over them, its confusion of caves, staircases, suns, kiosks, vending machines'.[49] After a whirlwind journey, the fleeing passengers are ejected at Hammersmith station where the train suddenly terminates. On the platform, Zamiatin observes 'the top hats and huge white hats' of the middle classes which 'clung to the blindingly white wall and merged with the raspberry and green posters, with the faces speeding motionlessly in the Rolls-Royce car, with the automatic sun. In the white, tiled catacombs a crowd of strange Christians out of posters were taking refuge'.[50]

In this passage, the Futurism of Nevinson is combined with the Fauvism of Laurence; the painting with the publicity poster. Zamiatin's snapshot of the tube is a roller-coaster ride into a vortex of colour, sound and movement in a place where a 'muffled, iron rumble could be heard coming down the lift-shafts and staircases'.[51] Zamiatin approved of Russian Futurism's stress on sound as well as their 'intensified use of the device of brief, momentary impressions [and] choice of subjects primarily from big city life, with its feverish movement and flicker'.[52] He provides an early indication of the modernist image of mechanical noise and movement of air as an unleashed force that is found in many later accounts of the Tube. The posters on the Tube seem to come to life in a weird exchange between reality and representation and the Tube is a place of refuge

---

46   E. Zamiatin, 'Autobiography, 1929', in *A Soviet Heretic: Essays by Yevgeny Zamyatin*, trans. M. Ginsburg (Chicago: University of Chicago, 1970), pp. 7–14, p. 13.

47   E. Zamiatin, 'Contemporary Russian Literature', in *Soviet Heretic*, pp. 34–50, p. 42.

48   E. Zamiatin, 'The Fisher of Men' (1918), in *Islanders and The Fisher of Men*, trans. S. Fuller & J. Sacchi (Edinburgh: Salamander Press, 1984), pp. 75–95, p. 84.

49   Zamiatin, 'Fisher of Men', p. 90.

50   Zamiatin, 'Fisher of Men', p. 91.

51   Zamiatin, 'Fisher of Men', p. 91.

52   Zamiatin, 'Contemporary Russian Literature', p. 49.

for the first time, pointing prophetically towards its role in the Second World War. Zamiatin was able to use the devices of modern painting in this story, rendering the psychological through the visual.

'The Fisher of Men' appears to be the *only* fictional account of the use of the underground as shelter in the First World War, a curious rarity considering that 4.25 million people used it in the four years of the war in response to 31 aerial attacks. Both the Underground Group and the authorities had immediately allowed people to shelter in the system in 1914 in stark contrast to their refusal in 1939, posting up notices saying:

> AIR RAID SHELTER
> PERSONS MAY SHELTER HERE AT THEIR OWN RISK AFTER THE TAKE
> COVER NOTICE HAS BEEN GIVEN
> Persons sheltering are not allowed to take Birds, Dogs, Cats
> and other Animals, as well as Mailcarts, on to the Company's
> premises.[53]

The Underground had even gone as far as advertising the virtues of using the tubes for shelter from the bombing saying, in a deliberate echo of the pre-war publicity poster by Marc Laurence:

> Never mind the dark and dangerous streets
> Underground
> It is warm and bright
> Be comfortable in well-lit trains and read the latest war news.[54]

As many as 12,000 people sheltered in Finsbury Park station and 9,000 at King's Cross in the first raids of the war rising to an estimated 120,000 in 1917, and it was only in that year with heavy aircraft attacks that a system was devised to cope with regular sheltering. The Underground Group provided 86 stations with an estimated capacity of 250,000 people but tried to impose restrictions as large crowds began to descend before air-raid sirens sounded. Nevertheless, there was considerable public outcry over the lack of anti-aircraft protection and one recent historian of the war suggests that the aircraft raids 'brought London to the brink of collapse'.[55]

Sheltering was also recorded in the painting *The Underworld* (1918) by Walter Bayes. Tube shelterers are depicted at Elephant and Castle station, appearing

---

53   J. A. Hamilton, *Britain's Railways in World War I* (London: Allen & Unwin, 1967), p. 92.
54   Quoted in C. Wolmar, *The Subterranean Railway* (London: Atlantic Books, 2004), p. 211.
55   N. Hanson, *First Blitz* (London: Doubleday, 2008), p. 342.

in a number of poses within a Vorticist composition with women dominating the foreground. Through an exit can be glimpsed a cavernous background with bright light illuminating more standing figures. A cross-section of social classes is represented and there are several vignettes of conversation within the picture, even if the general demeanour of the shelterers suggests distraction, boredom, and fatigue.[56] An example of the influence of underground writing is shown in Bayes' use of the title *The Underworld* which suggests that the shelterers are in Hades. This had appeared in the wartime short story called 'The Eighth Lamp' (1915) by Roy Vickers which made the Tube into a portal to Hades and was one of the earliest stories to feature railway workers. Pete Comber, a train driver, is killed by George Raoul, a signalman on the Circle line at 'Cheyne Road' station. Raoul is then terrorized by a phantom train driven by Comber that eventually leads him to his own death on the track. There is a 'faint luminosity in the driver's window'[57] of this ghost train and Raoul is fatally drawn to it as it stops at the platform at Cheyne Road. Raoul is found in a 'disused hole [in] the tunnel from Cheyne Road to Baker Street'.[58] The war only appears in a brief passage when Raoul glimpses a recruiting poster in which 'the beckoning smile of a young soldier seemed like the mirthless grin of a death mask'.[59] But this is definitely an artificial environment akin in some ways to the Western Front and, as the title of the story suggests, each light on the platform is extinguished until the final eighth lamp leaves Raoul in darkness.

The sheer physical impact of this mechanical environment affected other writers, notably Percy Wyndham Lewis and D. H. Lawrence. They were both drawn to the Futurist agenda although they rejected what Ezra Pound called its 'accelerated impressionism'.[60] Lewis, as we have seen, believed that Futurism was obsessed with technology, whilst Lawrence argued, in a letter to Edward Garnett, that it would 'progress down the purely male or intellectual

---

56 Two of the posters on the platform wall represent the very vivid lithograph used to advertise an exhibition by C. R. W. Nevinson entitled 'War: Pictures by Nevinson Official Artist on the Western Front'. Bayes' picture was exhibited in the same year that Nevinson (who had taken shelter in the tube during raids in 1917) staged a protest against government censorship of his painting *Paths of Glory* (1917). Bayes' painting is in the Imperial War Museum.

57 R. Vickers, 'The Eighth Lamp' (1915), in R. Holmes (ed.), *Macabre Railway Stories* (London: W. H. Allen, 1982), pp. 77–90, p. 84.

58 Vickers, 'The Eighth Lamp', p. 90.

59 Vickers, 'The Eighth Lamp', p. 78.

60 Quoted in R. Mengham, 'From Georges Sorel to *Blast*', in J. Howlett & R. Mengham (eds.), *The Violent Muse: Violence and the Artistic Imagination in Europe, 1910–39* (Manchester: Manchester University Press, 1994), pp. 33–44, p. 37.

or scientific line [...] That is it exactly—a great mechanism'.[61] But both Lewis and Lawrence had been attracted by the 'Futurists' massive investment in the principle of dynamism'[62] albeit for different reasons: Lawrence because it offered the general lines of an intuitive 'physiology of matter'[63] and Lewis because of its shattering of the private world of art. Before the war, Lawrence Rainey suggests, the Futurists had taken art out of the '"private" gallery, the polite salon, [into] the concert hall and mass-circulation newspaper that would serve as the new agora of cultural debate'.[64] During the war, the Italian Futurists enthusiastically entered into the conflict but Lewis and Lawrence were affected in very different ways. Whilst Lewis served in an artillery battery, Lawrence was rejected for military service but both writers believed that postwar culture was a battleground of contending social tendencies that had been accelerated by the war. Lewis was important in his highlighting of the role of poster art and in 1915 called for a more 'public' art in his notes to the catalogue of the first Vorticist exhibition: 'were the walls of London carpeted with abstractions [...] the Public taste would thus be educated in a popular way to appreciate the essentials of design better than picture-galleries have ever done'.[65] In the autobiographical *Blasting and Bombardiering* (1937), Lewis acknowledged that the underground had achieved this aim by commissioning poster designs which were on display at stations throughout the capital.[66] He also recalled a member of the newly formed postwar 'X Group', E. McKnight Kauffer, who became 'the Underground poster-king: he disappeared as it were belowground, and the tunnels of the "Tube" became thenceforth his subterranean picture galleries'.[67] McKnight Kauffer was one of the leading iconic poster artists in the interwar years, particularly through his designs for the underground after 1915. As Richard Cork concludes in his study of Vorticism, 'the principal way in which the lessons of Vorticism were to be disseminated in England after the war was through the outstanding posters by McKnight Kauffer for newspapers, department stores and the Underground'.[68]

---

61   D. H. Lawrence, 2 June 1914, in *The Letters of D. H. Lawrence*, eds. G. Zytaruk & J. Boulton, 8 vols. (Cambridge: Cambridge University Press, 1981), vol. 2, p. 181.

62   Mengham, 'From Georges Sorel to *Blast*', p. 37.

63   Lawrence, 5 June 1914, in *Letters*, vol. 2, p. 183.

64   L. Rainey, 'The Cultural Economy of Modernism', in M. Levenson (ed.), *The Cambridge Companion to Modernism* (Cambridge: Cambridge University Press, 1999), pp. 33–69, p. 39.

65   P. W. Lewis, 'Notes to the Catalogue for Vorticist Exhibition' (1915), in Cork, *Vorticism*, vol. 1, p. 280.

66   P. W. Lewis, *Blasting and Bombardiering* (1937; London: Calder & Boyars, 1967), pp. 212–13.

67   Lewis, *Blasting and Bombardiering*, p. 212.

68   Cork, *Vorticism*, vol. 1, p. 280.

Poster art on the underground was given a tremendous boost during the war as it was quickly perceived as a major opportunity for pro-war propaganda. Lewis was effectively opening up a 'cultural front' and during the war, the Underground Group was already putting his advice to good use by commissioning patriotic posters. These posters also helped to place the underground at the heart of the war effort by showing how important transport services were in the smooth running of the capital. There is a sense of militaristic duty and purpose to many of them that contrasts with *Punch*'s mildly mocking cartoons of the pre-war era with one in April 1902, for example, featuring a conversation between two lift men at Chancery Lane station on the Central line. The first lift man's idea of a change of scene is being transferred to Bank station, one stop down the line.[69] By October 1914, the boredom of Tube work was changing. *Punch* was swinging behind the war, placing an entirely different slant on the world of the lift with a cartoon proclaiming 'We are All Drilling Nowadays' as a bowler-hatted gent bawls out an order to a crowd waiting for a lift in parade-ground fashion: 'Form—two deep!'[70]

Whilst the war benefited the Underground Group in dealing with its financial problems, it also fuelled the notion that the underground was an overcrowded place—a kind of overflow for London. The poet Siegfried Sassoon, for example, referred to the 'congested Tubes'[71] during the Armistice celebrations in 1918 as though the tube was the capital's pulmonary system, and he was himself caught up in an air raid on Liverpool Street station in 1917.[72] Wyndham Lewis, in 'The Crowdmaster' (1914), imagined the crowd formed in London: 'It serpentines every night, in thick well-nourished coils, all over town'.[73] H. G. Wells, in *Mr Britling Sees It Through* (1916), saw London as a place of 'great unrest' in 1914 noting that there were 'fewer omnibuses and less road traffic generally, but

---

69 *Punch*, 9 April 1902, vol. 122, p. 262.

70 *Punch*, 14 October 1914, in J. A. Hammerton (ed.), *Mr Punch in London Town*, 20 vols. (London: Educational Book Co., 1985), vol. 15, p. 144. The figure of the Tube lift-man appeared many years later in the biting satire of war *In Parenthesis* (1937) by David Jones. In the freezing cold of the trenches, a well-muffled officer approaches soldiers to ask if anyone has seen a Liaison Officer and is met with blank stares 'as one who asks of the Tube lift-man at Westminster the whereabouts of the Third Sea Lord' (D. Jones, *In Parenthesis* (1937; London: Faber & Faber, 1963), p. 97).

71 S. Sassoon, 11 November 1918, in *Siegfried Sassoon Diaries, 1915-1918*, ed. R. Hart-Davies, 3 vols. (London: Faber & Faber, 1983), vol. 3, p. 282.

72 S. Sassoon, *Memoirs of an Infantry Officer* (1930; London: Faber & Faber, 1965), p. 208.

73 P. W. Lewis, 'The Crowdmaster' (1914), quoted in P. Peppis, *Literature, Politics and the English Avant-Garde: Nation and Empire, 1901–1918* (Cambridge: Cambridge University Press, 2000), p. 94.

there was a quite unusual number of drifting pedestrians'.[74] For Wells, this was a feminized environment full of women who 'seemed to have drifted in from the suburbs and outskirts of London in a state of vague expectation, unable to stay in their homes'.[75]

Women played a very prominent part in the wartime London underground by working there as 'gatewomen', guards, porters and ticket clerks. Lift men were also replaced by women during the course of the war, illustrated in an underground publicity lithograph called *War Work—Playing the Game: Lift Girl* (1919) by Archibald Standish Hartrick.[76] These women all wore uniforms, as shown by the woman depicted in *The Bystander* magazine in 1918 who, under the heading 'The New Gallant', is in the act of giving up her seat for another woman in the Tube.[77] The mainly male commentators of the time were clearly disturbed by this newly feminized workforce who even had the temerity to go on strike for equal pay at the end of the war: the 'Bakerloo Girls', as they were dubbed by the press, went on unofficial strike for three days in 1918 in order to win the war bonus payment that men were receiving. They were at least partially successful in this campaign and once more confirmed that women were a presence, albeit temporary, on the railways.[78] Even as they lost their jobs at the end of the war, some women workers defended their right to stay in the industry, arguing that the 'only winners in the scramble for bread between working men and women would be the employers'.[79] Jennifer Poulos Nesbitt suggests that the First World War can be seen as 'a consolidating moment for all those forces—education, employment, and philanthropy—that had been slowly drawing middle-class women into the streets [amplifying] anxieties about what their presence meant'.[80]

The new Tube lines that brought women into work were acting as blood

---

74   H. G. Wells, *Mr Britling Sees It Through* (1916; London: Odhams Press, undated), p. 168.

75   Wells, *Mr Britling*, p. 168.

76   London Transport Museum Collection. This was one of a number of commemorative lithographs issued by the Underground Group to indicate the contribution to war work made by its staff. Other posters showed women painting a stairwell and collecting tickets, while men are depicted working a signal box and driving a bus. All of these subjects are superimposed on images of the trenches.

77   'The New Gallant', *The Bystander*, 6 February 1918.

78   See S. R. Grayzel, *Women's Identities at War: Gender, Motherhood and Politics in Britain and France during the First World War* (Chapel Hill: University of North Carolina Press, 1999).

79   Quoted in P. Graves, *Labour Women: Women in British Working-Class Politics 1918–1939* (Cambridge: Cambridge University Press, 1994), p. 15.

80   J. P. Nesbitt, *Narrative Settlements: Geographies of British Women's Fiction between the Wars* (Toronto: Toronto University Press, 2005), p. 29.

vessels drawing the inhabitants of the suburban periphery into the centre of the city. The war seemed to revive organic images of transport and social movement, as though the human body needed to be asserted against the mechanical features of war. London was transformed by war, shown by the vague worries of Wells' Mr Britling being turned into concrete fears with the destruction of his dreams 'of great cities, the splendid freedoms, of a coming age [...] Had the war done more than unmask reality?'[81] London therefore came to represent a different world as the war progressed with the 'Home Front' seen by front-line writers as cut off from the real experience of conflict in mainland Europe, an idea conveyed by Wells when Mr Britling's son joins the army. London's inevitable progress towards modernity was now increasingly flawed for liberals like Wells because it seemed to symbolize an artificial society that sanctioned the killing on the Western Front. The war exposed the contradictions embodied in the ever-increasing mechanization of society, a sign welcomed by Marinetti who believed war to be a necessary purgation of decadent societies but inspiring dismay in those who saw only a deepening cycle of destruction. There are two kinds of modernity in conflict here: on the one hand, that of the Home Front with its false images and desperate clinging to novelty and normality, exemplified by cinema, ragtime, the gramophone and congested tubes; on the other hand, that of the Western Front utilizing images of tanks, gas, artillery fire, trenches and tunnels. Siegfried Sassoon, in his poem 'Blighters' (1917) wanted that most *modern* of machines, the tank, to destroy the crowds in the London music halls:

> I'd like to see a Tank come down the stalls,
> Lurching to rag-time tunes, or 'Home, sweet Home',
> And there'd be no more jokes in Music-halls
> To mock the riddled corpses round Bapaume.[82]

The Tube carried the people of London to and from their war work, maintaining the killing across the Channel through the most *normal* of activities. Was the Tube any different from the replica trench system and Tank-Bank display in Trafalgar Square in 1916, mocked by the front-line writers who regarded them as a cruel mimicry of warfare?[83] The real tanks that appeared on the streets were reflected on the London stage in October 1916 in the revue

---

81   Wells, *Mr Britling*, p. 207.

82   S. Sassoon, 'Blighters' (1917), in *Collected Poems 1908–1956* (1947; London: Faber & Faber, 2002), p. 19.

83   See P. Wright, *Tank* (London: Faber & Faber, 2000), chapter 6, pp. 81–100.

Hello Tanko and in the film *The Advance of the Tanks* (1917). The tank 'sensation' temporarily displaced the train from its central role as symbol of technological power. It resembled the Tube train in many ways—its coiled power clad in a metallic carapace, with its hidden driver and erratic jerking movements, and above all, in the way it loomed out of the landscape like the train from the darkened tunnel. Even 'F-stock' trains on the District line were dubbed 'tank stock' because of their likeness to the newly invented war machine.

Writers described London as a kind of subworld colonized by the war but also, paradoxically, as an ersatz world that could only be a false and distorted image of front-line realities. The 'war poets' referred to tunnels and tunnelling in their descriptions of the Western Front experience where images of tunnels could mean journeys into hell or the undermining or 'sapping' of the stable world.[84] The association between tunnels and infernal underworlds was renewed, as can be seen in Siegfried Sassoon's bitter poem 'The Rear-Guard' (1917) in which a soldier escapes from the horror of underground death when he finds

> Dawn's ghost that filtered down a shafted stair
> To the dazed, muttering creatures underground.

In the last line of the poem the soldier climbs

> through darkness to the twilight air,
> Unloading hell behind him step by step.[85]

As we have seen with their *War Work—Playing the Game* posters, the Underground Group actively encouraged the linking of the trenches on the Western Front with typical scenes featuring transport workers. Ironically, one version of the popular army song 'I don't want to be a soldier' contained the line 'I'd rather hang around Piccadilly Underground' as the familiar sights (and its associations with prostitution) of Soho found an echo on the Western Front.

These similarities were superficial. The art critic Herbert Read recorded his anger whilst serving on the Western Front, referring to 'the Londoners [who] have no conception whatever of what war is really like and don't seem concerned about it at all. They are much more troubled about a few paltry air raids.'[86] The tunnels that tormented the war poets threatened to undermine

---

84   See E. Leed, *No Man's Land* (Cambridge: Cambridge University Press, 1979) and A. Barrie, *War Underground: The Tunnellers of the Great War* (1962; Staplehurst: Spellmount, 2000).

85   Sassoon, 'The Rear-Guard' (1917), in *Collected Poems*, pp. 63–64, p. 64.

86   H. Read, *The Contrary Experience: Autobiographies* (London: Secker & Warburg, 1973), p. 112.

London and alarmed those, like Richard Aldington, who in his poem 'London' (1915) found the capital's 'Imagist' beauty slipping away into 'a vision of ruins, / Of walls crumbling into the clay'.[87] Ivor Gurney, on the other hand, welcomed the possibility of London's demise: 'All London, save only the City and the Embankment might, almost, fall through to hell without a word of regret from me'.[88] The sense intensified that a whole world was being sapped by the process of endless warfare. According to D. H. Lawrence in the novel *Kangaroo* (1923): 'the old spirit of London collapsed [...] and became a vortex of passions, lusts, hopes, fears and horrors'.[89] Lawrence praised Mark Gertler's painting the *Merry-Go-Round* (1916) for its 'combination of blaze, and violent mechanised rotation',[90] implying that life on the Home Front had been recoded to perform endless warlike gyrations like those of the trains on the Circle line. Richard Aldington also recoiled from the life of the capital in *Death of a Hero* (1929). In this novel, London has become an unknowable city for those at the front as it is impossible to penetrate the tangled veins and 'viscera of underground railways'.[91] It is also an organic city that has 'passed its meridian of power', becoming mechanized and ossified by war;[92] the streets can only be understood using the vocabulary of the trenches so London's roofs are a 'no-man's-land'.[93] Like Lawrence, Aldington sees this as a new London, a city that has entered a new age which cannot be comprehended imaginatively in the old ways anymore.

Aldington's response to this city is also evident in his poem 'In the Tube' (1915), written a year before he enlisted in the army. In the midst of war, he records a journey through London:

> The electric car jerks;
> I stumble on the slats of the floor,
> Fall into a leather seat
> And look up.[94]

It is probably the most grittily detailed description in poetry of the London Tube—here is a car (the American term) *not* a carriage, it 'jerks' like Tube cars

---

87   R. Aldington, 'London' (1915), in *Collected Poems* (New York: AMS Press, 1981), p. 37.
88   I. Gurney, 28 August 1916 (?), in *War Letters* (1983; London: Hogarth Press, 1984), p. 99.
89   D. H. Lawrence, *Kangaroo* (1923; London: Martin Secker, 1932), p. 243.
90   Lawrence, 9 October 1916, in *Letters*, vol. 2, p. 660.
91   R. Aldington, *Death of a Hero* (1929; London: Hogarth Press, 1984), p. 118.
92   Aldington, *Death of a Hero*, p. 246.
93   Aldington, *Death of a Hero*, p. 118.
94   R. Aldington, 'In the Tube' (1915), in *Collected Poems*, p. 37.

do, the floor is made of (wooden) slats and the leather upholstery captures him. The poem goes on to describe 'a row of advertisements', echoing the observations of George Gissing in King's Cross underground station, and windows 'Set in brown woodwork, pitted with brass nails'. Aldington's Tube car has all the characteristics of the modern urban world as it sways against 'the flickering background of fluted dingy tunnel'. The poem conveys the movement of the train through the tunnel and of the poet's eyes as he takes in the scene. But in the second half of the poem Aldington turns to his fellow passengers as he matches the hardness of the surfaces with the 'Eyes of greed, of pitiful blankness, of plethoric complacency'.[95] The eyes he studies are 'immobile' and 'brasslike' and his evocation of the Tube car seems to follow Flint's pre-war account in 'Tube'. However, Aldington's poem reflects the impact of the conflict on the Home Front in its bitter rejection of the other passengers: they inspire

> Antagonism,
> Disgust,
> Immediate antipathy

and the poem ends with the rhetorical 'What right have you to live?'[96] Here, Aldington seems to contrast the grinding monotony of the daily Tube journey with the ceaseless carnage of the Western Front, recording a sense of desolation that would grow as the war continued.

The novelist Henry Williamson recorded a similar sense of urban desolation by turning London *into* the Western Front. In his retrospective novel *The Innocent Moon* (1961), Williamson's hero travels across the city during the war and comes to 'an Underground station, and with relief bought a ticket to Charing Cross. Crowds waited on platforms, dense and silent'.[97] Later, he travels through 'vapours more dense and choking than those which lay upon the metropolitan area; [...] the reports of detonators placed on railway lines as fog-signals brought back to him the illusion of sentries' rifles loosed off into No-man's-land'.[98] The crowds on the underground are like soldiers waiting for a troop train to the front; the fog lying across London and its river suburbs is like the poison gas that lay in the shell holes of the Western Front; detonators are like rifle shots. In Williamson's nightmare description any trace of a natural or organic world has vanished from the city. This is the city of the Un-Dead;

---

95   Aldington, 'In the Tube', p. 37.
96   Aldington, 'In the Tube', p. 37.
97   H. Williamson, *The Innocent Moon* (1961; London: MacDonald & Co., 1985), p. 242.
98   Williamson, *The Innocent Moon*, p. 242.

those who carry out their tasks mechanically according to the orders of some monstrous or demonic force—capitalism, in this case. The steam demon has become part of the Tube train and controls the commuters who mindlessly travel in its clutches each day. Of course, Williamson's perspective came many decades later after he had flirted with the ideology of Oswald Mosley's Blackshirts in the 1930s. But the shift in the imaginative perception of the machine during the war can also be illustrated by comparing E. M. Forster's approach to technology in *Howard's End* (1910) and D. H. Lawrence's response during the war. Forster had invented a restless 'shadow city' in *Howard's End* in which the encroachment of the urban world on the countryside is represented by what Forster called a 'red rust'.[99] In the novel, London is in a process of constant upheaval and change, and the Dent clock above King's Cross station represents these mechanical forces in a similar way to the motor car. The clock is 'a second moon'[100] that rivals the natural one in the sky above the station. During the war, Lawrence was writing to Ottoline Morrell in 1915 that 'the moon is not Queen of the sky by night [...] it seems the Zeppelin is in the zenith of the night, golden like a new moon'.[101] This suggested that the fears of technology expressed in Forster's novel were no longer tied up with railways but with aerial warfare. The Zeppelin has replaced the railway/underground as the technological spectre, contributing to a whole raft of interwar science fiction that saw aerial bombardment as the main threat to London. Nevertheless, a link had been made between the underground and the arrival of an aerial threat.

The development of air warfare and the clear threat it posed to large urban regions may have softened attitudes towards the more earthbound technology of the tube during the interwar period. As early as 1895 in H. G. Wells' short story 'The Argonauts of the Air', the Argonauts had flown 'not eighty feet above the East Putney station, on the Metropolitan District line, to the screaming astonishment of a platformful of people'.[102] In W. Wood's *The Enemy in our Midst* (1906), German residents in Britain were busy making secret preparations for invasion: 'the capacities of the railways were known to a truck; the tubes were understood throughout every yard of their length'.[103] During the war, a patriotic German postcard showed terrified Londoners streaming down into

99   E. M. Forster, *Howard's End* (1910; Harmondsworth, Penguin, 1941), p. 329.

100   Forster, *Howard's End*, p. 95.

101   Lawrence, 9 September 1915, in *Letters*, vol. 2, p. 390.

102   H. G. Wells, 'The Argonauts of the Air' (1895), in *Selected Short Stories* (Harmondsworth: Penguin, 1958), pp. 212–23, p. 222.

103   Quoted in I. F. Clarke, *Voices Prophesying War, 1763–1984* (London: Oxford University Press, 1966), p. 149.

an underground station during an air raid (an image that reappeared in the film *Things to Come*, 1936). Offering apparent evidence of the collapse of civilian morale, its message certainly reflected the growing dangers of civilian panic after incidents at Mile End and Bishopsgate in which people were crushed to death.[104] But, as recorded by Wilfred Owen in a letter to his mother in 1916, when he was trapped in the underground at Liverpool Street for three hours during a Zeppelin raid, the tubes were widely perceived as a place of refuge.[105] This would remain the case even after the death of a Russian woman and a child as a result of a crush at that same station a year later in 1917.[106] The increased use of the underground as a subterranean public space did not suit the authorities. They were already concerned about both the volume and type of person using the underground for shelter on the pretext that legitimate travellers were being inconvenienced, and began to increase xenophobia by targeting 'aliens' as habitual shelterers. Most personal accounts of sheltering suggest that conditions were very poor, especially during the Gotha/Giant raids of 1917–18 shown, for example, in the description of Leicester Square station by Elizabeth Fagan: 'It was horrible that platform. The poor folk from the surrounding district who had taken refuge there [...] were lying all over it [...] and wherever there was an inch of platform uncovered by human beings, there was broken food, banana skins, orange peel—and worse than that too!'[107] Siegfried Sassoon, who was caught up in a Gotha air raid on Liverpool Street station in June 1918, also registered the full force of these attacks. He later wrote that 'This sort of danger seemed to demand a quality of courage dissimilar to front-line fortitude [...] here one was helpless; an invisible enemy sent destruction spinning down from a fine weather sky'.[108]

The underground offered H. G. Wells a location for these conflicting perspectives in his postwar novel *The Dream* (1924). Here they collide in 'a brightly lit first-class carriage' of the underground in what is described by the hero Sarnac as 'a sort of transport drain'.[109] The insulated world of the Home Front with its revellers 'going out to dinner and to the theatre' is invaded by

---

104 The British government rather ineffectually hit back with moralistic propaganda posters depicting German generals glorying in the monstrous achievements of their aviators or 'Knights of the Air'.

105 See W. Owen, 3 February 1916, in *Wilfred Owen: Selected Letters*, ed. J. Bell (Oxford: Oxford University Press, 1985), p. 178.

106 See Wolmar, *The Subterranean Railway*, p. 213.

107 Elizabeth Fagan, *Evening News*, 1 March 1935, quoted in Hanson, *First Blitz*, p. 207.

108 Sassoon, *Memoirs of an Infantry Officer*, p. 208.

109 H. G. Wells, *The Dream* (1924; London: Hogarth Press, 1987), p. 237.

soldiers 'muddy from the trenches',[110] reflecting the fact that men in uniform travelled free on tubes and buses. Underground trains are no longer the symbols of either individual freedom or progress as Wells had argued in *Anticipations*, but a sign of a modern world of irreconcilable forces, a machine-driven society at war with other machine-led societies and with itself. Wells seems to find reconciliation only in the fortieth century when a 'two thousand years old' tunnel[111] is discovered in Italy that contains a train full of mummified bodies preserved by the effects of poison gas in a tomb-like environment. Sarnac observes sagaciously: 'Those poor wretches caught in the tunnel! But everyone in that age must have felt caught in a tunnel'.[112] The railway carriages in this case seem to represent a whole epoch of human failure, a monument to a war that overcame civilization, with London as its doomed city. The war had brought about a shift towards a more mystical or religious solution for humanity, but *The Dream* also points to a general shift in thinking about technology in the interwar period.

The war, Daniel Pick remarks, reinforced the notion of an 'atomised rootless modernity'. It was a conception of 'technological progress and scientific acceleration deemed inseparable from the exercise of destructive power' which increasingly informed the often negative response of writers to the city.[113] Certainly the presence of troop and ambulance trains on underground lines through the capital would have reinforced the impact of warfare.[114] The railways as a whole and the underground in particular seemed to have combined man and machine as Futurism had demanded but at a terrible cost. It was certainly not a comfortable ride, as Karel Čapek, the author of the dystopian play *RUR* (1921), recorded in a letter during a visit to London after the war. Čapek reported being thrust into 'a barred cage which looks like scales for weighing cattle [...] through an ugly steel-plated-well'. He was then confronted by 'a snorting train [...] the train flew on; [...] thereupon they took me out and rushed me here through new catacombs to a moving staircase which clatters

---

110 Wells, *The Dream*, p. 237.

111 Wells, *The Dream*, p. 14.

112 Wells, *The Dream*, p. 17.

113 D. Pick, *War Machine: The Rationalisation of Slaughter in the Modern Age* (New Haven: Yale University Press, 1993), p. 204.

114 The most important link was the steam-operated 'widened lines' that brought trains through Farringdon Street and Moorgate Street and over the well-known bridge at Ludgate Hill. The West London Railway and its extension also carried many military trains from North Pole Junction to Addison Road (Olympia) and Lillie Bridge and towards the Thames at Chelsea. The East London Railway connected six railway companies, including the Metropolitan and the District, with Liverpool Street services.

like a mill and hastens people upwards on it'.[115] Here, Čapek suggests an impersonal mechanical world that could take over human beings and direct them like cattle. The lift plays an important role in this process, resembling a pit cage but descending into a catacomb rather than a coal seam. The train, which is electric, snorts like *Punch*'s steam demons. The escalator 'clatters' like an industrial mechanism as it draws passengers onto its moving belt almost like the belt used to feed ammunition into a machine gun.

The aggressive marketing strategy embodied in Tubism could be construed by writers as a sign of this tendency. *The Dream* is one of a number of parables in futuristic fiction which features a world created by technological disaster. But on this occasion the symbolic railway tunnel is dead, prehistoric and the result of the technology of twentieth-century warfare. It is a closed episode, hermetically sealed like a Pharaoh's tomb and seems to suggest that the impact of war had undermined Wells' belief in a purely technological solution to human problems. Wells discarded his utopian ideas of vast underground cities in order to concentrate on smaller scale municipal improvements and the reform of existing urban structures through organizations like the Design and Industries Association. Wells had prefigured aerial attacks on London in *The War in the Air* (1908) but this was no longer dystopian fiction, as in Forster's 'The Machine Stops', because the city had entered the historical record as a target for aerial bombardment. It was an idea that George Orwell was to make full use of in his novel *Coming Up for Air* (1939) where the London periphery would be simultaneously assaulted by bombers and underground-directed suburbanization.

FABRIC CLAMPED WITH BOLTS OF IRON: THE INTERWAR TUBE OF VIRGINIA WOOLF AND ARNOLD BENNETT

I n 1907 Virginia Woolf noted in her diary that the 'Twopenny Tube has now burrowed as far as Golders Green' on the Northern line. She went on to add that 'sinking into an earth laid with pavement & houses at one end, you rise to soft green fields at the other; the ashen dark & the chill & the cold glitter of electricity is replaced by the more benignant illumination of daylight'.[116] The 'Twopenny Tube' was, of course, a reference to the Central

---

115 K. Čapek, *Letters from England*, trans. P. Selver (London: Bles, 1925), p. 26.
116 V. Woolf, *Virginia Woolf, A Passionate Apprentice: The Early Journals, 1897–1909*, ed. M. A. Leaska (London: Harvest, 1990), p. 365.

London Railway but Woolf was using the term in its newly generic sense to describe the growing Tube railway. In this entry Woolf revealed a fascination with the Tube that would continue throughout her adult life: the strange notion of descending into the earth beneath the capital's dense carpet of buildings followed by a re-emergence in a pastoral world; the fearful cold and darkness of the tunnel with its eerie 'glitter' of artificial electric power followed by the familiar sunlight at the surface. Woolf quickly became a seasoned underground traveller, establishing a relationship with the system that was to take its most vivid shape in her fiction, drawing on many aspects of the Tube. If any one writer of the first half of the twentieth century can be described as the fictional chronicler of the Tube it is surely Virginia Woolf.

Woolf's interest in the Tube may also be linked to the Post-Impressionists exhibition mentioned at the start of this chapter. Featuring work by Cézanne, Manet, Van Gogh, Gauguin and Picasso amongst others, the exhibition was mainly representative of continental painting from the last two decades of the nineteenth century. But for the advocates of this visionary movement these painters were true innovators. As Roger Fry put it, they 'are cutting away at the merely representative element in art to establish more and more firmly the fundamental laws of expressive form at its barest, most abstract elements'.[117] For Clive Bell, Post-Impressionism was 'a return to first principles'[118] in art, a harbinger of the Arts and Crafts Movement's new life that Morris and others had struggled for in the socialist revival of the 1880s. Cézanne, one of the major painters in the exhibition, was hailed by Bell as a saint who had a 'revelation that set the gulf between the nineteenth century and the twentieth'.[119] Woolf's pinpointing of the exhibition as a watershed moment in the emergence of modernism was an acknowledgement of a break in the ways of seeing the world and an indication of the many variants of modernism that would follow. Woolf would try to incorporate the Tube as a machine into her work just as Lily Broscoe would try to create a Post-Impressionist painting in the novel *To the Lighthouse* (1927). The use of the Tube in her fiction was an attempt to deal with the machine in an abstract form. Michael Saler's argument that the essential continuity in the artistic lineage of the Tube in 'Fitness for Purpose' lay in the Arts and Crafts Movement[120] does not take into account the fact that Woolf and others redirected the ethos of Arts and Crafts into the channels of modernism. Woolf's moral and political responses to the Tube were partly determined by

---

117 R. Fry, 'The Grafton Gallery I', *Nation*, no. 8, 19 November 1910, p. 332.
118 C. Bell, *Art* (1914; New York: Capricorn Books, 1958), p. 38.
119 Bell, *Art*, p. 140.
120 See Saler, *The Avant-Garde in Interwar England*, pp. 25–43.

the broad currents of late-nineteenth-century socialism as embodied in Morris, but she fashioned these impulses in a radical way that drew on the legacy of Post-Impressionism.

What sort of machine was the Tube train that so impressed Woolf? In these decades it offered a thoroughly new environment for travel. The war had brought a halt to the speculative Tube construction started in 1903 that had begun the consolidation of separate lines into a unified system, and had created most of today's Tube stations in central London. But following the 1921 Trade Facilities Act, the Underground Group began the modernization of its Tube stock as well as building extensions to serve the developing suburbs and London County Council housing estates. One of the most revolutionary changes was in the design of its Tube trains. The original version had been likened to a 'padded cell'[121] with limited passenger comfort and poor visibility, but by the time the Central London Railway opened in 1900 the Tube car was better designed with large windows, rattan seating and stuffed armrests. Nevertheless, all Tube trains were formed of manually operated 'Gate Stock' cars, so-called because of the gates at each end of the car which were the sole means of entry and egress. In the 1920s such Gate Stock cars were being replaced by carriages with brand new air-operated automatic sliding doors. The very first Tube car to be designed in this way was the 1920 Tube Stock model that was ordered for the Piccadilly line. The last Gate Stock cars were finally removed from the Bakerloo line in 1929 and not until 1938 from the older District line, but what were to become known as Standard Stock trains established the type of Tube car with which we are still familiar today. Both the interior and exterior of cars were radically altered by the introduction of two sets of automatic sliding doors and, from 1930, single-leaf doors instead of the gates at the ends of each car. This meant that passengers could now enter and leave the train more freely and swiftly although congestion still occurred on packed trains. There was also a significant reduction in the number of staff on each six-car train from a guard, four 'gatemen' and a motorman down to two guards and a motorman.[122] The loss of three on-board staff was a radical shift in the relationship between passengers and the Tube car in which they travelled, particularly as the former were used to a visible human presence throughout the length of the train.

This was the environment in which passengers like Virginia Woolf travelled. However, the detailed picture of a Tube car interior in Richard Aldington's

---

121 See M. Horne & B. Bayman, *The First Tube: The Story of the Northern Line* (Harrow Weald: Capital Transport Publishing, 1990), p. 10.

122 The gatemen were responsible for supervising the loading and unloading of passengers on each car and ensuring that everyone was safely on board before manually closing the gates.

1915 Imagist poem 'In the Tube' was not repeated in writing. The type of Tube car that Aldington had described was disappearing by the mid-1920s and Modernist writers did not focus on the specific detail of their replacements but increasingly turned to the inner experience of *being* in a Tube car. One reason for this loss of grainy surface detail may lie in the collapse of the avant-garde's fetishism of the mechanized world, a change evident in the Vorticist sculpture *Rock Drill* (1913–15) by Jacob Epstein. The frighteningly mechanized figure produced by Epstein could be likened to the Tube train's powerful metallic frame into which human beings were crushed every day. It seems that he later destroyed much of the original sculpture because he felt that it celebrated the machine violence that had led to the war. Some writers believed that a machine-based society was leading towards a dystopian robot-controlled world. As A. E. Heath noted in a review of *Joy in Work* by Henri de Man, 'Our age is remarkable for combining active enjoyment of all the fruits of mechanisation with an unquenchable taste for denouncing it'.[123] Heath invoked Karel Čapek's play *RUR* as the source of much of this ambivalence and it was frequently cited in the BBC's magazine the *Listener* as an influential model for many contemporary commentators who seemed obsessed with this robot world.

By the mid-1920s Tubism had successfully aligned transport demand with technological innovation, presenting an image of almost unlimited progress. The response of writers was to survey this terrain, subjecting it to perspectives drawn from a number of disciplines. Some writers simply appropriated the Tube for the purpose of metaphorically consigning the whole paraphernalia of railway transport to the past—burying trains, tunnels and stations, a whole mode of transport in a time capsule. This was an approach we have seen in H. G. Wells' novel *The Dream* where Wells had declared that his own society would one day be perceived as an aberration. Others were not confident that progress would be resumed after the war and concluded that the modern world was a desert of broken images and artifacts:

> For two gross of broken statues,
> For a few thousand battered books

as Pound wrote in 'Hugh Selwyn Mauberley' (1920).[124] Pound also transferred the hell of the Western Front to London in this poem mentioning the soldiers who:

---

123   A. E. Heath, Review of *Joy in Work* by Henri de Man, *Listener*, vol. 2, 14 August 1929, p. 213.
124   E. Pound, 'Hugh Selwyn Mauberley' (1920), in *Selected Poems*, pp. 173–87, p. 176.

> walked eye-deep in hell
> believing in old men's lies, then unbelieving
> came home, home to a lie,
> home to many deceits,
> home to old lies and new infamy.[125]

T. S. Eliot declared London to be the 'Unreal City' through which:

> Under the brown fog of a winter dawn,
> A crowd flowed over London Bridge, so many,
> I had not thought death had undone so many.[126]

These images suggested that the liberal vision of progress had failed. The death of the natural landscape in the hell of war had been extended to the daily journey of the morning rush-hour crowd emerging from London Bridge station on the south side of the Thames and crossing the river to head towards the City. Such images suggest a truly Dantean vestibule to Hell that imprinted itself on modernist sensibilities. The crowd

> Flowed up the hill and down King William Street,
> To where Saint Mary Woolnoth kept the hours

on the corner by Bank tube station.[127] This topography is as precise as George Gissing's but Eliot offers no escape from the abyss, including death, as this crowd is already dead. The railways play a sinister role in this Dantean city, bringing generations of office workers into the centre from the suburbs.

Another approach was to make the railway journey a metaphor for a psychological account of change. Ford Madox Ford moved from the pastoral underground of his poem 'Finchley Road' to a narrative of fragmentation with his trilogy *Parade's End* (1924–28). *Some Do Not*, the first part of the trilogy, opens in the comfortable security of an Edwardian railway compartment on a pre-war journey from London to Rye in Sussex. The two passengers, Christopher Tietjens and Edward Macmaster sit 'in the perfectly appointed railway carriage [...] the train ran as smoothly—Tietjens remembered thinking—as British gilt-edged securities'.[128] Ford's message was that the war accelerated the social

---

125 Pound, 'Hugh Selwyn Mauberley', p. 175.

126 T. S. Eliot, 'The Waste Land' (1922), in *Selected Poems* (London: Faber & Faber, 1954), pp. 51–74, p. 53.

127 Eliot, 'The Waste Land', p. 53.

128 F. M. Ford, *Some Do Not* (*Parade's End*, vol. 1) (1924; Harmondsworth: Penguin, 1948), p. 11.

and economic change that would relegate the English gentleman, in this case Tietjens, to the sidings of history and elevate the more modern managerial figure typified by Macmaster to dominance in the harsh commercial world of the 1920s. The train in which they travel represents the death-knell of the old world and, as Sara Haslam points out in her discussion of Ford's fictional approach, 'appear perfectly on time when there is trauma at hand'.[129] As she notes, Tietjens travels on a train with Mrs Duchemin, bringing about gossip that he is sexually involved with her;[130] Edward Ashburnham in *The Good Soldier* (1915) is indiscrete during a train journey;[131] John Dowell cannot control the running of trains in the same novel[132] and William Sorrell in *Ladies Whose Bright Eyes* (1911) is involved in a railway accident.[133]

Virginia Woolf used a similarly Edwardian railway compartment on a journey from Richmond to Waterloo in her essay 'Mr Bennett and Mrs Brown',[134] although it was probably less well appointed and more suburban in character. In choosing to include a train journey in her essay Woolf was drawing attention to the solid realities to be found in the popular fiction of Arnold Bennett, John Galsworthy and H. G. Wells. Her comments suggest that modern fiction not only needed to break from its realist past but also that the certainties and solidities of that past were giving way to a more fluid and open-ended present. Woolf's article, which appeared in *The Criterion*, was a response to a provocative attack on her method of character-drawing by Bennett who, in a discussion of her novel *Jacob's Room*, had accused Woolf of creating characters that 'do not vitally survive in the mind because the author has been obsessed by details of originality and cleverness'.[135] And yet, barely six years earlier, Bennett chose to defend his own approach in a short article entitled 'Is the Novel Decaying?' following criticism of his work, along with that of Shaw, Wells and Conrad, by

---

129 S. Haslam, *Fragmenting Modernism, Ford Madox Ford, the Novel and the Great War* (Manchester: Manchester University Press, 2002), p. 190.

130 Ford, *Some Do Not*, p. 173.

131 F. M. Ford, *The Good Soldier: A Tale of Passion* (1915; Harmondsworth: Penguin, 1946), p. 51.

132 Ford, *The Good Soldier*, p. 49.

133 F. M. Ford, *Ladies Whose Bright Eyes* (1911; Manchester: Carcanet, 1988), p. 47.

134 Woolf, 'Mr Bennett and Mrs Brown', p. 321.

135 A. Bennett, 'Is the Novel Decaying?', *Cassell's Weekly*, 28 March 1923, quoted in L. Troman-hauser, 'Virginia Woolf's London and the Archaeology of Character', in L. Phillips (ed.), *The Swarming Streets: Twentieth-Century Literary Representations of London* (Amsterdam & New York: Rodopi, 2004), pp. 33–43, p. 36. Woolf was stung by Bennett's comments: she admitted she had no 'reality' gift in her *Diaries* (V. Woolf, 19 June 1923, in *The Diaries of Virginia Woolf*, ed. A. Bell, 5 vols. (London: Penguin, 1975–82), vol. 2, p. 248).

Ezra Pound. Most readers, Pound had argued, would find that 'there are values and tonalities to which these authors are wholly insensitive'.[136]

Woolf was significant amongst the novelists of the interwar period in her attempts to describe this new world of modernity in fiction. As Michael Whitworth remarks, Woolf did not reject technological progress: 'In her alignment of modernity and the machine, Woolf curiously and unexpectedly resembles the Italian Futurists, who celebrated the car, the train and the automobile'.[137] The solid planes of the railway carriage that had carried generations of fictional characters from Charles Dickens to Arnold Bennett would have to be sidelined in modern fiction. The problem with such fiction, she said in a letter to Jacques Raverat in October 1924, was that the 'falsity of the past (by which I mean Bennett, Galsworthy and so on) is precisely I think that they adhere to a formal railway line of sentence'.[138] Instead, Woolf set out to highlight the episodic nature of the Tube journey as it offered a paradigm for writing by presenting the conflicting elements of chaos and order that were, in her view, the task of fiction to capture. Woolf might be described as having embraced Tubism whilst rejecting the Futurist formalism of its pre-war origins; the Tube became a key motif in her fictional vocabulary.

Woolf's fictional approach to the Tube can be illustrated by comparing it directly with the fiction of Arnold Bennett that she had attacked in 'Mr Bennett and Mrs Brown'. Bennett had published 'The Fire of London' in 1904 as one of six short stories in *The Loot of Cities* and, in this story, he unwittingly provided Virginia Woolf with ammunition in her battle against the old guard of fiction writers. Bennett's story is solidly realist, in particular his description of Devonshire Mansion which was 'a bright edifice of eleven storeys in the Foster and Dicksee style, constructional ironwork by Homan, lifts by Waygood, decorations by Waring, and terra-cotta by the rood'. Bennett characteristically went on: 'It is a composite building. Its foundations are firmly fixed in the Tube railway'[139]. Not only is this probably the first mention of the shortened version Tube (with a capital T) in fiction but also a perfect example of Bennett's inclination to use the underground as a securely material part of his fictional

---

136 Pound, 'Joyce' (1918), in *Literary Essays*, pp. 410–17, p. 412.

137 M. Whitworth, 'Virginia Woolf and Modernism', in S. Roe & S. Sellers (eds.), *The Cambridge Companion to Virginia Woolf* (Cambridge: Cambridge University Press, 2000), pp. 146–63, p. 155.

138 V. Woolf, 3 October 1924, in *The Letters of Virginia Woolf*, eds. N. Nicolson & J. Trautmann, 6 vols. (London: Hogarth Press, 1975–80), vol. 3, p. 135.

139 A. Bennett, 'The Fire of London' (1904), in M. Smith (ed.), *Golden Age Detective Stories* (Bath: Parragon, 1999), pp. 161–76, p. 165.

construction of the capital. Bennett utilized the history of the underground in its steam phase in his novel *Riceyman Steps* and also, after electrification, to convey the reality of life in King's Cross where 'the earth faintly throbbed: for, to the vibrations of traffic and manufacture, the Underground railway, running beneath Riceyman Steps, added the muffled uproar of its subterranean electric trains'.[140] In *The Pretty Lady* (1918), his novel about the war, Bennett used the location of Piccadilly Circus Tube station as a meeting place for his hero G. T. Hoape, a wealthy middle-aged bachelor, and the prostitute Christine, the 'Lady' of the title. Bennett describes the couple meeting during a Zeppelin raid, 'just beyond the knot of loiterers at Piccadilly Tube' who are clearly entering the Tube to take shelter. But the two characters do not join the shelterers inside the station: 'They went through the Tube station and were soon in one of the withdrawn streets between Coventry Street and Pall Mall East'.[141]

Thus for Bennett, Piccadilly Circus station is a place on the map of London, an architectural embodiment of urban functionalism linking his characters together in the West End and the suburbs. It has the solid identity of stations because it is part of the urban furniture. The Tube was a place of refuge with Bennett recording a number of 'strange journeys in Tube' in his war-time diary entry of 27 September 1917, focusing on the 'very poor women and children sitting on stairs (fear of raid)' and 'dreadful sights of very poor with babies in Tube',[142] sights which brought out class bigotry in middle-class users.[143] Translated into this wartime fiction, in *The Pretty Lady*, the façade of Piccadilly Circus Tube station is a portal to safety. For Bennett, the real underground was an essential underpinning of the capital and not a partial cause of its metaphorical collapse. This was a view he shared with Virginia Woolf, however different their respective fictional accounts of the underground system turned out to be.

By the time Virginia Woolf published *The Waves* (1931), Bennett's Piccadilly Circus station had been demolished and rebuilt as the imperial hub of a fast-moving transport system. Based on the recent successful reconstruction of Bank station, a large public concourse was created below ground with five subways connecting the elliptical hall to street level. The concourse included the latest

---

140   A. Bennett, *Riceyman Steps* (1923; London: Pan, 1964), pp. 2–3.

141   A. Bennett, *The Pretty Lady* (London: Cassell, 1918), p. 199.

142   A. Bennett, 27 September 1917, in *The Journals of Arnold Bennett*, ed. F. Swinnerton (Harmondsworth: Penguin, 1954), p. 307.

143   In the same entry, Bennett noted 'middle-class women saying to each other that if the poor couldn't keep to the regulations they ought to be forbidden the Tube as a shelter from raid', *Journals*, p. 307.

improvements in ventilation and artificial lighting in order to maximise its role as a place for both pedestrian and passenger traffic, including the provision of showcases for exhibitions. *The Waves* is centred on the voices of six people as they journey through life and Woolf's characters are often to be found on the Tube, in particular here at Piccadilly Circus station. At one point she places her character Jinny on the new concourse where 'Everything that is desirable meets—Piccadilly South Side, Piccadilly North Side, Regent Street and the Haymarket, I stand for a moment under the pavement in the heart of London [...] The great avenues of civilisation meet [...] and strike this way and that. I am in the heart of life'.[144] For Woolf, Piccadilly Circus station is a state of mind, a location for one part of a complex relationship between individual consciousness and the shifting world of modern London. It is also at the centre of a world empire that, as Woolf knew well, radiated far beyond London. The empire was consciously linked to the underground such as in the Ernest Dinkel poster *Visit the Empire* (1932) and Piccadilly Circus had a mural with five panels, one of which was in the form of a pictorial map of the world showing the station at the heart of the empire.[145]

Woolf's diary entries provide evidence that she drew on her experiences of underground travel for her fiction, especially from her use of the District line in the period 1915–24. Woolf commented on London's 'civilisation of life' in 1918—'what with fires, electric light, underground railways & umbrellas, how can one take notice of the weather'.[146] This echoed the poster *Winter's Discontent Made Glorious* (1909) which proclaimed the Tube's victory over the elements by showing a warm Tube car placed against a wild and windy landscape. Woolf also refers in her diary to 'a burst of summer heat' that forced 'people in the Tube' to pull blinds down to protect themselves from the hot sun.[147] This observation was reworked in *The Years* (1937) when Peggy wishes that 'there were blinds like those in railway carriages that came down over the light and hooded the mind',[148] thus placing the mundane experience of Tube travel on a psychological wavelength. It also offered a metaphor for the closing off of the constant bombardment of sensory impressions that was experienced by the modernist mind in the Tube. For Bennett and Woolf, the physical facts of

---

144 V. Woolf, *The Waves* (1931; Harmondsworth: Penguin, 1951), p. 165.

145 Produced in 1928–29 by Stephen Bone, the mural was placed above the escalators in the new station. See S. Taylor, *A Journey Through Time: London Transport Photographs, 1880–1965* (London: Laurence King, 1992), p. 67.

146 Woolf, 23 January 1918, in *Diaries*, vol. 1, p. 111.

147 Woolf, 5 April 1918, in *Diaries*, vol. 1, p. 131.

148 V. Woolf, *The Years* (1937; London: Granada, 1977), p. 296.

Tube travel were important and both writers were reacting to recent changes in the physical landscape above and below the surface. But the differences are striking: Woolf sought to dissolve the solidities of urban life in accord with what she considered the modernity of her times and drenched the urban reality in a kind of fictional acid bath. This meant shunting the Edwardian railway compartment of Bennett into the sidings of literary history along with his realism.

Woolf's approach to the underground is the most complex and multifaceted example of Tubism. During the war, Woolf's narrator in her short story 'The Mark on the Wall' (1917) had observed that life could be compared to being:

> blown through the Tube at fifty miles an hour—landing at the other end without a single hairpin in one's hair! Shot out at the feet of God entirely naked! [...] that seems to express the rapidity of life, the perpetual waste and repair; all so casual, all so haphazard ...[149]

And the Tube and buses became a thread in novels such as *Mrs Dalloway* (1925) and *To the Lighthouse* as well as *The Waves* (1931), with Woolf using London's public transport as a means of recovering and reordering experience. Woolf's narrator in 'The Mark on the Wall' signals this method of self-analysis, a kind of descent into the self: 'As we face each other in omnibuses and underground railways we are looking into the mirror; that accounts for the vagueness, the gleam of glassiness, in our eyes.'[150] But it can also mean a literal descent into the Tube station, in line with the more traditional infernal aspects of the tubes, as when Jinny in *The Waves* observes commuters going 'down the moving stairs like the pinioned and terrible descent of some army'[151] into Piccadilly Circus station. The multiple experiences of her six characters in *The Waves* are refracted through the Tube where all six—Louis, Neville, Rhoda, Jinny, Susan and Bernard—have a separate narrative focus. For example, for Louis the 'descent into the Tube was like death. We were cut up, we were dissevered by all those faces and the hollow wind that seemed to roar down there over

---

149   V. Woolf, 'The Mark on the Wall' (1917), in *A Haunted House and Other Stories* (1944; London: Hogarth Press, 1967), pp. 40–48, p. 41.

150   Woolf, 'The Mark on the Wall', p. 43.

151   Woolf, *The Waves*, p. 166. *The Waves* contains an extraordinary number of references to the Tube, making it one of the most underground-oriented novels of all. Woolf did not neglect London's bus services either, referring in *Mrs Dalloway* (1925; London: Hogarth Press, 1950) to journeys on a 'pirate' bus (pp. 148–49) and 'The British Middle classes sitting sideways on the tops of omnibuses with parcels and umbrellas' (p. 20).

desert boulders'.[152] For Jinny it means a descent into middle age as she reacts with self-disgust to her reflection in a mirror at Piccadilly Circus station: 'I am no longer young. I am no longer part of the procession. Millions descend those stairs in a terrible descent. Great wheels churn inexorably urging them downwards'.[153] Both comments suggest that Woolf has split the episodic nature of underground travel into many fragments so that we are seeing the experience of daily Tube travel in myriad ways. Each of Woolf's characters experiences the same Tube system but each finds a different meaning in that experience. The wind that blew across Gissing's characters in King's Cross underground station is still blowing in Woolf's Tube even though it not a real wind—in Woolf's novel it is 'hollow' or artificial. This wind roars over Eliot-like desert boulders; invisible wheels draw people into old age.

Woolf can reverse the process and direct her characters to ascend the escalator as when Rhoda 'rises to the surface, standing erect with the others at Piccadilly Circus'.[154] The underground exerts a rhythmic power over the city, as the 'lifts rise and fall; trains stop'.[155] The Tube regulates the city but does not inflict a hell-like penance on its commuters in the way that Gissing had suggested. 'The iron gates have rolled back' says Jinny and the 'abysses of space' can be defeated with 'rouge, with powder, with flimsy pocket-handkerchiefs'.[156] The Tube is a necessary part of modernity and it is simply a question of negotiating everyday life in this machine-built environment. The Tube reclaims the characters in *The Waves*: as Bernard says, 'One cannot live outside the machine for more perhaps than half an hour'.[157] This is the machine in which 'vast numbers of men [...] jostled and encountered in trains and tubes [exchange] the knowing wink of competitors and comrades with a thousand snares and dodges to achieve the same end—to earn our livings'.[158] Even Percival, the 'invisible' seventh character in the novel, is invoked as leading people, military-fashion, into the underground when Bernard says: 'At the same time let me tell you, men and women, hurrying to the tube station, you would have had to respect him. You would have had to form up and follow behind him'.[159] The Tube has been fully integrated with its commuters as it now regulates the tides

---

152 Woolf, *The Waves*, p. 153.
153 Woolf, *The Waves*, p. 165.
154 Woolf, *The Waves*, p. 167.
155 Woolf, *The Waves*, p. 167.
156 Woolf, *The Waves*, p. 196.
157 Woolf, *The Waves*, p. 132.
158 Woolf, *The Waves*, p. 224.
159 Woolf, *The Waves*, p. 131.

of the metropolitan world. Woolf's characters live in the machine but are not controlled by it, as suggested in one of her diary entries which recorded the view that *The Waves* must end to show 'that the theme effort, effort, dominates: not the waves: & personality: & defiance'.[160] In other words, the struggle for individual identity must prevail against the breaking waves and tides of the urban world. The Tube does not trap its commuters but gives them a part of their identity in the modern city.

Woolf was consciously reflecting on a question that was very much in the public domain, the same question that had been posed in late Victorian fiction and occasionally raised in visual terms before, during and immediately after the First World War. It asked not *whether* the Tube affected people and the city they lived in, but precisely *how* it affected them. The Tube offered Woolf an important metaphor for the modernizing impulses of the metropolis after the war. It also offered a continuity and regularity that brought order as well as changes that turned new corners in perception. Woolf shared with the ideologues of Tubism the premise that the underground was an important means of integrating the modern city but for her this integration was psychological rather than physical, geographical or geopolitical. This does not mean, however, that Woolf was not a social thinker. Kathy Phillips has discussed Woolf's ability to develop a cultural analysis of society and her involvement in politics, from her teaching at the Working Men's College in London to her membership of the Women's Co-operative Guild and secretaryship of Rodmell Labour Party.[161] This is confirmed by Woolf's description of the purpose of *Mrs Dalloway* when she said her aim was 'to criticise the social system, and to show it at work, at its most intense'.[162] The Tube also provided her with an explanation of how she tried to create characters in her fiction through what she described as 'my tunnelling process, by which I tell the past by instalments, as I have need of it'.[163] In an earlier diary entry about her novel *The Hours*, Woolf had outlined 'how I dig out beautiful caves behind my characters; I think that gives exactly what I want; humanity, humour, depth. The idea is that the caves shall connect, & each comes to daylight at the present moment'.[164]

The Tube enabled Woolf to excavate her characters' lives, as Vicki Tromanhauser notes: 'this method of character development allows her to dig into

---

160 Woolf, 22 December 1930, in *Diaries*, vol. 3, p. 339.

161 See K. Phillips, *Virginia Woolf Against Empire* (Knoxville: University of Tennessee Press, 1994).

162 Woolf, 19 June 1923, in *Diaries*, vol. 2, p. 248.

163 Woolf, 15 October 1923, in *Diaries*, vol. 2, p. 272.

164 Woolf, 30 August 1923, in *Diaries*, vol. 2, p. 263.

the discrete pasts of individual characters [whilst] the labyrinthine network of tunnels that results connects up diverse social classes and experiences much like London's tube system'.[165] There can be no doubt that Woolf saw the Tube as a democratic form of travel because it joined socially as well as geographically disparate urban spaces and that its appearance in *The Waves* offers a common linkage of subterranean space for her six main characters. They are often joined by the image of a ring or circle as when 'the omnibuses were clogged; [...] stopped with a clink, like a link added to a stone chain'.[166] There is poignant moment when 'The circle is destroyed. We are thrown asunder' and 'now the circle breaks. Now the current flows'.[167] In a novel with so many references to the underground system it would seem possible that she was thinking in terms of the Circle line with its unifying and seemingly perpetual motion—but it is an electrical universe, perhaps an eternity in which 'the light on the electric rails flashes'.[168]

For Tubism, particularly in its Futurist forms, it was the hardware—trains, signals, stations—that supplied that totality of the experience in the city. For Woolf, the software was the key, enabling the direct experience of thinking and feeling in the city unmediated by formalism. Woolf rejected the masculinism inherent in much of the modernist project including the anti-feminist aspects of Futurism. She would have agreed with Dorothy Richardson's character Miriam in *Pilgrimage* when she complains about 'Men. All the things men have invented, trains and cannons and things that make a frightful noise'.[169] Woolf rejected the formalism but not the way that both objects and feelings were linked: the hardware and software of the Tube were inseparable elements of the modern world and of modern art, as she suggests in Lily Broscoe's description of her paintings in *To the Lighthouse* (1927) as 'feathery and evanescent, [...] like the colours on a butterfly's wings; [...] but beneath the fabric must be clamped together with bolts of iron'.[170] The posters that flapped from their moorings in this underground 'art gallery' concealed the iron panels of the Tube's tunnels. Woolf's writing described what made Tubism so successful as an entire package of ideas about London's transport.

Woolf was not always comfortable with the impact of the hardware on the subjective world, and she sometimes recoils from the dehumanizing effects of

---

165 Tromanhauser, 'Virginia Woolf's London', p. 37.
166 Woolf, *The Waves*, p. 240.
167 Woolf, *The Waves*, p. 122.
168 Woolf, *The Waves*, p. 197.
169 D. Richardson, *Pilgrimage* (1938), 4 vols. (London: Virago, 1979 & 1992), vol. 1, p. 327.
170 V. Woolf, *To the Lighthouse* (1927; Harmondsworth: Penguin, 1964), p. 264.

Tube transit. Neville, in *The Waves*, observes 'people pouring profusely out of the Tube when the day's work is done, unanimous, indiscriminate, uncounted', and the horrific mass of 'scarcely formulated faces that bubble up out of the doors of the Tube'.[171] Both images are organic, suggesting blood emerging from a wounded or damaged body, and may be linked with fears about London's vulnerability to air attack. Andrew Thacker has pointed to Woolf's description of the faces in a 'tube carriage [as] grey, sodden, brave, disillusioned' in a diary entry of January 1924.[172] Citing her novel *Jacob's Room* (1922), he argues that Woolf disliked the underground, preferring the street level journey of the omnibus: 'Beneath the pavement, sunk in the earth, hollow drains lined with yellow light for ever conveyed them this way and that' but Woolf went on: 'and large letters upon enamel plates represented in the underworld the parks, squares, and circuses of the upper'—a clear echo of Ford Madox Ford's description.[173] For Woolf the Tube system represented a world of complex events, concepts and activities which combined to give a modern meaning to the metropolis.

Woolf's ambivalence about the Tube may be explained by some of the ways in which London was conceived in the metaphor of the human body. She was aware of the many instances of the capital being seen as a vulnerable organic form—open to external attack as we have seen or from internal collapse brought about by mechanization. There was no mechanical carapace available for the protection of London, a problem mockingly alluded to in Siegfried Sassoon's poem 'An Unveiling' (1947) in which 'The President' plans

> to rebuild, for What-they-died-for's sake,
> A bomb-proof roofed Metropolis, and to make
> Gas-drill compulsory.[174]

---

171   Woolf, *The Waves*, pp. 168 & 208.
172   Woolf, 24 January 1924, in *Diaries*, vol. 2, p. 286.
173   V. Woolf, *Jacob's Room* (1922; Oxford: Oxford University Press, 2000), p. 88. See A. Thacker, *Moving Through Modernity: Space and Geography in Modernism* (Manchester: Manchester University Press, 2003), chapter 5 for an interesting discussion of Woolf's 'literary geography'. Thacker's analysis would be enhanced by reference to real transport developments in London. He analyses a passage in *Mrs Dalloway*, noting the 'fanciful image of the bus as "a pirate"' (p. 169) but this is not a 'fanciful' image but simply a reflection of the fact that London's streets in these years were invaded by a flood of 'pirate' or private buses, similar to the situation in many British cities since deregulation of bus services in the 1980s. We should never underestimate Woolf's powers of social observation in the real as distinct from the imaginary city.
174   Sassoon, 'An Unveiling' (1947), in *Collected Poems*, pp. 187–88, p. 188.

The railway train could be invoked as a piece of subversive ordnance that would 'explode in the flanks of the city like a shell in the side of some ponderous, maternal, majestic animal'[175] as Woolf put it in *The Waves*. A similar image was taken up four years later by Elizabeth Bowen in *The House in Paris* (1935) in which 'everyone waited for the train to impale them on London'.[176] Such violent images were not solely the product of the First World War as Arnold Bennett, for example, had likened trains leaving King's Cross station to shells emerging from a magazine in his pre-war novel *Hilda Lessways*. Woolf therefore had to struggle with a legacy of negative images centred on the future of the capital, a city that she cared deeply about throughout her life. Nevertheless, Woolf's diaries suggest how valuable, in a practical sense, the underground was to her as a lifeline into central London from her Richmond home in the period 1915–24. She noted, for example, 'a conspiracy of fog, frost, strike on Tube railways',[177] the latter disrupting District line services for seven days in February 1919 and again in September of the same year when 'the entire railways of England are on strike'.[178] The Tube also seemed to denote a kind of efficiency, as when Mr Ramsey, in *To the Lighthouse*, compared Shakespeare and the Tube liftman, describing the latter as an 'eternal necessity' representing the 'slave class' required by any society to sustain 'civilisation'.[179] This clearly draws on a passage in Woolf's diary of 1918 in which she recorded the Fabian theorist Sidney Webb's comments on the key role of the 'Railway Guard' as 'the most enviable of men. He has authority & he is responsible to a government. That should be the state of each one of us'.[180] This suggests that Woolf believed the Tube was essential for the survival of a whole way of life but was also a progressive force in society. It is even invoked when Lily Broscoe is considering the balance of gender roles in *To the Lighthouse*: she says she would expect Mr Tansley to rescue her if 'the Tube were to burst into flames'.[181] Charles Tansley is a member of the lower middle class like the 'young man carbuncular' in Eliot's 'The Waste Land' but he is improving himself. Lily Broscoe later remembers that he 'had got his fellowship. He had married; he lived at Golder's Green',[182] the Northern line suburb that Woolf had mentioned approvingly in her diary 20 years earlier. These Fabian expectations

---

175   Woolf, *The Waves*, p. 95.
176   E. Bowen, *The House in Paris* (1935; London: Jonathan Cape, 1949), p. 80.
177   Woolf, 4 February 1919, in *Diaries*, vol. 1, p. 238.
178   Woolf, 28 September 1919, in *Diaries*, vol. 1, p. 301.
179   Woolf, *To the Lighthouse*, p. 50.
180   Woolf, 18 September 1918, in *Diaries*, vol. 1, p. 194.
181   Woolf, *To the Lighthouse*, p. 105.
182   Woolf, *To the Lighthouse*, p. 223.

are an important part of Woolf's literary landscape—Lily is one of the New Women whose political demands had succeeded in extending the franchise to women and nearly a quarter of a million of them had flocked to join labour or socialist organizations after the war.

Woolf was following the many writers and artists who had observed the world from a train window, as does Bernard in *The Waves* when he stands in the train to London and observes the 'Blank expectant faces [that] stare at us as we rattle and flash through stations'.[183] Like Sherlock Holmes who had enthusiastically pointed out to Watson the new Board Schools from a railway compartment in 'The Adventure of the Naval Treaty' (1893),[184] Woolf's characters frequently observe urban landscapes. In *The Years* (1937) another journey is recounted: 'They were leaving London behind them; that blaze of light which seemed, as the train rushed into the darkness, to contract into one fiery circle'.[185] Eric Ravilious's painting *Train Landscape* (1939) portrays an empty third-class compartment with a view of the White Horse of Uffington on the Wiltshire Downs. As Ian Carter has pointed out, this echoes many previous images of the compartment, such as Robert Musgrave Joy's *Tickets Please!* (1851), Augustus Egg's *The Travelling Companions* (1862) and John Tenniel's curious 'Looking-Glass Insects' (1872)[186] and so perhaps sums up the idea of the train compartment interior framing the outside world. Meanwhile in poetry, Stephen Spender described how:

> I was on a train. Like the quick spool of a film
> I watched hasten away the simple green which can heal
> Sadness[187]

and Louis MacNeice opened his poem 'Autumn Journal' (1939) on a railway journey:

> And I am in the train too now and summer is going
> South as I go north.[188]

---

183 Woolf, *The Waves*, p. 95.

184 A. Conan Doyle, 'The Adventure of the Naval Treaty' (1893), in *Sherlock Holmes: The Complete Illustrated Short Stories* (London: Chancellor Press, 1985), pp. 394–420, p. 405.

185 Woolf, *The Years*, p. 207.

186 I. Carter, *Railways and Culture in Britain: The Epitome of Modernity* (Manchester: Manchester University Press, 2001), chapter 10.

187 S. Spender, 'Preludes' (1930–33), in *Collected Poems 1928–1953* (London: Faber & Faber, 1955), p. 24.

188 L. MacNeice, 'Autumn Journal' (1939), in *Collected Poems of Louis MacNeice*, ed. E. R. Dodds (London: Faber & Faber, 1966), pp. 101–53, p. 102.

Woolf's relationship with the streets helps us to understand her view of the Tube. There is a considerable body of scholarly opinion dealing with Woolf's 'street haunting': her own personal accounts of walking through the streets of the capital and of her characters' journeys. In her essay *Street Haunting: A London Adventure* (1927) Woolf tells us that the 'greatest pleasure of town life' is 'rambling the streets of London'.[189] Ford Madox Ford had noted that 'the Londoner comes to forget that his London is built upon real earth: he forgets that under the pavements there are hills, forgotten water courses, springs and marshland',[190] and Woolf combines the vastness of the metropolis with the particular 'Londons' with which each Londoner identifies. Her character Clarissa Dalloway observes London life 'in people's eyes, in the swing, tramp, and trudge; in the bellow and the uproar; in the carriages, motorcars, omnibuses, vans, sandwich men shuffling and swinging'.[191] This is the contrast between primeval and modern London that Woolf found attractive because it could be observed by means of walking or from the top deck of a bus. The Tube, on the other hand, posed a problem: it was not possible to observe the exterior urban world of the centre of London from within a Tube car. In *The Waves*, Jinny notes that there 'will be no reflections in window-panes in dark tunnels' as though there is not even a reflected image in the Tube car windows, so instead she will 'look into faces, and I shall see them seek some other face'.[192]

Woolf's fictional journeys on the Tube, particularly in *The Waves*, were a means by which she could undermine the notion of the unitary self, allowing her to decompose character into stylized fragments as suggested to her by the first Post-Impressionist exhibition. Her fiction produced the most completely modernist vision of the Tube as a world of the sharp and sudden disquieting detail. Whilst Woolf eschews the explicit piling up of surface detail that she attacked in 'Mr Bennett and Mrs Brown', she does not, as we have seen, abandon her long-standing concern for the social or cultural issues surrounding the Tube. Woolf had a theory about the role of transport in the city which underpinned her writing of fictional journeys—a history that coloured each individual's 'pane of glass'[193] as they made those journeys in real life.

---

189 V. Woolf, *Street Haunting: A London Adventure* (1927; London: Penguin, 2005), p. 1.
190 Ford, *The Soul of London*, p. 102.
191 Woolf, *Mrs Dalloway*, p. 6.
192 Woolf, *The Waves*, p. 166.
193 Woolf, *Jacob's Room*, p. 49.

AMONG THE TERMITES:
REJECTING THE TUBIST UTOPIA

Whilst many novelists of the interwar decades probably shared Woolf's belief in transport organizations as the necessary *economic* underpinning of modern cities, they do not identify with the cultural arguments. Aldous Huxley, in his novel *Crome Yellow* (1921), mocked the philosophy of Tubism through his character Mr Scogan. I. F. Clarke suggests that Scogan is introduced 'as a means of exposing the positivist delight in technological progress and social regimentation' with Huxley setting out an anti-Tubist agenda.[194] Scogan declares that 'Nature, [...] disturbs me; it is too large, too complicated, above all too utterly pointless and incomprehendible. I am at home with the works of man [...] That is why I always travel by Tube'.[195] For Scogan, the Tube represents a social order in which human beings can feel at home with their creation, a kind of hermetically sealed environment which is 'recognisably human' as well as 'comfortable and secure'.[196] Scogan argues that the passengers on the Tube contrive 'to forget that all around them stretches the blind mass of earth, endless and unexplored. Yes, give me the Tube and Cubismus every time; give me ideas, so smug and neat and well made'.[197] Huxley demolishes the cultural baggage associated with the Tube. Travel by Tube, Scogan says, and 'you see nothing but the works of man—iron rivetted into geometrical forms, straight lines of concrete, patterned expanses of tiles'.[198]

Huxley's argument against Tubism in *Crome Yellow* is part of a wider debate on modernity or 'living modernly' as Lucy Tantamount calls it in Huxley's later novel *Point Counter Point* (1928).[199] This novel explores the fashionable aristo-cratic world of London with its moral vacuity and 'progressive' ideas. The main character, Walter Bidlake, travels regularly by Tube from Chalk Farm, where he lives discontentedly with his wife Marjorie, to Leicester Square to visit his lover Lucy Tantamount. Walter rejects the old world, feeling angry when he glimpses a placard outside Chalk Farm station because its headline screams: 'SOCIALIST ROBBERY SCHEME, FIRST READING',[200] an attack on the proposed nationalization of

---

194 I. F. Clarke, *The Pattern of Expectation, 1644–2001* (London: Jonathan Cape, 1979), p. 245.
195 A. Huxley, *Crome Yellow* (1921; Harmondsworth: Penguin, 1937), p. 199.
196 Huxley, *Crome Yellow*, p. 199.
197 Huxley, *Crome Yellow*, p. 199.
198 Huxley, *Crome Yellow*, p. 198.
199 A. Huxley, *Point Counter Point* (1928; London: Chatto & Windus, 1971), p. 18.
200 Huxley, *Point Counter Point*, p. 18.

the mines. But on the Tube, Walter is confronted with a real proletarian when a 'wizened little man with a red handkerchief round his neck'[201] sits down next to him at Camden Town on the Northern line. On the older underground lines such as the Metropolitan, class barriers remained in place throughout the interwar period, as *Punch* skilfully noted in a cartoon showing the amused plight of two proletarians in a first-class carriage of top-hatted gents and highly respectable ladies.[202] Whilst class barriers have apparently disappeared in this case, Walter's progressive views become enmeshed in a pointless debate about the man sitting next to him. Walter wishes 'he could personally like the oppressed and personally hate the rich oppressors'[203] but he then drifts into thoughts about Lucy. The episode ends abruptly at Leicester Square station where Walter leaves the train: '"All tickets, please!" [...] the liftman slammed the gates. The lift ascended. In the street he hailed a taxi' to Lucy's house.[204] A similar point is made in Eric Siepmann's novel about the movie business in London, *Waterloo in Wardour Street* (1936). In this novel, a character called the Communist finds that 'Every little incident, each contact with a human being [involved him] in a complicated process of nervous reactions'.[205] This is exemplified for him on the Tube: 'He had only to buy a ticket on the Underground to experience alternations of hatred and self-reproof of the ticket-buying queue'.[206] Both Walter Bidlake and the Communist appear to express the idea of fashionable and hypocritical progressivism, based on an apparently naive belief in human perfectibility. Walter unthinkingly returns to the world of privilege by catching a cab to Lucy's house; the Communist works in the highly paid fantasy world of the film industry.

The cinema had actually caught up with the underground by 1928, the year *Point Counter Point* was published. That year, the silent film *Underground* by Anthony Asquith featured the story of a shop-girl (Elissa Landi) who is involved with two men: an underground porter (Brian Aherne) and an electrician (Cyril McLaglen). Asquith had directed a short 35 mm black-and-white documentary in 1910 that featured a journey from Baker Street to Uxbridge and Aylesbury but *Underground* broke new ground in British cinema with a full-length fictional treatment filmed on location. With shots of the rush-hour Tube, Asquith's film put the underground firmly on the cinematic map, followed a year later by

---

201 Huxley, *Point Counter Point*, p. 19.
202 *Punch*, 1909, in Hammerton, *Mr Punch in London Town*, vol. 15, p. 69.
203 Huxley, *Point Counter Point*, p. 19.
204 Huxley, *Point Counter Point*, p. 22.
205 E. Siepmann, *Waterloo in Wardour Street* (London: Chatto & Windus, 1936), p. 63.
206 Siepmann, *Waterloo in Wardour Street*, p. 63.

scenes in Tube trains travelling 'up west' for an evening out in Hitchcock's *Blackmail* (1929), in which Hitchcock makes a characteristic cameo appearance, this time as a passenger in a Tube car reading a book. *Bulldog Jack* (1935) was a film inspired by the closure of British Museum station in 1933 and featured the fictional 'Bloomsbury' station. Here was a distinctly modern underground, a location full of atmosphere, noise and the bustle of the rush-hour city. Tube trains and escalators offered perfect vehicles for cinematic action whilst cavernous underground walkways and sinister emergency staircases offered spaces for tension and pursuit. Both aspects of the Tube were more evident in fiction than film throughout the interwar years, and both reflected the typically mundane rhythms of urban life as well as the more edgy world of crime and violence. It was an underground that would continue to be 'modern' until the 1960s and 1970s when technological change once again began to disrupt the imaginative world to be found in fictional and cinematic coverage. The more futuristic motion picture *The Fugitive Futurist* picked up the Wellsian thematic in 1924, portraying a London with the River Thames drained and converted into a railway and Tower Bridge as a stop on a vast monorail system. In this cinematic vision railways have come to dominate the city. But once the cinema discovered the Tube, its qualities of modernity including speed and disconnection would increasingly offer familiar scenes to film audiences.

If the cinema made the underground actually move, writing took up the ambiguities of modern urban life. As Malcolm Bradbury points out in his discussion of modernism, *Point Counter Point* contains 'a vision of man as the Freudian hypocrite, a creature of self-delusion'. This vision, he argues, is set in an urban milieu of the 1920s that seems to undermine rationality.[207] In both *Crome Yellow* and *Point Counter Point*, Huxley contrasts the efficient and rational technology of the Tube—electric power, speed, lifts—with the failings of the human beings who inhabit this urban world. The Tube, Huxley believes, is simply an efficient façade behind which people can hide, a mechanical sheath that we can conveniently slip into during daily life. Huxley's attack on Tubism signals a wholesale rejection of its cultural project. This is amply demonstrated in his novel *Brave New World* (1932), in which public transport in the form of an ultra-modern monorail system carries 'crowds of lower-caste workers' home with their 'soma' ration after work in London. The booking clerk at Brentford station gives 'To each of them, with his or her ticket [...] a little cardboard

---

207 M. Bradbury, *Possibilities, Essays on the State of the Novel* (Oxford: Oxford University Press, 1973), p. 153.

pill-box' of the drug[208] thus fulfilling Marinetti's prophecy of the complete integration of worker and travelling machine through a chemical cocktail in which transport and drug-induced happiness are combined. Similarly, Huxley transformed Woolf's Tube liftman in *To the Lighthouse* into a soma-eating mechanical drone: 'The liftman slammed the gates, touched a button and instantly dropped into the droning twilight of the well, the twilight of his own habitual stupor'.[209] Huxley's exploration of the contradictions of modernity in these three novels leads to the conclusion that the Tubists' underlying belief that technology could successfully transform the metropolis was mistaken. Huxley's *Brave New World* was a 'technopolis' with the Charing-T Tower, a 'disk of shining concrete'[210] at its centre. The price for a stable social system, Huxley argues, is the subjection of the population and the subordination of the individual to the state.

The Tube could be a metaphor for the forms of urban and suburban life that seemed to be taking shape in and around the capital. In Wyndham Lewis's *The Apes of God* (1930) some tubes 'were worse than confusing, they led straight out into the wilderness right off the map into deserts of country'.[211] In 1918, by contrast, after his move to Marlow in Buckinghamshire, T. S. Eliot was writing that 'the relief of being out of London, getting away from it at the end of the day, is very great [...] The suburban traffic of London is tremendous—most 'city workers' people in offices, live out of town and commute every day, and I am sure it is better for one'.[212] This sense of a human tidal wave was one that Eliot deployed in 'The Waste Land' to great effect when he wrote of 'the crowd that flowed over London Bridge' on their way from the City to London Bridge station.[213] These workers could afford to commute as Eliot himself did regularly on the underground to Moorgate station for his job in Lloyds Bank Colonial and Foreign Department at 17 Cornhill from 1917 to 1920 and in Lombard Street from 1920 to 1923. Eliot acknowledged an important literary debt to John Davidson's poetic account of the 'Thirty Bob a Week' (1894) clerk, a figure who travelled 'like a mole'[214] on the underground and the

---

208 A. Huxley, *Brave New World* (1932; Harmondsworth: Penguin, 1955), p. 132.
209 Huxley, *Brave New World*, p. 56.
210 Huxley, *Brave New World*, p. 58.
211 P. W. Lewis, *The Apes of God* (1930; Harmondsworth: Penguin, 1965), p. 122.
212 T. S. Eliot, 9 June 1918, in *The Letters of T. S. Eliot, vol. 1, 1898–1922*, ed. V. Eliot (London: Faber & Faber, 1988), p. 234.
213 Eliot, 'The Waste Land', p. 62.
214 J. Davidson, 'Thirty Bob a Week' (1894), in J. Hayward (ed.), *The Oxford Book of Nineteenth Century English Verse* (Oxford: Oxford University Press, 1964), pp. 900–03, p. 901.

original model, it seems, for the 'young man carbuncular' of Eliot's 'The Waste Land'. Eliot was apparently persuaded by Ezra Pound to tone down some of the more acerbic references to the lifestyle of young clerks in the poem although he did admit, in a letter to Lytton Strachey, to 'sojourning among the termites', a clear indication of his personal subterranean travels.[215] Hugh Kenner points out Eliot was 'his time's chief poet of the alarm clock, the furnished flat, the ubiquitous telephone, commuting crowds, the *electric underground railway*' (my italics).[216] In fact 'The Waste Land' contains all the usual modernist suspects: ragtime, gramophones, condoms, typists, tins of food, sex and the 'sounds of horns and motors'[217] but has no direct references to the underground. It seems curious that Eliot does not refer to the Tube in this seminal work and it may be that we have simply come to expect him to be the poet of the Tube. We assume that 'The Waste Land' will include the Tube because it has modern twentieth-century objects in it, forgetting that underground writing stretches back to the 1880s. We have learned, with Eliot, to think of an 'Unreal City' as the poem proclaims but one that contains a Tube that is synonymous with the city. The components of Eliot's London underworld were held together by the journeys that the 'crowd' made every day, journeys that criss-crossed the city until their subjects surfaced in Eliot's poem. It seems that it was a 'silent voice' in this Dantean landscape, a sort of connective element in the metropolis, operating as one of the mechanisms required in order to ensure order and stability.

Eliot was struck by the way that the noises of the modern city could be turned into art. This was accentuated by those Futurist artists, such as Luigi Russolo, who energetically campaigned for music to incorporate 'dissonant, strange and harsh sounds'.[218] In 'The Art of Noises' (1913) Russolo called on audiences to 'cross a great modern capital with our ears more alert than our eyes [and to accept] orchestrations of the variety of din, from stations, railways, iron foundries, spinning mills, printing works, electric power stations and

---

215 Eliot, 1 June 1919, in *Letters*, vol. 1, p. 299.

216 H. Kenner, *The Mechanic Muse* (Oxford: Oxford University Press, 1987), p. 25.

217 Eliot, 'The Waste Land', p. 58. Henry Reed's parody of Eliot, 'Chard Whitlow' (1946), *does* contain the Tube: 'Or counting sleepless nights in the crowded Tube' (in T. S. Matthews, *Great Tom. Notes towards the definition of T. S. Eliot* (1973; London: Weidenfeld & Nicolson, 1974), p. 196).

218 L. Russolo, 'The Art of Noises' (1913), in Apollonio, *Futurist Manifestos*, pp. 74–88, p. 75. This was a period of experimentation with sound/noise in the arts with Russolo, Marinetti and Vertov in the USSR. See M. Gordon, 'Songs from the Museum of the Future, Russian Sound Creation, 1910–1930', in the interesting collection D. Kahn & G. Whitehead (eds.), *Wireless Imagination: Sound, Radio and the Avant Garde* (Cambridge, MA: MIT Press, 1992), pp. 197–244.

underground railways'.[219] The noise made by trains had come out of the war with a new meaning. T. E. Hulme likened the sound of a shell on the Western Front to a 'train high up in the air [...] then you hear the bang, then after that the whistling noise seems to stop'.[220] The sounds of the Tube came from the 'city routines, the daily rituals that shape the lives of people' that Mayer describes as characteristic of 'The Waste Land'.[221] By the time he wrote 'Burnt Norton' (1934), Eliot had put the underground into his poetry and invested it with a much more precise meaning. It is no longer simply a form of mass transportation but a 'cold wind / That blows before and after time' across 'the gloomy hills of London', hills that have been tunnelled through by tube lines.[222] For Eliot, the commuters on the tube are trapped in their daily routines in an urban desert full of 'Shrieking voices / Scolding, mocking, or merely chattering'.[223] Eliot, like the members of the Anti-Noise League (1933) was now asking 'Was man to be mutilated by the machines which he has invented, or was he to continue to use them for utility and enjoyment'?[224] He was convinced that the technology was only a symptom of the deeply flawed existence brought about by modernity. Eliot then went further, in the 'Choruses From the Rock' (1934) in which 'The desert is squeezed in the tube-train next to you'[225] and then later in 'Burnt Norton' he went on to describe the interior of a Tube car:

> Only a flicker
> Over the strained time-ridden faces
> Distracted from distraction by distraction
> Filled with fancies and empty of meaning
> Tumid apathy with no concentration
> Men and bits of paper, whirled by the cold wind
> That blows before and after time,[226]

Eliot's lines form the apogee of an underworld that the Tube had come to

---

219 Russolo, 'The Art of Noises', p. 85.

220 T. E. Hulme, 'Diary from the Trenches', 15 January 1915, in *The Collected Writings of T. E. Hulme*, ed. K. Csengeri (Oxford: Oxford University Press, 1994), p. 317.

221 J. Mayer, *T. S. Eliot's Silent Voices* (Oxford: Oxford University Press, 1989), p. 70.

222 T. S. Eliot, 'Burnt Norton' (1934), in *Four Quartets* (1944; London: Faber & Faber, 1970), pp. 13–20, p. 17.

223 Eliot, 'Burnt Norton', p. 19.

224 Quoted in T. Boon, 'Making the Modern World', *History Today*, vol. 51, no. 8 (August 2001), pp. 38–45.

225 T. S. Eliot, 'The Rock' (1934), in *The Complete Poems and Plays* (London: Faber & Faber, 1969), pp. 147–67, p. 149.

226 T. S. Eliot, 'East Coker' (1940), in *Four Quartets*, pp. 23–32, p. 28.

represent in its heyday. The factual world of the underground—the flickering effect of the Tube journey that had figured in Aldington's poem 'In the Tube' and the 'bits of paper'—is combined with the faces of the commuters that are 'empty'. Eliot does not even try to engage with the passengers as Aldington and Flint had done some 20 years before, because they have been carried away by the 'cold wind' into the realm of eternal time. Eliot then reverts to the more traditional underworld theme, a descent into Purgatory via Gloucester Road station:

> Descend lower, descend only
> Into the world of perpetual solitude
> World not world, but that which is not world.[227]

And 'Burnt Norton' suggests that the underground was part of a cycle of modern life that gives the illusion of security. The normality of Tube travel disguises the sweep of time, the commuters entering a shadowy underworld like the wraiths of the city who had crossed London Bridge in 'The Waste Land'. This is an explicit repudiation of modernity at the end of two decades in which Eliot had moved away from his earlier, more descriptive and detached idea of what the underground represented in the modern world, to a more religious view. In 'The Waste Land', Eliot merely identified the Tube as playing a key part in the shaping of the modern world; in 'Burnt Norton', its inner space has taken over the modern mind. For Eliot, the materialistic philosophy expressed in Tubism has come to dominate society whilst the Tube train is a symbol of the failure of modern urban life to recognize and accept the spiritual because the shock of discovery is repudiated by the commuter. Eliot's work exposed the principal contradiction in underground modernity and the Tubist mentality in saying that the Tube represented a dead end, that the materialism of modern life was leading towards human catastrophe with the likely result of civil strife and social collapse. The apparent consensus that the public transport machine could secure a safe and fully human metropolis had been challenged in much fiction following Huxley's lead, but in the 1930s it was to take on an increasingly sharper political edge.

---

227 Eliot, 'Burnt Norton', p. 18.

'OH, I CAN'T BEAR THE TUBE':
ORWELL AND OTHER TUBE TRAVELLERS

If Virginia Woolf is the modernist champion of the Tube, George Orwell is its most stubborn and persistent fictional critic. Orwell drew on the Tube in order to offer a devastating critique of the modern capitalist city in his novels *Keep the Aspidistra Flying* (1936) and *Coming Up for Air* (1939). For Orwell, the Tube is a key component of the metropolitan system, a machine for travelling in that condemns the commuter to a modern form of slavery. The transport system, now enshrined in the form of the London Passenger Transport Board,[228] is a symbol for Orwell of bureaucratic and authoritarian control over people. It offers integration, as Woolf believed, but only into capitalist degradation. Orwell explicitly rules out any utopian role for modern transport where it could act as a solution to the still urgent problems of urban living. In these novels, Orwell subscribes to the view, similarly expressed in the film *Metropolis* (1926), that human beings are being further enslaved under the logic of modern political and economic systems. His critique includes the impact of Tubism on both the countryside and the city itself. Orwell was the first twentieth-century novelist to confront Tubism in a sustained and consistent way, drawing together imaginatively much of the social and political criticism that was being levelled at public transport in the period. Orwell argued that, in the guise of 'Metro-Land', the underground had contributed to the destruction of London's outlying counties including Middlesex, Hertfordshire and Buckinghamshire, burying the countryside in 'a kind of volcanic eruption from the outer suburbs'.[229] Metro-Land was a term first used in publicity in 1915, after being coined by George Sims with his jingle 'Hearts are brighter, eyes are brighter / In Metroland-Metroland' to describe the Metropolitan Railway's hugely speculative expansion into property development along a north-western corridor from its headquarters at Chiltern Court next to Baker Street station.[230]

Evelyn Waugh, in *Decline and Fall* (1928) and *Vile Bodies* (1930), lampooned the values of the aristocratic Lord and Lady Metroland and their coterie who were profiting from the 'opportunist and sometimes flagrant disregard for

---

228 The London Passenger Transport Board was formed on 1 July 1933. It brought the underground, buses, trams and coaches into one publicly owned corporation.

229 G. Orwell, *Coming Up for Air* (1939; London: Secker & Warburg, 1986), p. 211.

230 D. Edwards & R. Pigram, *Metro Memories: A Pictorial History of Metro-Land* (London: Bloomsbury, 1977), p. 7.

the regional impact of [the Metropolitan Railway's] operations'.[231] Using the character of George (Tubby) Bowling in *Coming Up for Air*, Orwell followed Waugh's line but developed a sharper political critique from the left. In this novel, Orwell attacked everything in modern life that was 'slick and streamlined',[232] including, of course, the Tube which had recently undergone its most extensive modernization thanks to the Trade Facilities Act (1921), the Loan Guarantees and Grants Act (1929) and the New Works Programme (1935). These acts gave the underground sufficient government funding to finance the extension of lines like the Piccadilly and Central and the redesign of 35 stations including Oxford Circus and Piccadilly Circus. As we have seen, the underground was also transformed by technical innovations like escalators, faster lifts, air-powered train doors and the 'passimeter' for ticketing operations. In *Coming Up for Air*, Tubby Bowling travels westwards out of London to rediscover his past, making a journey through the wreckage of rural England that has become a hinterland of the capital. It seems to him a mere extension of an ersatz universe in which all is 'celluloid, rubber, chromium-steel everywhere, arc-lamps blazing all night, glass roofs over your head [...] no vegetation left, everything cemented over'.[233] Tubby mirrors Aldous Huxley's character Dennis Gumbril in *Antic Hay* (1923) who travelled out of London into the world of 'the business man, the holder of the season ticket'.[234] Tubby finds that Lower Binfield, where he was born and grew up, is full of 'fake-picturesque houses' and Upper Binfield is 'sham-Tudor'. Tubby, now a middle-aged insurance clerk who drives a car, cries out: 'But where is Lower Binfield? Where was the town I used to know? It might have been anywhere, all I knew was that it was buried somewhere in the middle of that sea of bricks'.[235] He later observes a 'stream of clerky-looking chaps in dark suits' who are hurrying 'just as if this had been a London suburb and they were scooting for the Tube'.[236] The countryside is being buried in much the same way as Clerkenwell was covered in the soot from the steam underground in the 1860s. The forces of modern technology, embodied in the concept of Metro-Land and the motor car, are turning the countryside into an industrial reservoir of labour for the capital, the 'Third England' that J. B. Priestley identified in his *English Journey* (1934). In this book,

231 P. L. Garside, 'West End, East End: London, 1890–1940', in A. Sutcliffe (ed.), *Metropolis, 1890–1940* (London: Mansell, 1984), pp. 221–58, p. 252.
232 Orwell, *Coming Up for Air*, p. 248.
233 Orwell, *Coming Up for Air*, p. 24.
234 A. Huxley, *Antic Hay* (1923; London: Chatto & Windus, 1949), p. 191.
235 Orwell, *Coming Up for Air*, p. 189.
236 Orwell, *Coming Up for Air*, p. 208.

Priestley entered the debate about England and the clash of traditional values with modernity and modernization, coming to the conclusion that a new form of society was emerging which combined both old and new values.[237]

Orwell's fictional view was different. Technology was responsible for the destruction of the countryside and the continuing spread of urban culture in the uncontrolled development of market capitalism, a process that could be traced back to the industrial revolution. Orwell saw it as his task to warn his readers that technology was a potent force and that it should be carefully restrained in the interests of human community and creativity. He was, Mark Connelly notes, sceptical about the 'queer spectacle of modern electrical science'.[238] In a review of Zamiatin's novel *We* (1924), Orwell remarked on the prescience of this 'study of the Machine, the genie that man has thoughtlessly let out of its bottle and cannot put back again'.[239] Clearly, as Alan Swingewood argues, novels like *We* argued that 'technology rather than liberating man from a lifetime of degradation and toil will only enslave him further so that he ceases even to be a human being'.[240]

Whereas the ruin of the countryside around London by Metro-Land was Orwell's target in *Coming Up for Air*, he turned to the heart of the capital in *Keep the Aspidistra Flying*. Here, the underground sustains a degraded and morally bankrupt system in which money has devalued all human contact, a system run by 'the money-priesthood, the pink-faced masters of the world. The Upper Crust'.[241] Orwell's novel explores the revolt of Gordon Comstock, an anti-hero who rejects the 'money-god' of commercial capitalism by quitting his job as a copywriter at the New Albion Publicity Company, journeying downwards through society like Gissing's Edwin Reardon in *New Grub Street* in order to satisfy his own stubborn assessment of life in the contemporary

---

237 See J. B. Priestley, *English Journey* (1934; Harmondsworth: Penguin, 1977).

238 G. Orwell, *The Road to Wigan Pier* (1937; London: Secker & Warburg, 1980), p. 90. See M. Connelly, *Orwell and Gissing* (New York: Peter Lang, 1997), introduction.

239 G. Orwell, review of *We*, *Tribune*, 4 January 1946, in *The Collected Essays, Journalism and Letters of George Orwell*, eds. S. Orwell & I. Angus, 4 vols. (London: Penguin, 1970), vol. 4, pp. 95–99, p. 99. In this review, Orwell refers to Zamiatin's narrator as a 'sort of Utopian Billy Brown of London Town' (p. 97). Billy Brown was a cartoon Tube traveller who told passengers how to behave on the underground during the Second World War. Osbert Lancaster mocked Billy Brown. In a cartoon set in a Tube car, a ferocious upper-class gent says to Billy: 'I don't care, sir, if you're Mr Brown of Timbuctoo—if I want to stand in the doorway I shall!' (O. Lancaster, *Osbert Lancaster Cartoons* (Harmondsworth: Penguin, 1945), p. 18).

240 A. Swingewood, *The Novel and Revolution* (London: Macmillan, 1975), p. 166.

241 G. Orwell, *Keep the Aspidistra Flying* (1936; Harmondsworth: Penguin, 1962), p. 160.

metropolis. Comstock is confronted with the underground as an oppressive and all-pervading system which offers an escape only for the wealthy who can afford to live outside the city, and who are destroying the countryside in their Metro-Land retreats. Orwell's protagonist owes a debt to Gissing's original in *New Grub Street* for, just as Reardon seems to welcome his descent into the abyss, Comstock's 'reaction to poverty [...] is that of a man whose previous lifestyle and experience lead him to a set of expectations which the ordinary person does not have'.[242] Orwell appears to deny Comstock the escape route that Gissing had offered some of his characters, the idea that culture could be salvaged by an escape into the suburbs via the underground. Orwell was an admiring student of Gissing but insisted nonetheless that Gissing's London was 'almost as distant as that of Dickens'.[243] Instead, the Tube underpins the entire corrupt, materialist, money-centred system with its artificial loveless life of respectability, mortgages and grinding anomie. Comstock feels the power of this system through the pavements of the city, generating a nightmare vision: 'something deep below made the stone street shiver. The tube-train, sliding through middle earth. He had a vision of London, of the western world; he saw a thousand million slaves toiling and grovelling about the throne of money'.[244] The underground train is like a malevolent mole which is about to penetrate the surface of the capital, impaling its inhabitants and heralding the downfall of any civilized society and the establishment of the complete rule of money.[245] Nevertheless, the Tube continues to carry 'the strap-hanging army that swings eastward at morning, westward at night, in the carriages of the Underground'[246] in the relentless rhythms of metropolitan life. It helps to trap people like Comstock's sister Julia who is working a 'seventy-two hour week' in a 'nasty ladylike little teashop'[247] in Earl's Court. Like another oppressed heroine, Ella, in Patrick Hamilton's *The Plains of Cement* (1934), she also endures a life of 'slavery [...] exacted by the Underground Railway on her way to NW3' every day.[248]

---

242 R. Williams, 'Observation and Imagination in Orwell', in R. Williams (ed.), *George Orwell: A Collection of Critical Essays* (Englewood Cliffs, NJ: Prentice-Hall, 1974), pp. 52–61, p. 57.

243 G. Orwell, 'George Gissing', in *Collected Essays*, vol. 4, p. 485.

244 Orwell, *Keep the Aspidistra Flying*, p. 160.

245 This image would recur in the adaptation of Nigel Kneale's *Quatermass and the Pit* (1967) by Roy Ward Baker when the devil (a Martian) takes up residence in a fictional Tube station in Knightsbridge called Hobbs Lane, during the excavation of a Central line extension.

246 Orwell, *Keep the Aspidistra Flying*, p. 54.

247 Orwell, *Keep the Aspidistra Flying*, p. 50.

248 P. Hamilton, *The Plains of Cement* (1934), third book in omnibus edition *Twenty Thousand Streets Under the Sky* (London: Hogarth Press, 1987), p. 464.

Orwell found the underground full of rampant commercialism and Comstock's self-imposed 'exile' from respectable wage slavery is prompted by his own Tube journeys when he finds that 'all modern commerce is a swindle [...] it was the advertisements in the Underground stations that first brought it home to him'.[249] The Tube is therefore another component part of an oppressive metropolitan system, simply an organization through which the commuter is transported each day whilst being bombarded with advertising messages. Orwell implies that it is no longer possible to live outside the Machine. The transport system offers only integration into capitalist degradation, not a utopian solution to the deep-seated problems of urban life. Orwell's hero embraces 'social death', the loss of respectability and status that occurs in the descent from the aspidistra world of the 'law-abiding little cit like any other law-abiding little cit—a soldier in the strap-hanging army'.[250] Comstock opts for the 'smoke-dim slums of South London'[251] and here Orwell invents an underworld which is entirely free of the many links with the actual underground. Orwell counter-poses a 'kingdom of ghosts'[252] or shadow world to the materialistic struggle for survival that is played out every day on the underground. The slums to which Comstock descends are 'Under-ground, under-ground! Down in the safe soft womb of earth',[253] the only refuge for the thinking person, the only way out of an oppressive and alienating existence— for Comstock 'Down there you had no contact with money or with culture'.[254] Orwell has completely severed the two concepts of underworld and underground that had developed in the late Victorian decades. Fictionally, the underground system is for the first time open to an interrogation on its own (Tubist) terms and Orwell finds it culturally as well as socially bankrupt.

This descent allows Orwell to focus on Comstock's masculinity that is undermined by his lack of a job. Comstock travels to the pastoral Burnham Beeches with his long-suffering girlfriend Rosemary Waterlow, a trip undermined by Comstock's failure to purchase contraceptives. On their return to London after a day which is dominated by his lack of money, Rosemary catches the underground:

---

249 Orwell, *Keep the Aspidistra Flying*, p. 160.
250 Orwell, *Keep the Aspidistra Flying*, p. 254.
251 Orwell, *Keep the Aspidistra Flying*, p. 217.
252 Orwell, *Keep the Aspidistra Flying*, p. 219.
253 Orwell, *Keep the Aspidistra Flying*, p. 217.
254 Orwell, *Keep the Aspidistra Flying*, p. 218.

> He left her at the booking-office. When he had gone twenty yards he felt a hand laid on his arm. He turned sharply. It was Rosemary. She thrust a packet of twenty Gold Flake, which she had bought at the tobacco kiosk, into his coat pocket and ran back to the Underground before he could protest.[255]

And in this dismal parting, Orwell underlines the connection between money and transport in the city. Other novelists, from Forster to Hamilton, had focused on the costs of public transport as a significant factor in the struggle to survive in London; Comstock, like Forster's Leonard Bast in *Howard's End*, clearly cannot afford the Tube fare home and would be too proud to accept the fare. Instead, he trails 'homeward through the wastes of Marylebone and Regent's Park' whilst Rosemary takes the Tube home, returning to the 'feminised' world of work. As Sidney Dark observed in a radio talk in 1929, the modern world was one in which 'women are completely enfranchised, even the flapper has the vote, a distinguished woman is in the cabinet, a picture of Mrs Pankhurst hangs in the National Portrait Gallery, and most of the straphangers on the late train are girls. Equality is established'.[256] Rosemary is the Ariadne of *Keep the Aspidistra Flying* as she maintains the thread between Comstock and the 'normal' world that he has rejected. Whilst Comstock walks home in an exact repetition of Reardon's dreary walk to west London in *New Grub Street*, he is not cut off completely due to Rosemary's apparently trivial gesture of buying the Gold Flake. The tobacco kiosk on the Tube station entrance is a symbol of the materialist world but it offers Comstock a small but significant prize—a packet of cigarettes.

In the characters of Tubby Bowling and Gordon Comstock, Orwell was picking a fictional fight with Tubism and its philosophy of man and machine. Both novels offer a critique of an ideology which had come to dominate the biggest public transport authority in the world at that time, a public corporation that utilized a stylish public relations package to disguise some serious deficiencies in its transport policies. Orwell's novels contain the most thorough-going rejection of the Tubist mentality, suggesting the degree to which the underground was not merely an enduring and ubiquitous presence in the capital but also a powerful psychosocial force which anaesthetized the commuter. In Orwell's view, T. S. Eliot's patient 'etherised on the table',[257] now travelled the tubes, buses and trams of London, the psychologically Un-Dead. Orwell can only reply to Tubism with a *nostalgic rejection* of modernity. It was a fight that

---

255 Orwell, *Keep the Aspidistra Flying*, p. 159.
256 S. Dark, 'London Twenty Years Ago', *Listener*, 4 September 1929, p. 301.
257 T. S. Eliot, 'The Love Song of J. Alfred Prufrock' (1917), in *Selected Poems*, pp. 11–16, p. 11.

Orwell was unlikely to win as his target, the Transport Board, could command the huge resources of a public corporation in order to publicize its role 'as the framework upon which the town is built'.[258] Orwell's writing came at the high point in the career of Frank Pick, the high priest of Tubism. As a leading figure in the underground from 1906 to 1940, Pick was responsible for the transport renaissance in London as well as the successful repackaging of the entire transport system into one integrated whole through the slogan 'Fitness for Purpose'. Pick, who drew deeply on a long tradition of British artistic thinking, believed that 'Fitness for Purpose is the keynote of good design'[259] in a self-regulating community based on a synthesis of Christian and classical Greek values. He argued, in 1926, that London was 'sprawling out amoebalike surrounding and absorbing the villages that lie on its borders'. It was necessary to 'make all this London a single ordered community, which is much more a problem of organisation than propinquity'.[260]

Pick believed in the unity of man and machine, which could be demonstrated in terms of the functionalist design of transport technology. He promoted the underground in the most vigorous ways through the standardization of lettering, station furniture and poster placement. He argued that this should be done within a commercial context of a privately owned underground consortium and only with some reluctance did he accept the model of a public corporation imposed by government in 1933. This approach was that of 'conservative modernity', which Alison Light defines as 'a contradictory and determining tension in English social life in the period'.[261] Just as these years witnessed the unprecedented growth of images of Englishness being reflected back to the population via the cinema, radio, press, loudspeaker or poster, the underground system also reflected back images of England to the commuter. This included the commissioning of poster art which would promote English values embodied in traditional views of a timeless countryside including, for example, the Thames riverside; sailing ships at Wapping; the county of Surrey in the first set of posters commissioned from McKnight Kauffer in 1916 and

---

258 F. Pick, quoted in C. Barman, *The Man Who Built London Transport: A Biography of Frank Pick* (London: David & Charles, 1979), p. 73.

259 F. Pick, 'The Meaning and Purpose of Design', *Listener*, 28 June 1933, pp. 1016–18, p. 1017.

260 F. Pick, 'Growth and Form in the Modern City', for the Institute of Transport, 3 January 1926 (Frank Pick Collection, London Transport Museum, unpublished typescript, 1926), p. 27.

261 A. Light, *Forever England: Femininity, Literature and Conservatism Between the Wars* (London: Routledge, 1991), p. 11.

the patriotic posters of the First World War. As N. Dutton concluded in 'Art and Industry' (1946), 'LT design is supremely impersonal, and at the same time convincingly English'.[262] This was essentially an adoption of the aesthetics of Futurism developed by Marinetti and Wyndham Lewis as a promotional strategy, but with the content of the message drawn from the English roots of the Arts and Crafts Movement.

A second element in Alison Light's analysis helps us to understand other aspects of Tubism: the ways in which conservative modernity allowed for 'new kinds of consensus, confidence and power' in the cultural world of the middle class.[263] The starting point for this process was the rejection of Victorianism— a view shared by Pick in his attempt to mould public behaviour within the travelling environment. The inside of the Tube car was to be emblematic of an orderly domestic interior with stylish art deco lighting, abstract designs on moquette fabric by artists like Marion Dorn and Enid Marx for seating, and chromium-plated window frames and sprung ball-ended strap hangers. The exterior of the Tube train was to be as experimental as possible with, for example, the futuristically streamlined design of trains introduced on the Piccadilly line in 1935 or the general simplification of Tube cars from 1938 based on the work of William S. Graff-Baker. The station platform was to represent an uncluttered, utilitarian place resembling the modern domestic kitchen with its latest gadgets like fridges and vacuum cleaners. Pick believed that design had an integrating effect despite the fact that the economic power of public transport and its technological stability were being eroded by newer forces like the motor car.

It seems unlikely that Orwell would have accepted any attempt to develop a strategy for managing the inevitable changes brought by technology. Orwell was more secure when he was contemptuously comparing the work of a miner to a 'City man's daily ride in the Tube' in *The Road to Wigan Pier* (1937).[264] Orwell focused on the ways in which the Transport Board was altering the relationship between the city and its surrounding countryside, engulfing and breaking down older rural communities through speculative house-building. Orwell's critique suggested, although it did not spell it out in detail, the idea that public transport and housing development could be harmonized in a way reminiscent of the Garden City movement. Furthermore, it challenged the technological determinism that underpinned the success of Tubism. He

---

262 N. Dutton, 'Art and Industry', *Special L.T. issue*, vol. 4, no. 244, October 1946, pp. 98–122, p. 98.

263 Light, *Forever England*, p. 11.

264 G. Orwell, *Road to Wigan Pier*, pp. 30–31.

considered the effects of Tube transport on human beings, suggesting that the regimentation of travel was helping to create conformity and obedience to the capitalist system.

A number of other writers of this period were also critical of Tubism. J. B. Priestley, Rose Macaulay, Jean Rhys, Graham Greene and John Sommerfield all explored the relationship between human beings and technology, finding the underground a fictional vehicle for a wide-ranging debate. These writers accepted that the modern metropolis needs a complex system of mass transportation and, like Orwell, they articulated the feelings that people have inside that machine. These feelings range from alienation to fear to anger and frustration but they offer a uniquely human dimension to the modernization process. In J. B. Priestley's novel *Angel Pavement* (1930), Miss Matfield declares: 'Oh, I can't bear the Tube' as she enters the offices of Twigg and Dersingham and, in a few words, the 'whole vast organisation' of transport in London is annihilated.[265] Priestley expresses the plight of the daily commuter who is trapped and buffeted by the journey to and from work. Miss Matfield feels like 'a shivering and bruised ant'[266] and Turgis, the main character in the novel, is regularly swept into Moorgate Tube station 'a monster sucking them down into its hot rank inside',[267] a demonic visual image. Like many other writers of the period, Priestley is able to articulate in fiction a sense of the massive pressures exerted by the transport system on those who simply have no alternative to using public services. Priestley's characters *have* to survive in the system as they do not have Gordon Comstock's option of rebellion. But, Priestley says, they *do* survive because they have developed survival mechanisms, like Miss Matfield's declaration of war on the Tube. The ability of characters to deflect the daily barrage of Tube travel in terms of information, delays, noise and crowdedness is a new feature of underground writing. A Select Committee report of 1919 had condemned public transport in the capital, describing it as a 'public scandal'. When public funding was poured into the system throughout the 1920s and 1930s, it suburbanized the tubes to an extent never before possible under purely private financial arrangements. The effect of this change in policy was, however, to increase the pressure on the central parts of the Tube system and to generate even greater overcrowding particularly during the rush hours.

In *Angel Pavement*, Miss Matfield feels that the evening rush hour is like fleeing from the front line of a war as she travels across London on the Tube

265 J. B. Priestley, *Angel Pavement* (1930; London: Heinemann, 1938), p. 16.
266 Priestley, *Angel Pavement*, p. 402.
267 Priestley, *Angel Pavement*, p. 158.

arriving at 'a Paddington that suggested that some invading army had already reached the Bank'.[268] Turgis is submerged in a vast organization, 'just a chap in the crowd [...] the young men who were forever packing themselves into tubes and buses'.[269] Like Orwell, Priestley attacks the obedience to money and materialism symbolized in the ritualistic purchase of tickets and other goods on stations. Turgis is only 'noticed when he bought something, when he turned himself into a customer'.[270] He is only singled out by Mr Park, the communist, who is on the look-out for potential party members but otherwise Turgis spends 'hour after hour in the very thick of packed humanity without exchanging a single word with anybody'.[271] Priestley was reflecting a level of discontent that could now be focused by the Communist Party as well as informed liberal opinion such as that of Clough Williams-Ellis. He asked 'Can We Scrap London?' (1938) in the *Spectator*, pointing out that the Transport Board 'actually promotes [itself] along its new tube extensions as may best suit its own sectional convenience, regardless of whether the fortuitous additions it thus makes to London are socially desirable or make sense from a town-planning point of view'.[272] Both private housing developers and transport authorities were blamed for the absolute increase in passenger journeys from 2,800 million in 1921 to 4,000 million in 1937 when Turgis is caught up in *Angel Pavement*. He spends much of his time away from the office 'in a crowd somewhere, getting back to his lodgings in the packed Tube, returning to the thronged streets'.[273]

The Communist Party was a major critic of the Transport Board, making a bitter attack on a five per cent fare increase in its 1938 pamphlet 'More Fares Please'. It argued that the Board was 'an inhuman machine which drags every available penny of profit out of the travelling public and its own employees'.[274] In its attempts to appeal to office workers like Turgis, the Communist Party argued that the directors of the transport undertakings were intent on offering a 'Square Deal' for the stockholders rather than looking after the needs of the commuter. Turgis and the other office workers in *Angel Pavement* are caught up

---

268 Priestley, *Angel Pavement*, p. 403. The world of the strap-hanger was also to be found in *Strap-Hangers, A Novel*, by N. C. James (London: Duckworth, 1934).

269 Priestley, *Angel Pavement*, pp. 326–27.

270 Priestley, *Angel Pavement*, p. 327.

271 Priestley, *Angel Pavement*, p. 327.

272 C. Williams-Ellis, 'Can We Scrap London?', *Spectator*, vol. 161, July–December, 11 November 1938, p. 805.

273 Priestley, *Angel Pavement*, p. 326.

274 Communist Party of Great Britain (CPGB), *More Fares Please* (London: London District Committee, CPGB, 1938), p. 14.

in a predatory takeover battle in their timber-dealing firm with predictably savage results, giving the novel a sharp political message about capitalist 'restructuring' when the workers lose their jobs. In the light of this account, it is possible to understand the many contradictions in the image of the Tube as the daily struggle to get to work is linked with the general insecurity of nine-to-six work itself. Notwithstanding all the glossy propaganda that flowed from Frank Pick's public relations office, the average experience of daily Tube travel in the 1930s can hardly be described as pleasant. The situation deteriorated so much that the first recorded protest sit-ins on the Tube occurred in 1937. It is no wonder that Priestley doesn't attempt to include any Tube-based 'episodes' in *Angel Pavement*!

IT'S A BATTLEFIELD: THE MAPPING OF LONDON

Fiction was offering a totally different account of the Tube from that of the corporate organization that was running it, repeating the divergence between official and literary views that was evident in the late Victorian period. In the 1930s, however, the official view of public transport was more persuasive than that of 50 years previously due to its more effective use of propaganda to defend corporate interests and the greater resources it could command. Fiction was a more critical force in the hands of novelists like Orwell and Priestley, particularly when it could draw on contemporary political comment. The modernizing aspects of the underground were recorded in Graham Greene's *It's a Battlefield* (1934) and John Sommerfield's *May Day* (1936), both novelists grasping the fact that transport was one of the most important industrial organizations in the capital. Public transport takes on a regulatory role in Greene's novel, a metaphorical force that underpins the circulation of people and ideas. Public transport—Tube, bus and tram—is mentioned no less than 26 times in this short work, suggesting its ubiquitous role in the daily life of the metropolitan world. The main protagonists live on 'the front line [...] where the trams screamed down the Embankment and the buses circled Trafalgar Square',[275] an image which suggests that a war of attrition is going on. The reader is reminded of the sheer power of public transport to move the population around the city and to rearrange the balance of forces in this invisible war. It is the first example of an all-encompassing mechanical network

---

275   Greene, *It's a Battlefield*, p. 136.

that occupies both central and suburban streets and the subterranean world beneath those streets.

The London of Greene's novel is one in which two rival forces, the ruling class and the working class, appear to be ranged in preparation on the 'battlefield' of Greene's title. The story is centred on a communist bus worker who is condemned to death for the murder of a policeman but in the background is the class struggle. Greene places the personal story of his characters in the context of urban insurrection, using the example of revolutionary Paris as a touchstone for modern London, from 'the Emperor to Sedan, from Sedan to Paris, from Paris to Commune',[276] thus turning London into a geopolitical terrain similar to Paris in 1870. *It's a Battlefield* suggests that the development of public transport in London has fundamentally changed the relationship between social classes in the capital, placing the working class at a strategic advantage leading both *The Times* and the Marxist journal *Viewpoint* to think that Greene was making an explicit statement about class warfare. The Assistant Commissioner of Police is responsible for the protection of order in the city and, in this figure, Greene echoes the ideology of the Transport Board. When the Assistant Commissioner meets Conrad Drover, the brother of the condemned busman, he is said to be 'safe in the capital of Empire, safe at the heart of civilisation'.[277] However, transport modernization has made London a contested terrain because the great powerhouses of the industrial working class, the docks and factories of the East End, have been extended across the whole city through public transport innovations. It is essentially a panoramic novel of London, tracing the lives of his characters as they interact with each other with public transport performing the ambiguous function of regulation or revolution.

Greene seems to be saying that public transport has 'invaded' the whole city as an industrial force, stretching the metropolis so much that, in the event of a communist insurrection, the defenders of capitalism would be unable to prevent the victory of proletarian actions. In a twist to William Morris's fable *News from Nowhere*, Greene no more than sketches in the possible conjunction of forces that would bring about the overthrow of the system in the capital, whereas for Morris it was triggered specifically by a series of uprisings in Trafalgar Square in the distant year of 1952. Greene points to the enormous growth in the regulatory role of public transport services since Morris's time and in this scenario, technological change—electrically powered tubes, the petrol-driven

---

276 Greene, *It's a Battlefield*, p. 35.
277 Greene, *It's a Battlefield*, p. 171.

omnibus and the electric tramway—has transformed the metropolis, giving it a unity impossible in the past. In Orwell's fiction, transport gives the urban world a false unity, in Greene's novel, transport integrates the city as a social institution: 'At each station on the Outer Circle a train stopped every two minutes' and 'the buses roared up Parliament Street and swung in a great circle'.[278] The Outer Circle is no longer the limit of a Dantean hell but can be the starting point, in Greene's view, of a communist takeover as Parliament Street, the home of bourgeois government, can be encircled by proletarian power.

Greene's thriller attempts to put some fictional flesh onto a broadly communist analysis of capitalism and draws strongly on contemporary events. The death of a policeman at a political rally in Hyde Park, for example, is based on a real demonstration in October 1932 where 15 people had been injured, including two policemen. The crimes described in the novel are realistic: a trunk murder at Paddington station, a girl killed on Streatham Common in south London. Choosing public transport as the thread around which to structure the story was a reflection of the growing body of real social analysis that had emerged in the 1930s. The Labour Research Department argued, in 1932, that 'the organisation of the Trade Union movement is probably stronger in the London Traffic Combine than in any other vast capitalist unit in the whole of Great Britain'.[279] The London District Committee of the Communist Party agreed, saying in the mid-1920s that 'it would be well to give special attention to these workers—such as Transport workers, Railwaymen, Dockers etc, power-station men, arsenal workers etc., who occupy strategically important positions'.[280] The significance of these powerful sections in London was not lost on Greene who described *It's a Battlefield* as his first overtly political novel and accordingly focused on the failings of the capitalist system. In the novel, the government worries about strike action by busworkers in support of Drover and even the personal alienation of the busworker is introduced as Drover sits in prison in a rigid bus-driving position, interested only in his own route. The outcome of the novel, however, is ambiguous as the tides of urban transport that pound and invade the social order do no more than threaten to overthrow it. Greene concludes with the view that it is hard 'to get a clear idea

---

278 Greene, *It's a Battlefield*, pp. 19 & 1.
279 Labour Research Department, *The London Traffic Combine* (London: London Research Department, 1932), p. 16. The London Traffic Combine later became the London Passenger Transport Board—see above, p. 137.
280 Communist Party, London District memo, quoted in K. Morgan, *Labour Legends and Russian Gold* (London: Lawrence & Wishart, 2006), p. 223.

of a war carried out in this piecemeal way throughout a city'[281] and there is no clear-cut resolution to the social or psychological turmoil. It is, however, the single most extensive statement of the imaginative power of public transport in fiction.

Similar political observations are made in Patrick Hamilton's trilogy *Twenty Thousand Streets Under the Sky* (1929–34) which conceives of London as a vast if stretched canvas of communications and micro-environments. Tube stations play an important role in Hamilton's three novels at both surface and subterranean levels. In the first novel, *The Midnight Bell* (1929), the strong lights of the lift at Hampstead station 'glare' on his characters and the noise of the train they take to Warren Street station obliterates 'any feeling of any kind'.[282] The Tube seems to offer no way out of the slavery that Hamilton suggests is imposed on the commuters, drawn as they are through a complicated apparatus of trains and termini in respiratory metaphors or in traffic 'coursing through the veins of the West End' as part of the bloodstream of the city.[283] At the same time, Hamilton's imagery in these novels identifies Tube stations as important nodules in a vast urban network, particularly as they supply public telephone boxes that form a link running in parallel with the Tube system. The telephone box at Great Portland Street station appears in the novel while the station is also used as a meeting place.[284] Hamilton's use of the Tube, particularly at street level, implies a political approach to the city as he seems to be making the point that a vast system of public transportation is also locally based. Another 'Soho Noir' novelist, James Curtis, used Tube stations to similar effect in *The Gilt Kid* (1936). The eponymous hero of the novel is a Marxist petty criminal who lives on the Soho margins and attacks the Communist Party for its failure to lead the working class effectively. Like Hamilton, Curtis uses Tube stations as a kind of communication network for his characters even if they rarely use the Tube itself. At one point, the Kid escapes into Piccadilly Circus station but does not hang around as he is afraid of being caught loitering there: 'dollars to doughnuts he would be arrested [...] he left by another exit, not bothering to look which'.[285] These West End Tube stations were one of the battlegrounds on which the criminal underworld encountered the forces of law and order in the capital. Later, 'His eyes, sharpened and wary to city sights as those of

---

281 Greene, *It's a Battlefield*, p. 136.

282 P. Hamilton, *The Midnight Bell* (1929), first book in *Twenty Thousand Streets Under the Sky*, p. 115.

283 Hamilton, *The Midnight Bell*, p. 333.

284 Hamilton, *The Midnight Bell*, p. 479.

285 J. Curtis, *The Gilt Kid* (1936; London: London Books, 2007), p. 109.

a gamekeeper are to the woodland', he spots 'a couple of detectives standing near the mouth of the Tottenham Court Road Underground Station'.[286] The Tube station has become too dangerous for the Kid as he is on the run from the police, choosing instead to take buses or taxis. This Piccadilly Circus station is very different from that of Virginia Woolf and closer to the more seedy picture of the West End as painted by Arnold Bennett. These novels suggest an organic model of the urban system in which stations are integrated into the landscape for those who live on the margins. Loitering is not solely the preserve of the middle-class *flâneur* as these figures in the criminal underworld operate at the interstices of tube stations. However, neither the telephone system nor the Tube offers the dubious characters in these novels effective communication in the metropolis.

Within this model there is a change which is illustrated in a number of other novels of this period. It is found in Rose Macaulay's *Crewe Train* (1926) when her characters Denham and Audrey find the spectacle of commuters using escalators perplexing: 'people crawled slowly down them, even when their trains were just coming in […] it seemed queer that so many apparently able-bodied people enjoy moving like invalids'.[287] Escalators were a major feature of the tubes after the war, giving the interface between train and street, surface and subsurface, a new dimension. For Macaulay, the figure of the commuter has lost its independence, becoming a mechanized puppet like Graham Greene's bus worker in *It's a Battlefield*. The commuter is subjected to the demands of the Tube, performing a series of rituals that deny his or her individual autonomy. Denham arrives in London a rebel and nonconformist but is forced to submit to the demands of society on women and stifles her inner nature. At the end of the novel, Arnold and Denham 'Go and Live in Metro-Land', 'catching an electric train to Baker Street five mornings a week, an electric train back from Baker Street five evenings'.[288] But Macaulay's earlier novel *Told by an Idiot* (1923) literally revolves around a fantasy world of the Tube. Macaulay's narrative of the Garden family contains an outline of world events spanning over four decades, a story suggesting flux and perpetual change in the lives of her characters. This results in their search for coherence, a quest which, as David Pike notes, in

---

286 Curtis, *The Gilt Kid*, pp. 109 & 200. See also M. Doriel Hay, *Murder Underground: Death on the Hampstead Tube* (London: Skeffington & Son, c.1930). I am indebted to Caroline Brick at the London Transport Museum Library for this and other references.

287 R. Macaulay, *Crewe Train* (1926; London: Methuen, 1985), p. 43.

288 Macaulay, *Crewe Train*, p. 249.

the 'perpetual motion of the Circle line—[is an] abstract reverie made real'.[289] Macaulay's teenage characters Imogen (an autobiographical character) and Tony seek the pattern in their lives of the perfect circle: 'Round the world for ever and aye, ROUND THE WORLD FOR EVER AND AYE [...] Oh joy! Sing for the circle completed, the new circle begun'.[290] They go on a Circle line journey, starting at: 'Sloane Square. Two penny fares. Down the stairs, into the delicious, romantic, cool valley. The train thundered in, Inner Circle its style'.[291] They travel through intermediate stations, changing compartments at Paddington. They continue on round the Circle line via King's Cross and 'the wild, romantic stations of the east: Liverpool Street, Aldgate, and so round the bend, sweeping west like the sun'.[292] They travel round the Circle a second time and then re-emerge at Sloane Square in 'the upper air, hot and elated'.[293] A similar fantasy world emerged in Rebecca West's *Harriet Hume* (1929). Here the ticket-collector on the underground will 'throw aside that pert, snapping metal thing, and pop down on his knees, disclosing himself to be the Prince of Wales' in order to propose marriage to a passenger.[294] Such Cinderella-like images would have fittingly graced a romantic film comedy—a projection of the strange imaginings of West's main characters.

In *Keeping Up Appearances* (1928) Macaulay returned to the underground as it figured in the upper and middle-class world of metropolitan life. She spends an entire chapter on Mrs Arthur of East Sheen and her use of the underground during a day at the sales in London. After a visit to Harvey Nichols she telephones her daughter Ada; then, following a trip to Swan and Edgar's, she phones her son Edward from Piccadilly Circus station. Bond Street station is the next port of call where she phones her other daughter Daisy and finally a call from Sloane Square to her husband in Baker Street. Later that day, she travels from Sloane Square to Oxford Circus station and then to Great Russell Street station[295] to visit Daisy at Maynard Buildings in Bloomsbury. This is an extraordinary use of Tube stations as communication nodes in the city—as Macaulay says earlier in the novel, 'each day was a little train running along

---

289 D. L. Pike, 'Modernist Space and the Transformation of Underground London', in P. K. Gilbert (ed.), *Imagined Londons* (Albany: State University of New York Press, 2002), pp. 101–19, p. 110.

290 R. Macaulay, *Told by an Idiot* (London: Collins, 1923), pp. 201–02.

291 Macaulay, *Told by an Idiot*, p. 200.

292 Macaulay, *Told by an Idiot*, p. 201.

293 Macaulay, *Told by an Idiot*, p. 202.

294 R. West, *Harriet Hume* (1929; London, Virago, 1980), p. 30.

295 Probably British Museum station which closed in 1933—a station used as a set for the imaginary 'Bloomsbury' station in the film *Bulldog Jack*.

well-known rails'.[296] But these novels reflect a deeper question for their women characters, because, as Nicola Beauman has pointed out, 'women writers gradually began to write about basic, everyday middle-class female preoccupations [...] describing the pleasures and pains of a generally rather steadfast daily life'.[297] The women upon whom such characters were based were themselves regular users of the underground if they lived in London or came up for the sales. The feminist writers of the 1920s and 1930s wanted these women to break out of the narrow channels of male-dominated, middle-class and family-obsessed society but wrote honestly of the difficulties of doing this. The changes that had occurred after the war meant that women's use of the Tube was now vastly different from that of Gissing's heroines and this was reflected in the fiction of these decades. But for some observers, the feminizing of the Tube, which would be completed during the Second World War, was double-edged. Pioneering suffrage-fighters who had stormed the tubes before the First World War had given way to the hordes of 'girls who travel on crowded tramcars and Underground trains among hordes of plain young men', girls who were 'depressed and disgruntled' about their lives.[298] The obvious 'modernity' of these years did at least seem to suggest that standards of living were rising for those in regular work—the apparent paradox being that the apogee of 'Fitness for Purpose' came in the midst of the Depression. And this period did bring many new jobs to the outskirts of London, along with a new female workforce that increasingly travelled on the Tube. These women were the first female generation to read hardback and to a lesser extent paperback fiction on the Tube and although it was likely to be romantic and escapist in content, it signalled a new proficiency which would be vastly expanded after the Second World War with the growth of paperback novels. So whilst these women were not necessarily the 'Old Feminists' of the pre-war era, they were a generation that opened up the underground system to working-class women. It is not a paradox that the upper-middle-class Virginia Woolf identified so strongly with the Tube as it was, after all, a system primarily designed with the middle class in mind. But Woolf was enough of a 'New Feminist' to insist on a democratic future.

For some writers the teeming streets and underground stations were part of a process that was undermining the city, as in Stephen Spender's *The Burning Cactus*

---

296 R. Macaulay, *Keeping Up Appearances* (1928; London: Methuen, 1986), p. 55.

297 N. Beauman, *A Very Great Profession: The Woman's Novel, 1914–39* (London: Virago, 1983), p. 95.

298 A. C. Ward, *The Nineteen-Twenties: Literature and Ideas in the Post-War Decade* (London: Methuen, 1930), p. 193.

(1936) where there is a 'hammering with [its] traffic' against the foundations of the city.[299] In these evocations of public transport the commuter is reduced to a cipher—a 'face' in the crowd controlled by the timetables of the underground. The office workers in Evelyn Waugh's *Vile Bodies* are 'hurrying with attaché cases and evening papers to catch their evening train home coughing and sneezing as they went'[300] whilst guests at 'a swish London party' are compared in the same novel to the 'emergence of City workers from the Underground'.[301] John Carey argues that this view of urban culture is irrevocably split between the mass of commuters who cannot exist outside the rituals and performances of work and travel and the minority who can.[302] An example of this can be found in W. H. Auden's 'Letter to Lord Byron' (1936) with its commuter:

> The bowler hat who straphangs in the tube,
> And kicks the tyrant only in his dreams,

a person who cannot escape from the city, the

> abstract space imposed upon fields
> Destroying that tie with the nearest which in Nature
> rules.[303]

The upward travel of a lift spells out the difference between the two states of mind when, in Auden and Isherwood's play *The Ascent of F6* (1936):

> everything is emphatically provided:
> The Dial Exchange and the voices in the lift
> We must accept them all and there is no one to thank.[304]

In the 'Last Days of Binnacle' (1926) by Gerald Bullett, the straphanger is literally torn to pieces by his commuter train. Percy Binnacle is the archetypal bank official who travels into London each day from the suburbs but, on this occasion, he meets his nemesis in the rush hour at Tottenham Court Road Tube

---

299   S. Spender, *The Burning Cactus* (London: Faber & Faber, 1936), p. 96.

300   E. Waugh, *Vile Bodies* (1930; Harmondsworth: Penguin, 1982), p. 126.

301   Waugh, *Vile Bodies*, p. 77.

302   See J. Carey, *The Intellectuals and the Masses* (London: Faber & Faber, 1992).

303   W. H. Auden, 'Letter to Lord Byron' (1936), in *W. H. Auden Collected Longer Poems* (London: Faber & Faber, 1974), pp. 35–76, p. 52.

304   W. H. Auden & C. Isherwood, *The Ascent of F6 and On the Frontier* (1936–38; London: Faber & Faber, 1958), p. 18. An imaginary tube even appeared in the 'Kingdom of Ostnia' in their play *The Dog Beneath the Skin* (1935; London: Faber & Faber, 1958), p. 52.

station on the Central line. Binnacle rushes at the closing tube gates: 'Was he to be shut out of the paradise of his daily routine by this soulless contrivance, this thing of iron, this piece of detestable modern gimcrackery?' but they close on him and 'Like gigantic fingers, like the talons of fate, they seized the little man, nipped him smartly, and held him, all wriggling arms and legs, in their cruel grip'.[305] In the ultimate expression of technological homicide, Binnacle's legs are cut off just above the knees. Binnacle's train is like Orwell's: 'a mechanical worm twisting and crawling for ever in a black infinity'[306] but despite his death he continues on his journey towards the Bank station. Binnacle's ghostly form finishes its trip at Liverpool Street station regardless of the attentions of other passengers and the guard. As a humorous reminder of the power of the train to consume the traveller, Bullett's short story evokes the guillotine—like the 'Railway Demon' of the early Victorian era. But it is also a rare fictional description of a Tube journey in the 1920s, bringing to life the mundane realities of the rush hour. The operation of the typical Tube car is stylishly evoked when, for example, the conductors or 'gatemen' close the gates: 'the sound of the other closing gates, in a diminishing series, crashed like surf up the length of the platform'.[307]

The loss of personal autonomy implied in these descriptions of commuters is taken a step further in the intense psychological world of Jean Rhys's novel *After Leaving Mr Mackenzie* (1931). The London of this novel is explicitly labelled, from Acton to a funeral in Golders Green and a boarding-house in Notting Hill Gate. The underground is a place of heightened psychological awareness, a location in which sound and sensation are strangely magnified. Rhys successfully brings out many of the most extreme moments of tension in the simplest of everyday activities, and in the process stretches the reader's own perception of the Tube. Julia Martin, Rhys's heroine, comes to London for ten days to see friends and family but her visit is highly charged and she feels an existential angst in the city. She switches from normality to paranoia when she journeys from Notting Hill Gate station on the Central line. Julia has to retain her sense of self during these journeys as, for example, in an encounter with a stranger: 'the girl standing next to her in the lift stared at her persistently. She grew angry and thought: "Well, I can stare too, if it comes to that"'.[308] After the lift has deposited her on the platform and she takes her train, Julia is able to return

305 G. W. Bullett, 'Last Days of Binnacle' (1926), in *The Baker's Cart and Other Tales* (Freeport, NY: Books for Libraries Press, 1970), pp. 143–72, pp. 146–47.

306 Bullett, 'Last Days of Binnacle', p. 164.

307 Bullett, 'Last Days of Binnacle', p. 163.

308 J. Rhys, *After Leaving Mr Mackenzie* (1931; Harmondsworth: Penguin, 1971), p. 86.

to normal: 'she stopped thinking of the people around. She became calm'.[309]
Later, Julia has a tense encounter on the Central line with a South African man
who is travelling to Oxford Circus. Both characters are strangers to London but
the man appears to be lost and asks Julia for directions. A train appears and 'he
followed her into a carriage which was nearly empty', sits next to her and soon
asks her out to dinner. He gives her his card but 'When the train stopped at
Notting Hill Gate station she got up quickly, and the card fell from her lap'.[310]
The Tube car, with its 'two men with their eyes fixed upon their newspapers,
and a woman with a large attaché case'[311] conveys the sometimes surreal quality
of Tube travel as well as its threatening ambience. In these two episodes, Rhys
is using the Tube to mark out events in her characters' lives but these events are
coterminous with life on the streets of the city. The underground does not offer
relief from inner turmoil although the motion of the train induces a temporary
respite. It is not possible to escape from the pressures of the inner psychological world in the 'underworld' of the Tube, and it is not the refuge anyway
that Wells seemed to imply in his social novels or the unifying world that Woolf
offered in *The Waves*. In fact, the streets of Notting Hill to which Julia escapes
from the Tube are 'like the streets of a grey dream—a labyrinth of streets, all
exactly alike',[312] and one street is like the Tube: 'a dark tunnel between the
high walls of the houses'.[313] Even when Julia travels on the top deck of a bus
from Oxford Circus she closes her eyes to the panoramic landscape below.

Julia's disorientation is in stark contrast to the orderly simplicity of the new
Tube map that appeared only three years after Rhys's novel in 1933. This map,
designed by Harry Beck, offered a supremely rational picture of the underground as a single system unifying the sprawling metropolis, a supremely clever
piece of corporate cartography. Beck enlarged the central area and placed all
lines on a horizontal, vertical or 45 degree axis giving the appearance of an
electrical circuit board. The new map ironed out the physical complexities of
the metropolis through its ingeniously simple reordering of the Tube system.
It could not, however, straighten out the tangled psychological viscera that
existed in underground writing. Julia, in Rhys's novel, does not need a Tube
map, as, like most regular Tube travellers, she has a mental map of the parts
of the system that she uses. This can also be seen in Rhys's novel *Voyage in the
Dark* (1934), the title of which points to the problems of navigating the city

---

309 Rhys, *After Leaving Mr Mackenzie*, p. 86.
310 Rhys, *After Leaving Mr Mackenzie*, p. 102.
311 Rhys, *After Leaving Mr Mackenzie*, p. 102.
312 Rhys, *After Leaving Mr Mackenzie*, p. 84.
313 Rhys, *After Leaving Mr Mackenzie*, p. 103.

even when it is mapped. Set chronologically in the years 1912–14, the novel has a dream motif in which Rhys's heroine Anna Morgan is travelling in psychologically unknown territory in parallel with her actual physical journeys. She comes to live in London from the Caribbean but admits: 'I don't like London. It's an awful place; it looks horrible sometimes. I wish I'd never come over here at all'.[314] Nevertheless, the Tube is always present in the background of the story. Anna lives 'in Adelaide Road, not far from Chalk Farm Tube station'[315] and she travels frequently on the Central and Northern lines to Marble Arch and Tottenham Court Road stations. For Anna, the Tube is an essential part of her life even if it is lived on the margins of conventional society and therefore subject to all the social and economic pressures that come with survival in the city. Like many other fictional women of these years, Anna's physical life in London is located very firmly on the grid of the Tube system but her reliance on it has made her, like Patrick Hamilton's heroine Ella, the prisoner of an exploitative urban world. Interestingly, Rhys pointed to the same regularity and mapping in the novel *Good Morning, Midnight* (1938) in which her character Sasha reflects on her life 'coming out of the Metro station at the Rond-Point every morning at half-past eight', apparently the first time that the Paris Métro is mentioned in a British novel.[316] But in that novel Rhys also writes the first dream sequence about the London Tube where Sasha dreams that she is 'in the passage of a tube station in London. Many people are in front of me; many people are behind me. Everywhere there are placards printed in red letters: This Way to the Exhibition, This Way to the Exhibition'.[317] And in a frightening reversal of Woolf's account, Sasha wants to get out and the man in front of her 'points to the placards and his hand is made of steel'. In a final horrific moment, her father appears with blood streaming from a wound in his forehead.[318] Rhys was an 'outsider' who explored the oppressive nature of the imperial capital and the surreal traumatic world of the underground. Another colonial 'outsider', C. L. R. James, who came to Britain from Trinidad in 1932, frequented the 'Russell Square tube café' and described how colour prejudice could be found on the Tube. The racism he found there led him to caution his readers in Port of Spain to 'watch your step' in England.[319]

---

314 J. Rhys, *Voyage in the Dark* (1934; Harmondsworth: Penguin, 1969), p. 40.

315 Rhys, *Voyage in the Dark*, p. 34.

316 J. Rhys, *Good Morning, Midnight* (1939; Harmondsworth: Penguin, 1969), p. 15.

317 Rhys, *Good Morning, Midnight*, p. 12.

318 Rhys, *Good Morning, Midnight*, p. 12.

319 C. L. R. James, *Letters from London* (1932), ed. N. Laughlin (Oxford: Signal Books, 2003), p. 190.

Survival in this city was perhaps enhanced by Beck's Tube map. It was the epitome of Tubism in the sense that it brought order to the underground. The map might be seen as ending any fictional doubts about the Tube system, as the writing of the Tube would be reduced to a simple simulacrum of the system. Fiction would no longer be required to describe the Tube as the map would henceforth speak for it with the voice of authority. Only a year before the map appeared J. B. Priestley explored the Tube in 'Man Underground' (1928), a short essay in which he asked why people 'groused' about the crowded tubes. Priestley admitted the 'indignity of those rush hours [in which] human beings, yourself included, are suddenly turned into parcels' (he had evidently been reading Ruskin).[320] He compared his own travels with Bulwer Lytton's futuristic novel *The Coming Race*, but concluded that 'nothing in that story was as fantastic as this journey from Hampstead to Oxford Circus'.[321] Priestley refused to 'be alarmed about the future' as a result of Tube travel, saying that 'there is such a thing as progress and [...] it is still happening'.[322] Priestley's novel *They Walk in the City* (1936) reworked this material when he describes the disorientation of the commuter. Edward, the hero of the novel, is 'shot through the very bowels of the Bloomsbury he had just left [...] until he came to the mysterious foundations of King's Cross'.[323] This underground station is a strange 'subterranean kingdom' because of the curious experience of being shunted around beneath the ground in 'echoing tunnels of corridors, designed for midnight murders'.[324]

A very modern underground had reappeared in fiction only three years after Beck's map promised psychological security: the underground of political crime. Graham Greene's agent 'D' in *The Confidential Agent* (1939) is pursued through the underground by would-be assassins. Greene's protagonist comes to London on a secret mission to gain assistance for a beleaguered European liberal government, 'D' being the representative of the type of government mocked by Rex Warner in his novel *The Professor* (1938). This 'balanced' government seeking to enshrine the classical values of the Greek *polis* in a contemporary context, was an idea shared by Frank Pick in his approach to the building of the 'good city'. The impact of the Spanish Civil War is registered with incredible clarity as 'D' is hunted by the forces of fascism and faces a frightening journey

---

320   J. B. Priestley, 'Man Underground' (1928), in *Self-Selected Essays* (London: Heinemann, 1932), pp. 75–80, p. 75.
321   Priestley, 'Man Underground', p. 77.
322   Priestley, 'Man Underground', pp. 79–80.
323   J. B. Priestley, *They Walk in the City* (1936; London: Heinemann, 1936), pp. 207–08.
324   Priestley, *They Walk in the City*, p. 208.

on the Tube from Russell Square station to Hyde Park Corner. The Tube is not a place of safety for 'D' but the reader is never sure whether he is really in danger during the journey. It is clear, however, that for Greene the Tube combines all the real and imagined terrors of the period; the walls of the lift at Russell Square station 'sail up around him' and when it reaches the bottom of the shaft 'He was underground'. Soon, he feels 'the dry stale wind of a distant train' and, a minute later, 'D' is herded into a train by a woman and her sticky seven-year-old son as she intones the advertising slogan 'It's quicker by underground' in a ghoulish caricature of Pick's orderly world.[325] As the train roars into the tunnel, agent 'D' is reminded of high explosive shells in another grim image of war. In this very powerful passage, Greene comes closest to producing a picture of real fear magnified by the mundane world of Tube travel, and although agent 'D' does not have to be physically assassinated, the sheer fear of the Tube journey with all its warlike associations is enough to heighten the tension and strengthen the message. Greene links the psychological dislocation and disorientation frequently found in fiction to political violence and terror. The woman and child represent the mundanity and normality of Tube travel that is suddenly overthrown by panic and paranoia; fears heightened by the glib sloganizing of the underground. Ironically, Greene points directly to the greater political and military terror that would be inflicted on the city. Only one year after the publication of *The Confidential Agent*, such a terror would turn the Tube from a world of disorientation into a world of security.

The most explicitly political recasting of the past is found in John Sommerfield's novel *May Day* (1936). The underground is a central motif alongside other forms of public transport on the one day in May of the title, playing the role of the normally invisible connective tissue of the metropolis. Sommerfield focuses on the modernizing impact of transport technology using some elements of Orwell's critique of modernity but does not reject what he believes is the liberating potential embodied in the Tube. He draws on the building of the subway in Moscow which had begun in 1931 and opened (partially) in May 1935, an example for western communists of the success of the Soviet Union under Stalin.[326] Sommerfield's novel incorporates into fiction the political critique articulated by the Communist Party but in a more explicit way than Graham Greene does in *It's a Battlefield*. In its 1938 pamphlet 'More Fares Please', the London District Committee of the party condemned the new

---

325 G. Greene, *The Confidential Agent* (1939; London: Vintage, 2002), pp. 92–94.

326 B. Bobrick, *Labyrinths of Iron: A History of the World's Subways* (New York: Newsweek Books, 1982), chapter 9, pp. 271–82.

London Passenger Transport Board as a 'financial dictatorship [...] which is strangling the proper development of London's transport system'[327] although it was not alone in making this kind of assessment. Ernest Bevin, the leader of the Transport and General Workers Union, called the new Transport Board 'positively the worst form of public control. We desire municipal control'.[328] Another trade union leader, John Bromley of the Associated Society of Locomotive Engineers and Firemen (ASLE&F), was dismayed: 'Heaven help us when a Labour Government cuts out all idea of Socialist ideals, and tells the world that only businessmen can secure our future'.[329]

The public debate over the ownership and future direction of London's public transport unfolds in *May Day* through the device of a bus strike that threatens to paralyse the city. Sommerfield picks up many of the threads in Greene's *It's a Battlefield* but shifts the focus from the orthodox thriller plot-line. Sommerfield is more interested in the modernity of the Transport Board with images of the underground as a vast interlocking system of power which pulsates with electric energy beneath the streets, a fictional counterpart to McKnight Kauffer's or Alan Rogers' Tubist posters such as *Power* (1931) and *Speed* (1930).[330] For Sommerfield, the continued modernization of the underground (now including fully electromagnetic doors on trains, remotely controlled interlocking machine rooms, automatic working of junctions and programme machines for train timetabling) was an important new stage in capitalism. It meant a greater oppression of the workforce as they were subjected to a speeding up of their work rates, higher productivity and job losses as technology reduced staffing levels. This also involved the greater subordination of passengers to the capitalist system of private profit as they could be more efficiently 'processed' on the journey to and from work. *May Day* is a fictional polemic modelled on the arguments of those like Arthur Downton who asserted in a 1936 pamphlet *The LT Scandal* that the 'new' London Passenger Transport Board was 'using every device of capitalist managerial "science" to intensify the working condi-tions'.[331] The Transport Board was a state capitalist institution, according to the Communist Party and it was also, according to Felicity Ashbee, rigidly

327 CPGB, *More Fares Please*, p. 16.

328 Quoted in A. Bullock, *The Life and Times of Ernest Bevin*, 3 vols. (London: Heinemann, 1960–83), vol. 1, p. 510.

329 J. Bromley, 'General Secretary Remarks', *The Locomotive*, June 1931, p. 238, quoted in N. Riddell, *Labour in Crisis: The Second Labour Government, 1929–31* (Manchester: Manchester University Press, 1999), p. 71.

330 London Transport Museum Collection.

331 A. Downton, *The LT Scandal* (London: London District Committee, CPGB, 1936), p. 14.

right wing in its refusal to display three posters calling for humanitarian aid to Republican Spain during the Spanish Civil War. As a young member of the Communist Party, she had designed the posters for the underground but was told by the authorities that they were 'political' and therefore not allowed on the Tube.[332]

Technology is the key thread in *May Day*. It enabled the tubes to descend deep 'Under the clay [where] crowded trains burrowed their wormy courses, and far from sight and sound of natural things, in a steel cased electric day'.[333] In this artificial environment in which commuters are cut off from the natural world above, there is also a rift between people. The electric light 'burned precariously in the dark and fearful subterranean darkness, [and] thousands of living human beings sat thinking their lonely thoughts'.[334] The electric light here seems like the illuminating light bulb in Picasso's painting of the Spanish Civil War *Guernica* (1937), only in Sommerfield's hands it throws light down into a Tube car as it rattles through an unending night. Sommerfield said that passengers are locked into an oppressive social and economic system that generates increasing power as 'dynamos are switched over to a fuller load, louder and faster'.[335] On the tubes themselves such power was translated into higher average train speeds and much shorter boarding times. Sommerfield asserts that, at the same time, there are greater and greater contradictions building up in a system where technological progress might also be harnessed for building a more humane society. The full implications of Wells' Fabian belief in the utopian role of technology are drawn out in *May Day* but in an account that accepts the need for revolutionary change led by the Communist Party. *May Day* attempts to demonstrate, in fiction, that the alternative to this chaos is social revolution: 'only the mathematics of class struggle can make order and design out of this seething chaos of matter in motion'.[336]

Sommerfield places his characters against the political backdrop of a planned bus strike in London with the streets of the capital being described as thoroughfares only navigable by buses and trams. The No. 7 bus journeys along 'the dangerous river of Oxford Street' and through 'the whirlpool around the island of Marble Arch'.[337] The class stratification of public transport is

---

332 E. Adams, M. Tyler, A. Santana & J. Moreno, *Echoes of Spain 1936–1939* (London: Gloucester Court Reminiscence Group, 2008), pp. 14–15.

333 J. Sommerfield, *May Day* (1936; London: Lawrence & Wishart, 1984), p. 70.

334 Sommerfield, *May Day*, p. 70.

335 Sommerfield, *May Day*, p. 79.

336 Sommerfield, *May Day*, p. 171.

337 Sommerfield, *May Day*, p. 54.

highlighted when one of the characters leaves the No. 7 bus at the corner of the Harrow Road and turns down Praed Street to 'where the tramlines begin'[338] in a reminder that trams were not allowed into the West End. The novel also contrasts the private cars of the wealthy boss Sir Edwin Langfier who 'glides' through Hyde Park in a 'dark blue Daimler'[339] and his son Peter Langfier who drives a 'long, low Bentley'[340] with the public transport used by workers. *May Day* demonstrates that the committed socialist fiction of the 1930s was drawn into the writing of the underground on the basis that the most modern transport systems offered opportunities to highlight the contradictions of capitalist society.

None of these writers accepted Tubism although it was in many ways the most successful concept of modernity to emerge from a tangled bundle of intellectual, ideological and aesthetic sources in this period. But even the staunchest Tubist writers like Woolf found themselves examining the internal contradictions of the Tubist mentality, a process which was sharpened by the impact of the First World War. The Tube was under greater scrutiny in the 1920s and 1930s, particularly as public perceptions were revised under the impact of overcrowding, delays and other crises. With the help of the Tubist project, the London Passenger Transport Board was able to navigate the fine line between social acceptability and imaginative condemnation. But Tubism effectively disappeared in 1940 as the Tube system was rapidly adapted to the need for shelter and security as the city and its underground were transformed into a battleground during the long days of the Blitz. In 1940 Virginia Woolf described the effects of the bombing in a letter to Ethel Smyth: 'the passion of my life, that is the City of London—to see London all blasted, that too raked my heart'.[341] As Vicki Tromanhauser concludes in her study of Woolf's London: 'that vast network of the underground railway tunnels that had once forged the bonds of Eros now became a last refuge from the assault of the air raids'.[342]

---

338 Sommerfield, *May Day*, p. 55.
339 Sommerfield, *May Day*, p. 17.
340 Sommerfield, *May Day*, p. 59.
341 V. Woolf, 11 September 1940, in *Letters*, vol. 6, p. 431.
342 Tromanhauser, 'Virginia Woolf's London', p. 43.

Chapter Four

THE KINGDOM OF INDIVIDUALS: SAFETY AND SECURITY ON THE TUBE IN THE SECOND WORLD WAR

Still the walls do not fall,
I do not know why;

H. D., 'The Walls Do Not Fall'[1]

When Henry Moore completed his *Shelter Sketchbooks* in 1940–41, he had created a vision of the capital—unparalleled in underground writing—that unified the subterranean world and the streets. His work echoes the prints and photographs of the building of the Metropolitan Railway in the Victorian period by showing people on Tube platforms, but now the people of the city are no longer just spectators. The trains have disappeared completely from Moore's drawings, leaving the people centre stage. Moore was not alone in his creation of what has been called an 'abiding city' in wartime. Many of the parallels of wartime London are expressed through its Tube system: first, the underground continued to provide London with a functioning transit system which was less subject to the disruptions caused by bombing that often disabled both public and private transport systems at street level. It acted as a unifier of the metropolis during the various phases of the Blitz, linking the city together in a way that offered continuity and stability to a population under siege. Secondly, the underground played a key role as shelter for around four per cent of London's population with up to 177,000 people sheltering during the worst phases of the Blitz. Whilst it had also provided shelter for people in the First World War, this had not been culturally and socially transformative

---

1   H. D. (Hilda Doolittle), 'The Walls Do Not Fall', in *H. D. Collected Poems, 1912–1944*, ed. Louis L. Martz (New York: New Directions, 1986), pp. 507–43, p. 542.

but now the Tube became a world beneath the city. In the Second World War, the role of the underground became one of the shaping episodes of the Home Front, embracing a national as well a metropolitan dimension within the mythology of wartime Britain. This was a city under siege, suffering a most intense, unpredictable and seismic bombardment during the Blitz. It was an underground that attained an unparalleled cultural visibility through the drawings of Henry Moore, documentary photography and writing.

Tubism, the cultural form of modernity on the underground, collapsed as a result of this process as the London Passenger Transport Board was transformed into a wartime organization and stripped of its corporate status. The underground ceased to be a beacon for urban capitalism becoming, instead, a symbol of social solidarity and harmony. This was a world away from the streamlined corporatism of the interwar years with its emphasis on efficiency, rationalization and 'Fitness for Purpose'. Underground writing found a number of reference points in the attempt to describe what was happening to the city during the Blitz. It could not supply the full range of responses to these experiences and there was some reworking to meet the urgent needs of war. The paradox was that the underground achieved its clearest unity with the city just at the point when its cultural form became loose, surreal and disjointed. Most of the writers of the war made the underground into a symbol of stability, reliability or human solidarity but they also undercut these images by presenting it as a detached realm in which normality broke down. This was hardly surprising given that the underground system was subjected to incredible pressures, both from the bombing raids on the capital and the effects of these raids on London's population. In wartime, underground writing was deployed in order to describe extreme situations. Writing itself was therefore stretched in order to cope with the stresses and strains of the wartime city, laying bare in only a few years the complexity of the cultural life of the system.

One reference point was massive change whether brought about by disruptions at surface level due to intensive bombing or other reorganizations of social and economic life. The underground system continued to function throughout the bombing campaigns, attaining a level of metropolitan integration as it offered a means of travelling across London when surface forms of transport were disrupted. If it was to perform this role effectively, the underground had to be dislocated or cut off from the surface of the city, and so the new relationship between surface and subterrain became critical. The new social phenomenon of Tube sheltering erased many of the distinctions between the public and private spheres, giving the underground an almost revolutionary modernity. During the two phases of the Blitz, many underground platforms, escalators and other station areas became the sites of social interaction that merged the public and private realms of the metropolis for many of its inhabitants and even those who declined to use the tubes as shelter could not fail to be aware of this fact. The essentially private and individual nature of Tube travel that had been such an important part of writing in the past was challenged by the development of mass sheltering. At another level, the question of what constituted public ownership of the Tube system was reopened as the 'public' reclaimed it from the authorities. Two undergrounds emerged during the war, both of them mythical and both deeply rooted in the past. One final major point of reference centred on the sheltering communities themselves. They gave rise to a large number of documentary, fictional, poetic and visual treatments that offered an entirely new interpretation of the Tube system.

Most writers were united by their wartime experiences of London in a way not possible before. The sense of wartime writing confers a kind of unity of purpose that infuses their depiction of the underground: it is an experience shared—metaphorically if not literally—amongst writers such as Elizabeth Bowen, Charles Williams, Graham Greene and George Orwell as well as a number of poets and dramatists including T. S. Eliot, Louis MacNeice, Nicholas Moore and Christopher Hassall. But there is no uniformity in the way they report the relationships between people and their need for safety and security with most novelists or poets placing some distance between themselves and the shelter experience, often using this sense of detachment as an opportunity for ironic reflection or commentary on pre-war class distinctions. Other commentators, like Vera Brittain, Sefton Delmer and the part-time participants in the Mass Observation surveys, produced documentary accounts of the underground experience which if they were realistic in their treatment of shelter life, were undeniably propagandistic in their effect. However, because they embodied many of the elements in the previous writing which were then overlaid by the new experience of sheltering, they became more contradictory and even subversive in their message. Another account comes from the oral tradition which has recorded individual shelterers' views of their experiences during this period, a unique social and cultural perspective on the Tube that will undoubtedly grow in importance.

THE LUNAR WORLD OF LONDON

For Elizabeth Bowen, the underground emerged as the only truly organic part of the capital in the early part of the Blitz. The urban landscape takes on a lunar quality in Bowen's short story 'Mysterious Kôr' (1944): 'London looked like the moon's capital—shallow, cratered, extinct'.[2] The surface of the metropolis is like a stage set for a science fiction film, a place from which the urban inhabitants have fled. This curiously Wellsian world is silent, strange and unnatural; a mechanical place in which traffic lights go 'through their unmeaning performance of changing colour'.[3] Pioneered by the underground, the traffic lights now metaphorically exercise their authority over the moonlit world above. This is surely the moon of H. G. Wells' short story 'The First Men in the Moon' where the Selenite colony has left the surface. Wells was much invoked during the war, for example by Vera Brittain when she described a journey through the East End of London as being like 'a nightmare fantasy by H. G. Wells',[4] a reference to the film *Things To Come* (1938), based on Wells' novel. In Bowen's story, the subterranean world has become the unseen public space which continues to function normally whilst the streets are deserted and in darkness except for the brilliant moonlight. The underground railway which runs through this subterranean city allows communication and interaction to take place both day and night whilst the surface of the city is locked in and privatized in domestic and public shelters. Whilst most shelters required people to be static, the Tube combined movement with shelter during traffic hours.

The relationship between surface and subterranean is modified during the war. The world of work and domestic life on the surface is more directly linked to the underground. Tube trains now regulate not only the daily journey to work of the commuter but signal the beginning and end of the day because when traffic starts and ceases, station platforms perform two different roles. The underground imposes its own regime on the social life of the city by making waking and sleeping hours entirely dependent on the movement of trains and the 'normal' routines of the transport system. The underground differs from Wells' Selenite colony or Forster's dystopian city because it is not enclosed and shut off from the surface—it is not merely a place of safety but a fully functioning underground metropolis which has to be connected to the surface even though that surface world is now a place of danger. The war could

---

2   E. Bowen, 'Mysterious Kôr' (1944), in M. Bradbury (ed.), *The Penguin Book of Modern British Short Stories* (London: Penguin, 1988), pp. 32–45, p. 32.

3   Bowen, 'Mysterious Kôr', p. 32.

4   V. Brittain, *England's Hour* (1941; London: Futura, 1981), p. 153.

not force a complete disjuncture between surface and subsurface worlds even though, in real terms, the two worlds had to be separated in the consciousness of the thousands of travellers and shelterers. The importance of this separation is illustrated in the comments of Tube shelterers such as Win Parker: 'we was terrified of the guns going off and the bombing, we decided to sleep down the tube [Caledonian Road] as you couldn't hear anything down there. The liftman was ever so nice and friendly'.[5]

The separation that opened up between the two levels led to a fracture in cartographic writing as writers like Bowen attempted to describe this wartime experience in terms of the past. For Bowen, to be underground is to be guided securely to your destination. She noted how 'one was always making one's own new maps of a landscape convulsed by some new change'.[6] In 'Mysterious Kôr' Bowen brings into play both the imperial city of Rider Haggard's *She* and the modern threat of fascism. The triangle of three characters Pepita, Arthur and Callie is pulled this way and that by the war: for Pepita the city of Kôr is a 'completely forsaken city, as high as cliffs and as white as bones, with no history'.[7] Ascending from the underground is like entering unknown territory because of the changes wrought by the bombing. Arthur recognizes this new reality when he says to Pepita: 'You ought to know the place, and for all I could tell you we might be anywhere: I often do have it, this funny feeling the first minute or two when I've come up out of the Underground'.[8] The Tubist concept of easy access from subsurface to street level has been disrupted by the bombing, leaving London's inhabitants in a state of bewilderment when they reach the surface. The underground has not altered during their journey but the streets of the city have lost their shape and meaning. The brick walls that were erected outside stations were as much cultural as physical barriers in that they distanced pre-war London from its wartime form. Bowen's short story observes that when the 'All Clear' sounded, 'a trickle of people came out of the Underground, around the anti-panic brick wall' as though entering a stage on which they were merely visitors.[9] Indeed, without lights the city at night lost its three-dimensional depth with the photographer Bill Brandt recalling how 'houses looked flat like painted scenery and the bombed ruins made strangely

---

5   D. Welsh, *Talk About a Liberty: An Oral History of Tube Sheltering In London, 1939–1945* (London: unpublished transcripts, 2006–08).

6   Bowen, 'Mysterious Kôr', p. 78.

7   Bowen, 'Mysterious Kôr', p. 33.

8   Bowen, 'Mysterious Kôr', p. 32.

9   Bowen, 'Mysterious Kôr', p. 33.

shaped silhouettes',[10] a view echoed in Edith Sitwell's Blitz poem 'Lullaby' which proclaims that 'There is no depth, there is no height' as the 'steel birds' fly over the capital.[11]

Underground stations serve as exits to the devastated and changed surface but they also function as beacons at street level. Stations such as Leicester Square and Charing Cross furnish a psychological link with pre-war London, an attempt, in the fragmented city, to grasp at notions of normality. These two stations appear in Charles Williams' *All Hallows' Eve* (1945) and they are important landmarks for the character Lester Furnival who in this novel is one of those killed in the war. She observes 'the entrances to the Leicester Square Tube Station' and remembered they had meant to go somewhere by Tube when she meets another of the dead, her friend Evelyn, in the street.[12] The Tube station is a sign of the normal processes of the pre-war city, for example in the habits exhibited by Richard Furnival, Lester's husband, 'in the Tube while he read the morning paper'.[13] This theme also emerges in the short story 'The Hours of Darkness' (1945) by Roger Anscombe where the 'sparks' on board a merchant ship in a North Atlantic convoy in 1940 registers his nostalgia for London's 'underground trains, bright red and warm, full of people in the morning, fresh-smelling of shaving, folded newspapers; full of different people in the evenings, going home, going to shows and dances and meetings'.[14] Similarly, in A. W. Baird's short story 'A Spiv on the Steppe' (1945), the Blitz is recalled by a soldier in Egypt whose 'Mum spent the nights in the tube [amongst] the mess the bleeders 'ave made of Befnal Green'.[15] These narratives suggest that whilst the underground was fragmenting, one of its most coherent and lasting elements was the myth of the interwar Tube. Anscombe's comments lay out the precise ways in which the interwar Tube would be mythologized after the war itself had ended. The myth of the Tube also pointed to its integrative function in bringing the underground into a harmonious relationship with the metropolis during wartime. In *All Hallows' Eve*, the Blitz evokes an image of London dissolving into its past: 'another London, say—other Londons, into

10 B. Brandt, *Camera in London* (London: Focal Press, 1948), p. 19.

11 E. Sitwell, 'Lullaby' (1940), in *Collected Poems* (London: Papermac, 1982), pp. 274–75, p. 275.

12 C. Williams, *All Hallows' Eve* (London: Faber & Faber, 1945), pp. 15 & 17.

13 Williams, *All Hallows' Eve*, p. 27.

14 R. Anscombe, 'The Hours of Darkness', in J. Lehmann (ed.), *The Penguin New Writing 25* (Harmondsworth: Penguin, 1945), pp. 175–81, p. 181.

15 A. W. Baird, 'A Spiv on the Steppe', in J. Lehmann (ed.), *The Penguin New Writing 23* (Harmondsworth: Penguin, 1945), pp. 37–46, p. 43.

which her own London opened or with which it intermingled'.[16] Despite the 'tubes and tunnels filled with horrors',[17] the end of the novel brings a journey of the dead towards redemption or respite: 'matter was purified and earth was free, [...] instead of the tunnels flowed the inexorable river'.[18] Here, the Tube integrates the present with the past—it has truly become one of the natural features of the urban world. More importantly perhaps, the Tube has shed images as the passageway of the dead, becoming instead part of a mythical underworld which ensures a gateway to eternal life. The underworld found in Gissing's fiction has been transformed, as a result of the war, into a profoundly positive pathway to redemption.

Even within this fragmented form, underground writing achieves a brief moment of integration with the metropolis at mythical as well as material level. Tubism gained its ultimate utopian goal of uniting the transport system with the city but this goal was achieved as myth rather than reality. In Williams' novel, the underground transports the souls of dead Londoners towards their eternal resting place but could only do so in the extreme conditions of war. Likewise, Anscombe's description of the Tube was one of recollection *in extremis*. After the war, the myth of integration remains strong in fiction but is nevertheless a fantastic version of a more complex and flawed past. The surface of London is, in these short stories and novels, a phantom city which abides in an after-image as the real fabric of London is destroyed by the bombing. Bowen described London in 1947 as an 'ephemeral city [...] with a doom ahead'; but fictionally it was London 'as Kôr with the roots on'.[19] In other words, the city that was anchored by its organic communities was exposed to the public gaze, with the underground as a principal part of this organic landscape being particularly vulnerable to the glare of publicity. The image of the uprooted city was familiar in fictional perspectives of the underground. The urban landscape was transformed by the external and aerial threat of bombing rather than the more internal forces of urban modernity that had demolished homes or exposed their interiors in the past. The speed of this process produced a much sharper, broader and instantaneous reaction on the part of writers and commentators. In Nicholas Moore's poem 'The Flag' (1941), for instance, the bombs are 'Talking

---

16 Williams, *All Hallows' Eve*, p. 167.
17 Williams, *All Hallows' Eve*, p. 211.
18 Williams, *All Hallows' Eve*, p. 211.
19 E. Bowen, 'Radio broadcast on *She*' (28 February 1947), in *The Mulberry Tree, Writings by Elizabeth Bowen*, ed. H. Lee (London: Virago, 1986), pp. 246–50, p. 249.

to the town with abandon' as Aladdin-Hitler 'Rubs his lamp over London'.[20] In Norman Cameron's poem 'Punishment Enough' (1941), a house is

> sliced like a cheese
> Displaying its poor secrets—peeling walls
> And warping cupboards.[21]

Another poet, Bertram Warr, found abandoned houses in 'Stepney 1941' (1943):

> But it's empty; no door even
> To knock at. And this too; the whole row
> And not a soul, All empty and windowless,
> With walls standing around regarding one another
> Naked.[22]

The opening up of the city to the public through the media of poetry, photographs, newsreels and cartoons is a major feature of wartime. The restructuring of the urban environment in the darkness of night is a condensing of the upheavals in the Victorian city in which gaslight had illuminated the streets. But that restructuring had been described in more disturbed ways in fiction. In wartime, representation of the city in poetry and fiction was as factual as censorship and paper availability allowed, but wartime writing still tried to capture the impact of light on a darkened and impenetrable landscape. For Paul Dehn, like Bowen, traffic lights (restricted to illuminated crosses) and tramlines appear to offer the only guide for pedestrians in this ruined city. His poem 'New Age' records how the lights 'ripen from green to yellow; / And I, with a cobweb of rain in my hair, Trudge between tram-lines' and the wind 'comes streaming up the road / Like the train in the tube'.[23] For even the gaslights, the 'biddable, domesticated stars' that R. L. Stevenson had celebrated in 'A Plea for Gas Lamps' (1881) were now extinguished as the city returned to its past forms of illumination. Stevenson had gone on to predict that electric

---

20 N. Moore, 'The Flag' (1941), quoted in A. Sinclair, *War Like a Wasp: The Lost Decade of the 'Forties* (London: Hamish Hamilton, 1989), p. 67.

21 N. Cameron, 'Punishment Enough' (1941), quoted in Sinclair, *War Like a Wasp*, p. 61.

22 B. Warr, 'Stepney, 1941', in K. Rhys (ed.), *Poems from the Forces* (London: Routledge, 1941), p. 127.

23 P. Dehn, 'New Age', in *The Fern on the Rock: Collected Poems 1935–65* (1951; London: Hamish Hamilton, 1965), pp. 72–73, p. 72.

lighting would be 'a lamp for a nightmare'[24] and on the surface of London this was indeed the case in 1940. The city was diminished by the lack of light after dark leaving the writer, as Stevenson noted, to be 'beleaguered by goblins'.[25] Only the underground burned with electric power all day and night, its modernity defying the return of the 'goblins' of pre-Victorian London.

This was a vindication of those writers and artists like John Sommerfield and E. McKnight Kauffer who had highlighted the sheer technological power of the Tube system. Neon lighting was given its first trials on Tube trains in 1944 although it had been switched off at cinemas at the beginning of the war and was not allowed again until 1949. But the Tube was still restricted in its use of light because trains ran without lights in open sections of track and 'Osglim' light bulbs, which gave off a blue glimmer, were fitted. Trains must have resembled, in some respects, the 'padded cells' of the original Tube. Carriage windows were covered by a sticky netting to catch glass if it was shattered but this meant that there was no view of the outside until small rectangular shapes were cut into the centre. Sheila in Monica Dickens' novel *The Fancy* (1943) discovers this when she has to 'peer through the diamond opening in the window netting in the window to watch [her future lover David] walk up the platform'.[26] Evoking a similar sense of throwback to a more distant past, Graham Greene described the 'obliterated acres of Paternoster Row'[27] in his novel *The Ministry of Fear* (1943). This was 'like a Pompeian landscape'[28] after the bombing, with 'shops [which] were reduced to a stone ground-plan like those of Pompeii',[29] a city now smothered by ashes rather than the smoke from steam locomotives, factories and domestic fireplaces. Greene identifies that 'Knightsbridge and Sloane Street were not at war, but Chelsea was and Battersea was in the front line'.[30] A front line reminiscent of Greene's novel *It's a Battlefield*, but now the line is drawn not by the dynamics of the domestic class struggle but by the external Nazi enemy. The Circle line, which had drawn a militant proletarian ring of steel around the inner part of the capital, is now a defensive bulwark set against the collapse of the city.

Everything is reversed in the wartime city. John Heath-Stubbs records that

---

24 R. L. Stevenson, 'A Plea for Gas Lamps' (1881), in *Virginibus Puerisque: and other papers* (London: Chatto & Windus, 1905), pp. 189–93, p. 192.

25 Stevenson, 'A Plea for Gas Lamps', p. 189.

26 M. Dickens, *The Fancy* (1943; Harmondsworth: Penguin, 1964), p. 88.

27 G. Greene, *The Ministry of Fear* (1943; London: Penguin, 1963), p. 178.

28 Greene, *Ministry of Fear*, p. 178.

29 Greene, *Ministry of Fear*, p. 42.

30 Greene, *Ministry of Fear*, p. 85

> Passing through those streets was rather like
> The jaunt that Dante took through the Inferno[31]

while Bowen noted that the streets were paved with broken glass and 'the whole length of Oxford Street, west to east, is empty, looks polished like a ballroom, glitters with smashed glass'.[32] The domed glass city constructed by H. G. Wells in *When the Sleeper Wakes* has been shattered by the bombing with glass cascading onto the streets, ending the vision that had come to play such an important part in creating a functional city of the future. Bowen described London during the Blitz as a 'network of inscrutable canyons',[33] a view broadly confirmed in documentary accounts. Miles Mordaunt described how 'The familiar London of streets rapidly disappeared and one became used to a nightmare landscape consisting of sand dunes from burst sandbags, and heaps of rubble where houses had been'.[34] The streets have come to resemble the walls of tunnels which loom up around London's inhabitants and collapse onto people. This is an enclosed world over which, Orwell noted, 'flights of bombers drown the nightingales'.[35] His observation was reiterated in Greene's *The Ministry of Fear* when 'another raider came up from the south-east muttering to them both like a witch in a child's dream, Where are you? Where are you? Where are you?'[36] The 'raiders' now form the skyward boundary of the city. The more fearful and dangerous imagery of the underground that had emerged in writing is being transferred to the surface of the city and, correspondingly, the underground loses its threatening roles.

Bowen, in *The Heat of the Day* (1949), found that the 'city at war ticked over' and, in an organic metaphor, described the 'unintermittent pumping of traffic through arterial streets into arterial roads' coupled with a 'jarring at the periphery'.[37] It is as though London as an organic social body is attempting to survive a series of shocks to its limbs and nervous system. This likening of London's streets to a social body under enormous external pressures is also found in Nigel Balchin's *Darkness Falls from the Air* (1943). In this novel, Bill

31 J. Heath-Stubbs, 'Letter to David Wright' (1982), in *Collected Poems, 1943–1987* (Manchester: Carcanet, 1988), pp. 111–13, p. 112.

32 E. Bowen, *Collected Impressions* (London: Longmans, 1950), p. 217.

33 Bowen, *Collected Impressions*, p. 52.

34 M. Mordaunt, quoted in C. Fitzgibbon, *The Blitz* (1957; London: Corgi, 1974), p. 178.

35 G. Orwell, 'As One Non-Combatant to Another' (1943), in *The Collected Essays, Journalism and Letters of George Orwell*, eds. S. Orwell & I. Angus, 4 vols. (London: Penguin, 1970), vol. 2, pp. 342–46, p. 343.

36 Greene, *Ministry of Fear*, p. 30.

37 E. Bowen, *The Heat of the Day* (1949; London: Reprint Society, 1950), p. 82.

Sarratt, a cynical civil servant, travels across this nightmare world in cabs and on foot until he reaches the East End where his wife Marcia has been fatally injured in a raid. After witnessing his wife's death, Balchin's character travels back to Islington where he suddenly realises that he could have used the Tube as a quicker route to the East End during the raid: 'I saw the Tube station and it struck me that maybe the Tube would be quite all right and that I was a fool not to have used it going'.[38] The Tube represents an open pathway of communication beneath the city which is relatively unimpeded by the effects of bombing, a signal of the normality that lies beneath the surface of the metropolis. Bill returns home on the Tube 'as though nothing were happening outside. I went to sleep on the way'.[39] He then travels to the Embankment which, as Greene notes in *The Ministry of Fear*, is a place of 'would-be suicides'.[40] Instead of committing suicide in despair, he extinguishes an incendiary bomb with a sandbag: 'It went out, and then it was darker than ever'—the closing words of the novel.[41] In Balchin's story, the Tube appears to symbolize an oddly banal return to unthinking normality after the traumatic events of the night. The Tube shuts off its users from the reality of the Blitz, apparently returning characters to a time and place before the war when mental as well as physical safety was assured. The relationship between street and underground levels is also vividly highlighted in a short story called 'King's Evidence' (1944) by Algernon Blackwood. Originally broadcast on BBC radio, this murder mystery was set in fog-bound London during the war. An underground journey from Regent's Park to South Kensington by a young Canadian soldier suffering from agoraphobia is uneventful because 'there are no open spaces on the Underground'.[42] On leaving the station he is plunged into the gloom of a city with no landmarks and is engulfed in a nightmare. As in Balchin's novel, the Tube system is portrayed as a solidly mapped place that contrasts with the uncertain and threatening world at street level.

The underground registers the normal and orderly operations of the city in Christopher Hassall's poem 'Tube Shelter Leicester Square, 1941' when:

---

38   N. Balchin, *Darkness Falls from the Air* (1943; London: Pan, 1969), p. 196.

39   Balchin, *Darkness Falls from the Air*, p. 196.

40   Greene, *Ministry of Fear*, p. 94.

41   Balchin, *Darkness Falls from the Air*, p. 204.

42   A. Blackwood, 'King's Evidence', in H. Brown (ed.), *Best Broadcast Stories* (London: Faber & Faber, 1944), pp. 147–55, p. 147.

> Exactly fitting, a train slows from the tunnel;
> Ingenious doors divide, at the gaps of light
> A shuffle of shoulders.[43]

The importance of orderly movement is highlighted in London Transport's wartime poster campaign. The posters of Eric Kennington (*Seeing It Through*, 1942) and Fred Taylor (*They Also Serve*, 1944) both featured the contribution of staff to the war effort in terms of keeping the system moving.[44] Another artist known as Fougasse (Cyril Kenneth Bird), produced a series of cartoon information posters that encouraged passengers to be aware of the need for order on the underground.[45] This thread in the writing can be found in Monica Dickens' *The Happy Prisoner* (1946) when breaking the rules is indicated by the comment that 'He's the sort of man who always walks on the right in the Underground'.[46] In Bowen's 'Mysterious Kôr', trains send out a reassuring, stabilizing and regulatory message during the raids: 'Now and then under the streets and buildings the earth rumbled: the Underground sounded loudest at this time.'[47] The people who sheltered in their basements could hear 'the Underground Railway below',[48] according to Vera Brittain, suggesting that they were suddenly more aware of the subterranean tunnels and felt the reassurance of the normal movement of trains in the tunnels. Such observations underline the important fact that the underground carried on working during the Blitz, bringing 'a degree of mobility not possible above ground'.[49] The underground functioned with an incredible degree of normality in providing services, despite the fact that 15 miles of platforms, subways and tunnels and 79 stations were used by shelterers. As John Gregg notes, despite the serious disruption caused by direct hits at stations like Bounds Green, Balham, Bank, Moorgate and Trafalgar Square, plus the longer suspension of services on the Northern line between October 1940 and May 1941, 'the service remained indispensable for many Londoners throughout the conflict'.[50] Vera Brittain recorded in *England's Hour* (1941) that the 'District Railway' was 'operating with

---

43   C. Hassall, 'Tube Shelter Leicester Square, 1941', in *The Slow Night, and Other Poems, 1940–1948* (London: Arthur Baker, 1949), pp. 23–24, p. 23.

44   London Transport Museum Collection.

45   London Transport Museum Collection.

46   M. Dickens, *The Happy Prisoner* (1946; London: Book Club, 1948), p. 86.

47   Bowen, 'Mysterious Kôr', p. 32.

48   Brittain, *England's Hour*, p. 102.

49   *Manchester Guardian*, 19 November 1940.

50   J. Gregg, *The Shelter of the Tubes* (Harrow Weald: Capital Transport Publishing, 2001), p. 86.

determined regularity behind boarded-up offices and matchwood partitions'[51] after a series of raids. Louis MacNeice's wartime radio drama 'Cook's Tour of the London Subways' (1941) is full of the sounds of Tube trains entering and leaving stations and contains an explicit emphasis on the normal operations of the system. For example, a conductor (guard) announces 'That's right! Change at Oxford Circus […] etc. Oh, I couldn't say […] I think there's an Alert on'.[52] Monica Dickens, in her autobiographical portrait *An Open Book* (1978), recalled regular journeys across London. Dickens was a west London habitué, being familiar with the 'filthy old lift' at Notting Hill Gate station and noting the people who were 'already coming down with blankets and pillows, staking out claims to the painted rectangles on the platform that were their beds night after night during the raids'.[53]

Bowen's *The Heat of the Day*, written after the war, also makes this clear as her central character, Stella, arrives at King's Cross station after witnessing 'ruins [which] began to string out along the main line'[54] as the train travels through the suburbs. The novel presents parallel female lives in London: Stella is from an upper-middle-class background working at the War Office whilst Louie Lewis is an uneducated factory worker. A third female character, Connie, is an ARP warden and becomes entangled with the other two through wartime work. All three characters walk the streets but represent a powerful assertion of women's wartime working roles in the bombed city. Stella escapes a companion at King's Cross by making 'a loop through the crowd and […] into the Underground'.[55] Later in the same novel, Connie has to direct people who are strangers to London, answering typical questions like: 'Was the Underground running? which way to the West End? where was Waterloo?'[56] In other words, Bowen's female characters can take command of the whole city, both at underground and street level in the present (the novel starts in summer 1942) and are not locked in a mythical past like many of her male characters.[57] In Bowen's novel, the dead continue to make their presence felt on the streets, moving in 'shoals through the city day, pervading everything to be seen or heard or felt'.[58] But

---

51   Brittain, *England's Hour*, p. 107.
52   L. MacNeice, 'Cook's Tour of the London Subways', *Listener*, 17 April 1941, pp. 554–55, p. 555.
53   M. Dickens, *An Open Book* (1978; Harmondsworth: Penguin, 1980), p. 101.
54   Bowen, *Heat of the Day*, p. 82.
55   Bowen, *Heat of the Day*, p. 82.
56   Bowen, *Heat of the Day*, p. 151.
57   See K. A. Miller, *British Literature of the Blitz: Fighting the People's War* (Basingstoke: Palgrave Macmillan, 2009), chapter 1.
58   Bowen, *Heat of the Day*, p. 86.

the underground is a place in which the business of living is conducted: 'the very soil of the city at this time [1940] seemed to generate more strength' and 'London's organic power [...] boiled, surged and, not to be dammed up, forced for itself new channels'.[59] The power of the subterranean world in these novels and poems reflects the highly charged atmosphere of wartime London. For writers, this energy was directed towards the reconstruction of urban life, a reconstruction that would occur through the reserves of an organic society as expressed in its myriad communities. The underground effectively joined these reserves together in a vast network, giving the city a mythical unity based on pre-war stability especially as it was the only reliably functioning part that remained of the old networks. Many Tube scenes were observed by 'outsiders' who travelled through London. In 1941, Naomi Mitchison noted the Tube 'indigenes' 'reading the papers, drinking tea from mugs, knitting, doing their nails, gossiping'[60] and Zelma Katin 'stared unashamedly at the families bedding down for the night on the three-tier bunks'.[61]

The underground allows those who have experienced disrupted sleep and shattered nerves to recompose themselves during the daylight hours. Arthur Rowe, the chief character in Graham Greene's *The Ministry of Fear*, spends much time both on and in the underground during the Blitz. Rowe does not appear to seek shelter in the tubes, even though several commentators assume that he does so. Indeed, he is reluctant to use shelters at all until he is forced to obey 'Hilfe's advice and at last [go] underground'.[62] He points out that 'I'm hiding underground, and up above the Germans are methodically smashing London to bits all around me'.[63] Significantly, Greene points to the important role of the underground system in reconstituting the everyday world that must continue despite the bombing. Rowe analyses his shelter 'dreams' whilst travelling on the Tube as though now in a position to think rationally about them in an atmosphere of normality. Rowe is guilt ridden about the mercy killing of his wife and wants to 'get out of London and let the fools scrap it out'.[64] He travels obsessively on the Tube but believes he cannot escape pursuit for this act: 'He

---

59   Bowen, *Heat of the Day*, p. 86.
60   N. Mitchison, *Among You Taking Notes: The Wartime Diary of Naomi Mitchison, 1939–1945*, ed. D. Sheridan (London: Gollancz, 1985), p. 115.
61   Z. Katin, *'Clippie' The Autobiography of a War Time Conductress* (1944; Ipswich: Adam Gordon, 1995), p. 96.
62   Greene, *Ministry of Fear*, p. 67. The shelter described by Rowe in Greene's novel is a public shelter. Andrew Sinclair, in *War Like a Wasp*, believes it is a Tube shelter but it is clear from the text that this is not in the underground.
63   Greene, *Ministry of Fear*, p. 69.
64   Greene, *Ministry of Fear*, p. 81.

analysed now—an unshaven man in dusty clothes sitting on the tube between Stockwell and Tottenham Court Road. (He had to go a roundabout route because the tube had been closed at many stations)'.[65] Greene uses the plot of a thriller to underline the shifting and often tortuous psychological relationship between Rowe's normal life and wartime life. The Tube in this novel is a powerful device holding Rowe's two lives together, making *The Ministry of Fear* both mundane and terrifying. In this novel, as in Balchin's *Darkness Falls from the Air*, the ordinary and everyday aspects of the Tube bring into relief the horrors of the bombing campaign.

A CALCULATED CLASS POLICY:
THE STRUGGLE FOR SHELTER IN THE TUBE

This sense of the ordinary operation of the Tube in the midst of war is particularly significant in the light of the pre-war debates over the use of the underground as possible deep-level shelter in the event of aerial attack. The fear of attack was a common theme in the fiction of the 1930s, as I. F. Clarke comments: 'The vision of a desolate city and its mutilated inhabitants was the image of a contemporary fear, common to all these writings, that air bombardment could destroy such conurbations as London within hours'.[66] The danger of London being the target of aerial attack was a feature of debates in cabinet. A highly pessimistic scenario was broadly accepted that some 20,000 to 150,000 casualties could be sustained in one week alone and that London would be disabled as a strategic centre for Britain during the early months of a war. Contemporary official wisdom ruled out the use of the underground as shelter accommodation on the grounds that this would impede transport services in the capital. This view was expressed in an officious notice posted at Tube stations at the start of the Blitz:

WAR EMERGENCY: UNDERGROUND STATIONS MUST NOT BE USED AS AIR RAID SHELTERS—
The public are informed that in order to operate the Railways for essential movement, Underground Stations cannot be used as air raid shelters. In any event a number of stations would have to be cleared for safety in certain contingencies.[67]

---

65   Greene, *Ministry of Fear*, p. 77.
66   I. F. Clarke, *Voices Prophesying War, 1763–1984* (London: Oxford University Press, 1966), p. 170.
67   I. Grant & N. Maddren, *The City at War* (London: Jupiter Press, 1975), p. 41.

And fiction had tended to agree with the official view of Tube sheltering, partly shaping government policy in Uri Bialer's view.[68] From Le Queux's *The Invasion of 1910* (1906) which featured Londoners panicking in the East End and Soho and being trapped on the underground 'like rats in a hole'[69] to Addison's *The Battle of London* (1923) and Southwold's *The Gas War of 1940* (1931), which had prophesied London's destruction, the verdict of science fiction suggested that the underground would not be a refuge but a tomb. Londoners would not be safe from gas warfare either, as Black's *The Poison War* (1933) had:

> Oxford Street, Piccadilly, the Mall, Trafalgar Square, the Strand, Fleet Street, Ludgate Hill [...] carpeted with the dead. The entrance to every tube station was piled high with the bodies of those who had made one last mad effort to escape from the poison gas.[70]

One pre-war perspective in the writing of the underground suggested an ambiguous relationship with the metropolis in peacetime conditions, highlighting the alienating and negative social and psychological roles it played in the lives of London's population. But during the war, it was the *only* viable and completely safe environment in which to shelter. Despite how obvious a solution the Tube provided, it is important to note that only four per cent of London's population used the Tube in this way during the war and that the vast majority of the city's inhabitants did not use public shelters at all during the Blitz. In Greene's *The Ministry of Fear* his character Rowe walks past 'the blackened chimneys of Lots Road',[71] a reference to the power station in Chelsea that supplied electricity to the underground system. He hears a voice saying 'They can't spoil Whistler's Thames [...] It's safe underground',[72] in a curious echo of Greene's earlier novel *The Confidential Agent* when a woman says 'It's quicker by underground'.[73] Lots Road power station represented the symbolic power of the Tube to keep the lifeblood of the city flowing during the raids. This was embodied in a London Transport poster by Walter Spradbery,

---

68   See U. Bialer, *The Shadow of the Bomber: The Fear of Air Attack and British Politics 1932–39* (London: Royal Historical Society, 1980).

69   W. Le Queux, *Battle of Royston from The Invasion of 1910* (1906; London: Ellisons' Editions, 1984), p. 346.

70   L. Black, *The Poison War* (1933), quoted in M. Ceadel, 'Popular Fiction and the Next War, 1918–39', in F. Gloversmith (ed.), *Class, Culture and Social Change: A New View of the 1930s* (Brighton: Harvester, 1980), pp. 161–84, p. 161.

71   Greene, *Ministry of Fear*, p. 97.

72   Greene, *Ministry of Fear*, p. 97.

73   G. Greene, *The Confidential Agent* (1939; London: Vintage, 2002), p. 94.

The Proud City: Chelsea Power House (1944), that silhouetted the power station against the devastated streets and confirmed the significance of technology in maintaining London's war effort. Frank Pick, chief advocate throughout the interwar years of the philosophy of 'Fitness for Purpose', argued the case for putting transport at the heart of the organic metropolis during wartime and after. In a 1939 article entitled 'War as an Educator', Pick pointed out that 'To keep London fit and convenient to live in at all times and in all circumstances, which means keeping London free to move, is a considerable contribution towards the conduct of the war'.[74] These words suggest that Pick did not consider that the underground could possibly sustain a sheltering role in the event of bombing, underlining his boss Lord Ashfield's point-blank refusal to open the tubes for sheltering.[75] It seems clear that both Pick and Ashfield shared the view that the underground's priority during wartime was to keep the capital moving, especially as they believed that street-level public transport would be severely disabled by bombing. This view was perfectly consistent with the pre-war role that Pick had advocated, with the underground playing a key role in the city as its main arterial system. Pick's 'conservative modernism' was confronted in 1940 with the most serious change of use ever placed on the agenda of London's transport system.

Government policy endorsed a highly pessimistic view of the likely effects of severe bombing in the capital, confirming its belief in Pick's pristine modernism and rejecting the clearly chaotic, random and unplanned nature of sheltering in the system. The question of sheltering threw into sharp relief the conflict between the legacy of Tubism as the institutional form and the more fragmentary, surreal and dissonant elements which were always present in writing. For Pick, sheltering represented a failure to plan for the effects of war on the capital. Pick and the ideologues of Fitness for Purpose wanted to impose order on the city by using its transport system to shape population movement, housing and industrial development. Design literacy was an integral part of this project but, given the political and policy restrictions of the interwar period, became the only vehicle for this strategy. Pick wanted the imagination to shape the city using the underground as the principal tool in the creation of the aesthetics of the modern metropolis. This was, inevitably, a long-term process. In 1929 Pick had noted that 'The metropolitan city is still in the experimental

---

74   F. Pick, 'War as an Educator', *Pennyfare, London Transport Staff News*, no. 2 (War Series), November 1939, p. 1.

75   Ashfield had previously gone on record as believing that the entire Tube system would have to be closed in the event of war.

stage. It is full of accomplishment but it is not accomplished. It serves many purposes but it has failed so far to serve that overriding purpose'.[76]

The war confirmed that Pick's strategy was incapable of being achieved by halting the development of the Tube system. Once the physical and geographical reach of the underground was stopped, albeit temporarily, the whole dynamic of the system was lost. Pick refused to acknowledge this fact when he looked forward to the role that the London Passenger Transport Board would play after the war 'in the labour of reconstructing a better Transport Board as a contribution to a better world'.[77] Pick was sacked from London Transport in April 1940 and quietly moved to a job at the Ministry of Information, an indication that his role as mentor and defender of the Tubist vision was no longer viable in wartime when confronted with the realities of metropolitan security and the human need for safety. With Pick gone, a new world came into existence on the tubes in 1940 but it was not the world that he and other advocates of Fitness for Purpose had imagined. It was, however, a world often displayed in writing, a subterranean place that contained all the elements of social dislocation, disorder and human distress. Furthermore, it was a world that threatened to overturn the normal workings of the capital city as much as the bombing on the surface. The government now took direct control over the capital's transport system, an issue that Pick and Ashfield had been extremely sensitive about in the interwar years. This was effectively the end of a socially and culturally unifying vision of the Tube within the overall urban system, paving the way for a less dynamic and more pragmatic notion of postwar reconstruction.

Sheltering reawoke many of the images and descriptions of the underground system as subterranean nightmare. This world was quickly recognized by a number of commentators, including Mollie Panter-Downes who described a 'new race of tube dwellers'[78] and Vera Brittain who witnessed 'London's poorer population, like melancholy troglodytes'.[79] Initial reactions to Tube sheltering were frequently negative, triggering fears of mass panic or epidemics of diphtheria, pneumonia or influenza. The former *Daily Express* journalist and wartime political intelligence officer, Sefton Delmer, described the 'panic slum on the Underground [...] those able-bodied proletarians absenting themselves

---

76   F. Pick, quoted in C. Barman, *The Man Who Built London Transport: A Biography of Frank Pick* (London: David & Charles, 1979), p. 250.

77   Pick, 'War as an Educator', p. 1.

78   M. Panter-Downes, *London War Notes 1939–1945*, ed. W. Shawn (Harlow: Longman, 1972), p. 112.

79   Brittain, *England's Hour*, p. 190.

from their workshops while they lay on their mattresses in the Underground, publicly copulating on the platforms and blocking up the stations for those who had to go to work'.[80] Vera Brittain fulminated against the type of London parent which 'still persists in taking its young children each night into the germ-infested atmosphere of the Underground'.[81] Peter Richards remembered a 'rather shamefaced man [who] emptied the contents of a chamber pot onto the line'[82] and many shelterers recall the oppressive smell. The *Picture Post* weighed in with a double-page spread by John Langdon-Davies on the urgent need for sick bays and shelter kitchens in Tube stations, using before and after illustrations of an improved Tube platform in order to make its case more graphically.[83] Such comments suggest that Tube sheltering quickly crossed the boundary of temporary respite from bombing to Tube dwelling on a more permanent basis. It proved impossible to prevent people occupying the tubes as they were a very public and collective space beneath the city. The transport authorities attempted to stop any form of sheltering, temporary or permanent, but were confronted with a series of mass actions all over the system which signalled the determination of shelterers to ignore the Home Secretary Herbert Morrison's warnings against using the Tube as shelter. Indeed, Morrison was quickly forced to climb down after the Communist Party helped to organize the breaking open of Tube stations in the East End, an action leading the way to further illegal occupations of stations. The *Daily Worker* denounced the authorities, arguing that 'The shelter policy is not just a history of incompetence and neglect. It is a calculated class policy, a determination not to provide protection because of profits being placed before human lives'. It added: 'They occupied the Tubes in the teeth of a Government order to the contrary—and they have got them still'.[84] The alternative, to stand firm on official shelter policy, would have almost certainly sparked off serious unrest in the capital. Even Unity Theatre's topical play *Jack the Giant Killer* (1940), which ran during the Blitz, contained references to Baron Mouthpiece who, in the role of Wicked Uncle, brushes aside demands to open the tubes to shelterers.[85]

---

80   S. Delmer, quoted in P. Ziegler, *London at War, 1939–1945* (London: Sinclair-Stevenson, 1995), p. 136.

81   Brittain, *England's Hour*, p. 202.

82   P. Richards, *Bombs, Bullshit and Bullets … in roughly that order* (London: Athena Press, 2007), p. 20.

83   J. Langdon-Davies, 'Against Epidemics—No. 1', *Picture Post*, vol. 9, 16 November 1940, pp. 18–19.

84   *Daily Worker*, 7 September 1940 and 23 September 1940.

85   See C. Chambers, *The Story of Unity Theatre* (London: Lawrence & Wishart, 1989), chapter 6. The Transport Workers Union (TWU) on the New York subway had developed an

It was Tube dwelling that marked a significant turning point in attitudes towards this change of use for the system, as it seemed to confirm the view that morale would fail to hold up amongst the metropolitan population under sustained aerial attack. A further consideration in official circles was the political impact of Tube sheltering. Left-wing politicians were not slow to point out that an illegal action had been required to achieve shelter, which was essentially a public service, demonstrating the failures of pre-war policies of preparation and pointing to the need for change after the war. Tube sheltering, Antony Hern wrote in *Tribune*, represented 'the biggest working-class demonstration London has seen', and by 'occupying the tubes they have given an overwhelming reply to the official attitude'.[86] Stephen Spender, in his 1945 *Citizens in War—And After*, struck a similar note in his comments on the 'crisis [...] when the people started to make use of the London tubes'.[87] Spender added that 'in Civil Defence, we see barriers break down, in order to meet the problems of war' and asked, pointedly, 'Can they remain down; in order that people may co-operate as effectively to meet the problem of maintaining peace?'[88]

Tube communities began to develop a political cohesion thrown up by the need to pressurize the authorities for better conditions and facilities. The shelterers soon boasted an impressive array of committees and newsletters, indicating that a kind of grass-roots democracy was becoming an important feature of wartime life. The various station committees, for example at Swiss Cottage, produced regular bulletins, foreshadowing later pressure groups like Capital, *Tubewatch* and the Campaign Against Tube Privatisation. For the first time, a widespread debate on the nature of public transport in the city was possible, especially as the underground was part of a public corporation. It had been the flagship of public ownership as conceived by Labour's Herbert Morrison in his earlier post as Minister of Transport. Tube sheltering, with its mass occupation of the stations, stretched the boundaries of this concept as it became clear that the shelter population was developing a sense of communal

education programme in the 1930s which included an art exhibit—'Art for the Subway'— and a play called *A Nickel Pusher's Delirium* written by a subway worker. See M. Denning, *The Cultural Front: The Laboring of American Culture In the Twentieth Century* (London: Verso, 1996), chapter 2 and, for the history of the TWU, see J. Freeman, *In Transit: The Transport Workers Union in New York City, 1933–1966* (New York: Oxford University Press, 1989).

86   A. Hern, 'The People of the Tubes' (27 September 1940), in D. Hill (ed.), *Tribune 40: The First Forty Years of a Socialist Newspaper* (London: Quartet, 1977), pp. 29–31, p. 30.

87   S. Spender, *Citizens in War—And After* (London: Harrap, 1945), p. 21.

88   Spender, *Citizens in War*, p. 17.

purpose. There was no collapse into the psychological 'shelter mentality' predicted by the authorities and portrayed in more dystopian writing. Peter Ritchie-Calder in an article in the *New Statesman and Nation* described the 'shelter committees' as the 'new units of democracy'. Commenting on the progress that had been made, Ritchie-Calder argued that such activities suggested that 'democracy and free criticism have proved themselves in a way in which public demand has humanised the conditions'. For Ritchie-Calder, Tube sheltering represented the true values embodied in democracy's struggle against fascism, with a reliance on common sense rather than bureaucracy, officialdom and red tape. He described the initial 'cesspool conditions' in the shelters, pointing out that the Communists had tried to 'nobble' the newly emerging shelter committees. But he also criticized the authorities for having an 'all-too-ready distrust of [the committees] as "Communist cells"'.[89] For the Communist Party itself, the fight to open the tubes for shelter use was a major boost in its rearguard action against the war and an opportunity for political intervention within the shelter communities. The Trotskyist left, after a debate over whether support for Tube occupation was to support the imperialist war by implication, wisely threw its weight behind the shelterers. Harry Ratner of the tiny Workers International League recalled his attempt to intervene at Hampstead Tube station where he 'dossed down nightly, I participated in the formation of a [shelter] committee [...] Here was I, still a callow youth, with no experience of mass political agitation, entirely on my own and without the support of any organisation, trying to create, single handedly a mass movement of shelterers!'[90]

The media played a crucial role in focusing public attention on the plight of the shelterers despite the Transport Board's initial attempts to downplay the daily occupation of the tubes. The mainstream news media, after the interventions by the left-wing press, played an important part in the creation of a positive image for Tube sheltering, through newsreels, feature articles, personal accounts, documentary and the regular Mass Observation surveys. Contemporary literary representation was only one of the many views of sheltering available and such representation was usually oblique because of the relatively short time-frame involved, especially as many literary magazines ceased to function during the war years. The mainstream news media were therefore in the vanguard of constructing a new public image for the tubes in a way similar

89   P. Ritchie-Calder, 'Shelters', *New Statesman and Nation*, 8 March 1941, pp. 235–36.

90   H. Ratner, *Reluctant Revolutionary: Memoirs of a Trotskyist 1936–1960* (London: Socialist Platform, 1994), p. 35.

to how they had done so in the earliest period of the underground. Journalism had been consistently active in the construction of a positive image of the system at other critical points such as the transition from steam to electric traction, demonstrating how much more suited it was to dealing with sudden developments. Press intervention at such watershed moments in underground history were, however, a reinforcement of official policies but, on this occasion, the media was instrumental in gainsaying official policy and advocating an alternative.

The reason for this reversal was the sheer weight of public opinion coupled with the obvious failings of government shelter policy. A range of newspapers, from the *Daily Worker* to the *Daily Express*, applied pressure with the latter taking up the now popular line that 'The government were caught unaware by the rush of people to find room in the tubes. Now, let the people stay. Why not make a good job of it? Bunks, canteens, sanitation first'.[91] The *Picture Post* continued the attack on government inaction with an article in November 1940 under the banner headline 'A Question for Mr Morrison'.[92] Antony Hern, in *Tribune*, argued that the shelterers were 'the advance guard of London's underworld'[93] shifting the usual cultural meaning of the term 'underworld' to a new political level of urban civil disobedience on a mass scale.

The occupation of the tubes was effectively the end of the Tubist vision. The Tube could no longer be insulated from the social effects of aerial bombardment and Pick's legacy of modernization required urgent modification to meet the needs of wartime. The Tube had to be wrenched from the hands of Ashfield and Pick in order to achieve a reordering of priorities and integration into the national war effort: in effect, the full nationalization of the London Passenger Transport Board that would be institutionalized in the postwar British Transport Commission. During the Blitz, the underground was one of the symbols of Britain's will to continue fighting the war and it therefore became a mythical community of war workers and transport workers who struggled through adversity to keep the capital alive in its role as national heart in the war effort. In underground writing, this was firmly underlined in

---

91 *Daily Express*, 1 October 1940. David Low mocked the government in his 1940 cartoon 'London Sleeps' in which Colonel Blimp portentiously declares: 'Gad, Sir John, Beaverbrook is right. We must show Hitler we have command of the air, the seas, the land and the underground'. He is seated amongst Tube shelterers on the platform of a station dubbed 'Dreamland' (D. Low, *Years of Wrath. A Cartoon History 1932–1945* (London: Victor Gollancz, 1986), p. 138).

92 *Picture Post*, 9 November 1940, vol. 9, pp. 14–15.

93 Hern, 'People of the Tubes', p. 30.

Monica Dickens' novel *The Fancy* in which one of the main characters works in a factory at 'Collis Park'. Sheila first sets eyes on her future lover David on the underground at Earl's Court station where he alights from the train twice a week. She has done 'nine months of this tedious journey [to the factory], she knew all the stations by heart, so when the train stopped at Earl's Court, she allowed a decent interval for him to get up and walk to the door'.[94] On this occasion, however, David stays on the train to 'Collis Park' and goes to her factory. The underground allows them to meet (without sharing any words) at the romantic level of the story but it also plays a key part in keeping wartime production going.

This mythical community came to occupy a central place in the London of the Blitz and the iconography of *London Can Take It* (1940).[95] The Ministry of Information stressed that the Blitz was an attack on 'the people' who occupied the 'Home Front' and endured a common suffering irrespective of class location. The act of resistance to authority represented by the occupation of the Tube could be transformed into an act of symbolic resistance to Hitler whilst independence of national character could be demonstrated by such a powerful act of defiance which would never be possible in the Nazi conformist state. Similarly, a threatening 'foreign voice' booms out of the void in MacNeice's 'Cook's Tour of the London Subways', saying 'You're deep down now but soon you will be deeper … Yes, my good people, your day is over. You are a nation doomed to oblivion'.[96] But MacNeice's shelterers answer Hitler's threats by forging a strong British identity which in turn strengthens the war effort. MacNeice underlined the role of the underground when suggesting that the city itself now made more sense: 'London since the Blitz has become more comprehensible. Because this great dirty, slovenly, sprawling city is a visible and tangible symbol of freedom'.[97]

The underground could also embody the alliance between the wartime state and the people, an alliance made necessary by the demands of war production and organization. The government had clearly failed to prepare for aerial attacks on cities, ruling out the use of the underground, and left-wing critics of the establishment, like Orwell, MacNeice and Henry Moore could be co-opted (albeit temporarily) into the national war effort against Nazism. In a manner that would iron out all the ambiguities of Tube sheltering, they allowed

---

94   Dickens, *The Fancy*, p. 88.
95   *London Can Take It* (1940), GPO Film Unit, for Ministry of Information.
96   MacNeice, 'Cook's Tour', p. 555.
97   L. MacNeice, 'The Way We Live Now', in J. Lehmann (ed.), *The Penguin New Writing 5* (Harmondsworth: Penguin, 1941), pp. 9–14, p. 13.

the recuperative power of propaganda to produce a sanitized icon of popular endurance. Inevitably, the human interest story of the tubes predominated in the mainstream media, constructing a new image of the situation within the parameters of Ministry of Information control and propaganda requirements. Initially taking a critical stance, most of the news media moved rapidly towards stories and pictures of the Tube shelterers as a steadfast national community under siege. Mollie Panter-Downes, for example, describes the scene on underground stations with their 'double rows of men, women, and children—eating, drinking, sleeping, reading papers, and just sitting: all part of the most extraordinary mass picnic the world has ever known'.[98] However, when news media stepped beyond such boundaries they were sharply rebuked with the *Daily Worker* being shut down for its anti-imperialist stance and anti-government polemic. The *Picture Post* was also pressurized over its persistent criticisms of the government's Home Front policy and a Special Branch raid on the Workers International League attempted to stop its production of leaflets printed for distribution in Tube stations.[99]

On the other side of the Atlantic, Hollywood contributed to this imagined Tube with a 1941 film *Confirm or Deny* about the wartime romance of an American news reporter, 'Mitch' Mitchell (Don Ameche) and his British government minder, Jennifer Carson (Joan Bennett). Scenes of shelterers in the Tube were constructed as the two leads are caught up in an air raid but such scenes were carefully edited to maximize the sense of order prevailing amongst the stiff-upper-lipped Londoners. Several stills from the film were reproduced in *Picture Post* under the headline 'Battle of London Fought Again in a Film about US Newsman' and the magazine captioned one of them, 'A Picture for Londoners to Study: The Ace Reporter Shelters in a Tube'.[100] The irony here lies in the fact that the Tube enters Hollywood cinema as part of a story for the first time during the most extreme and unusual set of conditions created by wartime bombardment. The scenes in the Tube station are curiously formalized and unreal so that anyone with personal experience of sheltering could not have found them anything but amusing.[101] The wartime underground in film

---

98   Panter-Downes, *London War Notes*, p. 112.

99   See Ratner, *Reluctant Revolutionary*, for background discussion.

100   *Picture Post*, 7 March 1942, vols. 13–14, October–March 1942, p. 10.

101   The film *Confirm or Deny* was followed by *Seven More Stations*, about the Central line, which premiered in London in 1948. From this point onwards, the Tube began to feature fairly regularly in films with, for example, *Under Night Streets* (1958) and *All That Mighty Heart* (1962). One interesting aspect of *Confirm or Deny* is that the heroine, Joan Bennett, is *protected* by the railway rather than threatened by it. Shelterers also appeared in the British film

could not reflect everyday life because sheltering and bombing were abnormal, but it could mask a sense of dislocation and oddness. This was an imagined, manufactured and mythical place; a subterranean world that paradoxically elevated Tubism to its highest level except that this was Tubism without the Tube trains. Newsreels regularly portrayed the new sheltering communities dovetailing with the everyday needs of the travelling public as though Tube dormitories were a completely normal feature of underground travel. Nevertheless it was an odd experience, the architect Sidney Toy comparing the scenes on platforms to a night out at the theatre: 'when [the train] stopped at a station and the doors were opened from the centre the effect was remarkably like that of a stage when the curtains are raised. Here was a stage, brilliantly lighted, and packed with humanity in all stages of animation'.[102] The writer and diarist Denton Welch captured something of this environment when he noted a journey 'fantastically through the bowels of the earth' during the Blitz. 'People were thronging, laughing, lusting, looking sad. We saw strange old women sleeping in the bunks that lined the wall [...] one bunk was draped in sacking, but I could just see sticking out a delicate child's leg'.[103]

The media put particular stress on the creation of an organic community in the Tube, making it literally a stage for national reconstruction of community in wartime, for example in the pages of the *Picture Post*. Community spirit on the underground was a compound of domestic life and the profoundly feminized world of sheltering accomplished through the medium of the urban working class as the most visible element in the Tube shelters. As it was impossible to deny that the majority of shelterers *were* working class, it was, as *Tribune* and the *Daily Worker* noted, an illegal invasion of state property and a daily occupation of stations that threatened to disrupt the old class-based boundaries of the urban world. Basing her comments on Mass Observation reports from the fairly typical Central line station at Holland Park, Constantine Fitzgibbon, in her postwar account *The Blitz*, confirmed that 'most of the shelterers were working-class people'.[104] Fitzgibbon added that shelterers were for the most part 'from the neighbouring streets'.[105] The Tube, renowned for its reinforcement of social

---

   Gert and Daisy's Weekend (1943), an attempt to reconcile class conflicts within the unifying notion of the Home Front. See C. Brunsdon, *London in Cinema: The Cinematic City Since 1945* (London: British Film Institute, 2007), p. 136.

102   S. Toy, quoted in Fitzgibbon, *The Blitz*, p. 159.

103   D. Welch, *The Journals of Denton Welch* (1952), ed. M. De-la-Noy (Harmondsworth: Penguin, 1987), p. 8.

104   Fitzgibbon, *The Blitz*, p. 161.

105   Fitzgibbon, *The Blitz*, p. 161.

barriers, became a place sheltering forced changes such as those reported by Winifred Bryher in *The Days of Mars* (1946): 'one of the taboos that the Blitz was breaking down was that it was wrong to speak to strangers'.[106] In public underground shelters like the Tube it was much more difficult to maintain the old social proprieties beloved of *Punch* in the Victorian period although the lower middle classes could and did continue to 'keep themselves to themselves'[107] by sheltering in their homes. This change was also noted by the American reporter Ed Murrow who, in his radio broadcasts to the United States during the first 16 months of the war, made great play of the fact that Londoners were becoming 'more human, less reserved and less formal. There's almost a small-town atmosphere about the place. Sometimes strangers speak to you in the bus or subways'.[108]

Phyllis Bottome's novel *London Pride* (1941) pinpoints the class topography of the East and West Ends that still dominated London, with the working-class Mrs Barton who cannot do her 'charring' for 'her Kensington ladies' because 'buses weren't running and the Circle *was* held up'.[109] Bottome notes that the 'only safe shelters were the Tubes [but] they were not handy'[110] for her fictional East End family. However, East End children can invade the West End during the Blitz in order to loot from shops. Bottome used the theme of looting as a means by which the working-class family could recuperate from their experience of war, demonstrating how the bombing 'enobled' the working class. In a less serious vein, the invasion of the city by the working class was signalled in a short story by Margery Sharp in the popular magazine *Lilliput*. 'Night Engagement' (1941) is centred on the sheltering experience with a strong romantic motif when the main character Doris Catchpole announces to her mother that she will 'try the Tube' in her search for 'Mr Right'. Doris goes off 'in her siren-suit with half the sandwiches and a bottle of tea'.[111] Doris does meet 'a nice young fellow'[112] named Harry in the Tube shelter but her mother insists on going with her daughter on their next 'date'. Harry disappears after meeting Doris's mum and, although she is unsuccessful in using the Tube in her quest for a husband, Doris

106 W. Bryher, *The Days of Mars: A Memoir, 1940–1946* (London: Calder & Boyars, 1972), p. 17.

107 Bryher, *The Days of Mars*, p. 17.

108 E. Murrow, *This is London* (1941), ed. E. Davis (New York: Schocken Books, 1989).

109 P. Bottome, *London Pride* (1941; London: Faber & Faber, 1947), p. 66.

110 Bottome, *London Pride*, p. 75.

111 M. Sharp, 'Night Engagement' (1941), in K. Webb (ed.), *Lilliput Goes to War* (London: Hutchinson, 1985), pp. 205–08, p. 205.

112 Sharp, 'Night Engagement', p. 206.

does meet another man who 'works on the Railway'.[113] The story underlines the important role of working-class people in all public sheltering but it also places the focus on working-class women.

Mass Observation discovered that Tube dwellers were, in fact, living in the underground rather than merely sheltering there even as late as 1943—creating a 'new society' in which working-class matriarchy flourished. A Mass Observation investigator picked out the figure of Auntie Mabel to exemplify this phenomenon, a 'small, spry woman of about 45'.[114] Auntie Mabel has become the mother-figure and leader of a station microcommunity in the tubes that parallels the hierarchy of the Tube as a workplace. She has emerged from 'being a nonentity of a London side-street',[115] as the investigator condescendingly puts it, to assume a key role in the war effort. In another Tube station, an investigator found the family atmosphere 'quite remarkable'[116] with much discussion of children and new-born babies. Bernard Kops, who as a child did not find Tube sheltering a positive experience, nevertheless testified to the ways in which families adapted to this new environment. It was, for him, 'a whole network, a whole city under the world'.[117] Shelterer Ros Tankard recalled that whole families turned the Tube 'into a way of life' and how 'you get off the tube and there's a whole bedroom in front of you'.[118] Pamela Frankau recorded what sheltering looked like in 1944 in her novel *The Willow Cabin* (1949). Through her character Caroline, Frankau registers the permanence and solid presence of the shelterers at Tottenham Court Road station: 'people on the platforms, sitting on wire bunks'.[119] Later, Caroline comments on 'the packed shapes on the platforms at night, the bunks all filled, beyond the bunks the people lying on mattresses and quilts'.[120] Caroline is not a Tube shelterer but the Tube seems to represent a way of hiding from 'the tightening and slackening of terror, the inevitable return from the lull to the panic, like a hateful dance that must never stop'.[121] The bombing has unnerved her but she reflects on 'her desire to be each one of these people [in the Tube] to share it and understand'.[122] For

---

113 Sharp, 'Night Engagement', p. 206.
114 A. Calder & D. Sheridan (eds.), *Speak for Yourself: A Mass Observation Anthology, 1937–1949* (London: Jonathan Cape, 1984), p. 103.
115 Calder & Sheridan, *Speak for Yourself*, p. 103.
116 Calder & Sheridan, *Speak for Yourself*, p. 104.
117 B. Kops, *The World is a Wedding* (1963; London: Mayflower, 1970), p. 69.
118 Welsh, *Talk About a Liberty*, unpublished transcripts.
119 P. Frankau, *The Willow Cabin* (1949; London: Pan, 1954), p. 215.
120 Frankau, *The Willow Cabin*, p. 216.
121 Frankau, *The Willow Cabin*, p. 216.
122 Frankau, *The Willow Cabin*, p. 216.

Frankau's character, the Tube symbolizes the means of achieving a collective shield against the terror of war even if she herself cannot participate in it. Frankau's novel illustrates the way that the highly visible collective nature of Tube sheltering often made a dramatic impact on outside observers.

David Matless has outlined the impact of the Blitz on the sense of national community and the ways in which London 'as an organic whole rises out of the bombsites'.[123] During the Blitz, he argues, a 'metropolis of suburban community was created',[124] a metropolis that writers like Graham Greene and Elizabeth Bowen outlined in fiction. Greene, in *The Ministry of Fear*, noted that 'London was no longer one great city: it was a collection of small towns',[125] while Bowen described London as a 'city of villages—almost village communes',[126] with the clear political implication of a kind of autonomous control by citizens. There can be no doubt that many local areas of the capital—both in the centre and on the periphery—developed a sense of community, purpose and comradeship that sustained life during the months of the Blitz. In addition, a sense of local autonomy was a powerful corrective to the growth of centralized state control that came with the war, giving local residents and workers a genuine role in the running of their own lives. For anti-fascist writers like Greene and Bowen, a key element in the war was the development of compact, committed and, above all, organic communities with their own voice. The underground city identified by Bernard Kops was one of these 'suburban communities'. It embodied all the features of Matless's metropolis with myriad small communities based on stations; loose federations linking these stations together like the interstation conference of Tube shelterers, a sharp sense of fair-mindedness and grass-roots democracy and a collective identity based on the conditions faced by all Tube shelterers. All these elements could be found in the slogan coined by the *Swiss Cottager* bulletin: 'Sleepers of the Underworld Unite!'[127]

The 'underworld' defiantly proclaimed by the *Swiss Cottager* bulletin is a graphic reminder that sheltering communities were aware of their place in history as well as its Dantean associations. Their historical significance was certainly clear to Mollie Panter-Downes who proclaimed, in one of her letters to the *New Yorker*, that 'If history is being torn up by the roots in London, history is also being made. The new race of tube dwellers is slipping a fresh page into the record; nothing has ever been seen like the concourse of humanity that

---

123 D. Matless, *Landscape and Englishness* (London: Reaktion Books, 1998), p. 187.
124 Matless, *Landscape and Englishness*, p. 187.
125 Greene, *Ministry of Fear*, p. 73.
126 E. Bowen, 'London, 1941', in *The Mulberry Tree*, pp. 21–25, pp. 23–24.
127 Quoted in Gregg, *Shelter of the Tubes*, p. 69.

camps underground every night'.[128] Tube shelter bulletins such as the *Swiss Cottager*, *The Subway Companion*, *The Holborn Shelter News* and *The Station Search-light* were organs of communication and morale-building but they also represented an entirely new public face for the underground. The 'editors' of such bulletins gave a new dimension to writing by giving the underground its own public voice and profile for the first time since the building of the Metropolitan Railway. A mixture of reports, stories, instructions, health articles and general observations, the bulletins were also the vehicle for sharp polemic against the authorities as shown in an 'editorial' from the *Swiss Cottager* No. 4. It outlined the 'battle against apathy, indifference amounting almost to callousness, neglect for elementary human decencies, against red-tape, authority and officialdom'.[129] *The Subway Companion*, whilst keen to allay fears that it was 'a fanatical revolutionary sheet',[130] was nevertheless more than willing to broadcast its grievances to the widest possible audience; in other words, to create a public identity for the shelterers. The shelter committees and the bulletins they produced represented the fullest development of the *public* nature of public transport, an important lesson for those who advocated postwar nationalization of the public transport system. The political importance of the shelterers' organizations was so great because they were the Chartists of the Tube, with a set of demands that amounted to social control of the underground. As such they were also the inheritors of the many debates around London's public transport which had informed underground writing since Gissing. The 'underworld' of the *Swiss Cottager* was also highly public in other ways. A 1940 article on 'Shelter Life' in *Picture Post* highlighted the interior of a typical shelter as the 'strangest sight in London [...] Here all one's life is public. Privacy, so cherished by Britons, is gone [...] Here nothing is intimate. One talks, eats, sleeps, lives with a hundred, a thousand others'.[131] The underground exhibited its shelter dwellers to the non-sheltering travelling public in a way that other public shelters did not, a fact which shocked Mass Observer Naomi Mitchison when she visited London in 1941 and found people 'sleeping on the bunks, and some had put coats across the lower ones to screen the light'.[132] For other commentators, Tube trains showed 'sights we dared not see, for we were pleasure bound

---

128 Panter-Downes, *London War Notes*, p. 112.
129 Quoted in Gregg, *Shelter of the Tubes*, p. 66.
130 Quoted in Gregg, *Shelter of the Tubes*, p. 66.
131 *Picture Post*, vol. 9, no. 4, 26 October 1940, p. 9.
132 Mitchison, *Among You Taking Notes*, p. 121.

[...] through humanity spurned'.[133] The lower-middle-class office-worker Mr Bunting, in Robert Greenwood's novel *Mr Bunting at War* (1941), continues to travel into the capital from the suburbs by train during the Blitz. He feels sympathy for the 'Londoners who night after night endured the terror [...] they had to sleep in shelters and dug-outs, or gregariously in tubes'.[134] It is interesting that Mr Bunting's comment precisely echoes that of Hugh Carnaby in Gissing's *The Whirlpool* except of course that this modern vortex is a very real one: the Blitz.

This elision of private and public worlds threw into sharp relief the normal role of the underground as a form of transit and its unprecedented new function as dormitory. The tension between male and female roles in the public sphere that had previously been explored was now lost in the nightly mixing of male and female bodies on platforms, exits, passageways and escalators. Bill Brandt's caption for his photograph of Liverpool Street Tube shelter published in *Lilliput* magazine described how 'the long alley of intermingled bodies, with the hot, smelly air and continual murmur of snores, came nearest to my pre-war idea of what an air-raid shelter would be like'.[135] In his poem 'Tube Shelter Leicester Square, 1941' (1949) Christopher Hassall noted people 'Sadly arrayed like junk for sale, defeated' and:

> Obliged to accept an unwonted privilege
> We see other men's wives as their husbands see them,
> Touzled with sleep.[136]

And the poet and broadcaster M. J. Tambimuttu described the:

> Knees, necks, a litter of loose arms,
> Awaiting to-morrow in yesterday's clothes, privacy's
> Last surrender[137]

Antonia Lant argues that these public representations of women in shelters attempted to reinforce traditional gender roles when, for instance, *Picture Post* (1940) shows women engaged in feminine activities such as applying lipstick. Lant concludes that 'Wartime ideology, the discourse that explains

---

133 F. Smewin, 'Blitz Dinner', in K. Rhys (ed.), *More Poems from the Forces* (London: Routledge, 1943), p. 265.

134 R. Greenwood, *Mr Bunting at War* (London: Dent, 1941), p. 203.

135 B. Brandt, in Webb, *Lilliput Goes to War*, caption to photograph, p. 210.

136 Hassall, 'Tube Shelter Leicester Square', p. 23.

137 M. J. Tambimuttu, radio talk 'The Man in the Street', in *Talking to India* (1943), quoted in Sinclair, *War Like a Wasp*, p. 54.

mobilization, recruitment, fighting, and killing, runs up against the peacetime ideology of separate spheres for men and women'.[138] Tube sheltering, above all, threatened to erode these spheres as the underground was still largely a male environment in 1939, but now women of all social classes were using it for shelter in a seemingly indiscriminate way. Women predominate in most of the posed photographs of Tube sheltering, a clear indication of the massive gender changeover from male to female occupancy that occurred every day of the Blitz following the male-dominated evening rush-hour period. Equally, photographs showing passengers alighting from or entering trains are invariably male, supporting Lant's contention that wartime ideology tried to stabilize traditional gender images. In addition, the authorities attempted to dissuade 'able-bodied men from using Tube stations as air-raid shelters, except in cases of urgent necessity'[139] and some photographs may have been reproduced with this in mind. In reality, this appears to have had little effect although the slogan 'Be a Man and Leave it to Them'[140] was recorded by Mass Observation. Pamela Frankau used the obviously real scene of a woman ticket collector in the Tube 'screaming angrily at a white-faced boy, be a man and get up them stairs'[141] in her novel *The Willow Cabin*.

The balance of gender forces on the Tube clearly also changed with women being a significant part of the workforce in a wide range of duties. Whilst some of these were traditional—supplying food and drink to shelterers—women played a key role as Tube shelter wardens as recorded by Betty Penn-Bull in a wartime letter. She described her duties as 'a Shelter-Warden on the underground station for six nights a week from either 7 p.m. or 8 p.m. alternate nights until 6.30 a.m. the following morning.'[142] Getting to work was obviously important for the women who performed an essential service in London's front-line hospitals. Eileen Hands worked at St George's Hospital and recalled her daily journey from South Ealing straight to Hyde Park Corner and up the stairs. All blacked out, of course. You were staggering about in the pitch dark at night'.[143]

Such changes brought about a subtle shift in the means by which the Tube was

---

138 A. Lant, *Blackout: Reinventing Women for Wartime British Cinema* (Princeton: Princeton University Press, 1991), p. 17.

139 Gregg, *Shelter of the Tubes*, p. 25.

140 Gregg, *Shelter of the Tubes*, p. 25.

141 Frankau, *The Willow Cabin*, p. 216.

142 B. Penn-Bull, *War Letters* (Windsor: Penn-Bull, 1991), p. 94.

143 Trades Union Congress Library Collections, *The Workers' War: Home Front Recalled* (London: Trades Union Congress, 2006; www.unionhistory.info/workerswar/).

portrayed in fiction during the Blitz. The private dialogues on station platforms that had been such an important feature of underground scenes in the novels of Gissing and others could no longer be sustained in the fiction of the 1940s when space on station platforms was so often at a premium. It is difficult to imagine the conversations of Victorian characters being repeated in the stations of the Blitz although two cartoon penguins managed it in the traditional setting of a railway carriage in a 1939 edition of *Penguin Short Stories*.[144] The fictional role of the private sphere and interior monologue on the Tube for both male and female characters as found in the work of Virginia Woolf in the 1930s is clearly rendered much more difficult by air raids and sheltering. Even on board Tube trains and buses, 'careless talk' was discouraged by the authorities as shown in the famous 1940 cartoon by Fougasse with Hitler and Goering seated attentively behind two female passengers who are enjoined to remember that 'You never know *who's* listening!'[145] Shelter wardens were alert to the dangers of defeatist talk and the threat of fifth columnism and were known to deal harshly with potential 'troublemakers' on their stations. T. S. Eliot's passengers in his 1940 poem 'East Coker' might likewise be even less talkative when their Tube train 'stops too long between stations'.[146] This suggests less existential angst than the consciousness that Tube journeys were subject to disruption and, in a number of cases such as the direct hit at Balham Tube station on the Northern line, could even be fatal. The Tube's former social role had been modified by sheltering and the air raids, being less about the individual private sphere and more concerned with the need for public and collective security. As Antonia Lant concludes in her discussion of wartime film-making, the 'war demanded attention to communal rather than individual matters'.[147]

The sheer scale of Tube sheltering helped to produce both new and recycled images. Within four years the volume of often contradictory or conflicting images of the Tube in writing surpassed any previous period. Much of this was found in the mass media as it attempted to gloss over the conditions on the underground for propaganda purposes with, for example, a company called Evans Immunological Products utilizing an image of Tube shelterers in order

---

144 See A. Steele (ed.), *Selected Modern Short Stories I* (1937; Harmondsworth: Penguin, 1939), end pages.

145 Fougasse (Cyril Kenneth Bird), 'Careless Talk Costs Lives' (1940), for Ministry of Information.

146 T. S. Eliot, 'East Coker' (1940), in *Four Quartets* (1944; London: Faber & Faber, 1970), pp. 23–32, p. 28.

147 Lant, *Blackout*, p. 146.

to advertise its syringes in the fight against 'the fifth column of infection'.[148] This could be so successful that the media was able to give accurate shape to the Tube shelters *in advance of* personal observation. This was noted by Mass Observer Jack Atkins: 'All new experiences today seem to be spoiled by *Picture Post* [the Tube shelters] were exactly like what he had imagined and seen pictures of'.[149] This merely earned the scorn of critics like George Orwell who reflected on the huge gap between the image as presented by the media and their own personal experience of the system. Tube shelters were 'taken in hand' by the authorities and supplied with improved resources and facilities but this did not alter the incredibly cramped and difficult conditions faced by the shelterers themselves. For Orwell, it seems likely that this credibility gap helped to promote a profound scepticism about 'newspaper-talk' which he would later dub 'Newspeak' in *Nineteen Eighty-Four* (1948). Furthermore, the state moved directly to influence public opinion and morale with the Ministry of Information commissioning official war artists such as Moore, Kapp, Topolski and Ardizzone in order to convey the 'right' message about Tube sheltering to a wider national audience. The *New Statesman and Nation* welcomed the decision to send six exhibitions of shelter drawings on a tour in 1941 but was quick to remind its readers that the original condition of the tubes before the drawings were completed was 'an untidy confusion of empty tins and bits of orange peel'.[150] And other observers, like the engineering worker Eddie Menday, recalled that 'We'd see [shelterers] all getting their beds down and the trains would come through. It was always a bit of a worry'.[151] Di Grover similarly did not enjoy the sheltering experience: 'We took blankets and we went down to Stockwell tube. It was terrible […] It was claustrophobic'.[152]

---

148   F. A. Mercer (ed.), *Modern Publicity in War* (London: The Studio Pubs., 1941), p. 68.
149   A. Calder, *The Myth of the Blitz* (1991; London: Pimlico, 1992), p. 143.
150   *New Statesman and Nation*, 1 March 1941, p. 207.
151   TUC Library Collections, *The Workers' War*.
152   TUC Library Collections, *The Workers' War*.

THE UTOPIAN UNDERWORLD:
HENRY MOORE AND AFTER

enry Moore's drawings and sketches were to become the most famous images of the Tube shelterers, eclipsing all other representations of the period. His *Shelter Sketchbooks* include many sequences on the Tube, for example 'Tube Shelter Perspective' (1940–41), 'Grey Tube Shelter' (1940) and 'Shelterers in the Tube' (1941).[153] Moore's images have been subjected to considerable critical comment that has focused on the contradictory nature of his figures. They stand out from all exterior detail in a way unique to shelter drawings and it is sometimes difficult to tell that it is the Tube rather than another type of public shelter. The figures are rooted, sedentary and often seem to be dead; they sit or sleep on platforms with distant tunnel openings in the background or the Tube roundel high on the wall behind them glowing like the sun in some instances. They are extremely stylized figures in a complex interplay with a bare environment. As Moore commented: 'I had never seen so many rows of reclining figures and even the holes out of which the trains were coming seemed to me like the holes in my sculpture'.[154] As one of a number of official war artists, he reflected on the private world that was now public, noting that he could not do sketches of the shelterers in the stations as this seemed an invasion of their privacy. Moore observed 'Children fast asleep, with trains roaring past only a couple of yards away [...] cut off from what was happening above'.[155] A photograph showing Moore busily sketching shelterers in Holborn Tube station was actually posed, with Moore explaining that he did the sketches at home after observing the sleeping shelterers:

> I never made any sketches in the Underground [...] Instead of drawing, I would wander casually past a group of people [...] I went up to London for two days each week, spending the nights in the Underground [...] Then I would go back to Much Hadham and spend two days making sketches.[156]

And he was shown again in this role in Holborn Tube station in September 1943 as part of the filmed reconstruction of his work in *Out of Chaos*, a documentary

---

153 H. Moore, 'Tube Shelter perspective' (1940–41), Henry Moore Foundation; 'Grey Tube Shelter' (1940), Tate, London; 'Shelterers in the Tube' (1941), Tate, London.

154 H. Moore, quoted in J. Andrews, *London's War. The Shelter Drawings of Henry Moore* (2002; Aldershot: Lund Humphries, 2005), p. 36.

155 Quoted in Sinclair, *War Like a Wasp*, p. 154.

156 H. Moore, quoted in F. Carey, *Henry Moore: A Shelter Sketchbook* (London: British Museum Publications, 1988), pp. 9–12.

about war artists by Jill Craigie. Moore's sketches represent the many contradictory elements in the development of this new sheltering community and
demonstrate the ways in which this instant construction of the wartime Tube
was, in many ways, a reconstruction which drew on many stored images and
ideas of the past. The sedentary figures reflect the static nature of the shelterers
counterposed to the (offstage) movement of trains and passengers; the shelterers
are becalmed and no longer in the daily rush of Tube travel. Moore's figures
thus embody one of the paradoxes of the Tube during the war in its dual role
as unifier of the metropolis through transport efficiency and as shelter for some
of the capital's population. His portrayal of the figures in 'Devastated Buildings
and Underground Platform Scene' (1940–41) and 'Wrecked Omnibus and
Figures in Underground Shelter' (1940–41)[157] is a remarkable statement of
his wartime work as the pieces unify Tube shelterers (from the world above)
with the subterranean transport system. Both drawings place his figures below
ground whilst above them the streets are torn apart by bombing.

The sketches bring together many of the constructed images of the underground. The historical background to these images provided a link between
the fear of aerial vulnerability induced by the First World War and the idea of
subterranean Tube sheltering. Vera Brittain made the connection explicit in
her autobiographical account *England's Hour* (1941).[158] Several First World War
poets, for example Edmund Blunden and Alfred Rosenberg, described soldiers
as mummified figures, an image picked up by Louis MacNeice in his 'Cook's
Tour of the London Subways' in which Tube shelterers are 'like a thousand
mummies'.[159] Moore's figures draw on these images of trenches and tunnels of
the First World War, particularly in their mummy-like shape and drapery. This
is, of course, a deeply ambiguous image: the soldiers of the Western Front were
'mummies' because they were dead rather than sleeping. However, the concept
of an underworld that was so familiar in the iconography of the Tube system
suggests that Moore's visual world could accommodate the contradictory
impulses of death and life in his depiction of the shelterers. The underground
could be seen as a kind of purgatory, as in T. S. Eliot's *Four Quartets* (1944). The
figures in Moore's sketches could also be viewed as the trapped 'undead' in a
labyrinthine underworld and this is certainly how some commentators have
reacted to his images. On the other hand, the figures may represent a sense of

157 H. Moore, 'Devastated Buildings and Underground Platform Scene' (1940–41), British
     Museum; 'Wrecked Omnibus and Figures in Underground Shelter' (1940–41), British
     Museum.
158 See Brittain, *England's Hour*, chapter 11 for details.
159 MacNeice, 'Cook's Tour', p. 554.

strength, solidarity and endurance in adverse conditions, an interpretation that was certainly favoured by Moore's official sponsors. MacNeice's 'Cook's Tour' expresses similar sentiments uttered on the underground with its defence of 'Liberty, Equality, Fraternity—someone or other said they are empty words. Empty words—unless you fill them'.[160] The shelterers in MacNeice's play have banished Hitler in a song:

> Go away you bad dreams
> Go away Berchtesgaden
> Go away you bad dreams
> Worry someone else.[161]

In other words, MacNeice's shelterers, like Moore's sleeping figures, are not condemned to a living death but are representatives of a human community that is rooted in a certain form of life and society. A form of life that can undergo tremendous shocks but is capable of adaptation by using the most humdrum and mundane defensive system: the London tubes.

It is hardly surprising that Moore's shelter drawings contain a number of contradictory elements, as much wartime writing uneasily combines striking opposites. Like the work of Topolski in another major visual record of the tubes, Moore's work is not a documentary of life in the underground but a composition rooted in the underworld that had been repeatedly constructed in underground writing. In *Picture Post* (1941), Topolski was praised as a 'portrayer of the London scene' and compared with Doré, Hogarth and Daumier in conveying the reality of a 'strange and terrible period'.[162] Wartime Tube illustrators like Topolski, Edward Ardizzone and Milein Cosman were in the unique position of describing real scenes of the impact of war on urban populations rather than imagining a projected future world. Such scenes combined gritty detail with a social message about the survival of certain values. Their work is informed by a moral fable about endurance and solidarity in a harsh environment and therefore embodies some of the optimism of those writers who had focused on the positive aspects of public transport in the metropolis.

According to Barnett,[163] Moore's images of passive suffering and endurance

160 MacNeice, 'Cook's Tour', p. 555.
161 MacNeice, 'Cook's Tour', p. 555.
162 *Picture Post*, 1941, vol. 9, October–December 1940, p. 32.
163 A. Barnett, 'The Shape of Labour', *Art Monthly*, October 1986, pp. 4–8. See also A. Lewis, 'Henry's Moore's "Shelter Drawings": Memory & Myth', in P. Kirkham & D. Thoms (eds.), *War Culture: Social Change and Changing Experience in World War Two Britain* (London: Lawrence & Wishart, 1995), pp. 113–27.

also reflect an important strand in the more recent past, that of the ideology of interwar socialism. Moore described the inhabitants of his Liverpool Street 'Tube Shelter Perspective' as having 'been sleeping and suffering for hundreds of years'[164] thus establishing a link with the historical tradition of the left that united many of the commentators on the crisis brought about by war. Louis MacNeice, who had returned from the United States on the eve of the Blitz, offered an important perspective on the ways in which the war had clarified this tradition and seemed to present a serious vision for the future. In his 'Reflections from the Dome of St Paul's, June 1941', MacNeice argued that 'Most individuals in and after an air-raid are not less individual, but, if anything, more individual than they were in peace-time [...] it concentrates, rather than disperses, peoples' essential personality'.[165] In this passage, MacNeice rejects the idea that the external dangers of the Blitz induce a kind of social conformity but equally embraces the view that the security of the shelter offered by the tubes nourishes individuality. The experience of Tube sheltering bore out MacNeice's optimism, a view shared by others like George Orwell, Julian Symons and Stephen Spender. For these writers, the experience of war was forging a new consciousness of the kind that Orwell had witnessed in republican Barcelona during the Spanish Civil War. The creeping materialism that Orwell had lambasted in the 1930s was being replaced by a shared collective endeavour that would translate into the building of a genuine socialist society in Britain. MacNeice's 'Cook's Tour' is the clearest example of the practical egalitarianism that writers like Julian Symons and Stephen Spender felt was emerging in wartime London. Symons recalled the sense of change—the capital was 'in many ways an ideal city [...] The sense of two "real" worlds, openly repressive and equalitarian, struggling with each other, was exhilarating'.[166] MacNeice's play builds around these themes and takes its main character, Mrs Van Winkle Brown, on a tour of the underground after she has woken from a ten-year-long sleep in 1941. In an echo of MacNeice's 1939 poem 'Autumn Journal', she is guided into the underground by a Mr Cook who takes her 'down the moving stairs, the moving stairs, the moving stairs'.[167] They meet a chorus of shelterers who explain the new world of the Tube communities with its sense of endurance, new-found optimism and social solidarity. In the words of the Irish woman: 'it's seventeen years I am living in

---

164 H. Moore, quoted in Webb, *Lilliput Goes to War*, p. 211.
165 L. MacNeice, 'Reflections from the Dome of St Paul's, June 1941', in *Selected Prose of Louis MacNeice*, ed. A. Heuser, (Oxford: Clarendon, 1990), pp. 131–36, p. 135.
166 J. Symons, *Notes from Another Country* (London: London Magazine Editions, 1972), p. 92.
167 MacNeice, 'Cook's Tour', p. 554.

London itself, but I never seen the like of this before [...] People be laying in heaps away down under the earth [...] and never a body complaining'.[168]

Sheltering seemed to offer an important example of the new spirit that would be required to 'win the peace' and reconstruct Britain after the war. Orwell had suggested that England was a family with the wrong people in charge[169] and, in March 1941, he went on to say that 'what amounted to a revolutionary situation existed in England, though there was no one to take advantage of it'.[170] As late as January 1942, in a radio talk, Orwell was still convinced that the 'mere necessity of war' was 'bringing about in the English people a more creative attitude'. He continued: 'The people who were penned up in the Tube shelters for hours had nothing to do, and there were no ready-made amusements available. They had to amuse themselves, so they improvised amateur concerts which were sometimes surprisingly good and successful'.[171] Similarly, Stephen Spender recalled in his autobiographical *World Within World* (1966) a: 'classic example of something that the writers of the Left had spent so much time discussing during the 1930s: proletarian art, folk art even'.[172]

None of these writers were orthodox communists and MacNeice's poem 'The Kingdom' (1943) most clearly represents a particular strand of independent libertarian socialism that seemed the only alterative to the Stalinism of the Communist Party. 'The Kingdom' opens with the description of an underground world that shares a generalized scene found in Moore's sketches:

> Under the surface of flux and fear there is an underground movement,
> Under the crust of bureaucracy, quiet behind the posters,
> Unconscious but palpably there—the Kingdom of individuals.[173]

Here, MacNeice places together many of the themes of the wartime tubes that he had enunciated in 'Cook's Tour'. From within the sheltering community comes a seismic tremor that erodes the control of the authorities and threatens

---

168 MacNeice, 'Cook's Tour', p. 554.

169 G. Orwell, 'The Lion and the Unicorn' (1941), in *Collected Essays*, vol. 2, pp. 74–134, p. 88.

170 G. Orwell, 'London Letter' (1941), in *Collected Essays*, vol. 2, pp. 67–74, p. 67.

171 G. Orwell, 'Money & Guns', BBC Radio talk, 20 January 1942, in *Orwell: The War Broadcasts*, ed W. J. West (London: Duckworth/BBC, 1985), pp. 71–73, p. 73.

172 S. Spender, *World Within World: The Autobiography of Stephen Spender* (Berkeley: University of California Press, 1966), p. 277.

173 L. MacNeice, 'The Kingdom' (1943), in *Collected Poems of Louis MacNeice*, ed. E. R. Dodds (London: Faber & Faber, 1966), pp. 248–54, p. 248. MacNeice returned to the theme of the underground in his 1969 radio play *Persons from Porlock* (London: BBC, 1969), in which he links the Tube with Henry Moore.

the gross materialism that emerges from the advertising posters on platforms. Unlike 'Cook's Tour', MacNeice's poem is a more subversive summary of his beliefs and he is focusing on individuality rather than the faceless mummy-like figures of Moore. He goes on to talk about a 'different Order'[174] which inheres in the people of a London with its 'blistered cupola [...] moored balloons and the feathery tufts of searchlights'.[175] 'The Kingdom' is an extraordinarily imaginative statement of the hopes that emerged during wartime and which were anchored in an environment which offered security and a sense of identity to thousands of Londoners during the Blitz. As Edna Longley notes, 'The ideal of "The Kingdom of individuals" remains an ideal, or at best "an underground movement" [...] it reflects the communal experience of war in putting more flesh on the Utopian theme of Autumn Journal'.[176] But the poem puts 'flesh' onto ideas through the very real social processes that MacNeice observed during the sheltering period. In MacNeice's hands, the underground system fulfils the needs of Londoners as a place of security but also ushers in a social utopia hammered into existence by real individuals rather than conservative modernists like Pick, liberal modernizers like Wells or Communist Party writers like John Sommerfield.

Such optimistic visions of the underground were not convincing, however, for those writers who drew on the imagery and symbolism of hell in order to describe the experience of the Blitz. Just as the development of sheltering unleashed an avalanche of visual and printed commentary which was linked with an almost utopian social and political agenda, it also triggered apocalyptic writing. Valentine Ackland's poem 'War in Progress: A Running Commentary, Spring 1941' attacks the war because it sacrifices human beings in a pointless power struggle. The shelterers in the Tube are 'Drain-deep below the slums' where:

> another birth
> Sets angels singing—the other noise you hear
> May be the Warning, may be the All Clear.
> The shelterers are trapped in an underworld that will be their tomb:
> Comfort ye My people! These reflections
> Should help them politely who must die.[177]

---

174 MacNeice, 'The Kingdom', p. 250.
175 MacNeice, 'The Kingdom', p. 254.
176 E. Longley, *Louis MacNeice: A Critical Study* (London: Faber & Faber, 1988), p. 91.
177 V. Ackland, quoted in W. Mulford, *This Narrow Place, Sylvia Townsend Warner and Valentine Ackland: Life, Letters and Politics, 1930–1951* (London: Pandora, 1988), p. 210.

Thus the images represent the Tube shelterers as the helpless victims of capitalist warmongering now trapped in an underworld from which they would never emerge. In a similar vein, Stephen Spender's poem 'Abyss' (1945) reflected during 'the icy night' on our:

> Sulphurous nether fate, I saw
> The dead of all time floating on one calm tide[178]

Again, John Heath-Stubbs, in his poem 'Wounded Thammuz' (1942) described how

> All the year's gold and silver is gone underground
> Into your cold dark caves, you fortunate Dead.[179]

Louis MacNeice had been drawn to this more negative view in the 1930s when he wrote a number of poems which seemed to refer to a kind of purgatory or limbo in the Dantean sense used by Spender and others. In 'Autumn Journal', for example, MacNeice had described the Tube as drawing people down into a whirlpool of the psyche, although this pessimism is tempered by a sense of renewal:

> And so to London and down the ever-moving stairs
> Where a warm wind blows the bodies of men together
> And blows apart their complexes and cares.[180]

And in 'Letter to Graham and Anna' (1936) he had suggested that:

> we must keep moving to keep pace
> or else drop into Limbo, the dead space.[181]

In 'Christmas Shopping' (1936–38) MacNeice used the image of the wind blowing again:

> though the tubes of London
> The dead winds blow the crowds like beasts in flight from
> Fire in the forest[182]

---

178   Spender, 'Abyss' (1945), in *Citizens in War*, pp. 53–54, p. 53.
179   J. Heath-Stubbs, 'Wounded Thammuz' (1942), in *Collected Poems*, pp. 614–28, p. 615.
180   L. MacNeice, 'Autumn Journal' (1939), in *Collected Poems*, pp. 101–53, p. 103.
181   L. MacNeice, 'Letter to Graham and Anna' (1936), in *Collected Poems*, pp. 61–64, p. 63.
182   L. MacNeice, 'Christmas Shopping' (1936–38), in *Collected Poems*, p. 96.

but, unlike Eliot, he felt sympathy for the crowds who use it. MacNeice returned to these themes in a more pessimistic note towards the end of the war when, in the poem 'Hiatus' (c.1944–47), he notes that 'the sleepers in the Tube' are 'Wrapped in old quilts, no wonder they wake stiff'. The war itself now seems to have been a hiatus: 'years that did not count' and the shelterers have been brought from the past 'a long way to prove that civilisation is vain'.[183] Finally, in 'The Drunkard' (c.1944–47), for the drinker on the Tube:

> His last train home is Purgatory in reverse,
> A spiral back into time and down towards Hell
> Clutching a quizzical strap where wraiths of faces
> Contract, expand, revolve, impinge, disperse
> On a sickly wind which drives all wraiths pell-mell
> Through tunnels to their appointed, separate places.[184]

These extracts suggest a disintegration of the vision that MacNeice had constructed in the first years of the war. The return to a fragmented series of images of the Tube—a 'quizzical strap', a 'sickly wind', the 'wraiths pell-mell' flight through tunnels—seems to signal the victory of the surreal over the previously unified world of MacNeice's 'Cook's Tour'.

For Charles Williams, in his novel *All Hallow's Eve* (1945), the underground begins as a river of the dead, a place for all those killed in the city by the bombing. His character, Lester Furnival, wonders if the underground contains the dead: 'perhaps there the people, the dead people, of this empty City were; perhaps that was where the whole population had been lying, waiting for her too, the entrance waiting and all below the entrance'.[185] Tube station entrances are concealed by 'curtains of brick'[186] as if screening off a tomb or forbidden world in a horrifying inversion of the Tubist concept of access to Tube stations. But when Lester returns to the Tube later in the novel it is to discover a different, if more prosaic reality of wartime London: 'It was not the dead, as she had thought, it was the living who dwelled in those tunnels of earth—deep

---

183 L. MacNeice, 'Hiatus' (c.1944–47), in *Collected Poems*, p. 218.

184 L. MacNeice, 'The Drunkard' (c.1944–47), in *Collected Poems*, pp. 235–36, p. 235. MacNeice had felt this sense of despair in the 1930s when he published the poem 'Eclogue from Iceland' (1936), in which he wrote: 'Where any day now may see the Gadarene swine / Rush down the gullets of the London tubes / When the enemy, x or y, let loose their gas' (*Collected Poems*, pp. 40–47, p. 47). It can hardly be a coincidence that L. Black's novel *The Poison War*, published only three years earlier, had contained a similar prose passage.

185 Williams, *All Hallows' Eve*, pp. 17–18.

186 Williams, *All Hallows' Eve*, p. 15.

and O deep beyond any railways, in the tubes they themselves, thrusting and pushing, hollowed out for their shelter'.[187] In other words, the living have colonized the Tube, driving out the dead who have traditionally inhabited the underworld, bringing in their place the people of the 'città dolente [...] smooth or hairy, tusked or clawed, malicious or lustful, creeping and clambering up from the lower depths'.[188] Lester, who is herself one of the dead, is excluded from the living modern world, a shock to the assumed peacetime life signified by the daily journey to work.

Williams' novel couples Victorian notions of apocalypse brought by national crisis with Wellsian images of evolutionary reversion. He was not alone in reviving such constructions of London's fate in wartime. In some cases this was the result of the kind of class prejudice that Arnold Bennett had observed in the First World War. Tube sheltering could clearly be associated with a collapse of moral values and standards in a kind of post-Victorian 'nether' world. It was also perceived as an invasion of public space, thrusting the private and domestic world into an environment designed purely for transit purposes. One commentator believed that 'of the whole war [Tube sheltering] was the most *demoralising* and *depressing* sight I ever saw [...] I mean, one reads and knows about refugees from other countries, the sort that comes up against it, but you never expected to see your own people doing that' (italics in original).[189] The troglodyte existence of the shelterers also left a deep impression on Vera Brittain, who was typical of many commentators when she observed the 'mothers and children queuing [at Regent's Park station] with cushions and mattresses for their nightly occupation of the Tube'. Brittain went on to suggest that 'London's poorer population [...] will spend its whole life in the Underground'.[190] This pessimistic conclusion was tempered by her understanding that the Tube shelterers were the most obvious victims of the long decades of insecurity that had begun with the First World War. They were the victims of a failure to remedy an international economic and political system that was fundamentally flawed.

A Mass Observation report, *The Tube Dwellers* (1943), found that the communal atmosphere of the mainly working-class community was 'something of a new tradition in London's Underground'[191] because it had led to less constrained personal behaviour. The West End travellers in Fred Smewin's poem 'Blitz Dinner' (1943) feel the 'stench and heat and aching lights' of the Tube and

---

187   Williams, *All Hallows' Eve*, p. 83.
188   Williams, *All Hallows' Eve*, p. 17.
189   Quoted in Fitzgibbon, *The Blitz*, pp. 159–60.
190   Brittain, *England's Hour*, p. 190.
191   Quoted in Calder & Sheridan, *Speak for Yourself*, p. 104.

return home 'silent and ashamed'.[192] Orwell recorded 'disgusting scenes in the Tube stations at night, sordid piles of bedding cluttering up the passage-ways'.[193] Class prejudice was as clearly exhibited by some passengers as it was perceived by shelterers themselves: 'In the evenings you'd get ladies and gentlemen going home after the theatre and night-club people. And you felt they were sneering at you, as much to say, "look at them"'.[194] Such comments indicate that there were social and moral pressures on the shelterers to conform to norms that were class based, pressures from both passengers and the authorities. The tubes, after all, were still largely the domain of the middle-class commuter and there was clearly some resentment of the intrusion of the shelterers. Sidney Toy found the Tube shelters a cosmopolitan environment, describing Oval station in 1940: 'the platform was crowded with people from end to end about five feet deep, only a narrow pathway at the edge of the platform, two feet wide, being reserved for circulation. Here were people of every conceivable character, appearance and age—thousands of them'.[195] The use of the word cosmopolitan to describe the Tube shelterers could easily shade into a casual though mild form of anti-Semitism. Orwell, for example, recorded his observations of crowds sheltering in Chancery Lane, Oxford Circus and Baker Street stations as '*Not* all Jews, but I think a higher proportion of Jews than one would normally see in a crowd of this size. What is bad about Jews is that they are not only conspicuous, but go out of their way to make themselves so' (italic in original).[196] Anti-Semitism was one response to sheltering—blaming Jews for the 1943 Bethnal Green station disaster in the same way that 'aliens' had been targeted over the deaths at Mile End tube station in 1918.

'Burnt Norton' had highlighted T. S. Eliot's appreciation of the methods by which the London underground had come to shape perceptions of being in the city. For Eliot, the world ran on 'metalled ways' and his depiction of the underground in the garb of an underworld was an adoption of the strand within writing that had frequently invoked a subterranean hell. A decade before, he had predicted to Stephen Spender that the future of Europe would be 'internecine conflict [...] people killing one another in the streets'[197] and these lines

192 Smewin, 'Blitz Dinner', p. 265.

193 G. Orwell, 'London Letter' (1944), in *Collected Essays*, vol. 3, pp. 224–29, p. 228.

194 Quoted in J. Mack & S. Humphries, *London at War, The Making of Modern London 1939–1945* (London: Sidgwick & Jackson, 1985), p. 63.

195 S. Toy, quoted in Fitzgibbon, *The Blitz*, p. 152.

196 Orwell, *Collected Essays*, vol. 2, p. 428.

197 T. S. Eliot, quoted in S. Spender, 'Remembering Eliot' (1965), in A. Tate (ed.), *T. S. Eliot: The Man and His Work* (Harmondsworth: Penguin, 1971), pp. 42–68, p. 53.

on the Tube were perhaps symbolic of such a fatalistic conclusion prior to the outbreak of war. With 'Little Gidding' (1942) Eliot turned to the experience of wartime London, wanting to express a private experience in his wartime poetry:

> Not the expression of collective emotion
> Imperfectly reflected in the daily papers.[198]

Angus Calder suggests that Eliot's poem 'meditated about matters other than war, "above" the daily news bulletins [...] the poem, without literally stating them, appears to *endorse* central elements of the Myth [of the Blitz] extremely strongly'.[199] Eliot did not attempt to engage with the experience of Tube sheltering in 'Little Gidding' despite the huge impact it had on the system. He adopted, instead, the experience of the Tube journey from 'Burnt Norton' in order to signify the impact of the war on daily life in the capital. Eliot had focused on a journey that he himself would have made on many occasions during the 1920s, a journey that possessed no resonances other than that of familiarity and repetition. It seems likely that Eliot rejected the collective experience embodied in Tube sheltering and embraced the concept of the underworld/underground simply because the latter offered valid historical continuity. Eliot wanted to preserve the most mundane instance of the modern world in the form of the Tube journey, expressing this in the whole poem alongside his wartime observations on the Blitz. He also clearly opposed wartime controls, bureaucratic state power and militarism, believing in a Catholic vision of England rather than the secular collectivism of the left.

The underground was also an important feature of George Orwell's more pessimistic reassessment of the war after 1942. In his 'London Letters', Orwell wrote of his main impression of 'the immense stolidity of ordinary people, the widespread vague consciousness that things can never be the same again'.[200] At the same time in his diary he recorded walking 'through the Underground stations, sickened by the advertisements, the silly staring faces and strident colours, the general frantic struggle to induce people to waste labour and material by consuming useless luxuries or harmful drugs'.[201] For Orwell, like

---

198 T. S. Eliot, 'A Note on War Poetry', in S. Jameson (ed.), *London Calling: A Salute to America* (New York: Harper, 1942), pp. 237–38, p. 237. For an explanation of Eliot's decision, see S. D. G. Knowles, *A Purgatorial Flame: Seven British Writers in the Second World War* (Philadelphia: University of Pennsylvania Press, 1990), chapter 4, pp. 100–31.

199 Calder, *Myth of the Blitz*, p. 148.

200 Orwell, 'London Letter' (1941), vol. 2, p. 73.

201 G. Orwell, 'Wartime Diary, 1940', in *Collected Essays*, vol. 2, pp. 385–432, pp. 395–96.

MacNeice, the posters on the underground highlighted the ways in which the war effort was being impeded by capitalism, thereby delaying progress towards a new social system. This sense of frustration was heightened by the contrast between the adverts and the shelterers, many of whom were homeless and would have lost most of their material possessions. In this respect, Orwell was simply restating his powerful interwar critique of materialism. But the Tube was now, in the context of war, a location of a struggle between the human individual celebrated by MacNeice and the capitalist system that undermined the war effort to defeat fascism. Orwell noted the removal of railings from the private squares of London as a small victory of equality over privilege. The covering up of advertisements by shelterers as documented in contemporary photographs and in Christopher Hassall's poem 'Tube Shelter Leicester Square, 1941', in which shelterers are 'Hiding posters of dead plays',[202] could be a sign of the victory of the individual over the system of capitalist consumption. Orwell's response to the Tube in this passage places him much closer to Eliot's fatalism but Orwell retains a belief in the power of individuals to change their surroundings as the shelterers were able do during the Blitz.

Even in Orwell's *Nineteen Eighty-Four* (1949) this ambivalence is still evident. For Orwell, the world depicted in the novel is the result of the failure of libertarian socialism to achieve power during or after the war and here the Tube reverts to its former role as a symbol of mindless commuting, conformity and drudgery. Life for Orwell's hero Winston Smith is 'a matter of slogging through dreary jobs, fighting for a place on the Tube',[203] whilst journeys to the Ministry of Truth where he works mean 'the stench of the Tubes at the rush hour was a horror'.[204] There can be no question that the 'stench' to which Orwell refers is the Tube during the Blitz. In the novel, as in so much of Orwell's earlier fiction, the Tube forms a connecting link between a lost world of the past, the horrors of the Blitz and the terrors of the future imperialist division of the globe. When Winston Smith recalls his childhood, the Tube is clearly identified as a safe haven during the atomic war which ushers in the rule of Big Brother. He remembers going down 'a spiral staircase which rang under his feet [...] Finally they had emerged into a noisy, crowded place which he had realised to be a Tube station'.[205] Orwell then describes the Tube during the Blitz where there are:

---

202 Hassall, 'Tube Shelter Leicester Square', p. 23.
203 G. Orwell, *Nineteen Eighty-Four* (1949; London: Penguin, 1971), p. 62.
204 Orwell, *Nineteen Eighty-Four*, p. 121.
205 Orwell, *Nineteen Eighty-Four*, p. 29–30.

people sitting all over the stone-flagged floor, and other people, packed tightly together, were sitting on metal bunks, one above the other. Winston and his mother found themselves a place on the floor, and near them an old man and an old woman were sitting side by side on a bunk.[206]

The old man is also a voice from the Blitz when he cries out 'We didn't ought to have trusted the buggers',[207] recalling Orwell's own sentiments about the ruling class that had failed England in the interwar years.

Winston's childhood becomes an amalgam of the London Blitz projected into an atomic conflict when he remembers 'the rackety, uneasy circumstances of the time: the periodical panics about air-raids and the sheltering in the Tube stations, the piles of rubbish everywhere'.[208] Orwell was already thinking about the next war of the superpowers. Winston as an adult, like Gordon Comstock in *Keep the Aspidistra Flying*, experiences the London of the future as 'vast and ruinous, city of a million dustbins'.[209] The Tube continues to function in the same old ways in the projected year of 1984, a system which has survived nuclear war and is still being used as refuge by the city's inhabitants as rockets occasionally shoot overhead in the post-atomic conflict of the 1980s. The Tube offers shelter and security as well as transport in Orwell's future state, making permanent the twin roles that it had played during the Blitz. Orwell's novel implicitly rejects the myth of a golden age of the underground that would play such an important part in the cultural reconstruction of the tubes in the immediate postwar decades. Rather, the Tube remains forever locked in a wartime mode. Orwell's final verdict on the Tube is a fine blend of his pre-war revulsion against its subterranean world of materialistic conformity and human drudgery but it is also a vindication of the security role it had played during the war. The underground that Orwell constructed in *Nineteen Eighty-Four* was a shabby, dreary, monolithic hell in which the new bureaucrats of Oceania travelled each day. Its roots lay in the fiction of George Gissing but Orwell forecast what the system would be like in the three decades following the war, a system characterized by lack of investment, poor development, stagnation and 'quick-fix' solutions. At the same time, Orwell had envisaged the underground as a place of safety and security, based on his own experience of sheltering, a notion that reflected the experience of thousands of Londoners for whom the Tube was a solid, fixed and secure part of urban life.

---

206 Orwell, *Nineteen Eighty-Four*, p. 30.
207 Orwell, *Nineteen Eighty-Four*, p. 30.
208 Orwell, *Nineteen Eighty-Four*, p. 131.
209 Orwell, *Nineteen Eighty-Four*, p. 63.

Even though the authorities removed all traces of sheltering within weeks of the end of the war, the cultural memory of sheltering acted as a filter for the Tubism of the interwar years.

Orwell's novel appeared to have loosened the imaginative grip of the underground on the literary landscape of the city. There seems, after all, little more that might be said about a Tube system that is merely the drab counterpart of a totalitarian superstate. But Rose Macaulay's *The World My Wilderness* (1950) opened a doorway to postwar underground writing. The novel is poised between the 'wilderness' of blitzed London and the planned urban reconstruction of the postwar world. Centred on Cheapside in the City itself, the story features the lives of Barbary and her stepbrother Raoul who have come to London from France to live in their father's elegant house in the Adelphi. The novel is full of 'waste lands [...] deep chasms, the pits, the broken walls and foundations'.[210] Macaulay's characters journey through this world, painting the scenes and feeling the distant medieval past in 'the wrecked guildhalls that had belonged to saddlers, merchant tailors, haberdashers, wax-chandlers, barbers, brewers, coopers and coachmakers, all the ancient city fraternities'.[211] But although this excavated medieval and Roman city appears to be slipping back into chaos, towards the apocalyptic world of Gothic fiction, there is a constant reminder that the modern future world of cinemas, radio sets and real underground railways is also part of the ruined landscape. Charing Cross underground station appears early in the story and, towards the end, there is a journey 'home from Moorgate station across the ruins'.[212] The badly bombed Moorgate station was, like the rest of the City, already under reconstruction: 'civilized intelligence was at work among the ruins [...] cranes and derricks would make their appearance, sites would be cleared for rebuilding, tottering piles would be laid low, twisting flights of steps destroyed'.[213] Macaulay's novel is a lyrical evocation of a city hovering between past and future, an early illustration of just how much postwar fiction depicting life in the capital would use the underground system as a link between the knowable communities of the old London and the emergent writing of the postwar era.

---

210 R. Macaulay, *The World My Wilderness* (1950; Harmondsworth: Penguin, 1958), p. 46.

211 Macaulay, *The World My Wilderness*, pp. 94–95.

212 Macaulay, *The World My Wilderness*, p. 186.

213 Macaulay, *The World My Wilderness*, p. 187.

Conclusion

FROM BECK'S TUBE MAP TO BECKS ON THE TUBE

She would [...] take the tube, with all its history, its crowds, its announcements, its delays, and erase its existence from the face of London.

Rachel in Keith Lowe's *Tunnel Vision*[1]

U nderground writing did not end in 1945. George Gissing's King's Cross has moved westwards and been altered by new Tube intersections. It has recently undergone redevelopment and is no longer the smoky underworld of steam engines that characterized his fiction, even if the horrors of the King's Cross fire in 1987 remain a watershed in the history of the whole underground system. If writers from Gissing to Woolf were the first to integrate the underground into fiction as a metaphor for modern urban life, then later writing has transformed this vocabulary into an entire language. The Tube is a pervasive cultural metaphor, seen by some as representing the postmodern condition through its identification as a place where peoples' lives intersect, relationships are formed and the urban world defined. It is also perceived as a place where everything is fragmented, evanescent and contingent. A national if not global brand, it is a permanent referent for London with the ubiquitous logo and Beck's map garnering instant recognition on the English cultural landscape. This cultural underground has been deliberately manufactured, its artefacts and products to be found in the London Transport Museum and throughout the capital's tourist outlets. It was unified by the design philosophy of 'Fitness for Purpose', a unity that remains despite the fragmentation of the Tube system in recent decades. Every generation rewrites this cultural identity in its own image, as the Tube is reflected back as the stage for cultural interventions.

---

1   K. Lowe, *Tunnel Vision* (London: Arrow, 2001), p. 305.

Such interventions now consciously use the Tube for brand identity. Fashion collections such as Bella Freud's have featured in photo shoots on Tube trains for Sunday supplements; television documentaries have appeared such as 'Tube Night' on BBC 4 or drama with *Tube Tales*, and a whole new genre of Tube writing has been published like, for example, *From Here to Here* (2005) which features 31 stories written specifically about the Circle line.[2] In 2008 David Beckham appeared in Tube adverts with a shimmering image of a District line train in the background. We can travel around almost the entire Tube system in the imagination without actually entering the underground. More than ever before the Tube signifies London as a global capital, making it probably more famous than any other underground system.

So what legacy was left in underground writing after the Second World War? In the 1950s the Tube seemed to be reconnected with a localized London that seemed to emerge in the war-damaged and dislocated city. A highly romanticized image can be found in the work of John Betjeman in poems like 'The Metropolitan Railway' (1954),[3] 'Harrow-on-the-Hill' (1954)[4] and 'Middlesex' (1954).[5] Writers such as Monica Dickens wanted to reclaim the close-knit landscape, celebrated by Ford Madox Ford and G. K. Chesterton, of a Tube that was performing its wartime sheltering role by holding communities together or offering boundaries to London's villages, particularly in western suburbs like North Kensington. Monica Dickens' novel *The Heart of London* (1961) practically opens in the Tube as her character Arthur Sears glides 'down into the Underground, slipping sideways down the ironclad stairs as if they were a ship's ladder'.[6] Later in the novel, the first Tube riot in fiction occurs when, according to the morning newspapers 'debutantes battle with police in Underground bottle riot'.[7] A similar world was to be found in Colin MacInnes's *City of Spades* (1957) in which beginners 'discovered' the Tube in the 1950s. The impact of the opening lines of chapter two are a revelation: 'to go straight out by taxi [...] to the famous Piccadilly tube station where I took a one-stop ticket, went down the escalator, and then *ran up the same steps in the wrong direction*'

---

2   See J. Simmons, N. Taylor, T. Rich & T. Lynham (eds.), *From Here to Here. Stories Inspired by London's Circle Line* (London: Cyan Books, 2005).

3   J. Betjeman, 'The Metropolitan Railway' (1954), in *John Betjeman's Collected Poems* (1958; London: John Murray, 2001), pp. 169–70..

4   J. Betjeman, 'Harrow-on-the-Hill', (1954), in *Collected Poems*, p. 148.

5   J. Betjeman, 'Middlesex' (1954), in *Collected Poems*, pp. 163–64.

6   M. Dickens, *The Heart of London* (Harmondsworth: Penguin, 1961), p. 7. This localism is reflected in the film *Passport to Pimlico* (1949), when the community has to consider its borders *beneath* the streets on the underground.

7   Dickens, *The Heart of London*, p. 279.

(italics in original).[8] This small world was not always comfortable. V. S. Naipaul remembered the 'old-fashioned heavy vending machines [on underground stations] with raised metal letters. No sweets, no chocolates came from them now [...] no one had bothered to take them away'.[9] The eponymous character in *Mr Stone and the Knights Companion* (1963) thought that 'the entrance to [Earl's Court] underground station was filthy'.[10] Other immigrants adopted the Tube as their own, with Sri Lankan students using the Circle line as a classroom in the 1960s.[11] Sam Selvon memorably sketched what it was like to work on the Tube in the 1950s with his portrayal of Barbados-born character Small Change in 'Working the Transport' (1957). Selvon signalled the start of a major recomposition of the workforce, accurately forecasting how young workers (both black and white) would turn to working on London Transport over some three decades.[12] John Betjeman's romantic 'Metro-Land' was revived by Julian Barnes in his novel *Metroland* (1980) but was by this time a tale of two adolescent schoolboys. This does not make it any the less romantic, particularly when Barnes incorporates a brief history lesson on the underground, concluding that Metroland is a 'bourgeois dormitory'.[13]

A revival of the other utopian elements of the Tube moved away from the localized scenes of the past into a more playful cultural world, a place of irony and mocking leading directly to Hanif Kureishi's *The Buddha of Suburbia* (1990). Here, the District line is enthroned as the key to a new future with schooldays and adolescence being played out on underground trains.[14] Such Tube journeys were a magic carpet ride away from the dreary outer suburbs— not for nothing was Barbara Vine's novel about the Tube actually called *King Solomon's Carpet* (1991). Dedicated to the men and women of the underground, Vine's crime novel is a conscious celebration of the Tube as it was perceived in the postwar period down to about 1986.[15] Even Maeve Binchy's *Victoria Line*

8   C. MacInnes, *City of Spades* (1957; Harmondsworth: Penguin, 1964), p. 15.
9   V. S. Naipaul, *The Enigma of Arrival* (London: Penguin, 1987), p. 121.
10   V. S. Naipaul, *Mr Stone and the Knights Companion* (1963; Harmondsworth: Penguin, 1973), p. 26.
11   A. Arulambalam, *Memories*, compiled by K. Haynes, R@H Project (London: HISTORYtalk, 2002), p. 32.
12   S. Selvon, 'Working the Transport', in *Ways of Sunlight* (New York: Longman, 1987), pp. 120–26.
13   J. Barnes, *Metroland* (1980; London: Picador, 1990), p. 38.
14   H. Kureishi, *The Buddha of Suburbia* (London: Faber & Faber, 1990).
15   B. Vine, *King Solomon's Carpet* (1991; London: Viking, 1992). London Transport workers are more evident from the 1950s with films like *Under Night Streets* (1958), a 20-minute British Transport documentary, *City After Dark* (1955) which includes the 'fluffers' who cleaned the

(1983) attempted to humanize a fully automatic brand new Tube line.[16] And all of these novels were based on the same premise: that the Tube was a unified organization as it had been since 1933 and without that unifying factor such writing would have been impossible. This was a revival of the old debate about public and private ownership, reflecting how the nationalized Tube system had become embedded in writing. It is a debate that continues today.

These novels mediated the Tube to a new audience, helping it to navigate a system in a way similar to H. G. Wells. But the people who read these novels did not need a guide like Wells, because they were in control of their journeys on it (even if they came from Nigeria like Johnny in *City of Spades*). The Tube was a familiar not an alien place—after all, a generation of transport workers came from the Caribbean to work on it in the 1950s and their children travelled to school and then work on it in the 1960s and 1970s. In this sense the fiction of the postwar decades had more in keeping with the wartime role—the Tube went on providing shelter for writers and their characters long after the bunks had been ripped out. There were of course reminders of the alienation of the 1930s to be found in the writing of Doris Lessing and Russell Hoban.[17] The Tube proliferated in postwar writing, growing more quickly than the system itself in these decades of underfunding and neglect.

Seamus Heaney's poem 'District and Circle' (2006), with its modern Dantean journey on the underground, is a potent reminder of the multiple layers of underground writing. Heaney's poem has a knowing familiarity with real Tube travel: 'My watcher on the tiles', 'crowd swept, strap-hanging' and darting glances backwards towards the myths and visions of the imagined journey. Lines like 'underneath the vault', 'blasted weeping rock-walls./Flicker lit' are a compression of history.[18] The poem is a return to the thematics of the Victorian underground, a poetic development of the mainly fictional portrayals

tracks at night, and *The Irishmen: an impression of exile* (1965) which explores the building of the Victoria line, through to Molly Dineen's 1989 television documentary *The Heart of the Angel.*

16   M. Binchy, *Victoria Line* (1983; London: Coronet, 1984).

17   See D. Lessing, *The Golden Notebook* (St Albans: Panther, 1973), D. Lessing, 'In Defence of the Underground', in *London Observed: Stories and Sketches* (London: Flamingo, 1993), pp. 79–96 and R. Hoban, *Kleinzeit* (1974; London: Picador, 1976).

18   S. Heaney, *District and Circle* (London: Faber & Faber, 2006), pp. 17–19. In an interview in the *Guardian*, Heaney commented on the poem, saying that he wanted to convey the 'actual experience of an ordinary journey by tube' but that inevitably 'the classical echoes were going to be heard, and the underground/underworld/otherworld parallels come into play' (*Guardian*, 8 November 2008, pp. 2–4, p. 3).

of the Tube to be found, for example, in Tobias Hill's *Underground* (1999)[19] or Conrad Williams' *London Revenant* (2004).[20] Heaney's poem, however, draws together myth and the everyday details of underground journeys whilst the novels of Hill and Williams are richly dystopian in their creation of marginalized 'other' worlds in the Tube system. These poems and novels are examples of the contemporary re-articulation of the Tube, a process triggered during the 1980s when the underground entered a period of profound technological and political change. But at a wider cultural level, 'infotainment' stories continue to appear in the pages of London's free papers with front-page headlines that scream 'Giant Monsters on Tube', a massive front-page advert for that night's episode of the television series *Primeval*.[21] A dismembered insect leg is 'found' on a Circle line train, evidence of creatures that emerge from a mysterious portal found in a deserted Tube shelter. As well as utilizing the rush hour in order to distribute newspaper advertising for such television series, the producers of this episode of *Primeval* are combining a number of layers of Tube history both imaginative and real. Mysterious portals, frightful other worlds containing fiendish creatures and Second World War Tube shelters are all to be found here.

Contemporary underground writing has other continuities with the period covered by this book. It depicts the Tube in ways that undermine, contradict or question the notion that public transport is simply a managerial or technical question. It explores the relationship between urban government and transport needs, making us aware of the human dimension. Using the accessible forms of fiction and poetry, it reminds us of the historical legacy of the Tube that developed from Gissing to Woolf, public underground writing that cannot be contained within the 'heritage industry' or nostalgic affection for the 'Pick era'. Such new directions are notable in David Leavitt's 'postmodern' novel *While England Sleeps* (1993). Based on the gay relationship between a ticket-collector at Earl's Court station and an upper-class writer, it traverses the system of the 1930s with writing itself 'in transit' with a fictional author who is writing a novel about the Underground.[22] Furthermore, underground writing was from the start linked to socio-political issues and this remains a constant in the postwar period. A new strand in underground writing cannot be far off but in all likelihood it will take up the more utopian social and political themes that have largely disappeared from recent fiction. The Tube has become environmentally

19   T. Hill, *Underground* (London: Faber & Faber, 1999).

20   C. Williams, *London Revenant* (London: The Do-Not Press, 2004).

21   'Giant Monsters on Tube', *The London Paper*, 16 February 2007, p. 1.

22   See D. Leavitt, *While England Sleeps* (1993; Boston: Houghton & Mifflin, 1995).

central to the future of the capital and new Tube lines like Crossrail are being constructed which will affect car use and bring more passengers onto public transport. The need for integration with other services like buses and main-line trains is long overdue whilst the total failure of the government's public-private partnership scheme reopens the old debate over funding for the system. An integrated transport infrastructure for the capital may provide a new impulse that is far from the grim dystopian fiction of recent years. It will be uneven and contradictory just as the underground writing crafted by George Gissing coexisted with the utopian vision of H. G. Wells whilst Frank Pick's modernist philosophy of 'Fitness for Purpose' was embodied in Virginia's Woolf's novels but found its antithesis during the Blitz. When Gissing described the King's Cross underground station as a battleground, he was inventing an imaginative landscape that would play an increasingly significant role in the formation of the underground that transports three million people every day.

BIBLIOGRAPHY

A. E. Abbott, 'The Spawn of Fortune' (1896), in A. K. Russell (ed.), *The Rivals of Sherlock Holmes 2* (Secaucus, NJ: Castle Books, 1980), pp. 3–9.

C. S. Ackley (ed.), *British Prints From the Machine Age: Rhythms of Modern Life 1914–1939* (London: Thames and Hudson, 2008).

E. Adams, M. Tyler, A. Santana & J. Moreno, *Echoes of Spain 1936–1939* (London: Gloucester Court Reminiscence Group, 2008).

H. Adams, 'The Dynamo and the Virgin' (1900), in *The Education of Henry Adams* (1918), ed. I. B. Nadel (Oxford: Oxford University Press, 1999), pp. 317–26.

R. Aldington, *Collected Poems* (New York: AMS Press, 1981).

———, *Death of a Hero* (1929; London: Hogarth Press, 1984).

R. Allen (ed.), *The Moving Pageant: A Literary Sourcebook on London Street-Life, 1700–1914* (London: Routledge, 1998).

W. Allingham, *William Allingham: A Diary, 1824–1889* (1907), eds. H. Allingham & D. Radford (Harmondsworth: Penguin, 1985).

R. D. Altick, *The Presence of the Present: Topics of the Day in the Victorian Novel* (Columbus: Ohio State University, 1991).

G. Anderson, *Victorian Clerks* (Manchester: Manchester University Press, 1976).

O. Anderson, *Suicide in Victorian and Edwardian England* (Oxford: Clarendon, 1987).

J. Andrews, *London's War. The Shelter Drawings of Henry Moore* (2002; Aldershot: Lund Humphries, 2005).

R. Anscombe, 'The Hours of Darkness', in J. Lehmann (ed.), *The Penguin New Writing 25* (Harmondsworth: Penguin, 1945), pp. 175–81.

U. Apollonio (ed.), *Futurist Manifestos* (London: Thames & Hudson, 1973).

A. Arulambalam, *Memories*, compiled by K. Haynes, R@H Project (London: HISTORYtalk, 2002).

W. H. Auden, 'Letter to Lord Byron' (1936), in *W. H. Auden Collected Longer Poems* (London: Faber & Faber, 1974), pp. 35–76.

———, 'Thomas Epilogizes' (1926), in *Juvenilia: Poems 1922–1928*, ed. K. Bucknell (Princeton: Princeton University Press, 1994), pp. 146–49.

——— & C. Isherwood, *The Ascent of F6 and On the Frontier* (1936–38; London: Faber & Faber, 1958).

——— & C. Isherwood, *The Dog Beneath the Skin* (1935; London: Faber & Faber, 1958).

P. S. Bagwell, *The Railwaymen: The History of the National Union of Railwaymen*, 2 vols. (London: Allen & Unwin, 1963–82).

J. O. Bailey (ed.), *British Plays of the 19th Century* (New York: Odyssey, 1966).

A. W. Baird, 'A Spiv on the Steppe', in J. Lehmann (ed.), *The Penguin New Writing 23* (Harmondsworth: Penguin, 1945), pp. 37–46.

N. Balchin, *Darkness Falls from the Air* (1943; London: Pan, 1969).

E. Banton, 'Underground Travelling London' (1903), in G. R. Sims (ed.), *Edwardian London*, 4 vols. (London: Village Press, 1990), vol. 4, pp. 60–63.

E. Barkan & R. Bush (eds.), *Prehistories of the Future: The Primitive Project and the Culture of Modernism* (Stanford: Stanford University Press, 1995).

T. Barker, *Moving Millions, A Pictorial History of London Transport* (London: London Transport Museum, 1990).

T. C. Barker & M. Robbins, *A History of London Transport*, 2 vols. (London: Allen & Unwin, 1963–74).

C. Barman, *The Man Who Built London Transport: A Biography of Frank Pick* (London: David & Charles, 1979).

John Barnes, *The Beginnings of the Cinema in England, 1894–1901*, 5 vols., vol. 5 (Exeter: Exeter University Press, 1997).

Julian Barnes, *Metroland* (1980; London: Picador, 1990).

A. Barnett, 'The Shape of Labour', *Art Monthly*, October 1986, pp. 4–8.

A. Barrie, *War Underground: The Tunnellers of the Great War* (1962; Staplehurst: Spellmount, 2000).

N. Beauman, *A Very Great Profession: The Woman's Novel, 1914–39* (London: Virago, 1983).

M. Beaumont, *Utopia Ltd., Ideologies of Social Dreaming in England 1870–1900* (Boston: Brill, 2005).

M. Beerbohm, '1880' (1894), in *The Works of Max Beerbohm* (London: Heinemann, 1922), pp. 35–47.

C. Bell, *Art* (1914; New York: Capricorn Books, 1958).

E. Bellamy, *Looking Backward 2000–1887* (1888; Harmondsworth: Penguin, 1982).

W. Benjamin, 'The Storyteller' (1936), in *Illuminations* (London: Fontana/Collins, 1973), pp. 83–109.

A. Bennett, *Buried Alive* (1908; London: Methuen, 1913).

———, 'The Fire of London' (1904), in M. Smith (ed.), *Golden Age Detective Stories* (Bath: Parragon, 1991), pp. 161–76.

———, *Hilda Lessways* (1911; London: Eyre Methuen, 1976).

———, *The Journals of Arnold Bennett*, ed. F. Swinnerton (Harmondsworth: Penguin, 1954).

———, *A Man from the North* (1898; London: Hamish Hamilton, 1973).

———, *Our Women: Chapters on the Sex-Discord* (London: Cassell, 1920).

———, *The Pretty Lady* (London: Cassell, 1918).

———, *Riceyman Steps* (1923; London: Pan, 1964).

———, *The Sinews of War* (1906; London: Ayer Co. Pub., 1977).

R. Bessel, 'Transport', in C. Chant (ed.), *Science Technology and Everyday Life, 1870–1950* (London: Routledge, 1989), pp. 162–99.

C. L. Bernstein, *The Celebration of Scandal: Toward the Sublime in Victorian Urban Fiction* (University Park, PA: Penn State University Press, 1991).

J. Betjeman, *John Betjeman's Collected Poems* (1958; London: John Murray, 2001).

U. Bialer, *The Shadow of the Bomber: The Fear of Air Attack and British Politics 1932–39* (London: Royal Historical Society, 1980).

M. Binchy, *Victoria Line* (1983; London: Coronet, 1984).

A. Blackwood, 'King's Evidence', in H. Brown (ed.), *Best Broadcast Stories* (London: Faber & Faber, 1944), pp. 147–55.

C. S. Blum, *The Other Modernism: F. T. Marinetti's Futurist Fiction of Power* (Berkeley: University of California Press, 1996).

R. D. Blumenfeld, *R. D. B.'s Diary, 1887–1914* (London: Heinemann, 1930).

B. Bobrick, *Labyrinths of Iron: A History of the World's Subways* (New York: Newsweek Books, 1982).

T. Boon, 'Making the Modern World', *History Today*, vol. 51, no. 8 (August 2001), pp. 38–45.

C. Booth, *Improved Means of Locomotion as a first step towards the cure of the housing difficulties of London* (London: Macmillan, 1901).

M. Booth, *Theatre in the Victorian Age* (Cambridge: Cambridge University Press, 1991).

P. Bottome, *London Pride* (1941; London: Faber & Faber, 1947).

D. Boucicault, *After Dark; A Drama of London Life* (1868), in J. O. Bailey (ed.), *British Plays of the 19th Century* (New York: Odyssey, 1966), pp. 283–302.

E. Bowen, *Collected Impressions* (London: Longmans, 1950).

————, *The Heat of the Day* (1949; London: Reprint Society, 1950).

————, *The House in Paris* (1935; London: Jonathan Cape, 1949).

————, *The Mulberry Tree, Writings by Elizabeth Bowen*, ed. H. Lee (London: Virago, 1986).

————, 'Mysterious Kôr' (1944), in M. Bradbury (ed.), *The Penguin Book of Modern British Short Stories* (London: Penguin, 1988), pp. 32–45.

R. Bowlby, *Just Looking: Consumer Culture in Dreiser, Gissing and Zola* (New York: Methuen, 1985).

M. Bradbury (ed.), *The Penguin Book of Modern British Short Stories* (London: Penguin, 1988).

————, *Possibilities, Essays on the State of the Novel* (Oxford: Oxford University Press, 1973).

———— & J. McFarlane, *Modernism: A Guide to European Literature, 1890–1930* (Harmondsworth: Penguin, 1976).

B. Brandt, *Camera in London* (London: Focal Press, 1948).

P. Brantlinger, *Rule of Darkness: British Literature and Imperialism, 1830–1914* (London: Cornell University Press, 1988).

M. I. Bray, *Railway Picture Postcards* (Ashbourne: Moorland Publishing, 1986).

A. Briggs, *Victorian Things* (1988; Harmondsworth: Penguin, 1990).

V. Brittain, *England's Hour* (1941; London: Futura, 1981).

P. Brooker, *Bohemia in London: The Social Scene of Early Modernism* (Basingstoke: Palgrave Macmillan, 2004).

H. Brown (ed.), *Best Broadcast Stories* (London: Faber & Faber, 1944).

R. Brown, *The Art of Suicide* (London: Reaktion Books, 2001).

C. Brunsdon, *London in Cinema: The Cinematic City Since 1945* (London: British Film Institute, 2007).

W. Bryher, *The Days of Mars: A Memoir, 1940–1946* (London: Calder & Boyars, 1972).

S. Buck-Morss, *The Dialectics of Seeing: Walter Benjamin and the Arcades Project* (London: MIT Press, 1989).

F. T. Bullen, *Confessions of a Tradesman* (London: Hodder & Stoughton, 1908).

G. W. Bullett, 'Last Days of Binnacle' (1926), in *The Baker's Cart and Other Tales* (Freeport, NY: Books for Libraries Press, 1970), pp. 143–72.

A. Bullock, *The Life and Times of Ernest Bevin*, 3 vols. (London: Heinemann, 1960–83).

E. Bulwer-Lytton, *The Coming Race* (London: Routledge & Sons, 1891).

G. Byron & D. Punter (eds.), *Spectral Readings: Towards a Gothic Geography* (Basingstoke: Palgrave Macmillan, 1999).

A. Calder, *The Myth of the Blitz* (1991; London: Pimlico, 1992).

————, *The People's War: Britain, 1939–45* (London: Panther, 1971).

———— & D. Sheridan (eds.), *Speak for Yourself: A Mass Observation Anthology, 1937–1949* (London: Jonathan Cape, 1984).

J. Campbell, 'To London, for love', *Guardian*, 20 November 2004.

D. Cannadine & D. Reeder (eds.), *Exploring the Urban Past* (Cambridge: Cambridge University Press, 1982).

J. Cantlie, 'Degeneration Amongst Londoners' (1885), in L. Hollen Lees & A. Lees (eds.), *The Rise of Urban Britain* (New York: Garland, 1985), pp. 7–61.

K. Čapek, *Letters from England*, trans. P. Selver (London: Bles, 1925).

F. Carey, *Henry Moore: A Shelter Sketchbook* (London: British Museum Publications, 1988).

J. Carey, *The Intellectuals and the Masses* (London: Faber & Faber, 1992).

J. W. Carey & J. J. Quirk, 'The Mythos of the Electronic Revolution', *The American Scholar*, 39, no. 2, Spring 1970, pp. 219–41.

H. Carpenter, *A Serious Character, The Life of Ezra Pound* (London: Faber & Faber, 1988).

E. A. Carr, 'Criminal London' (1902), in G. R. Sims (ed.), *Edwardian London*, 4 vols. (London: Village Press, 1990), vol. 3, pp. 221–27.

N. Carrington, 'Need Our Cities be Ugly?', *Listener*, 22 January 1930, pp. 149–51.

L. Carroll, *Through the Looking Glass* (1872; London: Penguin, 1994).

I. Carter, *Railways and Culture in Britain: The Epitome of Modernity* (Manchester: Manchester University Press, 2001).

M. Ceadel, 'Popular Fiction and the Next War, 1918–39', in F. Gloversmith (ed.), *Class, Culture and Social Change: A New View of the 1930s* (Brighton: Harvester, 1980), pp. 161–84.

C. Chambers, *The Story of Unity Theatre* (London: Lawrence & Wishart, 1989).

C. Chant (ed.), *Science Technology and Everyday Life, 1870–1950* (London: Routledge, 1989).

G. K. Chesterton, *The Man Who Was Thursday* (1908; London: Penguin, 1986).

C. Christensen Nelson (ed.), *Literature of the Women's Suffrage Campaign in England* (Peterborough, Ontario: Broadview Press, 2004).

I. F. Clarke, *The Pattern of Expectation, 1644–2001* (London: Jonathan Cape, 1979).

————, *Voices Prophesying War, 1763–1984* (London: Oxford University Press, 1966).

H. Clout (ed.), *The Times History of London* (1991; London: Times Books, 2000).

M. Collie, *The Alien Art: A Critical Study of George Gissing's Novels* (Folkestone: Dawson, 1979).

G. Colmore, *Suffragette Sally* (1911), reissued as *Suffragettes: A Story of Three Women* (London: Pandora, 1984).

Communist Party of Great Britain (CPGB), *More Fares Please* (London: London District Committee, CPGB, 1938).

A. Conan Doyle, *Sherlock Holmes: The Complete Illustrated Short Stories* (London: Chancellor Press, 1985).

————, 'A Study in Scarlet' (1887), in *The Complete Short Stories of Sherlock Holmes* (Ware: Wordsworth Editions, 2007), pp. 13–93.

M. Connelly, *Orwell and Gissing* (New York: Peter Lang, 1997).

S. Connor, *The English Novel in History 1950–1995* (London: Routledge, 1996).

C. Cook, 'The Myth of the Aviator and the Flight to Fascism', *History Today*, vol. 53 (12), December 2003, pp. 36–42.

R. Cork, 'Art & the Underground', in E. Paolozzi, *Eduardo Paolozzi Underground*, ed. R. Cork (London: Weidenfeld & Nicolson, 1986), pp. 28–42.

————, *Vorticism and Abstract Art in the First Machine Age*, 2 vols. (London: Gordon Fraser, 1976).

P. de Coulevain, *The Unknown Isle* (French edition 1906, trans. 1911), in J. Coulter (ed.), *London of One Hundred Years Ago* (Stroud: Sutton, 1999), pp. 97–98.

J. Coulter (ed.), *London of One Hundred Years Ago* (Stroud: Sutton, 1999).

W. L. Courtney, 'The Soul of a Suffragette' (1913), in C. Christensen Nelson (ed.), *Literature of the Women's Suffrage Campaign in England* (Peterborough, Ontario: Broadview Press, 2004), pp. 313–25.

P. Coustillas (ed.), *Collected Articles on George Gissing* (London: Frank Cass, 1968).

T. W. H. Crosland, *The Suburbans* (London: John Long, 1905).

V. Cunningham, *British Writers of the Thirties* (Oxford: Oxford University Press, 1989).

J. Curtis, *The Gilt Kid* (1936; London: London Books, 2007).

C. J. Cutcliffe Hyne, 'London's Danger' (1898), in A. K. Russell (ed.), *Science Fiction by the Rivals of H. G. Wells* (Secaucus, NJ: Castle Books, 1979), pp. 341–48.

——, 'The Tragedy of a Third Smoker' (1898), in A. K. Russell (ed.), *The Rivals of Sherlock Holmes 2* (Secaucus, NJ: Castle Books, 1980), pp. 317–23.

N. Daly, *Literature, Technology and Modernity, 1860–2000* (Cambridge: Cambridge University Press, 2004).

——, 'Railway Novels: Sensation Fiction and the Modernization of the Senses', *ELH* (*English Literary History*), vol. 66, no. 2, Summer 1999, pp. 461–87.

S. Dark, 'London Twenty Years Ago', *Listener*, 4 September 1929, p. 301.

L. Davidoff, *The Best Circles: Society, Etiquette and The Season* (London: Croom Helm, 1973).

J. Davidson, *A Random Itinerary* (1894; Whitefish, MT: Kessinger Publishing, 2008).

——, 'Thirty Bob a Week' (1894), in J. Hayward (ed.), *The Oxford Book of Nineteenth Century English Verse* (Oxford: Oxford University Press, 1964), pp. 900–03.

J. Davies, 'Mechanical millennium: Sant'Elia and the poetry of Futurism', in E. Timms & D. Kelley (eds.), *Unreal City: Urban Experience in Modern European Literature and Art* (Manchester: Manchester University Press, 1985), pp. 65–79.

J. Day & J. Reed, *The Story of London's Underground* (Harrow Weald: Capital Transport Publishing, 2001).

P. Dehn, 'New Age', in *The Fern on the Rock. Collected Poems 1935–65* (1951; London: Hamish Hamilton, 1965), pp. 72–73.

P. Delany, *George Gissing A Life* (London: Weidenfeld & Nicolson, 2008).

M. Denning, *The Cultural Front: The Laboring of American Culture In the Twentieth Century* (London: Verso, 1996).

L. De Vries, *Victorian Inventions* (London: John Murray, 1971).

C. Dickens, *Dombey and Son* (1848; Harmondsworth: Penguin, 1970).

——, *The Letters of Charles Dickens*, eds. G. Storey, K. Tilliotson & N. Burgis, 12 vols. (Oxford: Clarendon, 1965–2002).

M. Dickens, *The Fancy* (1943; Harmondsworth: Penguin, 1964).

——, *The Happy Prisoner* (1946; London: Book Club, 1948).

——, *The Heart of London* (Harmondsworth: Penguin, 1961).

——, *An Open Book* (1978; Harmondsworth: Penguin, 1980).

G. Doré & B. Jerrold, *London: A Pilgrimage* (1872; New York: Dover, 1970).

M. Doriel Hay, *Murder Underground: Death on the Hampstead Tube* (London: Skeffington & Son, c.1930).

H. Douglas, *The Underground Story* (London: Robert Hale, 1963).

A. Downton, *The LT Scandal* (London: London District Committee, Communist Party of Great Britain, 1936).

T. Dreiser, *The Stoic* (1947; New York: Thomas Y. Crowell, 1974).

N. Dutton, 'Art and Industry', *Special L.T. issue*, vol. 4, no. 244, October 1946, pp. 98–122.

H. J. Dyos, 'Railways and Housing in Victorian London', in D. Cannadine & D. Reeder (eds.), *Exploring the Urban Past* (Cambridge: Cambridge University Press, 1982), pp. 101–18.

O. Eckhardt, 'The Underground Railway—As It Should Be' (1896), in J. Coulter (ed.), *London of One Hundred Years Ago* (Stroud: Sutton, 1999), p. 98.

D. Edwards & R. Pigram, *Metro Memories: A Pictorial History of Metro-Land* (London: Bloomsbury, 1977).

T. S. Eliot, 'Baudelaire', in *Selected Essays* (1932; London: Faber & Faber, 1972), pp. 419–30.

————, *Four Quartets* (1944; London: Faber & Faber, 1970).

————, *The Letters of T. S. Eliot, vol. 1, 1898–1922*, ed. V. Eliot (London: Faber & Faber, 1988).

————, 'London Letter', *The Dial*, vol. 71, no. 4, October 1921, pp. 452–55.

————, 'A Note on War Poetry', in S. Jameson (ed.), *London Calling: A Salute to America* (New York: Harper, 1942), pp. 237–38.

————, 'The Rock' (1934), in *The Complete Poems and Plays* (London: Faber & Faber, 1969), pp. 147–67.

————, *Selected Poems* (London: Faber & Faber, 1954).

P. Faulkner (ed.), *A Modernist Reader* (London: Batsford, 1986).

S. Faulks, *A Week in December* (London: Hutchinson, 2009).

C. Ferns, *Narrating Utopia* (Liverpool: Liverpool University Press, 1999).

P. Ferris, *The House of Northcliffe, The Harmsworths of Fleet Street* (London: Weidenfeld & Nicolson, 1971).

C. Fitzgibbon, *The Blitz* (1957; London: Corgi, 1974).

F. S. Flint, 'Tube', *The Egoist*, vol. 1, no. 1, January 1914, p. 14.

F. M. Ford (writing as Ford Madox Hueffer), *Collected Poems* (London: Max Goschen, 1914).

————, *The Good Soldier: A Tale of Passion* (1915; Harmondsworth: Penguin, 1946).

————, *Ladies Whose Bright Eyes* (1911; Manchester: Carcanet, 1988).

————, *Some Do Not (Parade's End*, vol. 1) (1924; Harmondsworth: Penguin, 1948).

————, *The Soul of London* (1905; London: Everyman, 1995).

E. M. Forster, *Collected Short Stories* (Harmondsworth: Penguin, 1954).

————, *Howard's End* (1910; Harmondsworth, Penguin, 1941).

J. Franch, *Robber Baron, The Life of Charles Tyson Yerkes* (Urbana & Chicago: University of Illinois Press, 2006).

P. Frankau, *The Willow Cabin* (1949; London: Pan, 1954).

J. Freeman, *In Transit: The Transport Workers Union in New York City, 1933–1966* (New York: Oxford University Press, 1989).

D. Frisby & M. Featherstone (eds.), *The Sociology of Georg Simmel* (London: Sage, 1997).

R. Fry, 'The Grafton Gallery I', *Nation*, no. 8, 19 November 1910, p. 332.

J. Galsworthy, *The Man of Property (Forsyte Saga*, vol. 1) (1906; Harmondsworth: Penguin, 1951).

————, *Swan Song (Forsyte Saga: A Modern Comedy*, vol. 3) (1928; Harmondsworth: Penguin, 1968).

P. L. Garside, 'West End, East End: London, 1890–1940', in A. Sutcliffe (ed.), *Metropolis 1890–1940* (London: Mansell, 1984), pp. 221–258.

B. Gates, *Victorian Suicide: Mad Crimes and Sad Histories* (Princeton: Princeton University Press, 1988).

P. K. Gilbert (ed.), *Imagined Londons* (Albany: State University of New York Press, 2002).

G. Gissing, *Born in Exile* (1892; London: Hogarth Press, 1985).

————, *By the Ionian Sea* (1901; Marlboro, VT: The Marlboro Press, 1920).

————, *The Collected Letters of George Gissing*, eds. P. F. Mattheisen, A. C. Young & P. Coustillas, 9 vols. (Athens, OH: Ohio University Press, 1990–97).

————, *The Crown of Life* (1899; Hassocks: Harvester, 1978).

————, *Demos* (1886; Brighton: Harvester, 1972).

————, *Eve's Ransom* (1895; London: Sidgwick & Jackson, 1911).

————, 'Humplebee', in *The House of Cobwebs* (1906; Edinburgh: Constable, 1926), pp. 68–87.

————, *In the Year of Jubilee* (1894; London: Hogarth Press, 1987).

————, *The Letters of George Gissing to Eduard Bertz, 1887–1903*, ed. A. C. Young (London: Constable, 1961).

————, *The Letters of George Gissing to Gabrielle Fleury*, ed. P. Coustillas (New York: New York Public Library, 1964).

————, *The Letters of George Gissing to Members of his Family*, eds. A. & E. Gissing (London: Constable, 1927).

————, *A Life's Morning* (1888; Brighton: Harvester, 1984).

————, *London and the Life of Literature in Late Victorian England, The Diary of George Gissing, Novelist*, ed. P. Coustillas (Hassocks: Harvester, 1978).

————, *The Nether World* (1889; London: Dent, 1973).

————, *New Grub Street* (1891; Harmondsworth: Penguin, 1968).

————, *The Odd Women* (1893; London: Virago, 1980).

————, 'On Battersea Bridge', in *Selections Autobiographical and Imaginative from the Works of George Gissing. With Biographical and Critical Notes by his Son* (New York: Jonathan Cape & Harmon Smith, 1925).

————, *Thyrza* (1887; Brighton: Harvester, 1974).

————, *The Unclassed* (1884; Brighton: Harvester, 1976).

————, *The Whirlpool* (1897; London: Hogarth Press, 1984).

————, *Will Warburton* (1905; London: Hogarth Press, 1985).

————, *Workers in the Dawn* (1880; Brighton: Harvester, 1985).

F. Gloversmith (ed.), *Class, Culture and Social Change: A New View of the 1930s* (Brighton: Harvester, 1980).

J. Goode, *George Gissing: Ideology and Fiction* (London: Vision Press, 1978).

————, 'Gissing, Morris and English Socialism' (1968), in *Collected Essays of John Goode*, ed. C. Swann (Keele: Keele University Press, 1995), pp. 247–71.

L. Gordon, *Eliot's Early Years* (Oxford: Oxford University Press, 1978).

M. Gordon, 'Songs from the Museum of the Future, Russian Sound Creation, 1910–1930', in D. Kahn & G. Whitehead (eds.), *Wireless Imagination: Sound, Radio and the Avant Garde* (Cambridge, MA: MIT Press, 1992), pp. 197–244.

S. Grand, 'When the Door Opened' (1898), in A. Richardson (ed.), *Women Who Did: Stories by Men and Women, 1890–1914* (London: Penguin, 2002), pp. 217–24.

I. Grant & N. Maddren, *The City at War* (London: Jupiter Press, 1975).

C. Graves, *London Transport at War, 1939–1945* (London: London Transport Publications, 1974).

P. Graves, *Labour Women: Women in British Working-Class Politics 1918–1939* (Cambridge: Cambridge University Press, 1994).

S. R. Grayzel, *Women's Identities at War: Gender, Motherhood and Politics in Britain and France during the First World War* (Chapel Hill: University of North Carolina Press, 1999).

Greater London Council, Popular Planning Unit, *Notes from the Underground* (London: GLC, 1986).

———, *One Man: 2000 Jobs* (London: GLC, 1986).

O. Green, *Underground Art* (London: Studio Vista, 1990).

H. Green, *Blindness* (1926), in *Nothing/Doting/Blindness* (London: Picador, 1979), pp. 343–505.

G. Greene, *The Confidential Agent* (1939; London: Vintage, 2002).

———, *It's a Battlefield* (1934; London: Heinemann, 1970).

———, *The Ministry of Fear* (1943; London: Penguin, 1963).

H. Greene (ed.), *The Rivals of Sherlock Holmes* (London: Bodley Head, 1970).

W. Greenslade, *Degeneration, Culture and the Novel, 1880–1940* (Cambridge: Cambridge University Press, 1994).

R. Greenwood, *Mr Bunting at War* (London: Dent, 1941).

J. Gregg, *The Shelter of the Tubes* (Harrow Weald: Capital Transport Publishing, 2001).

G. & W. Grossmith, *Diary of a Nobody* (1892; Harmondsworth: Penguin, 1965).

I. Gurney, *War Letters* (1983; London: Hogarth Press, 1984).

P. Haining (ed.), *Murder on the Railways* (London: Orion, 1996).

S. Halliday, *Underground to Everywhere* (Stroud: Sutton Publishing, 2001).

J. A. Hamilton, *Britain's Railways in World War I* (London: Allen & Unwin, 1967).

P. Hamilton, *The Midnight Bell* (1929), first book in omnibus edition *Twenty Thousand Streets Under the Sky*, (London: Hogarth Press, 1987).

———, *The Plains of Cement* (1934), third book in omnibus edition *Twenty Thousand Streets Under the Sky* (London: Hogarth Press, 1987).

J. A. Hammerton (ed.), *Mr Punch in London Town*, 20 vols., vol. 15 (London: Educational Book Co., 1985).

N. Hanson, *First Blitz* (London: Doubleday, 2008).

L. Hapgood, *Margins of Desire: the Suburbs in Fiction and Culture, 1880–1925* (Manchester: Manchester University Press, 2005).

———, 'The Unwritten Suburb: Defining Spaces in John Galsworthy's *The Man of Property*', in L. Hapgood & N. Paxton (eds.), *Outside Modernism, In Pursuit of the English Novel 1900–30* (London: Macmillan, 2000), pp. 162–79.

——— & N. Paxton (eds.), *Outside Modernism, In Pursuit of the English Novel 1900–30* (London: Macmillan, 2000).

D. Hardy, 'Brave New Worlds', *BBC History Magazine*, vol. 1, no. 8, December 2000, pp. 20–22.

T. Hardy, *Thomas Hardy: Selected Letters*, ed. M. Millgate (Oxford: Clarendon, 1990).

M. Harkness (writing as John Law), *A City Girl* (1887; London: Garland, 1984).

——— (writing as John Law), *Out of Work* (1888; London: Merlin Press, 1990).

B. L. Harman, *The Feminine Political Novel in Victorian England* (Charlottesville: University Press of Virginia, 1998).

D. Harvey, *The Condition of Postmodernity* (Oxford: Blackwell, 1990).

S. Haslam, *Fragmenting Modernism, Ford Madox Ford, the Novel and the Great War* (Manchester: Manchester University Press, 2002).

C. Hassall, 'Tube Shelter Leicester Square, 1941', in *The Slow Night, and Other Poems, 1940–1948* (London: Arthur Baker, 1949), pp. 23–24.

R. Haynes, *From Faust to Strangelove: Representations of the Scientist in Western Literature* (Baltimore: Johns Hopkins University Press, 1994).

——, *H. G. Wells, Discoverer of the Future: The Influence of Science on his Thought* (London: Macmillan, 1980).

J. Hayward (ed.), *The Oxford Book of Nineteenth Century English Verse* (Oxford: Oxford University Press, 1964).

H. D. (Hilda Doolittle), 'The Walls Do Not Fall', in *H. D. Collected Poems, 1912–1944*, ed. Louis L. Martz (New York: New Directions, 1986), pp. 507–43.

S. Heaney, *District and Circle* (London: Faber & Faber, 2006).

A. E. Heath, Review of *Joy in Work* by Henri de Man, *Listener*, vol. 2, 14 August 1929, p. 213.

J. Heath-Stubbs, *Collected Poems, 1943–1987* (Manchester: Carcanet, 1988).

E. Hepworth Dixon, *The Story of a Modern Woman* (1894; London: Merlin, 1990).

A. Hern, 'The People of the Tubes' (27 September 1940), in D. Hill (ed.), *Tribune 40: The First Forty Years of a Socialist Newspaper* (London: Quartet, 1977), pp. 29–31.

R. Hewison, *Under Siege: Literary Life in London, 1939–45* (London: Quartet, 1979).

J. Hewitt, 'Poster Nasties: Censorship and the Victorian Theatre Poster', in S. Popple & V. Toulmin (eds.), *Visual Delights: Essays on the Popular and Projected Image in the 19th Century* (Trowbridge: Flicks, 2000), pp. 154–69.

D. Hill (ed.), *Tribune 40: The First Forty Years of a Socialist Newspaper* (London: Quartet, 1977).

T. Hill, *Underground* (London: Faber & Faber, 1999).

R. Hoban, *Kleinzeit* (1974; London: Picador, 1976).

L. Hollen Lees & A. Lees (eds.), *The Rise of Urban Britain* (New York: Garland, 1985).

J. Hollingshead, *Ragged London* (London: Smith Elder, 1861).

P. P. Holman, *The Amazing Electric Tube: a history of the City and South London Railway* (London: London Transport Museum, 1990).

R. Holmes (ed.), *Macabre Railway Stories* (London: W. H. Allen, 1982).

M. Horne & B. Bayman, *The First Tube: The Story of the Northern Line* (Harrow Weald: Capital Transport Publishing, 1990).

W. D. Howells, *London Films* (London: Harper & Brothers, 1905).

J. Howlett & R. Mengham (eds.), *The Violent Muse: Violence and the Artistic Imagination in Europe, 1910–39* (Manchester: Manchester University Press, 1994).

H. F. Howson, *London's Underground* (1951; London: Ian Allan, 1986).

D. Hudson, *Munby Man of Two Worlds, The Life and Diaries of Arthur J. Munby 1828–1910* (Boston, MA: Gambit, 1972).

T. P. Hughes, *Networks of Power: Electrification in Western Society, 1880–1930* (Baltimore: Johns Hopkins University Press, 1983).

T. E. Hulme, *The Collected Writings of T. E. Hulme*, ed. K. Csengeri (Oxford: Oxford University Press, 1994).

L. Hunt Beckman, *Amy Levy: Her Life and Letters* (Athens: Ohio University Press, 2000).

V. Hunt, *My Flurried Years* (London: Hurst & Blackett, 1926).

J. Huntington, *The Logic of Fantasy: H. G. Wells & Science Fiction* (New York: Columbia University Press, 1982).

A. Huxley, *Antic Hay* (1923; London: Chatto & Windus, 1949).

——, *Brave New World* (1932; Harmondsworth: Penguin, 1955).

——, *Crome Yellow* (1921; Harmondsworth: Penguin, 1937).

————, *Point Counter Point* (1928; London: Chatto & Windus, 1971).

J. K. Huysmans, *A Rebours (Against Nature)* (1884), trans. R. Baldick (Harmondsworth: Penguin, 1959).

S. Hynes, *The Edwardian Turn of Mind* (London: Oxford University Press, 1968).

————, *A War Imagined: The First World War and English Culture* (London: Bodley Head, 1990).

A. A. Jackson & D. F. Croome, *Rails Through the Clay: A History of London's Tube Railways* (London: Allen & Unwin, 1962).

C. L. R. James, *Letters from London* (1932), ed. N. Laughlin (Oxford: Signal Books, 2003).

H. James, *The Letters of Henry James*, ed. P. Lubbock, 2 vols., vol. 1 (London: Macmillan, 1920).

————, 'A London Life' (1888), in *A London Life; and, The Reverberator* (Oxford: Oxford University Press, 1989), pp. 3–146.

————, *The Wings of the Dove* (1902; Harmondsworth: Penguin, 1965).

N. C. James, *Strap-Hangers, A Novel* (London: Duckworth, 1934).

F. Jameson, *The Political Unconscious: Narrative as a Socially Symbolic Act* (1981; London: Routledge, 1996).

S. Jameson (ed.), *London Calling: A Salute to America* (New York: Harper, 1942).

R. Jefferies, *After London or Wild England* (1885; Oxford: Oxford University Press, 1980).

————, *The Story of My Heart* (1883; London: Macmillan, 1968).

————, 'A Wet Night in London' (1885), in C. H. Warren (ed.), *The Open Air* (London: Eyre and Spottiswoode, 1948).

J. Jervis, *Exploring the Modern: Patterns of Western Culture and Civilisation* (Oxford: Blackwell, 1998).

P. Johnston, *Edward Johnston* (1959; London: Barrie & Jenkins, 1976).

D. Jones, *In Parenthesis* (1937; London: Faber & Faber, 1963).

D. Kahn & G. Whitehead (eds.), *Wireless Imagination: Sound, Radio and the Avant Garde* (Cambridge, MA: MIT Press, 1992).

Y. Kapp, *Eleanor Marx*, vol. 2, *The Crowded Years, 1884–98* (1976; London: Virago, 1979).

Z. Katin, *'Clippie' The Autobiography of a War Time Conductress* (1944; Ipswich: Adam Gordon, 1995).

J. Kellett, *Railways and Victorian Cities* (London: Routledge & Kegan Paul, 1969).

H. Kenner, *The Mechanic Muse* (Oxford: Oxford University Press, 1987).

S. Kern, *The Culture of Time and Space, 1880–1918* (London: Weidenfeld & Nicolson, 1983).

L. Kirby, *Parallel Tracks: The Railroad and Silent Cinema* (Exeter: University of Exeter Press, 1997).

P. Kirkham & D. Thoms (eds.), *War Culture: Social Change and Changing Experience in World War Two Britain* (London: Lawrence & Wishart, 1995).

S. D. G. Knowles, *A Purgatorial Flame: Seven British Writers in the Second World War* (Philadelphia: University of Pennsylvania Press, 1990).

B. Kops, *The World is a Wedding* (1963; London: Mayflower, 1970).

J. Korg, 'Division of Purpose in George Gissing', in P. Coustillas (ed.), *Collected Articles on George Gissing* (London: Frank Cass, 1968), pp. 64–79.

J. Korg, *George Gissing: A Critical Biography* (1963; Brighton: Harvester, 1980).

H. Kureishi, *The Buddha of Suburbia* (London: Faber & Faber, 1990).

Labour Research Department, *The London Traffic Combine* (London: London Research Department, 1932).

O. Lancaster, *Osbert Lancaster Cartoons* (Harmondsworth: Penguin, 1945).

J. Langdon-Davies, 'Against Epidemics—No. 1', *Picture Post*, vol. 9, 16 November 1940, pp. 18–19.

A. Lant, *Blackout: Reinventing Women for Wartime British Cinema* (Princeton: Princeton University Press, 1991).

B. Latour, *We Have Never Been Modern*, trans. C. Porter (Cambridge, MA: Harvard University Press, 1993).

D. H. Laurence (ed.), *Bernard Shaw Collected Letters 1874–1897* (London: Max Reinhardt, 1965).

D. H. Lawrence, *Kangaroo* (1923; London: Martin Secker, 1932).

———, *The Letters of D. H. Lawrence*, eds. G. Zytaruk & J. Boulton, 8 vols., vol. 2 (Cambridge: Cambridge University Press, 1981).

D. Leavitt, *While England Sleeps* (1993; Boston: Houghton & Mifflin, 1995).

W. Le Queux, *Battle of Royston from The Invasion of 1910* (1906; London: Ellisons' Editions, 1984).

S. Ledger, 'Gissing, the Shopgirl and the New Woman', *Women: A Cultural Review*, 6.3, 1995, pp. 263–74.

———, *The New Woman: Fiction and Feminism at the Fin de Siècle* (Manchester: Manchester University Press, 1997).

E. Leed, *No Man's Land* (Cambridge: Cambridge University Press, 1979).

J. Lehmann (ed.), *The Penguin New Writing 5* (Harmondsworth: Penguin, 1941).

——— (ed.), *The Penguin New Writing 23* (Harmondsworth: Penguin, 1945).

——— (ed.), *The Penguin New Writing 25* (Harmondsworth: Penguin, 1945).

D. Lessing, *The Golden Notebook* (St Albans: Panther, 1973).

———, 'In Defence of the Underground', in *London Observed: Stories and Sketches* (London: Flamingo, 1993), pp. 79–96.

W. R. Lethaby, *Form in Civilization: Collected Papers on Art & Labour* (London: Oxford University Press, 1927).

M. Levenson (ed.), *The Cambridge Companion to Modernism* (Cambridge: Cambridge University Press, 1999).

A. Levy, *The Romance of a Shop* (1888), ed. S. D. Bernstein (Peterborough, Ontario: Broadview Press, 2006).

———, 'Women and Club Life', *Woman's World I* (1888), pp. 364–67, reprinted in *The Complete Novels and Selected Writings of Amy Levy 1861–1889*, ed. M. New (Gainesville: University Press of Florida, 1993), pp. 532–38.

A. Lewis, 'Henry's Moore's "Shelter Drawings": Memory & Myth', in P. Kirkham & D. Thoms (eds.), *War Culture: Social Change and Changing Experience in World War Two Britain* (London: Lawrence & Wishart, 1995), pp. 113–27.

P. W. Lewis, *The Apes of God* (1930; Harmondsworth: Penguin, 1965).

———, *Blasting and Bombardiering* (1937; London: Calder & Boyars, 1967).

———, *The Enemy of the Stars* (1914; London: Desmond Harmsworth, 1932).

———, 'Notes to the Catalogue for Vorticist Exhibition' (1915), in R. Cork, *Vorticism and Abstract Art in the First Machine Age*, 2 vols. (London: Gordon Fraser, 1976).

———, 'The Review of the Great English Vortex 1' (1914), in P. Faulkner (ed.), *A Modernist Reader* (London: Batsford, 1986), pp. 42–46.

A. Light, *Forever England: Femininity, Literature and Conservatism Between the Wars* (London: Routledge, 1991).

J. N. Lockyer, 'Editorial', in *Nature*, 3 January 1901, p. 2.

E. Longley, *Louis MacNeice: A Critical Study* (London: Faber & Faber, 1988).

D. Low, *Years of Wrath. A Cartoon History 1932–1945* (London: Victor Gollancz, 1986).

K. Lowe, *Tunnel Vision* (London: Arrow, 2001).

R. Luckhurst, *Science Fiction* (Cambridge: Polity, 2005).

R. Macaulay, *Crewe Train* (1926; London: Methuen, 1985).

————, *Keeping Up Appearances* (1928; London: Methuen, 1986).

————, *Told by an Idiot* (London: Collins, 1923).

————, *The World My Wilderness* (1950; Harmondsworth: Penguin, 1958).

A. Machen, 'Opening the Door', in *Holy Terrors* (Harmondsworth: Penguin, 1946), pp. 54–65.

————, *The Three Impostors* (1895; London: Everyman, 1995).

C. MacInnes, *City of Spades* (1957; Harmondsworth: Penguin, 1964).

J. Mack & S. Humphries, *London at War, The Making of Modern London 1939–1945* (London: Sidgwick & Jackson, 1985).

C. Mackenzie, *My Life and Times, Octave One 1883–1891* (London: Chatto & Windus, 1971).

M. Mackintosh & H. Wainwright (eds.), *A Taste of Power: The Politics of Local Economics* (London: Verso, 1987).

L. MacNeice, *Collected Poems of Louis MacNeice*, ed. E. R. Dodds (London: Faber & Faber, 1966).

————, 'Cook's Tour of the London Subways', *Listener*, 17 April 1941, pp. 554–55.

————, *Persons from Porlock & Other Plays for Radio* (London: BBC, 1969).

————, 'Reflections from the Dome of St Paul's, June 1941', in *Selected Prose of Louis MacNeice*, ed. A. Heuser, (Oxford: Clarendon, 1990), pp. 131–36.

————, *The Strings are False* (London: Faber & Faber, 1965).

————, 'The Way We Live Now', in J. Lehmann (ed.), *The Penguin New Writing 5* (Harmondsworth: Penguin, 1941), pp. 9–14.

B. E. Maidment, *Reading Popular Prints, 1790–1870* (Manchester: Manchester University Press, 1996).

F. T. Marinetti, 'The Founding and Manifesto of Futurism' (1909), in U. Apollonio (ed.), *Futurist Manifestos* (London: Thames & Hudson, 1973), pp. 19–24.

————, *Marinetti: Selected Writings*, ed. R. W. Flint (London: Secker & Warburg, 1972).

J. Marlow (ed.), *Votes for Women: The Virago Book of Suffragettes* (London: Virago, 2000).

A. Martin, 'Going Underground', *Evening Standard Magazine*, 26 March 1999, pp. 12–15.

C. F. G. Masterman, *The Condition of England* (London: Methuen, 1909).

————, *From the Abyss: Of Its Inhabitants by One of Them* (1902; New York: Garland, 1980).

D. Massey, *Space, Place and Gender* (Cambridge: Polity, 1994).

D. Matless, *Landscape and Englishness* (London: Reaktion Books, 1998).

T. S. Matthews, *Great Tom. Notes towards the definition of T. S. Eliot* (1973; London: Weidenfeld & Nicolson, 1974).

J. Mayer, *T. S. Eliot's Silent Voices* (Oxford: Oxford University Press, 1989).

H. Mayhew, *The Shops and Companies of London and the Trades and Manufactories of Great Britain* (London: Strand, 1865).

J. Maynard, 'A Marxist Reading of "Snowed Up"', in J. Wolfreys & W. Baker (eds.), *Literary Theories: A Case Study in Critical Performance* (London: Macmillan, 1996), pp. 129–56.

J. P. McKay, *Tramways and Trolleys: The Rise of Urban Mass Transport in Europe* (Princeton: Princeton University Press, 1976).

O. Meier (ed.), *The Daughters of Karl Marx, Family Correspondence, 1866–1898* (Harmondsworth: Penguin, 1984).

R. Mengham, 'From Georges Sorel to *Blast*', in J. Howlett & R. Mengham (eds.), *The Violent Muse:*

Violence and the Artistic Imagination in Europe, 1910–39 (Manchester: Manchester University Press, 1994), pp. 33–44.

F. A. Mercer (ed.), *Modern Publicity in War* (London: The Studio Pubs., 1941).

K. A. Miller, *British Literature of the Blitz: Fighting the People's War* (Basingstoke: Palgrave Macmillan, 2009).

T. Miller, *Late Modernism: Politics, Fiction and the Arts Between the World Wars* (London: University of California Press, 1999).

M. Minden & H. Bachmann (eds.), *Fritz Lang's Metropolis: Cinematic Visions of Technology and Fear* (Rochester, NY: Camden House, 2000).

N. Mitchison, *Among You Taking Notes: The Wartime Diary of Naomi Mitchison, 1939–1945*, ed. D. Sheridan (London: Gollancz, 1985).

G. Moore, *Esther Waters* (1894; London: Dent, 1962).

F. Moretti, *Atlas of the European Novel, 1800–1900* (London: Verso, 1999).

K. Morgan, *Labour Legends and Russian Gold* (London: Lawrence & Wishart, 2006).

J. A. Morris, *Writers and Politics in Modern Britain (1880–1950)* (London: Hodder & Stoughton, 1977).

W. Morris, *The Collected Letters of William Morris*, ed. N. Kelvin, 4 vols. (Princeton: Princeton University Press, 1987).

———, *News from Nowhere* (1890), in *Three Works by William Morris* (London: Lawrence & Wishart, 1968), pp. 181–401.

———, *William Morris, Journalism: Contributions to Commonweal, 1885–1890*, ed. N. Salmon (Bristol: Thoemmes Press, 1996).

W. Mulford, *This Narrow Place, Sylvia Townsend Warner and Valentine Ackland: Life, Letters and Politics, 1930–1951* (London: Pandora, 1988).

E. Murrow, *This is London* (1941), ed. E. Davis (New York: Schocken Books, 1989).

V. S. Naipaul, *The Enigma of Arrival* (London: Penguin, 1987).

———, *Mr Stone and the Knights Companion* (1963; Harmondsworth: Penguin, 1973).

L. Nead, *Victorian Babylon: People, Streets and Images in Nineteenth-Century London* (New Haven & London: Yale University Press, 2000).

J. P. Nesbitt, *Narrative Settlements: Geographies of British Women's Fiction between the Wars* (Toronto: Toronto University Press, 2005).

O. S. Nock, *The Railways of Britain* (London: Batsford, 1949).

M. Nordau, *Degeneration* (1895; London: University of Nebraska Press, 1968).

R. Nye, 'Savage Crowds, Modernism and Modern Politics', in E. Barkan & R. Bush (eds.), *Prehistories of the Future: The Primitive Project and the Culture of Modernism* (Stanford: Stanford University Press, 1995), pp. 42–55.

E. Orczy, 'The Mysterious Death on the Underground Railway' (1901), in H. Greene (ed.), *The Rivals of Sherlock Holmes* (London: Bodley Head, 1970), pp. 217–37.

G. Orwell, *The Collected Essays, Journalism and Letters of George Orwell*, eds. S. Orwell & I. Angus, 4 vols. (London: Penguin, 1970).

———, *Coming Up for Air* (1939; London: Secker & Warburg, 1986).

———, *Keep the Aspidistra Flying* (1936; Harmondsworth: Penguin, 1962).

———, 'Money & Guns', BBC Radio talk, 20 January 1942, in *Orwell: The War Broadcasts*, ed W. J. West (London: Duckworth/BBC, 1985), pp. 71–73.

———, *Nineteen Eighty-Four* (1949; London: Penguin, 1971).

————, *The Road to Wigan Pier* (1937; London: Secker & Warburg, 1980).

W. Owen, *Wilfred Owen: Selected Letters*, ed. J. Bell (Oxford: Oxford University Press, 1985).

J. Oxenham, 'A Mystery of the Underground' (1897), in P. Haining (ed.), *Murder on the Railways* (London: Orion, 1996), pp. 340–68.

M. Panter-Downes, *London War Notes 1939–1945*, ed. W. Shawn (Harlow: Longman, 1972).

E. Paolozzi, *Eduardo Paolozzi Underground*, ed. R. Cork (London: Weidenfeld & Nicolson, 1986).

A. Parejo Vadillo, *Women Poets and Urban Aestheticism: Passengers of Modernity* (Basingstoke: Palgrave Macmillan, 2005).

P. Parrinder, *Shadows of the Future: H. G. Wells, Science Fiction and Prophesy* (Liverpool: Liverpool University Press, 1995).

D. L. Parsons, *Streetwalking the Metropolis: Women, the City and Modernity* (Oxford: Oxford University Press, 2000).

B. Penn-Bull, *War Letters* (Windsor: Penn-Bull, 1991).

P. Peppis, *Literature, Politics and the English Avant-Garde: Nation and Empire, 1901–1918* (Cambridge: Cambridge University Press, 2000).

K. Phillips, *Virginia Woolf Against Empire* (Knoxville: University of Tennessee Press, 1994).

L. Phillips (ed.), *The Swarming Streets: Twentieth-Century Literary Representations of London* (Amsterdam & New York: Rodopi, 2004).

R. M. Philmus & D. Y. Hughes (eds.), *H. G. Wells: Early Writings in Science and Science Fiction* (Berkeley: University of California Press, 1975).

D. Pick, *War Machine: The Rationalisation of Slaughter in the Modern Age* (New Haven: Yale University Press, 1993).

F. Pick, 'Art in Modern Life', *The Nineteenth Century and After*, February 1922, pp. 256–64.

————, 'At the Paris Exhibition', *Listener*, 19 May 1937, pp. 971–73.

————, 'Growth and Form in the Modern City', for the Institute of Transport, 3 January 1926 (Frank Pick Collection, London Transport Museum, unpublished typescript, 1926).

————, 'The Meaning and Purpose of Design', *Listener*, 28 June 1933, pp. 1016–18.

————, 'War as an Educator', *Pennyfare, London Transport Staff News*, no. 2 (War Series), November 1939, p. 1.

D. L. Pike, *Metropolis on the Styx, The Underworlds of Modern Urban Culture, 1800–2001* (London: Cornell University Press, 2007).

————, 'Modernist Space and the Transformation of Underground London', in P. K. Gilbert (ed.), *Imagined Londons* (Albany: State University of New York Press, 2002), pp. 101–19.

————, *Subterranean Cities, The World Beneath Paris and London, 1800–1945* (London: Cornell University Press, 2005).

————, 'Underground Theater: Subterranean Spaces on the London Stage', *Nineteenth Century Studies*, vol. 13, 1999, pp. 103–38.

S. Popple & V. Toulmin (eds.), *Visual Delights: Essays on the Popular and Projected Image in the 19th Century* (Trowbridge: Flicks, 2000).

B. Porter, *The Origins of the Vigilant State: The London Metropolitan Police Special Branch before the First World War* (London: Weidenfeld & Nicolson, 1987).

E. Pound, *Gaudier-Brzeska, A Memoir* (1970; New York: New Directions, 2009).

————, *Literary Essays*, ed. T. S. Eliot (London: Faber & Faber, 1954).

————, *The Selected Letters of Ezra Pound, 1907–1941*, ed. D. D. Paige (London: Faber & Faber, 1982).

————, *Selected Poems* (1928; London: Faber & Faber, 1968).

C. Prendergast, *Paris and the Nineteenth Century* (Oxford: Blackwell, 1992).

J. B. Priestley, *Angel Pavement* (1930; London: Heinemann, 1938).

————, *English Journey* (1934; Harmondsworth: Penguin, 1977).

————, 'Man Underground' (1928), in *Self-Selected Essays* (London: Heinemann, 1932), pp. 75–80.

————, *They Walk in the City* (1936; London: Heinemann, 1936).

Radclyffe Hall, *The Unlit Lamp* (1924; London: Jonathan Cape, 1933).

L. Rainey, 'The Cultural Economy of Modernism', in M. Levenson (ed.), *The Cambridge Companion to Modernism* (Cambridge: Cambridge University Press, 1999), pp. 33–69.

E. D. Rappaport, *Shopping for Pleasure, Women in the Making of London's West End* (Princeton: Princeton University Press, 2000).

H. Ratner, *Reluctant Revolutionary: Memoirs of a Trotskyist 1936–1960* (London: Socialist Platform, 1994).

H. Read, *The Contrary Experience: Autobiographies* (London: Secker & Warburg, 1973).

D. Reeder, *Suburbanity and the Victorian City* (Leicester: University of Leicester, 1980).

R. Rendell, 'A transport of love in the underworld', *The Guardian*, 17 October 1991.

G. W. M. Reynolds, *The Mysteries of London* (1845; Keele: Keele University Press, 1996).

J. Rhys, *After Leaving Mr Mackenzie* (1931; Harmondsworth: Penguin, 1971).

————, *Good Morning, Midnight* (1939; Harmondsworth: Penguin, 1969).

————, *Voyage in the Dark* (1934; Harmondsworth: Penguin, 1969).

K. Rhys (ed.), *More Poems from the Forces* (London: Routledge, 1943).

———— (ed.), *Poems from the Forces* (London: Routledge, 1941).

J. Richards & J. M. MacKenzie, *The Railway Station: A Social History* (Oxford: Oxford University Press, 1986).

P. Richards, *Bombs, Bullshit and Bullets … in roughly that order* (London: Athena Press, 2007).

A. Richardson (ed.), *Women Who Did: Stories by Men and Women, 1890–1914* (London: Penguin, 2002).

D. Richardson, *Pilgrimage* (1938), 4 vols. (London: Virago, 1979 & 1992).

N. Riddell, *Labour in Crisis: The Second Labour Government, 1929–31* (Manchester: Manchester University Press, 1999).

A. Rimbaud, 'Métropolitain', in *Rimbaud: Complete Works, Selected Letters*, trans. W. Fowlie (Chicago: University of Chicago Press, 1966), pp. 242–44.

P. Ritchie-Calder, 'Shelters', *New Statesman and Nation*, 8 March 1941, pp. 235–36.

M. Roberts, *The Private Life of Henry Maitland: A Portrait of George Gissing*, ed. M. Bishop (1912; London: The Richards Press, 1958).

A. Robinson, *Imagining London, 1770–1900* (Basingstoke: Palgrave Macmillan, 2004).

S. Roe & S. Sellers (eds.), *The Cambridge Companion to Virginia Woolf* (Cambridge: Cambridge University Press, 2000).

S. Rowbotham, *Edward Carpenter: A Life of Liberty and Love* (London: Verso, 2008).

E. Royston Pike, *Human Documents of the Age of the Forsytes* (London: George Allen & Unwin, 1969).

J. Ruskin, 'Fiction, Fair and Foul' (1880), in *The Genius of John Ruskin: Selections from His Writings*, ed. J. D. Rosenberg (London: Routledge, 1963), pp. 435–44.

————, 'The Study of Architecture in Our Schools' (1865), in *The Works of John Ruskin*, eds. E. T. Cook & A. Wedderburn, 39 vols., vol. 19 (London: George Allen, 1905), pp. 19–46.

A. K. Russell (ed.), *The Rivals of Sherlock Holmes 2* (Secaucus, NJ: Castle Books, 1980).

———— (ed.), *Science Fiction by the Rivals of H. G. Wells* (Secaucus, NJ: Castle Books, 1979).

L. Russolo, 'The Art of Noises' (1913), in U. Apollonio (ed.), *Futurist Manifestos* (London: Thames & Hudson, 1973), pp. 74–88.

M. Saler, *The Avant-Garde in Interwar England: Medieval Modernism and the London Underground* (Oxford: Oxford University Press, 1999).

S. Sassoon, *Collected Poems 1908–1956* (1947; London: Faber & Faber, 2002).

————, *Memoirs of an Infantry Officer* (1930; London: Faber & Faber, 1965).

————, *Siegfried Sassoon Diaries, 1915-1918*, ed. R. Hart-Davies, 3 vols., vol. 3 (London: Faber & Faber, 1983).

J. Schneer, *London 1900: The Imperial Metropolis* (New Haven: Yale University Press, 1999).

W. Schivelbusch, *The Railway Journey: The Industrialisation of Time and Space in the 19th Century* (1977; Leamington Spa: Berg, 1986).

G. R. Searle, *The Quest for National Efficiency: A Study in British Politics and Political Thought* (Oxford: Basil Blackwell, 1971).

R. Selig, *George Gissing* (Boston: Twayne, 1983).

S. Selvon, 'Working the Transport', in *Ways of Sunlight* (New York: Longman, 1987), pp. 120–26.

M. Sharp, 'Night Engagement' (1941), in K. Webb (ed.), *Lilliput Goes to War* (London: Hutchinson, 1985), pp. 205–08.

G. B. Shaw, *Bernard Shaw: The Diaries, 1885–1897*, ed. S. Weintraub, 2 vols. (London: Penn State University Press, 1986).

E. Sicher, *Rereading the City/Rereading Dickens: Representation, the Novel and Urban Realism* (New York: AMS Press, 2003).

E. Siepmann, *Waterloo in Wardour Street* (London: Chatto & Windus, 1936).

G. Simmel, 'The Metropolis and Mental Life', in D. Frisby & M. Featherstone (eds.), *The Sociology of Georg Simmel* (London: Sage, 1997), pp. 174–85.

J. Simmons, *The Victorian Railway* (London: Thames & Hudson, 1991).

J. Simmons, N. Taylor, T. Rich & T. Lynham (eds.), *From Here to Here. Stories Inspired by London's Circle Line* (London: Cyan Books, 2005).

G. R. Sims (ed.), *Edwardian London*, 4 vols. (London: Village Press, 1990).

A. Sinclair, *War Like a Wasp: The Lost Decade of the 'Forties* (London: Hamish Hamilton, 1989).

E. Sitwell, 'Lullaby' (1940), in *Collected Poems* (London: Papermac, 1982), pp. 274–75.

M. Slater, *An Intelligent Person's Guide to Dickens* (London: Duckworth, 1999).

F. Smewin, 'Blitz Dinner', in K. Rhys (ed.), *More Poems from the Forces* (London: Routledge, 1943), p. 265.

M. Smith (ed.), *Golden Age Detective Stories* (Bath: Parragon, 1999).

J. Sommerfield, *May Day* (1936; London: Lawrence & Wishart, 1984).

S. Spender, *The Burning Cactus* (London: Faber & Faber, 1936).

————, *Citizens in War—And After* (London: Harrap, 1945).

————, *Collected Poems 1928–1953* (London: Faber & Faber, 1955).

————, 'Remembering Eliot' (1965), in A. Tate (ed.), *T. S. Eliot: The Man and His Work* (Harmondsworth: Penguin, 1971), pp. 42–68.

————, *The Thirties and After: poetry, politics, people (1933–75)* (London: Fontana, 1978).

————, *World Within World: The Autobiography of Stephen Spender* (Berkeley: University of California Press, 1966).

J. Spiers (ed.), *Gissing and the City. Cultural Crisis and the Making of Books in Late Victorian England* (Basingstoke: Palgrave Macmillan, 2006).

G. Stedman Jones, *Outcast London: A Study in the Relationship between Classes in Victorian Society* (Harmondsworth: Penguin, 1991).

C. Steedman, 'Fictions of Engagement; Eleanor Marx, Biographical Space', in J. Stokes (ed.), *Eleanor Marx (1855–1898), Life, Work, Contacts* (Aldershot: Ashgate, 2000), pp. 2–39.

A. Steele (ed.), *Selected Modern Short Stories I* (1937; Harmondsworth: Penguin, 1939).

R. L. Stevenson, 'A Plea for Gas Lamps' (1881), in *Virginibus Puerisque: and other papers* (London: Chatto & Windus, 1905), pp. 189–93.

J. Stokes (ed.), *Eleanor Marx (1855–1898), Life, Work, Contacts* (Aldershot: Ashgate, 2000).

B. Stoker, *Dracula* (1897; London: Penguin, 1993).

L. Stratmann, *Whiteley's Folly. The Life and Death of a Salesman* (Stroud: Sutton Publishing, 2004).

J. Struther, *Mrs Miniver* (New York: Harcourt, Brace & Company, 1940).

H. L. Sussman, *Victorians and the Machine: The Literary Response to Technology* (Cambridge, MA: Harvard University Press, 1968).

A. Sutcliffe (ed.), *Metropolis, 1890–1940* (London: Mansell, 1984).

A. Swingewood, *The Novel and Revolution* (London: Macmillan, 1975).

J. Symons, *Notes from Another Country* (London: London Magazine Editions, 1972).

———, *The Thirties: A Dream Revolved* (1960; London: Faber & Faber, 1975).

H. Taine, *Notes on England 1860–1870*, trans. E. Hyams (London: Thames & Hudson, 1957).

A. Tate (ed.), *T. S. Eliot: The Man and His Work* (Harmondsworth: Penguin, 1971).

S. Taylor, *A Journey Through Time: London Transport Photographs, 1880–1965* (London: Laurence King, 1992).

L. Tickner, *The Spectacle of Women: Imagery of the Suffrage Campaign, 1907–14* (London: Chatto & Windus, 1987).

A. Thacker, *Moving Through Modernity: Space and Geography in Modernism* (Manchester: Manchester University Press, 2003).

E. P. Thompson, *William Morris, Romantic to Revolutionary* (London: Merlin, 1977).

E. Timms & D. Kelley (eds.), *Unreal City: Urban Experience in Modern European Literature and Art* (Manchester: Manchester University Press, 1985).

G. Tindall, *Countries of the Mind: The Meaning of Place to Writers* (London: Hogarth Press, 1991).

A. Trachtenberg, *The Incorporation of America: Culture and Society in the Gilded Age* (New York: Hill & Wang, 1982).

Trades Union Congress Library Collections, *The Workers' War: Home Front Recalled* (London: Trades Union Congress, 2006; www.unionhistory.info/workerswar/).

R. Trench & E. Hillman, *London Under London: A Subterranean Guide* (1984; London: John Murray, 1993).

A. Trollope, *The Claverings* (1886–87; Oxford: Oxford University Press, 1986).

———, *The Eustace Diamonds* (1873), ed. J. McCormack (Oxford: Oxford University Press, 1983).

———, *The Prime Minister* (1876), ed. J. Uglow (Oxford: Oxford University Press, 1983).

———, *The Way We Live Now* (1874–75; Indianapolis: Bobbs-Merrill, 1974).

L. Tromanhauser, 'Virginia Woolf's London and the Archaeology of Character', in L. Phillips (ed.), *The Swarming Streets: Twentieth-Century Literary Representations of London* (Amsterdam & New York: Rodopi, 2004), pp. 33–43.

M. Tropp, *Images of Fear: How Horror Stories Helped Shape Modern Culture, 1818–1918* (Jefferson, NC: McFarland & Co., 1990).

M. Twain, *The Selected Letters of Mark Twain*, ed. C. Neider (New York: Harper & Row, 1982).

R. Vickers, 'The Eighth Lamp' (1915), in R. Holmes (ed.), *Macabre Railway Stories* (London: W. H. Allen, 1982), pp. 77–90.

B. Vine, *King Solomon's Carpet* (1991; London: Viking, 1992).

J. R. Walkowitz, *City of Dreadful Delight: Narratives of Sexual Danger in Late-Victorian London* (London: Virago, 1992).

E. Wallace, *The Four Just Men* (1905; London: House of Stratus, 2001).

M. J. K. Walsh, *C. R. W. Nevinson: This Cult of Violence* (London: Yale University Press, 2002).

M. Walters, 'Introduction', in G. Gissing, *The Odd Women* (London: Virago, 1980).

A. C. Ward, *The Nineteen-Twenties: Literature and Ideas in the Post-War Decade* (London: Methuen, 1930).

B. Warr, 'Stepney, 1941', in K. Rhys (ed.), *Poems from the Forces* (London: Routledge, 1941), p. 127.

C. H. Warren (ed.), *The Open Air* (London: Eyre and Spottiswoode, 1948).

A. Warwick, 'Lost Cities: London's Apocalypse', in G. Byron & D. Punter (eds.), *Spectral Readings: Towards a Gothic Geography* (Basingstoke: Palgrave Macmillan, 1999), pp. 73–87.

E. Waugh, *Vile Bodies* (1930; Harmondsworth: Penguin, 1982).

B. Webb, *The Diaries of Beatrice Webb*, eds. N. & J. MacKenzie, 4 vols., vol. 1 (London: Virago, 1982).

———— (writing as Beatrice Potter), 'A Lady's View of the Unemployed', *Pall Mall Gazette*, 18 February 1886.

————, *My Apprenticeship*, 2 vols., vol. 2 (Harmondsworth: Penguin, 1938).

K. Webb (ed.), *Lilliput Goes to War* (London: Hutchinson, 1985).

S. Webb, 'Lord Rosebery's Escape from Houndsditch', in *The Nineteenth Century and After*, vol. 50, July–December 1901, pp. 366–86.

D. Welch, *The Journals of Denton Welch* (1952), ed. M. De-la-Noy (Harmondsworth: Penguin, 1987).

H. G. Wells, *Ann Veronica* (1909; London: Dent, 1966).

————, *Anticipations of the Reaction of Mechanical and Scientific Progress upon Human Life and Thought* (London: Chapman & Hall, 1902).

————, *The Dream* (1924; London: Hogarth Press, 1987).

————, *An Experiment in Autobiography*, 2 vols. (London: Gollancz, 1934 & 1966).

————, *The First Men in the Moon* (1901; New York: Airmont, 1965).

————, *The Island of Doctor Moreau* (1896; London: McFarland, 1996).

————, *Kipps* (1905; London: Fontana, 1961).

————, *A Modern Utopia* (1905; London: Thomas Nelson, undated).

————, *Mr Britling Sees It Through* (1916; London: Odhams Press, undated).

————, 'Mr. Wells Reviews a Current Film', in M. Minden & H. Bachmann (eds.), *Fritz Lang's Metropolis: Cinematic Visions of Technology and Fear* (Rochester, NY: Camden House, 2000), pp. 94–100.

————, *The New Machiavelli* (1911; London: Penguin, 2005).

————, 'The Rediscovery of the Unique' (1891), in R. M. Philmus & D. Y. Hughes (eds.), *H. G. Wells: Early Writings in Science and Science Fiction* (Berkeley: University of California Press, 1975), pp. 22–31.

————, *Selected Short Stories* (Harmondsworth: Penguin, 1958).

————, *The Sleeper Awakes* (1899; London: Sphere, 1976).

————, *Socialism and the Family* (London: Fifield, 1906).

————, *Tono-Bungay* (1909; Harmondsworth: Penguin, 1946).

————, *The War of the Worlds* (1898; New York: Tor Books, 1988).

————, *The World Set Free* (1914; London: Hogarth Press, 1988).

D. Welsh (ed.), *Fortress Britain: Working Lives and Trade Unions in World War II* (London: National Pensioners Convention, 2005).

————, *Talk About a Liberty: An Oral History of Tube Sheltering In London, 1939–1945* (London: unpublished transcripts, 2006–08).

R. West, *Harriet Hume* (1929; London, Virago, 1980).

M. Wheeler, *Death and the Future Life in Victorian Literature and Theology* (Cambridge: Cambridge University Press, 1990).

S. Whetlor, *The Story of Notting Dale* (London: Kensington & Chelsea Community History Group, 1998).

F. M. White, 'The Four Days' Night' (1903), in A. K. Russell (ed.), *Science Fiction by the Rivals of H. G. Wells* (Secaucus, NJ: Castle Books, 1979), pp. 441–53.

————, 'The Four White Days' (1903), in A. K. Russell (ed.), *Science Fiction by the Rivals of H. G. Wells* (Secaucus, NJ: Castle Books, 1979), pp. 457–68.

————, 'The Invisible Force' (1903), in A. K. Russell (ed.), *Science Fiction by the Rivals of H. G. Wells* (Secaucus, NJ: Castle Books, 1979), pp. 483–94.

M. Whitworth, 'Virginia Woolf and Modernism', in S. Roe & S. Sellers (eds.), *The Cambridge Companion to Virginia Woolf* (Cambridge: Cambridge University Press, 2000), pp. 146–63.

O. Wilde, 'The Decay of Lying' (1889), in *De Profundis and Other Writings* (Harmondsworth: Penguin, 1973), pp. 55–87.

Charles Williams, *All Hallows' Eve* (London: Faber & Faber, 1945).

Conrad Williams, *London Revenant* (London: The Do-Not Press, 2004).

C. Williams-Ellis, 'Can We Scrap London?', *Spectator*, vol. 161, July–December, 11 November 1938, p. 805.

Raymond Williams, *The Country and the City* (1973; London: Hogarth Press, 1985).

————, *Culture and Society 1780–1950* (1958; Harmondsworth: Penguin, 1963).

————, 'Culture is Ordinary' (1958), in *Resources of Hope: Culture, Democracy, Socialism*, ed. R. Gable (London: Verso, 1989), pp. 3–18.

————, *The English Novel from Dickens to Lawrence* (London: Hogarth Press, 1984).

———— (ed.), *George Orwell: A Collection of Critical Essays* (Englewood Cliffs, NJ: Prentice-Hall, 1974).

————, *The Long Revolution* (1961; Harmondsworth: Penguin, 1965).

Rosalind Williams, *Notes on the Underground: An Essay on Technology, Society and the Imagination* (Cambridge, MA: MIT Press, 1990).

H. Williamson, *The Innocent Moon* (1961; London: MacDonald & Co., 1985).

G. Winter, *A Cockney Camera* (Harmondsworth: Penguin, 1979).

J. Winter, *London's Teeming Streets, 1830–1914* (London: Routledge, 1993).

A. Wohl, *Endangered Lives: Public Health in Victorian Britain* (London: Methuen, 1983).

J. Wolfreys & W. Baker (eds.), *Literary Theories: A Case Study in Critical Performance* (London: Macmillan, 1996).

C. Wolmar, *The Subterranean Railway* (London: Atlantic Books, 2004).

L. Woolf, 'Politics in Spain', in *Nation and Athenaeum*, 21 April 1923, vol. 33, no. 3, pp. 74–75.

V. Woolf, *The Diaries of Virginia Woolf*, ed. A. Bell, 5 vols. (London: Penguin, 1975–82).

————, *Jacob's Room* (1922; Oxford: Oxford University Press, 2000).

————, *The Letters of Virginia Woolf*, eds. N. Nicolson & J. Trautmann, 6 vols. (London: Hogarth Press, 1975–80).

————, 'The Mark on the Wall' (1917), in *A Haunted House and Other Stories* (1944; London: Hogarth Press, 1967), pp. 40–48.

————, 'Mr Bennett and Mrs Brown' (1924), in *Collected Essays*, ed. L. Woolf, 4 vols. (London: Hogarth Press, 1966), vol. 1, pp. 319–37.

————, *Mrs Dalloway* (1925; London: Hogarth Press, 1950).

————, *Street Haunting: A London Adventure* (1927; London: Penguin, 2005).

————, *To the Lighthouse* (1927; Harmondsworth: Penguin, 1964).

————, *Virginia Woolf, A Passionate Apprentice: The Early Journals, 1897–1909*, ed. M. A. Leaska (London: Harvest, 1990).

————, *The Waves* (1931; Harmondsworth: Penguin, 1951).

————, *The Years* (1937; London: Granada, 1977).

P. Wright, *Tank* (London: Faber & Faber, 2000).

E. Zamiatin, 'The Fisher of Men' (1918), in *Islanders and The Fisher of Men*, trans. S. Fuller & J. Sacchi (Edinburgh: Salamander Press, 1984), pp. 75–95.

————, *A Soviet Heretic: Essays by Yevgeny Zamyatin*, trans. M. Ginsburg (Chicago: University of Chicago, 1970).

P. Ziegler, *London at War, 1939–1945* (London: Sinclair-Stevenson, 1995).

INDEX